MAP, SECTION OF GLENVILLE AREA, 1933

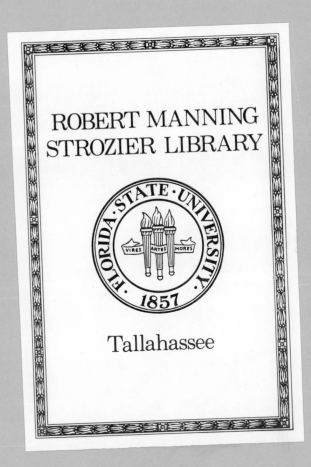

History of
The Jews of
Cleveland

Regional History Series of
The American Jewish History Center of
The Jewish Theological Seminary of America

EDITOR
MOSHE DAVIS

VOLUME ONE
The History of the Jews of Milwaukee
by Louis J. Swichkow and Lloyd P. Gartner
Published by The Jewish Publication Society of America, 1963

VOLUME TWO
History of the Jews of Los Angeles
by Max Vorspan and Lloyd P. Gartner
Published by The Huntington Library and
The Jewish Publication Society of America, 1970

VOLUME THREE
Immigrants to Freedom Jewish Communities in
Rural New Jersey Since 1882
by Joseph Brandes in association with Martin Douglas
Published by the University of Pennsylvania Press, 1971

VOLUME FOUR
History of the Jews of Cleveland

ודרשו את שלום העיר . . . .
כי בשלומה יהיה לכם שלום.

"And seek the peace of the city . . .
for in the peace thereof shall ye have peace."

JEREMIAH 29.7

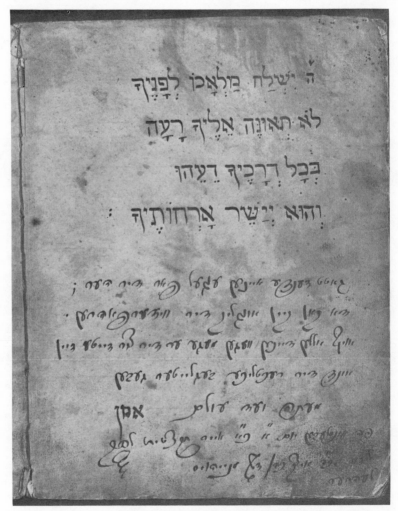

The opening page of the ethical testament given to the emigrants who left Unsleben for Cleveland 21 Iyar 5599 (May 5, 1839). "The blessing, written in Hebrew and repeated in German Yiddish, reads 'May God send His angel before you/ May no ill befall you/ In all your ways know Him/ And he will make your paths straight.' " (Jewish Community Federation)

History of The Jews of Cleveland

LLOYD P. GARTNER
Tel-Aviv University

A joint publication of
THE WESTERN RESERVE HISTORICAL SOCIETY
and
THE JEWISH THEOLOGICAL SEMINARY OF AMERICA

THIS VOLUME WAS PREPARED UNDER THE DIRECTION OF
THE AMERICAN JEWISH HISTORY CENTER OF
THE JEWISH THEOLOGICAL SEMINARY OF AMERICA
IN COOPERATION WITH
THE JEWISH COMMUNITY FEDERATION OF CLEVELAND

Library of Congress, Cataloging in Publication Data
Gartner, Lloyd P. , 1927-
    History of the Jews of Cleveland.

    (Regional history series of the American Jewish
History Center of the Jewish Theological Seminary
of America ; v. 4) (The Western Reserve Historical
Society publication ; no. 143)
    Includes bibliographical references and index.
    1. Jews in Cleveland—History. 2. Cleveland—
History. I. Title. II. Series: Jewish
Theological Seminary of America. American Jewish
History Center. Regional history series ; v. 4.
III. Series: Western Reserve Historical Society,
Cleveland. Publication ; no. 143.
F499.C69J545   977.1'32'004924   78-5868
ISBN 0-911704-17-5

Manufactured in the United States of America

For Ruth

"When she opens her mouth it is to
    speak wisely...
Many a woman shows how capable she
    is, but you excel them all."

Proverbs 31.26, 29.

Volume VIII in the Moreshet Series,
Studies in Jewish History, Literature and Thought

Foreword

IT is a distinct pleasure to be part of this scholarly publication. While many manuscripts have been submitted to the Western Reserve Historical Society for consideration, few have been as thoroughly researched and well-prepared as that of Dr. Lloyd P. Gartner. We anticipate that his study will prove to be a major contribution in the field of local history and will serve to enlighten its readers on the significant aspects of the development and impact of Cleveland's Jewish community.

We were fortunate to have the close cooperation of Sidney Z. Vincent and Judah Rubinstein of the Jewish Community Federation of Cleveland. In addition to their individual labors in the editorial process, these men were instrumental in bringing the Historical Society and The Jewish Theological Seminary of America together in this joint publishing endeavor.

It is particularly rewarding for us to note the fact that a large number of the original sources—newspapers, manuscripts, records, and the like—consulted by Dr. Gartner while undertaking this study are in the collections of the Historical Society's Library. And the number of collections pertinent to the study of Jewish history is growing, due to the establishment of the Cleveland Jewish Archives in the Library in 1976.

This Archives, this book, and the Historical Society's plans for future programs in the broad field of ethnic history are testimony to the fact that the Historical Society intends to support and cooperate and, when appropriate, take the lead in matters of substance relative to the preservation and dissemination of the history of northeastern Ohio.

Kermit J. Pike
Director of the Library

Author's Introduction

I have written about a group within a society which participates fully in that society's political, economic, and cultural life. Since it constitutes a visible, coherent group, retains considerable social separateness, and possesses independent, voluntarily supported institutions of its own, it may be called a community. Within a large city like Cleveland one may observe closely a community functioning while its members are part of urban society. To narrate and analyze the founding of such a community, the increase in its numerical size, its activities, and the symbols and inner communications it employs, appears to me as important an undertaking as most of those pursued by American historians.

The generalizing which is necessary in writing about society on the grand scale is no less necessary but is perhaps harder when the focus is on a limited group like a local community. The intimacy and sometimes the very pettiness of details about streets and individuals and organizations do not forbid generalization; they only remind the historian at every step what he is generalizing about. An all too easy mystification comes from the frequent appeal to terms like "process" and "movement" on the part of writers who deal with an entire country or people. Perhaps there is not much choice for those who seek to present an interpretation of general bearing. However, too many are lax in doing their local history homework, although I would like not to be harsh in judgment.

It seems to me that some of the Jewish historians who have long been poring over pamphlets and parliamentary debates concerning the propriety and desirable extent of Jewish emancipation could profitably direct more attention to Jewish emancipation in practice. Once Jews did receive emancipation, what they did afterwards has been too little noticed. Jewish history, especially most of what has been written under Zionist inspiration, has tended to study Jewish life in emancipated lands under the rubrics of radical assimilation and anti-Semitism. Sup-

posedly, emancipated Jews would assimilate totally, to the point
of the extinction of their Jewish identity, or were prevented
from accomplishing this only by anti-Semitic viciousness. In
other words, Jews would continue to be Jews only because of
external hostility. Others, far from Zionism, have thought likewise. I am convinced that this analysis is misleading. It may
bear mention here that only in Germany under Nazism was
Jewish emancipation actually revoked; the rest of the hideous
chronicle of European Jewry from 1933 to 1945 occurred under
Nazi German domination. As to assimilation, whereby Jews
became like the general population—or like some preferred part
of it—in the lands where they lived, that is a matter of degree. So
pervasive is assimilation in the post-emancipatory history of
Western Jewry that it requires a great deal of refinement and
sub-classification before the term can be profitably used. At all
events, radical assimilation and anti-Semitism, separately or in
combination, can not provide a sufficient framework for Jewish
history under emancipation. There has been considerable assimilation among Cleveland Jews, and they have known some anti-
Semitism, but to make those the governing factors would im-
poverish their history.

Several ways to write the history of a local Jewish community
may be employed. There is a method which would focus on the
development of Jewish religious, educational, social, and philanthropic institutions, or on prominent individuals, seeing in
them and their activities the expression of emancipated Jewish
life. While to my knowledge it has yet to be done, it should be
possible to apply the recently elaborated quantitative techniques
to the history of Jews in a given locality. Upon reflecting back
upon what I have written here, it seems to me that I have done
the history of the Jews' economic and cultural life, paying special attention to their immigration from Europe, which, before
approximately 1940, had the most influence in setting the course
of their lives. I have simultaneously been writing the history of
the Jewish community, more as a defineable entity than as a
gathering of institutions. Above all, I have attempted to tie social
and cultural to communal history. For example, I have treated
a synagogue not only as a place where Jewish beliefs and observances find expression. It is that to be sure, but the character

of a synagogue, and even the comparative weight assigned certain of these beliefs and observances, are strongly influenced by the social and cultural physiognomy of those who worship there. Again, the giving and receiving of charity has taken place within the Jewish community since ancient times, but who gives how much to which charity, and who receives charity and on what terms, are largely decided by the backgrounds of givers and receivers and by the wider environment they live in. It may also be mentioned that Cleveland's Jewish community has long played a notable role within American Jewry at large and even in world-wide Jewish affairs. This prominence has come mainly during the last forty years and is not only a result of contemporary Jewish history. It is also the outcome of the inner development of the Jewish community and of the unmistakable impact of several remarkable personalities who occupied key positions.

The history of Cleveland Jewry as I have written it attempts especially to make clear the social bearings of Jewish communal life and institutions. Even the conflicts acquire a significance beyond that of personal dislikes and institutional rivalries. I have also attempted to set the history of Cleveland Jewry where its Jews, like those of every American city, have always sought that it be, within the historic context of their city's life from the time the first known Jew appeared in Cleveland village in 1836. Of course the reader will judge, especially if he happens to live in Cleveland, how well I have succeeded in all this.

A word more may be said of the other ways to write a local Jewish history like this one. Much more attention could be devoted to particular institutions and individuals. On the other hand, what is called the new social history should find much of value in defining and analyzing Jewish social strata where possible in comparison with other Cleveland ethnic and religious bodies and other American Jewish local communities. The history of the lower, generally inarticulate classes might also be profitably investigated, especially since Jews of whatever class are rarely inarticulate, and sources exist for such a study. To trace Jewish families through several generations, which I wish I could have done here, appears to me a likely way of adequately answering perennial questions about Jewish birth rate, social and geographic mobility, marriage and intermarriage, and the continuity of Jewish identity in general. Having set forth these varied alternatives, I ought to express my own conviction that of the ways to write the history of a local Jewish community the present method of playing together the social and cultural with the communal is the best when a single choice is to be made.

This work was long in the making before it became my responsibility. A very small portion is derived from a partial, earlier manuscript by Charles Reznikoff, whose death in 1976 was a loss not only to American poetry but also to the writing of American Jewish history. Three outstanding American historians took an active interest in this project during its earlier phases. Let Harvey Wish, Carl F. Wittke (both of Case Western Reserve University) and Allan Nevins (Columbia University and Huntington Library) be thankfully remembered here. The participation of the late Rabbi Jack J. Herman is also recalled with gratitude. Just before he died last month I had two delightful, informative sessions with Ezra Z. Shapiro, President of Keren Hayesod, whose rich experience in Cleveland included leadership in the Jewish community besides service as Law Director and Acting Mayor during the 1930s.

To separate between the quick and the dead, I would like to offer my thanks to the Jewish Community Federation, which sponsored this work and left me free to write and form judgments as I saw fit. Mr. Sidney Z. Vincent, who has retired after many years of fine service as its Executive Director, was always kind and knowledgeable. Mr. Judah Rubinstein, the Federation's Research Director, has been informative and hospitable without stint. They and others were tolerant of an outsider's efforts to understand a Jewish community which they lived in and served. Their pictorial history of Cleveland Jewry, to appear soon, will be an interesting companion to the present work.

While he served as its associate director, Professor Stanley F. Chyet personally exemplified the cordiality and helpfulness for which the American Jewish Archives, under Professor Jacob R. Marcus' direction, enjoys deserved renown. I have also to thank Miss Miriam Leikind, The Temple, Cleveland; the library and archival staff of the Western Reserve Historical Society, Cleveland; the American Jewish Committee, New York;

the National Jewish Welfare Board, New York; the Historical
Society of Israel, Jerusalem; and Richard Karberg, photographer. Dr. Gladys L. Rosen cheerfully bore much of the administrative work at the earlier stages, and Mrs. Joan L.
Wettenstein was a patient, skillful typist. Professor Moshe
Davis, who long bore the cares of producing this book together
with Dr. Simon Greenberg, was again its editor par excellence
as he was in the other American Jewish local histories of this
series. I wonder whether this book would exist without my wife's
patience and support.

I have written this book in Israel, where I have lived since
1970. Has this location influenced my conception of American
Jewish history? Aside from the deeper perspective which distance and greater detachment can lend, I am not now consciously aware that it has. However, any reader who is so minded may
compare this with previous local histories where I was co-author.
But I shall say with certainty that American Jewish history can
be written in Israel, and more will come forth.

LLOYD P. GARTNER

Tel-Aviv University
June 1977/Tammuz 5677

Contents

PART ONE

The Founding Generation
1840–1870

I

Settling in an Expanding City

THE Cleveland that the first Jewish settler we know of came to in 1836 had been founded about forty years before. In 1795 the General Assembly of Connecticut had sold three million acres of its Western Reserve in Ohio for forty cents an acre to the Connecticut Land Company; and the Company had sent General Moses Cleaveland at the head of a survey party to explore what had been purchased unseen. In due course the General reported to the Company: "While I was in New Connecticut I laid out a town on the bank of Lake Erie, which was called by my name, and I believe the child is now born that may live to see that place as large as Old Windham."[1] Cleveland in fact grew slowly. Its population was under three hundred in 1810, and ten years later, after the pioneer settlement was laid out on the model of a New England village, there were but 600 inhabitants.

The first settlers were for the most part New Englanders. They were not particularly religious men; although the majority came from New England, they had not gone west to found a Christian commonwealth, as the Puritans did, but to better themselves.[2] There was a distillery in Cleveland before there was a school or church. But when later immigrants came, also chiefly from New England, bringing their wives and children as well as the school, the church, and the form of government the first immigrants had brought with them, Protestant Christianity began to take root and flourish.[3]

European immigrants were also among the first settlers. About 1830 Germans began to settle Cleveland. In 1836 they organized the German Society of Cleveland; it had fifty members in 1837. The first Irish immigrant to settle in Cleveland also came in 1830.[4]

The village of Cleveland, like a town of New England with its central green, grew slowly. When Captain Lewis Dibble visited the place shortly after the War of 1812, he found a

3

forest region with isolated pioneer clearings. But the village had already been incorporated, and the residents held their town meetings in a two-story log building, painted red. This was the courthouse. Here, too, the members of Concord Lodge No. 15 of the Masonic Order met. The schoolhouse was near Bank Street, where the Bank of Lake Erie conducted its business in a small parlor—before expiring in 1820. By that date Cleveland had its first newspaper, a regular stage line to Painesville, the Commercial Coffee House, an agricultural society, a bookstore with a bindery in back, and Trinity Church.

There was nothing yet to distinguish the village from dozens of small settlements in the vastness of the Western Reserve. The large towns lay further south, along the Ohio River, the great artery of commerce between the East and Middle West in the pre-railroad era. On the Ohio's banks stood Cincinnati, Queen City of the West, numbering 9,642 inhabitants in 1820, the year when the village on Lake Erie had 606.

In 1840 the population of Cleveland, at last larger than Old Windham, stood around 6,000 (Cincinnati numbered 46,000). It included a handful of Jews. The town was concentrated on the knob formed by the curving Cuyahoga River but was stretching out towards Clinton Street. Cleveland purchased its second school building that year. The new courthouse at the southwest corner of the public square had just been white-washed and the southern border of the square fenced in. Cleveland's first municipal market was completed, and the wagons with produce from the interior came up Prospect and Kinsman Streets.[5]

According to Cleveland's first directory, issued in 1837, there were then "four very extensive Iron Foundaries and Steam engine manufactories in this city." It also listed three soap and candle "manufactories," two breweries, a sash factory, two rope walks, one stoneware pottery, two carriage "manufactories," and two "French burr" millstone factories—all, the directory added, "in full operation." The directory also observed how Cleveland's trade "within the last few years considerably increased, owing to her peculiar and advantageous location at the termination of the Ohio Canal." Six stage companies and a number of forwarding lines on Lake Erie and the Ohio Canal—"Through in 80 hours" to Portsmouth—provided transportation. Charters had already been issued to railroad companies which were to link the city to Pittsburgh and Cincinnati. The line to Cincinnati, the directory announced, would "connect the two great commerical emporiums of the state." Most of the 250 sailing vessels on Lake Erie in 1841 stopped at Cleveland.[6]

As Cleveland became the leading town in the Western Reserve, the City Directory which listed its craftsmen and merchants also included the public institutions. There were nine congregations, as well as a number of societies and associations with purposes ranging from temperance "on the teetotal plan" to cultural pursuits and anti-slavery agitation. The directory noted, for example, that the Young Men's Literary Association, formed in 1836, had established a library and reading room in the Commercial Building on Superior Street. In the late 1830s Cleveland had a Hermonic Society with amateur performers, a Mozart Society to promote "Musical Science and the Cultivation of a refined taste," and the Cleveland Lyceum, which offered lectures to the townspeople. A regular lyceum speaker on hygienic subjects in 1838 and 1839 was Daniel L. M. Peixotto, M.D. (1800–1842), who had arrived in 1836 to become a professor at the newly founded Willoughby University Medical School (ultimately merged into Case Western Reserve University Medical School) just outside Cleveland. In 1836 Asa Gray (1810–1888), the botanist, spent some time in the town and wrote to a friend that Cleveland would "ultimately be a very pleasant place," adding "the people show some signs of civlization; they eat ice cream, which is sold in many places."[7]

In 1841 six newspapers, including the *Eagle-Eyed News Catcher*, made their initial appearance; the *Plain Dealer* in 1842 became a Democratic voice "in the wilderness of Whiggery." The last of the log cabins had been taken down. There was refinement enough in the middle 'forties to attract Madame Cinti Damoreau of the Opera Comique of Paris; to supply an audience for the newly formed Quartette Club; and to encourage Mr. and Mrs. E. Hosmer to open their Young Ladies' Institute. Part of Willoughby University Medical College moved into

Cleveland in 1844. The organization of the Academy of Natural Science took place in November, 1845.[8]

But Superior Street, Cleveland's main street, was not paved until 1842, when heavy planks were laid crosswise along the street from the Square to the river; this was the first attempt at paving within the city limits. The other streets were still deep in dust, except when they were deep in mud after a rain, or covered with snow. For days at a time the sky would be dark as millions of carrier pigeons flew overhead. Their wings, it was said, "sounded at the distance of miles like the heavy surge of Erie beating an iron-bound coast." One shot would bring down many, and peddlers sold them on the streets for food at less than a cent apiece.[9]

"A POLITICAL CANAAN"

Before any Jews appeared in the city, they were occasionally discussed in the local press. The discussions combined the tradition of Puritan New England with that of early American libertarianism. When the Maryland House of Delegates still refused in 1819 to grant Jews full political rights by altering the Christian wording of the oath of office, sharp reproof came from the *Cleaveland Register*:

> It is remarkable and indeed disgraceful . . . at a time when the bigoted monarchs of Europe are removing those lines of religious distinction which are inconsistent to a sincere devotion to the Almighty Father of all. When such proceedings once begin, there is no calculating where they will stop. If the legislature of Maryland have a right to disfranchise any portion of the Free-men of the State, because they believe in the God of Abraham, Isaac and Jacob, they may next decide which of the various sects are true Christians and disfranchise all the rest. . . .[10]

Soon thereafter the same newspaper quoted with apparent approval an address by the New York Jewish journalist and politician Mordecai M. Noah. He expressed surprise that "a greater number of the children of Israel have not found their way to these provinces where they would, it is to be hoped, find a sanctuary from prejudice, and [be] treated with that respect which the descendants of so renowned, and interesting, a people are so eminently entitled to. . . ."[11] In 1825 Noah proclaimed the establishment of Ararat, near today's Buffalo, as an asylum for persecuted Jews under his benevolent despotism. The *Cleaveland Herald* declared that "all will rejoice at the enterprise of Mr. Noah, if he improves the condition of his Jewish brethren by directing their steps from the intolerant kingdoms of the Old World to the political Canaan of the new."[12]

Invitations to emigrate to free, sparsely populated America did not exclude a feeling that the Jews were also destined to be restored to Palestine. This restoration was not consciously part of doctrines of the Second Coming or of a political program. Perhaps it was just regarded as a requirement of history during an optimistic age. At any rate, late in 1834, the Reverend Mr. Winchester spoke at a local church on the restoration of the Jews from the perspective of the Second Coming. The *Cleveland Whig* noted that "he proposes that the Jews be gathered there [in Palestine] under a temporal king, and take Jesus Christ as their Messiah." The newspaper was unimpressed. "Whatever credit he may gain, he reveals much zeal on the subject."[13] When Winchester spoke, no Jews yet lived in Cleveland. When the town's first synagogue, on Eagle Street, was dedicated in 1846, the (*Herald*) published an extended account of the event. It concluded on a note quite absent from the synagogue celebration: "A scattered and persecuted people, they with faith await the coming of their promised Messiah, and at the end of 6,000 years confidently expect to be restored to the privileges, the blessings and the land of their Fathers."[14] Jews had actually begun to dwell in Cleveland about ten years earlier.

The first notice of a Jew in Cleveland came in 1836, in a modest newspaper advertisement. Perez B. Walcott and William D. Colburn having withdrawn from their partnership, "the business of the concern will be settled by Lewis Joachimssen, who, jointly with Philip J. Joachimssen, will carry on the wholesale Grocery and Liquor Business at the old stand of Messrs. Walcott, Colburn & Co., under the form of Joachimssen & Co."[15] The new men were selling 4,000 pounds of Rio coffee and other provisions from their place of business on the dock. As customary during this period of banknote fever, they sold "for cash or approved notes."[16] Philip Joachimsen (the standard spelling; 1815–1890) was a native of Breslau three or four years in the United States, and Lewis may have been his brother. Philip fell foul of the Panic of 1837, for he, like many other local businessmen, was served with a writ of attachment for $500.[17] He left Cleveland and a few years later appeared in New York City, where he carved out a considerable career as a Civil War officer, judge, and Jewish communal personage.[18]

Joachimsen was the forerunner, and Dr. Peixotto, with his family, followed. Another Jewish settler, Simson Thorman, who in 1835 left his native Bavarian village of Unsleben, came to the town on Lake Erie in 1837. He must have written to his family in Bavaria; certainly the Thormans of Unsleben needed little persuasion to join their kinsman in America, since emigration fever coursed through German Jewry from about 1820 until the 1870s. Contemporary peasants, who abandoned their homeland by the millions, left mainly on account of land hunger, but the Jews were oppressed by different conditions. Already German in language, education, and general culture, they were restricted in the right to marry in order that the Jewish population be prevented from increasing, handicapped in acquiring legal domicile, unable to practice the trades they had learned, and kept down in other galling ways. German Jews no longer accepted such treatment as a predicate of their Judaism. Some fought on the liberal side for emancipation, while others made ready to emigrate to a free country. Correspondents to the weekly *Allgemeine Zeitung des Judentums* in Leipzig wrote much of emigration and movingly described the departure of groups of fellow villagers who were leaving behind sorrowful parents, brothers, and sisters.[19] Many families were to be reunited in America years later, but at parting the sense of loss reached very deep.

The village of Unsleben, with 225 Jews among its 930 inhabitants in 1837, was one of those infected by "America fever." Emigration was common among Unsleben's Jews; 48 of them left for America between 1834 and 1853. During the spring of 1839 a party of young people prepared to cross the Atlantic. Lazarus Kohn, the local Hebrew teacher, drew up for Moses Alsbacher, a dyer aged thirty-four, and his wife and companions a list of all the Unsleben Jews they were leaving behind. Three had already left for America, and two, Abraham Rosenbaum and Nathan Tuch, had already settled in Cleveland.

> I give you by way of saying goodby a list of names of the people of your faith with the dearest wish that you may present these names to your future heirs, yes, even to your great-grandchildren, of which may you have many, under the best family relationship and under pleasant economic circumstances.

Then he offered good wishes for the perilous voyage:

> I further wish and hope that the Almighty, who reigns over the ocean as well as over dry land, to whom thunder and storms must pay heed, shall give you good angels as travel companions, so that you, my dear friends, may arrive undisturbed and healthy in body and soul at the place of your destiny, in the land of freedom.

Kohn concluded with an ethical testament reminding Alsbacher and the other emigrants of their duties as Jews:

> Friends! You are traveling to a land of freedom where the opportunity will be presented to live without compulsory religious education. Resist and withstand this tempting freedom and do not turn away from the religion of our fathers. Do not throw away your holy religion for quickly lost earthly pleasures, because your religion brings you consolation and quiet in this life and it will bring you happiness for certain in the other life.[20]

The band, thus equipped with religious admonition as well as much baggage, headed for Meiningen, a three-day journey by stagecoach and a gathering point for emigrants from Bavaria and Saxony. Here, on May 6, 1839, a Jewish observer reported that almost one hundred newly arrived Jews were making joint arrangements for the trip to Hamburg. Scrutinizing their possessions and talking to the men, the correspondent noted a Torah scroll and other religious articles and discovered that the party included persons who were qualified to conduct various functions of their faith.[21] When Simson Hopfermann left Unsleben with the Alsbacher party, he, too, carried a scroll of the Torah, which he guarded on the trip up the Elbe to Hamburg and beyond.[22] The emigrants' ship, the *Howard*, sailed some time in June and arrived in New York on July 12, 1839. Captain Flor submitted to Customs the required Manifest of Passengers, 4 in cabin class and 111 in steerage. Eighteen came from Unsleben.

After entering the United States at the port of New York, Moses Alsbacher and his companions proceeded west by way of the Hudson River and the Erie Canal. They landed at the dock at the foot of Superior Lane in Cleveland late in the summer of 1839.

These first Jews, like most of their successors until the 1880s, came from German lands. However, there were Jews in Cleveland who bore names testifying to other origins. Dr. Daniel L. M. Peixotto's son, Benjamin Franklin Peixotto (1834–1890), was a native American Sephardi who came with his father in 1836. He returned "as a boy of 13 . . . to dwell near this [Woodland] avenue, then a forest. . . . " His Jewish business partner, George A. Davis, bore an un-German name and was in the city by 1850. The clever doggerel Massachusetts-born Isaac A. Isaacs composed to advertise his clothing store testifies to his native ease and fluency in English. Very likely Davis and the possessor of a name like Mosely Ezekiel were English Jews, who were among the first settlers of the Ohio Valley.[23] But these were the exception, for Cleveland Jewry remained Germanic for many years.

There probably were twenty Jewish families and perhaps as many unattached Jews among the 6,071 residents of Cleveland in 1840. By 1850, when there were 17,034 Clevelanders, 400 to 500 of them were Jews.[24]

Most of the known native places of immigrants of the 1840s are Bavarian: years later, their obituaries pointedly refer to birth in Bavaria, Hesse, or Rheinpfalz—seldom just Germany—and proudly give the year they settled in Cleveland. Samuel Loeb Kallman (later Colman), thirty-six years of age, from Geroda, arrived in 1840 together with Ella Strauss, fourteen years his junior and from Riedénberg; they were promptly married.[25] Louis Schwarzenberg, an immigrant of 1841, was born in the large Bavarian town of Fürth, and his bride, Phoebe Bloch, came soon after from her native Sloss (Floss?).[26] The first member of an important family of the future, Aaron Halle, was twenty-five years old when he left his native Willmars in Bavaria in 1840 and lived two years in America before settling in Cleveland.[27] Caroline and Jacob Weil came some time before 1847; her birthplace is not known, but his was Heigaloch (Hagenbach?), Bavaria.[28] Jacob Rohrheimer of Lorsch in Hesse Darmstadt also was in America for two years before reaching Cleveland in 1849, but his brother Bernhard came direct to join him in 1853.[29] And Rosa Hays, a girl of sixteen, ventured forth alone from Stormdorf in 1846, later to be followed by her brothers.[30]

Isidor Skotski (Skotsky), who probably arrived in 1850, may have been the first "Prussian" Jew in Cleveland.[31] At that time Prussia meant German Poland; it was long before the "celestial suffix" common in East European Jewry became so among Cleveland Jews.[32] Bohemian Jews, however, became an important segment of early Cleveland Jewry. Abraham Weidenthal, the first of a family which became conspicuous in journalism, arrived from Bohemia in 1849, aged twenty-two,[33] and a good many more followed during the 1850s. Probably the largest family to come to the city was that of Abraham Rosenwasser, who arrived from Bohemia in 1855 with his wife, five sons, and three daughters.[34] Also from the South German and Bohemian central reservoir of emigrants, Sam Wertheimer of Eichersheim, near Sinzheim, reached Cleveland in 1853.[35]

Very few immigrants could have come from Alsace, most of whose Jews tended to remain in France and settle in Paris. David Black came from Hungary to Cleveland in 1854, the first townsman from that land. His family became leading clothing manufacturers and civic figures.[36] The first local Jew of unmistakably East European birth was James Horwitz, M.D., born and raised in ancient Polish Cracow. He came in 1853.[37]

Many immigrants moved about the United States before settling in Cleveland, while for others Cleveland was not the ultimate destination. Kaufman Koch, for example, lived in the United States from 1834 to 1842 before returning to Germany, where he married. He was in Meadville, Pennsylvania, when his son Moses was born in 1846 and in the following year came to Cleveland, where he settled down and grew rich.[38] Frederick Muhlhauser, of the rare Swiss Jewish vintage, from Berne, lived in the United States from 1848 to 1854 and returned about 1860; he did not come to Cleveland until 1865.[39] Others may have had careers resembling former Private Jacob Arnstein's. As a twenty-five year old he enlisted in Cincinnati on May 6, 1847, and served in the Mexican War in Company G of the Fourth Regiment of Ohio Volunteers until his discharge on July 20, 1848. Arnstein moved to Cleveland, where he received the 160 acres of land to which his service entitled him on May 1, 1849. In 1850 we find him a charter member of the Tifereth Israel congregation.[40]

One way or another, Jewish immigrants reached Cleveland in ever increasing numbers. Even during the hopeful months of the revolution of 1848 a patriotic German writer had to acknowledge that "thousands upon thousands of countrymen . . . are eager to cross over to the great land in which millions of their brethren quietly and peacefully earn a good livelihood." In "their dear old home" they could not improve their economic status. The author, a Bavarian pastor, compiled a handbook of the state of Ohio for emigrants and included a few pages on Cleveland.[41]

Eighty Jewish families were reported in Cleveland in 1850. By 1852, when the city's population was estimated at 25,670, there were 120 families. The Jews numbered "about 200 families" in 1858, and in 1860, when the census recorded a Cleveland population of 43,883, there were reportedly "above 200 families," or "about 1,200 souls."[42] Thus the Jews constituted about three and one-half percent of the city's population. During the peak years of German and German Jewish migration in the 1850s, many families completed the migration which one member had begun earlier. Aaron Halle, who came in 1842, brought his brother Moses in 1848, Abraham in 1853, Joseph in 1854, and Loeb in 1855.[43] Sister Regina, to become Mrs. Reinthal, arrived in 1850.[44]

Kaufman Hays of Stormdorf, Hesse Darmstadt, was left motherless when he was nine years old, along with three (or four) elder sisters and a younger brother, Joseph. After leaving school, he worked for a cousin in the cattle business, while the eldest sister kept house for their father and two others "took places at Alsfeld." It was a rather sad and meager living. In a few years the odyssey of the Hays family began. As Kaufman Hays, full of years, wealth, and esteem, recorded on his seventy-fifth birthday in 1910:

> About 1850 sister Rosa with several other girls went to America, and in due course of time sent me a small sum of money. With this money and what money I had managed to save, [I] started for America, father and brother Joe going with me as far as Mainz. Took a boat for Rotterdam, thence by boat to London where I took a [cheaper] sailing vessel to New York which made the trip in forty-five days.[45]

In return for his voluntary service as a butcher, the boy of seventeen received better fare than his fellow-passengers. Apparently his good fortune continued after the arrival in America:

> We arrived in New York September 21, 1852. Had the address of Mrs. Alt who had worked for my mother when I was a baby, and she was delighted to see me. Visited there three days and then took an emigrant train to Buffalo, thence by boat to Cleveland. When we arrived at the dock, a lot of hotel runners took us —bundles and all—to a small hotel on River St., but [I] did not like its looks, so left my bundles and started up the street; made enquiry for a Jewish hotel and was directed to the Moses Boarding House on St. Clair St.

Samuel Moses, who was in Cleveland by 1850, might have been the proprietor; more likely, it was his wife, while Moses was away peddling.[46] It must have been a modest place, but it served the needs of single or travelling Jews who had no family to stay with. No further mention is made of Moses' boarding house; S. Stein's Hotel, however, was in operation by 1855, when it was thought suitable enough to accommodate the notables of the Cleveland rabbinical assembly at a banquet.[47]

In 1859 Baruch Marks advertised his Marx Hotel Boarding House, while L. Wolf was recommending "his commodious house to the Traveling public as well as to permanent boarders." Marks offered "a selection of refreshments," and Wolf announced that "a good lawful drink of excellent liquor" could be imbibed at his bar. C. Strauss' Cleveland House, "in the center of the business community," loftily declared that "the name of the proprietor is a guarantee."[48] The existence of at least three Jewish boarding houses strongly suggests many single and transient persons among Cleveland's approximately 1,200 Jews.

The days of a Hebrew Immigrant Aid Society and municipal supervision of railroad terminals where immigrants arrived lay many years off. Joseph Levy reportedly took in sixteen of his fellow Bohemian families when they first arrived in 1852, and other immigrant settlers also must have been kindly disposed.[49] There were family reunions like that of Kaufman Hays as he approached the Moses Boarding House:

> When I reached its door, some young man called, "Rosa, here is your brother." She came running and it was a happy meeting. She had come up for the holidays with the Hyman family who lived at Brimfield, Ohio. Although she knew I was on my way, [she] did not expect me then. I had a twenty franc piece when I reached this city.[50]

Four years later, Joseph Hays also arrived.

Like all new American cities, Cleveland sought immigrants, domestic and foreign. The city's increase from some 6,000 in 1840 to 43,000 twenty years later came from little else. Jews were of course in the foreign contingent, but native Americans also streamed towards the city, largely from the surrounding territories of Ohio (like Marcus Alonzo Hanna, industrialist and politician of the future) and upstate New York (like John D. Rockefeller, fourteen years old in 1853, with his family).

At first few Jewish families had children, but not many years passed before the single men and women married and formed families. Soon after Regina Klein came from Unsleben, she married Simson Thorman and gave birth to Samuel, the first Cleveland-born Jewish child, in 1840.[51] Isaac Alsbacher, born on October 8, 1840, was the second; he probably arrived before Moses Roskopf, a child apparently born in 1841.[52] Abraham Wiener, born in New York City, was brought to Cleveland "while still an infant," also in 1841.[53]

The early Cleveland Jews were prolific. This is seen from a sample of twenty-five obituaries of Cleveland Jews aged sixty or over who died between 1887 and 1910. The twenty-five—twenty men and five widowed ladies—had 131 living children at the time of their respective deaths. It is not possible to determine how many children they had lost at birth or afterwards, but under the conditions of the time the number must have been high. The distribution ranged from Ferdinand Strauss' one daughter to Simson Thorman's twelve children, Marx Joseph's and Kaufman Koch's ten, Abraham Deutsch's and Samuel Moses' nine, and Jacob Rohrheimer's and Babette Ullman's seven; the mean number is 6.8 living children.

The German Jews of Cleveland, like early Chicago Jewry, were more traditional in their habits than those, for example, of Milwaukee.[54] For example, of eighty-two Jews—sixty-one men and twenty-one women—who received informative obituaries in the Jewish and general press between 1880 and 1917, all but three of whom were immigrants arriving before 1860 or born in Cleveland before 1850, only one change of name is discernible —Schwarz of Hungary became Black of Cleveland. Otherwise they held fast to their foreign family names. The same may be said of forty-six names mentioned in Tifereth Israel's records during its founding year of 1850.[55] Given names were also profoundly traditional. Among the eighty-two, there were six Abrahams, six Moses, five Jacobs, and five Isaacs; altogether, forty-one men bore biblical Hebrew names, and four others bore Judaic ones. Only twenty men's names were not specifically Jewish. Names which became emblematic of pronouncedly Germanized Jewry—Adolf, Siegmund, Rudolf, Siegfried, Friedrich, Hermann, Erich—do not appear. Among the women it was rather different. Only two were biblically named (Rebecca, Hannah), but the names of most others were German adaptations of old Jewish cognomens: Rosa, Fanny, Jeanette, Babette, Betty.

The native tongue of the Jewish immigrants was of course German. Congregational affairs were conducted in German until well into the 1860s. The first English preacher arrived only in 1868. On the other hand, the Young Men's Literary Society, active from the mid-1850s, and the B'nai B'rith which succeeded it were English speaking. Kaufman Hays boarded with the family of Sam Loeb, whose "wife and children only spoke English" and so learned the language himself.[56] Samuel Colman required still less effort, for reportedly he "learned English before coming to America, and this language was spoken in the home instead of German."[57] On the other hand, Jacob Mandelbaum (1834–1915), an arrival of 1852, loyally supported the local German press and held stock in the *Wächter am Erie*, while Felix Rosenberg (1844–1916) arrived from the South around 1880 to undertake German journalism.[58] What we know suggests that very few Jews of Cleveland brought or developed the German cultural ideal which was a feature of Jewish life in cities like St. Louis, Baltimore, Cincinnati, and Milwaukee. Yet as late as 1891, H. Waldman was chairman and Walter Jacoby was secretary of the local German-American Association, the federation of Cleveland's German societies; Dr. Samuel Wolfenstein addressed the body on "The German as an American Citizen."[59] But then, it was not cultural expression, German or English, that occupied the waking hours of Cleveland's Jews six days a week; it was hard work and the hope of prosperity.

Work and its Rewards

When John D. Rockefeller graduated from Cleveland High School in 1855, he sought desperately to avoid his quixotic father's plan to take him along on his trips as a fellow pitchman.[60] Rockefeller's contemporary, Mark Hanna, who also achieved great wealth and power, likewise shunned the road.[61] Both young men, like so many future businessmen of those days, found clerical positions in business houses and began their ascent from that status.[62]

Some young German Jews also clerked, usually in the business of fellow German Jews who knew them, but a period on the road seems to have been standard. Again, Kaufman Hays' experience is instructive. Three days after his arrival he went to work in Sam Loeb's clothing store and boarded with Loeb's family. He left after a few months and for a while found work with a grocer named Wolf. Hays also left Wolf, saying he "did not like the way the business was conducted;" but perhaps the youth yearned for something broader than the little business premises of fellow immigrants:

Got some goods and peddled in the country. Started out Euclid Avenue way for the country and travelled many miles in the course of the next six weeks. Then I sold my pack boxes and all, clearing about $100.00. Did not like the business but made lots of friends among the people I stopped with over night and they later traded where I was clerking. I would help with the chores wherever I stayed, help milk the cows or feed the stock, and go to church with them on Sundays. Where I stayed once over night, they were glad to have me come again, and I remember kindly a Mrs. Maps of Mayfield who would bring me in one of her first pumpkin pies every year.

Simson Thorman, the 1835 arrival from Unsleben who came to Cleveland in 1837, dealt originally in furs and travelled as far west as St. Louis to buy from the Indians.[63] He is listed in an early directory as a grocer and dry-goods merchant at 7 Orange Street, but for most of his life he was in the wool and hide business. In 1860 he and his brothers, Meyer and Simon, together with Isaac Hoffman, Abram Klein, and Frederic Goldsmith, occupied three acres at the city's outskirts (at Croton Street and Case Avenue, now East 40th Street) with their cattle yard and slaughterhouse. Once, when a poorly built sewer dumped its filth on their premises, they sued and won a settlement.[64]

One reason for the heavy representation of Cleveland Jews in the meat business could have been the old Bavarian Jewish occupation of cattle dealing. *Peet's Business Directory* of 1846–1847, the second issued in Cleveland, lists eighteen Jews, of whom six were grocers, three were peddlers, two kept dry-goods stores, and two were in the clothing business. Simson Hopfermann (also known as Hoffman) was the first *hazzan* and *shohet*, but in addition was listed as a peddler. His son Isaac Hoffman (Seckel Hopfermann), who arrived with the Unsleben group in 1839 at the age of twenty-four, first kept a grocery and then became a butcher. When he died in 1890, his firm of I. Hoffman and Son, dealers in hides, had been in business for twenty-nine years, and he had lived forty years in the house where he died. Isaac Hoffman was also a professional *mohel* (circumciser) who performed his duties throughout Ohio and eastward to Meadville, Pennsylvania.[65]

Butchers and grocers and peddlers had little to advertise, but clothiers needed to be more aggressive. Few outdid that balladeer of early Cleveland haberdashery, Isaac A. Isaacs, who was in business from 1845 until he moved to New York in 1866. An early partnership with his brother George broke up in 1858, amid bitter recriminations which came to court. In the inventory taken at the dissolution, the clothing was assigned a cash value no less than $26,189.[66] Isaacs boasted that his was "the largest and most magnificent clothing wear house in the western country." He announced:

Glorious news for the people! Isaac A. Isaacs . . . will hereafter sell his cheap and fashionable ready made clothing at retail as well as wholesale. . . . On entering the tenth year of our establishment in Cleveland, we have many causes for congratulation. We congratulate the public on the perfection which we have attained in the manufacture of ready made clothing . . . and in confirmation of our assertion you have merely to contrast the appearance of the people of the present day with the dress of the same community ten years ago on the advent of Isaac A. Isaacs in Cleveland.

Of his abundant verse, two examples will do:

> I have only one objection,
>   Said a maiden to her lover;
> I have only one objection
>   To the matters you propose;
> I would no longer tarry,
>   I am ready now to marry;
> But I cannot wed a lover
>   In those unwelcome clothes. . . .
> He went back unto his charmer,
>   With a suit of Isaacs' latest,
> And the maiden filled with rapture,
>   In his open arms did fall. . . .

During the panic of 1857 Isaacs advertised:

> Give the producing classes help;
> Sustain the men of toil;
> Avoiding those who rob the till,

> Aid those who till the soil. . . .
> You have no cause to be alarmed,
> Except about your diet,
> If you should want a suit of Clothes,
> A little cash will buy it. . . .

But in December, 1857, he simply advertised "Panic Prices."

Isaacs also possessed sole local rights to sell Singer's sewing machine, an automaton pressman, and "Strong's Patent Army Trunk and Bed Combined." And he had sufficient personal standing in the community to be appointed in 1863 by the City Council as "school visitor" for the Third Ward.[67]

Rivalry, real and contrived, was also expressed in advertising. Sonneborn Brothers offered a reward "for the detection of the Thief" who stole their flag advertising a complete men's suit for three dollars.[68] A. Schwab declared himself "determined not to be undersold" but unfortunately declined in business from owner to agent around 1859.[69] Another local clothier was George A. Davis, who opened in 1847 "with heaps of ready made clothing which blocks up the entrance to his counters, vests, pants, coats, overcoats, etc." Some of his ready-made goods won an award when they were exhibited at a state fair in 1857. In 1859 Davis, Peixotto & Co. was the sole agent in Cleveland for a "life-preserving coat and vest" for merchants and commercial travellers who "at certain seasons of the year [are] subjected daily to danger of death by drowning." Davis left Cleveland for New York in that year, as Isaacs was to do in 1866 and Peixotto still later.

The Civil War's demand for military uniforms infused new life into Cleveland's Jewish clothing firms. In May, 1861, Davis, Peixotto & Co. filled an order from Camps Denison and Belair in Ohio for 2,000 uniforms for the newly recruited troops, and by September of that year they advertised that "within the past month" they had manufactured 500 officers' uniforms. Their "Good News for Working People" in 1862 was that they were about to resume manufacturing after an unexplained discontinuance and would take on two to three hundred workers. By 1867, however, the good years were over, and the firm liquidated.[70]

Siegmund Mann, manufacturing ready-made clothing since

1859 in the Superior Street store he had opened in 1855, also sought army business: "Parties forming themselves into military companies will be calling on us for their uniforms, save at least 20%, and will have a better fit than can be furnished elsewhere." Only one of the three floors and basement in Mann's establishment was devoted to retail; the rest of the business was wholesale. "He employs three cutters and about two hundred hands, constantly. . . ."[71]

Even those who became rich did not always have a smooth road to success and affluence. Kaufman Koch, listed in 1885 as a millionaire, lost his money in 1845 in Meadville, Pa. He then opened a store in Cleveland on Superior Street and succeeded. He sold both retail and wholesale in "one of the largest, finest and handsomest [stores] in the western country. . . ." Cloth was bought from the mills and cut in the store; it was then sent to the small shops of contractors to be made into suits. Koch employed coat and overcoat shops owned chiefly by Bohemians, trouser shops operated mostly by Germans, and vest shops of Hungarians and Germans. In August, 1863, he had a four-story building under construction, and by 1885 his firm ranked as one of the largest manufacturers of clothing in the state. Koch died in 1893, and in 1907 his old business became the Joseph and Feiss Company, one of the largest clothing concerns in the country.[72]

Success on a smaller scale, in the scrap steel business, was attained by Abram Block, L. H. Schwarzenberg, and Nathan New, who began together in the 1850s. Schwarzenberg bought out his partners, and after his death the business was run for many years by his widow.[73] The risks and frictions of small business are illustrated by the lawsuit of Moses Weiler in 1863. A debt he owed Mayer Rose, a jewelry dealer of Lafayette, Ohio, was to be paid by the sale of a horse Weiler turned over to Bloch Brothers. The proceeds of the sale were $80 less than what Weiler owed Rose, and Weiler then sued Bloch Brothers. We do not know the details of the case, which dragged on inconclusively for eighteen months.[74]

Another Jew on the *Plain Dealer*'s list of millionaires in 1885 was Simon Newmark, described as "a banker." About forty years earlier he had been in *Peet's Business Directory* as a grocer. He then went into the wool and hide business, and by 1865, at the age of fifty, he had made enough money to go into banking.[75]

Cleveland was to become a national center for women's ready-to-wear clothing. Its first manufacturer was David Black, who was also the city's first Hungarian, arriving with his family in 1852. At the outset he had a "market garden" near Willson and Woodland Avenues, but he began to make cloaks for women in 1874. After his death in 1880 his nephews Joseph Black and Louis Black (who was also his son-in-law) carried on the business.[76]

With their accumulated funds some Cleveland Jewish businessmen extended their interests into Lake Erie shipping and western Pennsylvania oil. Elias Cohen, a Bavarian who had sailed to Cleveland from Buffalo in 1846 and entered the clothing business, became financially interested in shipping in 1860. His steamer, *Lady Franklin*, was the first passenger steamer ("freight steamer" according to the *Plain Dealer*) to cross Lake Erie directly to Canada. Cohen also owned several freighters running from Buffalo to Duluth. During the Pennsylvania oil boom of the 1860s he was an organizer of the Cherry Valley Oil Company, which was capitalized at $100,000. Other leading Jews were in it: Benjamin F. Peixotto was president; Kaufman Koch, treasurer; S. Mann, one of the directors.[77] Manuel Halle, another prospering merchant, was also an oil investor.[78]

Not every business failure recouped his fortune as handsomely as had Koch. Nor were all Jewish immigrants successful, even the majority; extended obituaries are seldom written about the unsuccessful, and when one is written it is often merely said that "he engaged in various lines of trade." Thus, Aaron Lowentritt, a successful merchant and leader of Jewish community life during its first fifteen years, met with—to use the common expression—"business reverses" in 1858, which he was unable to recoup before his death in 1867. Even so, his son had a far different career. Myer—"Mike" to everyone—borrowed enough money on his twenty-first birthday in 1864 to reach Oil City, Pennsylvania, a boom town in those days. After working briefly in a clothing store, he took a job as a "pumper" at $2.50

a day and saved enough to buy an interest in the wells he was pumping. By the time of Myer Lowentritt's death—which occurred before 1899—he was vice-president of the Oil City Trust Company, president of the Oil City Building and Loan Association, part owner of the Oil City Opera House, and had interests in a Cleveland brewery and cold storage plant.[79]

Mobility did not always end with settlement in Cleveland. Isaacs and Davis moved to New York, and Benjamin Peixotto went from Cleveland to New York, San Francisco, Bucharest, Lyons, and, finally, New York again, where he died in 1890.[80] Two of the numerous Rosenwassers made notable careers for themselves in Omaha under the slightly changed name of Rosewater.

Edward Rosewater (1841–1906) worked for a while in Loeb Colman's store and became his employer's son-in-law. Meanwhile, he learned bookkeeping in a local "business college," and a friend taught him the rudiments of the new skill of telegraphy. Unable to secure a telegrapher's position in the railroad depot, he got permission to practice on the instruments in the depot office. He practiced diligently and won a position and then several promotions. Rosewater was the U.S. Army telegrapher who had the distinction of sending out Lincoln's Emancipation Proclamation on January 1, 1863. Settling in Omaha after the war, he became a reporter, then founded the Omaha *Daily Bee*, and lived to be one of the foremost figures in Nebraska. Edward Rosewater's younger brother Andrew (1849–1909) lived in Cleveland until he was fifteen, when he left with a surveying party for the West to lay out the route of the Union Pacific Railway. Most of his later life was devoted to municipal engineering; at his death he was city engineer of Omaha.[81]

Another immigrant only temporarily linked with Cleveland was Simon Wolf, who came to the United States with his grandparents in 1848. He passed through Cleveland en route to settle in Ulrichsville, where he worked in his uncle's store and helped ship produce to Cleveland by way of the Ohio Canal. Wolf presently had his own store but eventually moved to Cleveland to study law. Shortly after being admitted to the bar in 1861, he moved to Washington, D.C., where he began a long and successful career in law, politics, and Jewish communal affairs.[82]

CULTURE, POLITICS, AND EQUAL RIGHTS

Cleveland was a village when cultural institutions began to be established. Jews took part in them from early days. Very likely the first Jew to settle down in Cleveland was not a German immigrant or a trader, but a Sephardic Jewish physician from New York, where his father had been *hazzan* of Congregation Shearith Israel, Daniel Levi Maduro Peixotto (1800–1843). In July, 1835, the fledgling medical school of "Willoughby University of Lake Erie" made him Professor of the Institutes and Practice of Medicine. He was in town by 1836 and was listed on the faculty of the medical school when it opened in 1837.[83] Peixotto's Jacksonian Democratic principles included participation in popular cultural activity. After he resigned from the tottering medical school in 1838 he still spoke at the new Cleveland Lyceum on medical subjects.[84] In 1839 Peixotto appeared on the scientific program of the Ohio Medical Convention, meeting in Cleveland.[85] About 1841 he returned to New York, where he died of consumption in 1843.[86]

The young Jews of the town kept company in literary associations which resembled those in vogue throughout America. Their programs included lectures, readings, debates, dramatics, and German "songfests" for those with German immigrant memberships. It was their Jewish membership rather than the Jewish content of their programs which gave the societies their name "Hebrew."[87] The Young Men's Hebrew Literary Society was founded in 1860 with Benjamin Peixotto as its president. It planned to establish a library—Peixotto had been president of the Mercantile Library Association lyceum—and to meet weekly for the purpose of "literary culture and improvement" and for "the general diffusion of knowledge among the Jewish youth of both sexes." The following year the society had forty members and its own hall, "already embellished with several works of art," a library, a stage with scenery, and a wardrobe. But in 1864 Peixotto, who was also a leading member of B'nai

B'rith's Solomon Lodge and had just finished his term as national head (Grand Saar) of the Order, convinced the group to convert itself to B'nai B'rith Maimonides Lodge No. 54.[88]

The nation-wide growth of the Y.M.C.A., founded in 1851, encouraged some Jews to conceive of synagogue-centered sport and social clubs with cultural amenities like those of a literary society. A Hebrew Literary Association in 1869 decided "to function as the local organization corresponding to the Young Men's Christian Association."[89] Its leader, Rabbi Jacob Mayer of Tifereth Israel, tried to promote the study of Hebrew and religious literature, but although some members may have desired this, others wished to pursue their German. The Hebrew Literary Society's entertainments included one in 1868 for the "Poor Relief Fund" of the city.[90]

The musically talented Reverend G. M. Cohen established the Zion Musical Society, which may well have been the first Jewish musical group in the land. It presented a "vocal and instrumental concert" in Melodeon Hall in 1862, and the program probably contained some of Cohen's own compositions which he published in *The Harp of Judah* in 1864.[91] Cohen was also the force behind the Hebrew Young Ladies' Literary and Social Society, mentioned in several Jewish publications in 1870.[92]

The members of all these groups were middle-class unmarried young adults who had not yet fully entered the sphere of adulthood. Such groups had short lives. The longer-lived Phoenix Club was a merchants' group organized in 1869 "for the purpose of promoting sociability and enlightenment among the Israelites of this city, at the same time a happy resort to the stranger when visiting this city."[93]

It is remarkable how the children of centuries-old restriction and exclusion at once grasped their equal rights and used them to the full. This was partly because the Jewish communities of western Germany had lived with hopes of emancipation since the French Revolutionary era and had rejected the moral basis of their inferior status. Moreover, Cleveland, like most of the United States, was a new society which genuinely desired and welcomed industrious, ambitious white newcomers. The few court decisions which bore on Jewish status confirmed full

Jewish equality. Allen G. Thurman, then on the Supreme Court of Ohio and one of the foremost political figures in the state for many decades, spoke for that bench in 1853 when he interpreted the rigorous church-state separation clause in the Ohio Constitution to mean that

> neither christianity [*sic*] nor any other system of religion is a part of the law of this state. We sometimes hear it said that all religions are tolerated in Ohio; but the expression is not strictly accurate—much less accurate is it to say that one religion is part of our law, and all others are only tolerated. It is not by mere toleration that every individual here is protected in his belief or disbelief. . . . We have no union of church and state, nor has our government ever been vested with authority to enforce any religious observance, simply because it is religious.[94]

As if to implement these ringing words from the highest state court, Cleveland and other Ohio Jewish merchants who observed the Jewish Sabbath were allowed to open their premises on Sunday. In 1846, for example, a Cincinnati ordinance prohibiting trading on Sunday was held to exempt those "who conscientiously observe the seventh day of the week as the Sabbath," although the text of the ordinance did not appear to say this. It did exempt "common labor" from the Sunday rule, and this expression was held to include the work of the merchant in trading.[95]

There is very little evidence of friction or discrimination in daily life. Jewish and non-Jewish Germans of Cleveland may not always have dwelt in concord, however, and the close cultural connections between Jews and Germans in other cities are little mentioned in Cleveland. It was reported of the rabbi and German orator Jacob Mayer that "since his arrival in Cleveland the former antipathy had given way to the most friendly feeling between Jews and Germans."[96] Jews also fought against insurance companies which refused to issue policies to Jewish merchants. As was done in other cities, leading Jews of Cleveland met in 1867 to condemn the action as a "gross outrage upon the Jewish community of this country; one calculated to revive the prejudices of the dark ages, and not in keeping with the liberal institutions of America." They pledged "to cancel

all policies of insurance in companies which have refused to in-
sure the property of Israelites, and to withhold our patronage
from such companies."[97]

Occasional slights at the governmental level were largely un-
intentional. Governor Seabury Ford's Thanksgiving proclamation of 1850 spoke of "ancient Christian custom" continued in
Ohio, and enumerated "especially the Christian religion" and
the "principles of the 'everlasting gospel' " among the blessings
showered by Divine Providence upon the state. Jews were still
few and unimportant, and rhetorical Christianity was still pervasive. However, Governor Salmon P. Chase's 1856 Thanksgiving proclamation to the "Christian people" of Ohio drew a
sharp protest from the ever-vigilant Isaac M. Wise, an Ohioan
since 1854.[98] In 1857 Cleveland was one of the cities where mass
meetings were held to protest the discriminatory implications of the
Swiss-American Treaty. Benjamin Peixotto was the chairman.[99]
Another meeting, in 1859, supported the movement to restore
George Washington's home in Mount Vernon.[100]

With the approach of the Civil War, Jews in Cleveland sided
with their city in the Unionist but bitterly divided state.[101] In
the southern region of the state pro-Confederacy and Copperhead sympathies were rife during the war. Isaac M. Wise in
Cincinnati thought little of Lincoln and less of the war and
found it best to avoid the entire subject insofar as he could.[102]
The Democrats of Cleveland, however, though unhappy over
their leader's sponsorship of the Kansas-Nebraska Act of 1854,[103]
were of the Stephen A. Douglas school, which, with all its desire to compromise on slavery and the territories, was firmly
for the Union. Simon Wolf first became active in politics as a
Douglas Democrat, while Benjamin Peixotto became Associate
Editor of the *Plain Dealer*, a leading Douglas organ, in January, 1856. After Cleveland voted for Lincoln in 1860 and war
began in April, 1861, Peixotto joined Douglas—who died one
month later—and his editor, J. W. Gray, in unflinching Unionism. Unlike any other Cleveland Jew, Peixotto had a long family tradition in America; his father was an active Jackson Democrat who followed that doughty upholder of the Federal Union
during the 1830s, while his great-grandfather, the famed Reverend Gershom Mendes Seixas, firmly supported the Revolu-

tionary cause which had created the Union. When the *Plain Dealer* turned Copperhead after Gray's death in 1862, Peixotto had left the paper.[104]

The patriotism of Cleveland Jewry after Sumter found expression in the common flag-raising ceremonies. One was held in front of Anshe Chesed in Eagle Street. The young women of the congregation made the flag, and Peixotto and Wolf delivered appropriate addresses. During the war, when Union soldiers were encamped on "the Flats," B'nai B'rith members supplied them with food and delicacies.[105] Congregation Tifereth Israel joined a nation-wide movement of congregations in petitioning Congress to amend the laws permitting only Christian ministers to be chaplains. Long after the war it continued to hold special Fourth of July services.[106]

Bloodshed and prosperity mixed well; the tragic years of the Civil War were also a period of economic growth and booming profits. During these years Cleveland acquired a standard-gauge railroad connection with the eastern seaboard and become a major gateway between East and West. Streetcars were installed, churches and public buildings were erected, water supply expanded, and the ready-made clothing trade began its career in the city.[107]

Military service, the essence of war, drew 1,134 Ohio Jews into the Union Army. Fifty-two were killed in action. Henry Goldsmith of Cleveland served four years in the cavalry and was secretary to one of the officers of his company. He fought in twenty-nine battles. Moses Koch, Kaufman Koch's son born in 1846, served the duration of the war with the 190th Ohio Volunteer Infantry, Company F. Jonah Sloss who served in the 150th Ohio Regiment, Company A, was one of the "hundred day men" called for by Lincoln after Sumter. So was Louis Black. Joseph Black, of the same family, had fought as a boy with the Hungarians against the Austrians in 1848–1849; he enlisted in Company C, Second Tennessee Infantry, and rose to the rank of sergeant. Herman Stern entered the Union Army at seventeen and served three years. Lessman Strauss served throughout the war and marched with Sherman to the sea. Captain Nathan Strauss raised a company (113th Ohio Volunteer Infantry) and served until his health failed and he had to resign.

Abraham Strauss served in the same regiment.[108]

When the tragic news reached Cleveland of Lincoln's "startling and untimely death . . . by the hand of a ruthless assassin" just after the conclusion of the war, B'nai B'rith resolutions eulogized "the irreproachable character of Abraham Lincoln as a man, his purity of purpose as a statesman, his exalted patriotism, and his magnanimity in the hour of triumph. . . ." Believing, as was common in those fevered days, that "this most horrible and sacreligious act" was part of "the conspiracy aimed at the life of the Nation," they pledged "never to cease their efforts" to extirpate it. Benjamin Peixotto, who probably drafted these resolutions, led B'nai B'rith's Solomon and Montefiore lodges in the funeral procession when Lincoln's remains passed through Cleveland.[109]

The Unsleben families and those who followed them had ample reason to feel that they were persons of moral and economic worth in their adopted city.

II

The Establishment of a Community

THE pious teacher who exhorted the eighteen souls leaving Unsleben in 1839 might not have welcomed the zeal with which they pursued material life in a rude commercial town. This suggested unworthy attachment to "quickly lost earthly pleasures." He would have drawn solace, however, from witnessing their resolute efforts to implant Judaism as they knew it in the face of difficult obstacles. They did indeed withstand the "tempting freedom" to "turn away from the religion of [their] fathers. . . ."

The Jews who came from Bavarian and Posen birthplaces to America had been brought up in the centuries-old Judaism of those regions. In Bavarian villages like Unsleben as well as in larger places, Jewish children had been receiving a German education since the beginning of the nineteenth century, but Jewish life continued in its traditional manner. Reform Judaism made headway only after the 1840s, and then only in the large towns and cities. To most of the small-town and village Jews (*Dorfjuden*) who furnished thousands of immigrants to America, Judaism meant being governed in life's entirety by laws which were sacred and binding. Abraham Kohn, who left Bavaria in 1842 and ultimately settled in Chicago, described his trip to Bremen in his diary and added:

On Saturday morning at three o'clock we set out. . . . For the first time in my life I desecrated the Sabbath in such a manner, but circumstances left me no choice. My God, forgive me!

He later wrote:

Thousands of peddlers wander about America. . . . They no longer put on the phylacteries; they pray neither on working day nor on the Sabbath. In truth, they have given up their religion for the pack which is on their backs.[1]

29

Without doubt Kohn's feelings were those of innumerable young immigrants. But it is hardly less certain that many felt few such qualms, and others felt none. Men of all these types joined in founding the Jewish community of Cleveland.

The first corporate act by Jews was taken on July 7, 1840, by the Israelitic Society of Cleveland, apparently an unincorporated group founded sometime in 1839 by Aaron Lowentritt, Simson Thormann, and Isaac Hoffman (Hopfermann). It was the melancholy, simple step of purchasing a burial ground. The group purchased from Josiah Barber "part of Lot Number fifty-two (52) original Survey of said township . . . one acre which said society design for the use of a Cemetery, all "for the consideration of one hundred dollars received to my full satisfaction. . . ." The boundary lay along Willett Street, so the burial ground was known to succeeding generations by its principal bordering street.[2] The cemetery was required less for the burial of the young and hardy adults than for many of their infant children who failed to survive the rigorous climate and harsh environment. The Willett Street ground soon received its first interment. In mid-summer, 1840, on the fast day of the ninth of Ab, a man named Kanweiler, described as a "Rhinish [sic] Bavarian," was buried.[3]

The Torah scroll Isaac Hoffmann brought from Unsleben was the prerequisite for a proper congregation. Word was passed among the Jewish townspeople. An account sent to Isaac Leeser's *Occident* a few years later, in 1852, tells of the simple beginnings:

> Many young men joined the call; and public worship was first held in a private house. Mr. S. Hopfermann was engaged as Hazan and Shochet for the small salary of only fifty dollars; but the people proceeded at once to purchase a well-situated burial ground. The new congregation obtained a charter of incorporation, under the name of 'The Israelite Congregation, Cleveland, Ohio', and adopted the German mode of worship.[4]

A dwelling house at the corner of Water Street and Vineyard Lane was soon acquired and converted into a house of worship.[5] For some reason, most members left in 1841 to form Anshe Chesed ("Pious Men" or "Men of Good Faith," Isaiah 57:1).

They met in a rented room next to Masonic Hall, in Farmers Block on Prospect Street. They, too, were chartered in 1842. The schism in the small community probably had the usual causes—the character of the services.[6]

For four years the two little Orthodox congregations went their separate but parallel ways. In 1844 Anshe Chesed opened an elementary school, which may well have increased its attractiveness to parents in the Israelitic Congregation who had children of school age. Then, on February 5, 1845, the Water Street place of worship was destroyed by fire, a common occurrence in cities of the time; the Torah scroll from Unsleben was fortunately saved. Aaron Lowentritt pleaded in the *Occident* of Philadelphia and two London Jewish periodicals for donations to restore the small congregation. The results must have been meager, for the two bodies reunited under the compounded name, "The Israelitic Anshe Chesed Society of Cleveland." To this reunion Anshe Chesed brought forty-seven members and the Israelitic Society fifteen.[7] Thus commenced the unbroken institutional history of the city's oldest Jewish congregation. West of the Alleghenies, only Cincinnati's Bene Israel, dating to 1819, was older.

With new Jewish families arriving in Cleveland frequently, Anshe Chesed could well plan to erect a synagogue. Land was abundant, but it had to be near the homes of the Jewish residents and extensive enough to accommodate new arrivals as well. Since 1843 the Israelitic Society of Cleveland had possessed a plot of ground originally owned by a resident New Englander of notable family, John M. Woolsey. He was moved to present a tract for one dollar "whereon to erect and sustain a Synagogue or house of worship according to the rites and ceremonies of the Jewish or Hebrew religion. . . ."[8] After several exchanges involving Leonard Case, the future railroad builder and banker, the Israelitic Anshe Chesed Society at last possessed a plot of ground for its building on the south side of Eagle Street in the old First Ward. The cornerstone was laid on October 6, 1845. The *Herald* reported that the synagogue was "to be built in nearly the same style as the Baptist Church, and will be 35 feet front by 50 feet deep, and 32 feet high, with an 11 foot deep basement of stone." It would be "an ornament of

beauty to our flourishing city."[9] Since Cleveland had no archi-
tect, the plans were drawn by John B. Wigman, a master builder.
The Baptist church design was modified, for the synagogue had
such Romanesque elements as a round rather than a pointed
arch.[10] The congregation, now more than sixty strong, needed
ten months to finish its synagogue. The thanks offered at the
dedication to Congregations Mikveh Israel of Philadelphia and
Beth Elohim of Charleston "for the timely aid afforded" imply
that the project was no easy matter.

The mercantile town knew few public ceremonies in its bustling life, so the dedication of a synagogue—a ceremony which
few if any of the townspeople had ever seen—was a major public
event. The affair was held on Friday evening and Saturday
morning, August 7 and 8, 1846. There was no rabbi, so
knowledgeable laymen conducted both the regular and the
special services, as they had been doing for several years.
Aaron Lowentritt (1815–1867), one of the three founders and
"a well-known merchant," according to the *Herald,*

> delivered a sensible discourse in English. . . . He exhorted his
> brethren to illustrate and adorn their profession by living in the
> bonds of charity with all mankind. [Asher] Lehman the teacher
> followed with an address in German, the choir sang 'Mizmor Le
> David' (Psalm 29) and the ceremonies closed with a Psalm in
> Hebrew.

The reporter noticed an inscription on the wall, "A Testimonial
of Gratitude to J. M. Woolsey Esq., and Lady for their liberal
assistance in erecting this Edifice."[11] The *Herald's* comments
were flattering, but the *Plain Dealer's* description concluded
with a sour, Christological note:

> These deluded people are no doubt the genuine remnants of
> Israel. They have resisted the influences of Christianity for 1800
> yrs. and are still hoping for the restoration of the Holy City and
> the country of their promised Messiah.[12]

Land, a building, and regular worship represented a considerable accomplishment for a few dozen families, all recently

arrived foreigners engaged in wresting a living under exacting conditions.

Four years after the dedication of their Eagle Street synagogue, Anshe Chesed felt prosperous enough to engage a rabbi. He was Isidòr Kalisch (1816-1886), a native of Krotoschin, in Prussian Poland, who had pursued his Jewish studies at yeshivot and then studied at the universities of Berlin, Breslau, and Prague.[13] In 1842 Kalisch wrote a German patriotic poem, "Schlacht Gesang der Deutscher," which was set to music and widely sung. He became a journalist, expressing ideas that were radical for Germany of the 1840s. Perilously active in the Revolution of 1848, he eventually had to leave Germany. In America, Kalisch turned to the rabbinate and secured his first position as Cleveland's rabbi. But the Jews he served had more staid backgrounds and aspirations than his own, and after a few months the majority of the congregation decided upon his dismissal. About twenty thereupon left with Kalisch and formed a new congregation, Tifereth Israel (Glory of Israel). Did they leave because of personal differences, or perhaps because of loyalty to Kalisch, or were there intimations of a shift towards Reform? All three motives were probably present. Reform tendencies appeared sooner in Tifereth Israel than in the older Anshe Chesed, but both remained Orthodox for several years. Still, there are hints of religious differences between the two congregations—and also within them.

"On Sunday, the 26th of May [1850] the congregation was asked by Mr. A. Schwab to come together at Mr. S. Loeb's home for the purpose of deciding what action to be taken to found a new congregation by the name of Tifereth Israel." At that first meeting "Mr. Calisch [sic] then explained to the congregation what his intentions would be as cantor and teacher in the event he were chosen," and said that he would accept the position "under the condition that we decide to be present at services at least each Friday evening and Saturday morning."[14] Kalisch "was chosen as Chazan, Rabbi and Preacher and teacher until Pesach [Passover] of the year 1852 for the sum of $400 a year." He was to teach in the congregation's elementary school and to preach in German every Sabbath morning, "or to instruct the people through some exposition of the Bible." Two "assistant rabbis," whom he was required to consult at least once in four weeks, had to approve the form of worship and the employment of new officials.[15] Worship would follow the practice (*minhag*) of Frankfurt-am-Main, the principal community in the members' native region.

The ways of tradition were maintained in both congregations. Anshe Chesed provided a "conveniently arranged" ritual bath (*mikveh*) for women. True, Tifereth Israel engaged the local Gesangverein until its own members could be trained as a choir; but it also employed a *shohet* to provide kosher meats.[16]

As time passed, Anshe Chesed's improved finances and esthetic sense enabled it to abandon the public sale of synagogue honors.[17] It also took the first small steps towards altering traditional worship. Of contemporaneous meetings at Tifereth Israel, which also began to deal with changes in worship, it was recorded that "we parted as brothers with hearts full of peace and harmony," and, again, that "the congregation adjourned quietly and in unity."[18] This harmony was disrupted in 1852 by a novel proposal:

> A motion was made and seconded that no names were to be called to the Torah. Instead the president should be requested to call up by tickets, thus: 1, 2, 3. The numbers are written in Hebrew, *Rishon*, etc., which was accepted by a vote of 12 to 8. Then the president saw fit to adjourn the meeting because of the great disturbance caused by a few of the members.[19]

Debate could be vigorous in those early years. Anshe Chesed experienced "a little difficulty" one day in 1861, which culminated "in a lively knock down. The dispute arose from a difference of opinion as to who should preside over a business meeting." Three men "were consequently arrested on a charge of disturbing the peace."[20]

After Rabbi Kalisch and his supporters left, Anshe Chesed elected B. L. Fould (1812–1880) as rabbi. Like Kalisch, Fould had come from Germany in 1848, and his sympathies lay with moderate reform. On the other hand, the new rabbi had no record of political activity. A native of Muhlhausen, Bavaria, he studied at Fürth—probably at its yeshiva—and then at the

University of Göttingen. Unlike the fiery Kalisch, Fould appears to have been a quiet, reserved person. Kalisch continued at Tifereth Israel until 1855, while Fould remained at Anshe Chesed until 1858. Their later careers took them to various congregations until their deaths—Fould in Norfolk, Virginia, in 1880, and Kalisch in Newark, in 1886.[21]

The Reverend Isaac Leeser of Philadelphia, the traditionalist leader who published the *Occident* and wrote many books, found in 1857 that "all the communities [i.e., both synagogues] at Cleveland are orthodox and do not desire the modern reform; for though it too has its advocates there, it does not seem to have made rapid progress." And this was in the West, where he found that "unfortunately, the state of religion is in most cases very deplorable, the Sabbath being habitually profaned almost everywhere." Cleveland was an exception: "there are many who keep it holy."[22] Years later it was recalled how "it was the exception to break the Sabbath and dietary laws, and it was a pleasure to see the crowded *shuls*, and share in the happy social influences."[23] The mid-summer fast of Tisha b'Av was "observed in the prescribed manner," with a full service on its eve and the following afternoon.[24] The press regularly "noticed our Jewish stores closed, it being the commencement of their New Year. . . ."[25] Undoubtedly the atmosphere of Protestant piety had its effect upon the Jews. "Cleveland in the fifties was a religious community, full of churches, looking up to the ministers as community leaders, and much given to revivals."[26]

Tifereth Israel first used a little frame building on Lake Street (later Lakeside Avenue). Isaac Leeser addressed it in 1852 in "a large room in the Seneca Block" on Superior Street, which he thought was "handsomely fitted up."[27] The twenty-odd founders, aspiring to a full-fledged synagogue like Anshe Chesed's, appealed to the generosity of Jews in other towns. Elias Cohen (1824–1904), one of the founders, "was one of those who visited several cities to collect money for building the synagogue on Huron Street."[28] They probably did this during their peddling rounds.

Tifereth Israel resembled the Erie Street Baptist Church, founded in 1851 as an offshoot of the First Baptist Church. This Protestant congregation started with "forty-four devoted

Baptists . . . largely poor clerks, artisans and shopkeepers, and it had little money." Like Tifereth Israel it had to be satisfied with old buildings and hard struggles until one of its most faithful members, John D. Rockefeller, began to prosper exceedingly.[29] The Jewish congregation was fortunate sooner, for an altogether unexpected windfall came from one of the mail appeals. "Our much-esteemed fellow-citizen, George A. Davis, wrote to Judah Touro asking him to aid the Tifereth Israel Society of our city who were desirous of raising funds to erect a synagogue. No answer at the time was returned but recently Touro died and in his will he donated $3,000 to the Tifereth Israel Society." Delighted and no doubt astonished by this sum, huge for its time and place, the congregation recited one year's kaddish for the bachelor New Orleans philanthropist; forty years later his munificence was still recalled by a plaque in the congregation's Willson Avenue temple.[30]

A lot on Huron Street was bought for $4,200, and on January 4, 1856, Rabbi Isidor Kalisch presided over the dedication of Cleveland's second synagogue with "an oration in the vernacular of the country." Cleveland now had an architect, H. White, and his design of the "external architecture [was] that of a Greek temple; its interior the Hebrew style of finish and ornament." The resemblance to a Greek temple was somewhat remote, for the circular window over the entrance was divided into twelve lights, and the other windows were tall and narrow, giving the edifice its religious air.[31]

A Divorce and a Conference

Among the young German and Bohemian Jews of Cleveland a figure appeared who seemed patriarchal. Joseph Levy, born in 1797 in Pieseck, Bohemia, had studied at the yeshiva in Prague around 1811 to 1817 under that community's illustrious Talmudists, and held rabbinic ordination granted by the Rabbis of Pieseck and Bresnitz. "Chance led" him to Cleveland, he testified, to which he also brought his extensive library of rabbinic literature. Levy was happy to find that at Anshe Chesed, "the majority . . . are pious and attentive to the world of God." They received him "joyfully and respectfully . . . whilst I without fee or reward instruct them every Sabbath day in portions of the Law, in words of exhortation that draw the hearts of man to the fear of God and to His law." Soon, however, an act by Levy became the source of a vigorous dispute over the interpretation of that law.[32]

Around 1850 one Nathan Becker married civilly a Christian woman from Pennsylvania whom subsequently Rabbi Kalisch reluctantly consented to convert to Judaism. At the Jewish marriage ceremony Becker solemnly vowed, at Kalisch's insistence, that he would never divorce his wife.[33] About one year later, however, the *Plain Dealer* reported Cleveland's first Jewish divorce, explaining that "the 'old story' was the cause."[34] The legal act was administered by Joseph Levy, with a scribe to write the document of divorce (*get*) and a third person to constitute the required tribunal. Apparently no civil divorce had taken place at the time of issuance of the *get*. The *Asmonean* in New York, when it learned of the proceeding, indignantly denounced the practice of issuing divorces in unofficial fashion. Rabbi Kalisch, who very likely supplied that newspaper with some facts as well as interpretations of them, scoffed that "the Chief Rabbi was a grocer. . . . Of the other two Rabbis, one is a cigar maker, and the other a pedlar."[35] Actually, the cigar maker, Bernhard Weidenthal, had European rabbinic authorization to function as a scribe; the identity of the third person is not known.[36] Kalisch, infuriated at being disregarded, poured out his wrath and finally went so far as to declare the *get* "null and void" on the specious grounds that only three ordained rabbis could issue a valid one.[37]

Throughout 1852 the Cleveland divorce simmered in the two Jewish newspapers of the time, Robert Lyon's *Asmonean* in New York and Isaac Leeser's *Occident* in Philadelphia. The *Asmonean* and most of its correspondents denounced the act, while Leeser, notwithstanding his hatred of unofficial divorces, backed Joseph Levy. Probably reflecting the views of Anshe Chesed, Aaron Lowentritt also upheld their elder scholar. There is little doubt that the *get* episode soured inter-congregational relations.[38]

Three years after this turbulence, from October 17 to 20, 1855, Cleveland was the scene of one of the national events of antebellum American Jewry. The Cleveland Assembly, as it was known, was the most important of several early attempts to bring doctrinal unity and organizational cohesiveness to the 110 American Jewish congregations. The local participants constituted a creditable group. Besides Rabbis Fould and Kalisch, there were F. I. Cohen and Alexander Schwab representing Tifereth Israel, and Joseph Levy and Asher Lehman from Anshe Chesed. Schwab was pro-Reform, and Cohen had been a volunteer High Holiday cantor; Lehman, as we shall see, conducted a school. Isaac Wise, who had joined the attack on Levy a few years earlier, now described him affectionately as a "learned rabbinical Jew of the oldest stamp. The old gentleman is a Bohemian by birth. . . . he stands firm upon the basis of the rabbinical literature, and commands respect from [sic] his religious position by his simple, firm and decided language."[39] Wise was pleased that "the conference is a general concern" in the city,[40] as learned Jews debating abstruse matters impressed the newspapers:

> The speeches of the different parties represented were exceedingly able, and the debates remarkable for earnestness and learning. Conducted in the German language principally the Hebrew, Latin and Greek are frequently quoted and indeed, judging from the appearance of the assembly, we should say that our city has seldom been graced with a galaxy of more profound scholars or learned philosophers at any time during its existence.[41]

"There is much eloquence, talent and learning displayed . . . ," said the *Leader*.[42] The resourceful Wise exploited his visit to organize a branch of his Zion Collegiate Association, while the local synagogues "gave a great banquet . . . a feast of peace of all parties who joined hands fraternally."[43]

REFORM

After the stirring days of the meeting, the two synagogues in Cleveland returned to routine. Anshe Chesed elected Moses Kupfer its *shohet* in 1857 and required that he station himself behind the synagogue three mornings weekly from 7 A.M. to

9 A.M. "to kill the fowls for the members of the congregation at two cents a piece." Another *shohet*, Moses Openheimer, was probably empowered to slaughter cattle, while Isaac Wolf, Louis Schwarzenberg, and Simon Newmark were appointed "to see that the meat sold to members of the congregation bore the proper seal."[44]

Except for the short service of Elkan Herzman, the two congregations were served primarily by cantors. Jacob Cohen began at Tifereth Israel in 1857 at a salary of $75 which rose to $250 by 1864; he pleased his congregation, in Isaac Leeser's words, "with his unaffected reading, which was correct and devotional." He declined invitations to deliver sermons. Cohen was rewarded for his services with "the selection of any burial lot yet unsold."[45]

In 1860 the 110 members of Anshe Chesed enlarged their synagogue to provide at least 300 seats on the High Holidays. At the rededication not only did a choir sing but an organ accompanied them in Reform manner. Isaac Wise was present; his "surprise reached the highest pinnacle when on the next Sunday the money was subscribed to purchase the organ and leave it permanently in the synagogue; all this was done without a dissenting vote. Thus the Synagogue Anshe Chesed is permanently ours."[46] As cantor Anshe Chesed installed Gustavus M. Cohen (1820–1902), a native of Walldorf, Saxony, who had a German education in music and pedagogy and had been in the United States since 1844. Cohen was probably the first musically trained, modern cantor in the United States. As to rabbis, Wise noted that "unfortunately neither of the Kahals [congregations] seem to be sufficiently impressed with the importance of having such."[47] Cleveland's congregations moved towards Reform Judaism under lay leadership, thus demonstrating what Jews acting on their own desired in worship and observance.

Anshe Chesed held closer to religious tradition and had a larger membership than Tifereth Israel—about 130 in 1866 and 150 in 1870. The older congregation had forthright upholders of the halakhic standards, and in the absence of a rabbi these members' role was magnified.

Tifereth Israel, on the other hand, took a small step away from Orthodoxy by voting for slight alterations in the liturgy,[48] and then moved decisively toward Reform. Their renovated synagogue of 1861 incorporated an organ, and family pews instead of separation of the sexes. There apparently was internal struggle, reflected in several resignations, reelections, and declinations of office in the little congregation. Allegedly, three determined leaders—president Mosely Ezekiel[49] and trustees A. Schwab and J. Steiner—pressed hardest for reforms and finally "overwhelmed and outvoted" those "few members whose conscientious regard for the time-honored usages and principles of our religion would not permit them to sanction or assent to any wide departure from the faith of their fathers."[50] However, it was not a hard-core traditionalist raised in Europe who quit and sold his seat, but Benjamin Franklin Peixotto, probably the only American-born Jewish adult in the city, who had been treasurer and superintendent of the new Sunday school.[51]

Reforms continued to occur despite opposition. The cantor was told to "draw up a form of prayers to be suitable for and after the consecration"[52] of the renovated synagogue. Soon he was "directed to face the audience during all prayers,"[53] rather than the Torah ark like the worshippers. The congregation declined to shift to the Merzbacher prayer book in 1862,[54] perhaps because it was too outspokenly Reform, but it did decide "that the German prayer . . . be substituted in place of the Musaph and the latter dispensed with."[55] The purchase of the required citron for Sukkot was a see-saw question. "A question and vote . . . resulted in the negative, which upon motion was reconsidered, and Jacob Cohen appointed to buy the best Esrog he can find."[56]

Reform by no means coincided with the abandonment of personal religious observance. A petition concerning the Sabbath came before a congregational meeting in 1865:

> We the undersigned members of T.I. Congregation knowing and without hesitation admitting our violation of the Mosaic Law, in keeping our places of business open on the Sabbath day, whereby not only ourselves, but also our children become estranged from Judaism and trusting that our heavenly father, who ordained the seventh day as one of rest and meditation, will bless us with prosperity during the week days, deem it our duty and hereby promise, if all agree, to keep our business places closed on Saturday, and to attend regularly on that day divine worship.[57]

The president and S. Mann, "appointed a committee to circulate the same for signature," almost six months later had only "obtained some signatures." The congregation merely agreed "that the committee continue in their efforts."[58]

A significant step to detraditionalize and rationalize congregational finances was more successful: offerings and fees and assessments were abolished, and each member was classified in a dues-paying category—$150, $125, $75, $50, $25, or $20 yearly.[59] Tifereth Israel could then engage "a preacher of reformed principles at a salary of from $1,500 to $2,000."[60]

Comparatively little is known about Anshe Chesed while Tifereth Israel was adopting Reform. Certainly tradition was more widely upheld, although the evening service arranged by Cohen for Rosh Hashanah and Yom Kippur in 1863 began with a German song by his mixed volunteer choir "which fitted the solemnity of the day, and accompanied by the melodious sounds of the organ, no doubt impressed the hearers with pure and holy reflections."[61] Three strong traditionalists—F. I. Cohen, Joseph Levy and H. Rosenwasser—had extracted a promise from Cohen, as he recalled, to introduce no reforms in worship without their approval. The first Rosh Hashanah service won them over, however: "If this is what you call reform, we heartily agree with you."[62]

Probably this relative adherence to tradition provoked the crisis of 1865–1866. Thirty men of Anshe Chesed sought to join Tifereth Israel en bloc "on certain propositions," one of which apparently was the appointment of Gustavus Cohen as cantor. Tifereth Israel drew back from accepting the group on these terms, and Cohen meanwhile departed for Milwaukee. In June, 1866, thirty-four men presented a second petition. Such founders as Isaac Hoffman, Moses Alsbacher, and Moses Thorman were among the signers:

> This petition comes from a body of men, who come not merely because we have no shelter to lay our heads down, neither is it for our own aggrandizement, it is solely because we see that our hands are bound, and we are stopped in the way of progress, we have outlived the dark and superstitious ages. We are determined to raise the Congregation Tifereth Israel to the standard and to such a beauty as it will make it [*sic*] a joy and glory not only to ourselves as also to our sons and daughters. We wish to

Simson Thorman, 1812-1887, the first Jewish settler to remain in Cleveland (Jewish Review and Observer)

Nathan Strauss (1831-1905), captain, 113th Ohio Volunteer Infantry during the Civil War (Western Reserve Historical Society)

Kaufman Hays, 1835-1916, German Jewish immigrant merchant, financier and civic leader (Western Reserve Historical Society)

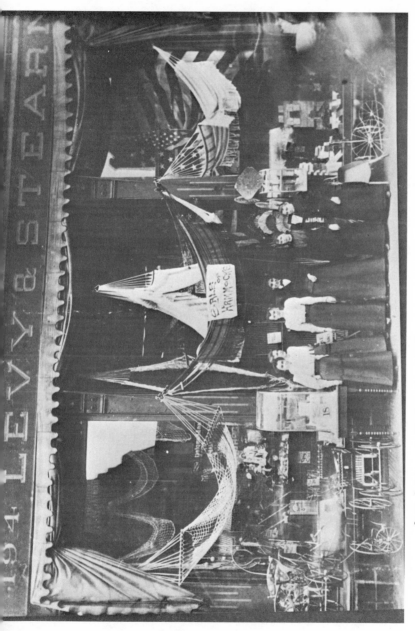

Isaac Levy's and Abraham Stearn's department store on Superior Avenue, ca. 1890 (Cleveland Public Library)

Main Building, Jewish Orphan Asylum, 5000 Woodland Avenue, ca. 1890 (Western Reserve Historical Society)

Moritz and Yetta Joseph's residence given in 1899 as the first home of The Council Educational Alliance (Western Reserve Historical Society)

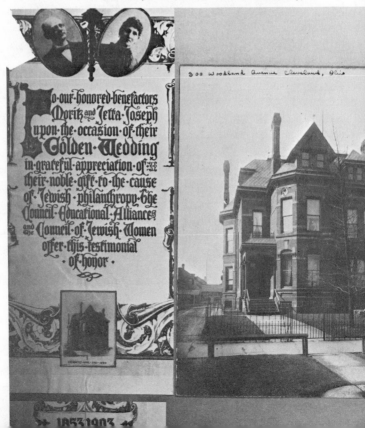

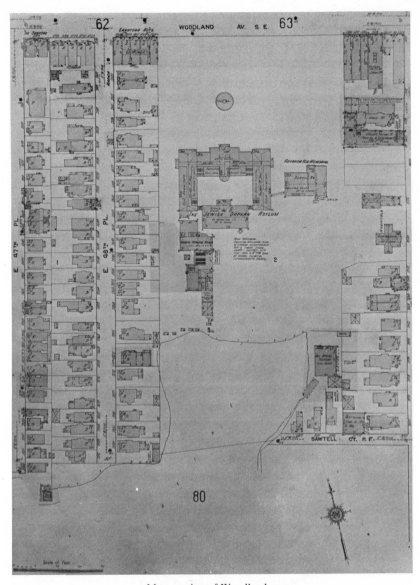

Map, section of Woodland area

Choir of the Shaarei Torah Congregation, 2357 E. 55th Street, 1912 (Western Reserve Historical Society)

The Tetiever Society in front of their synagogue, 2565 E. 40th Street, ca. 1916 (Mrs. Dorothy Beckerman)

Sarah Scher stands in the entrance of her Scovill Avenue confectionery. Above, to her right, is a Yiddish theater poster, while to her left in the newspaper rack is the local *Yiddishe Velt*, ca. 1910 (Mrs. Bernice Silver)

Nathan and Mary Kritzer and daughter Lillian in their bakery, 2944 Woodland Avenue, ca. 1907 (Mrs. Sol K. Marks)

have a good Sabbath and Holiday service as well as a good and
wholesome religious instructor. We will not ask any condition
from you, but our wish and prayer is to have Rev. G. M. Cohen
our Reader and leader of the Choir.[63]

All were accepted into Tifereth Israel, making its membership
eighty. Gustavus Cohen was to be cantor.

The next steps are not entirely clear, but it would appear that
Anshe Chesed, disturbed at the defections, advertised for a
"Preacher of Reformed principles" who could teach its children.
Tifereth Israel had lured Gustavus Cohen back from Milwaukee,
but now he was "urgently requested by letters and the personal visit of a committee of the most influential members
. . ." of Anshe Chesed. More to the point, at Anshe Chesed,
which retained 130 members, his salary would be raised from
$1,200 to $2,000. A Dr. Nathan then serving as preacher left
the scene.[64] Yet Cohen went to Tifereth Israel.

Increased membership—150 in 1870—compelled another addition to the Anshe Chesed synagogue in 1869. Now family pews
replaced the separation of the sexes, and the cycle of reading the
Torah was extended from one to three years.[65]

Yet Tifereth Israel moved more rapidly toward Reform. It too
decided to adopt the three-year cycle for Torah reading. "After
a lengthy debate" concerning the new prayer book to be adopted,
Wise's *Minhag America* was selected, and the Cincinnati Reformer was invited "to be present at as early a date as possible
to introduce his Minhag America."[66] During a festive weekend
which included sermons, a banquet, and the acceptance of a fine
gift, Wise commended the congregation as one which "has always been inclined to progress. . . . It only remains to do away
with the Aufrufen and the second holidays, to be as far as
other reform congregations."[67] (His proposal that the congregations merge went unheeded.[68]) Tifereth Israel strengthened its
Reform affiliation by electing on Wise's recommendation Jacob
Mayer of Cincinnati as its rabbi in 1867, at a salary of $2,500 the
first year and $3,000 thereafter.[69] Gustavus Cohen was dis-
charged and returned to Anshe Chesed, where he stayed until
1873.[70]

The Cleveland congregation loved Mayer at first sight. His
sermons, declared their resolution, were "instructive and

thoughtful, . . . [he] expounds the principles of our faith with a rare freedom of thought, that wins the hearts and convinces the minds of his hearers." His reading of the prayers reflected "an unsurpassable grammatical correctness and clearness of Hebrew reading. . . ."[71]

Mayer's reputation rapidly spread. In 1869 he preached on the *Kosmos*, Alexander von Humboldt's (1769–1859) systematic treatment of the totality of nature, calling its author "the messiah of the civilized world. . . ." He continued:

> With respect to the education of the future . . . the preference is to be given to Humboldt's *Cosmos*. The Bible bears some indelible features of beauty and art and the *Cosmos* is all beauty and naturalness. They never deny the old dame the respect which is due her.

Such statements of Mayer's nettled traditionalist Jews and met with sharp comment by some Cleveland Christians. The *Leader* snapped:

> So the Bible is an old dame to whom these self-styled men of the future are sensible and polite! . . . [Mayer] is merely polite towards the law of Moses and the prophets; and he is sensible to the extent of his position and its emoluments.

Few would notice such a statement had it been uttered by "some enthusiastic devotee of science" or "an avowed infidel," but "coming from an eminent and prominent Jewish Rabbi, it is calculated to arrest attention and excite inquiry."[72]

If he met with antagonism elsewhere, Dr. Mayer had the devotion of Tifereth Israel. When members of the congregation began to be troubled about the *Minhag America* prayer book, it was decided that Mayer should use such prayers as were "most suitable and best adapted." He was reputed "the best preacher in Cleveland." In 1870 he was re-engaged for ten years, although his term did not end until 1872.[73] His sermons lacked accuracy and substance, but they had a flashy brilliance which dazzled listeners who had come from villages and backward towns. They had been much too busy earning a living in the United States to learn much of anything except their own business, yet they had the Jewish regard for knowledge—particularly, in their case, knowledge of the great world outside.[74]

These revolutionary changes in Jewish religious life were at first little noticed outside the Jewish community. When Reform was already far advanced, the *Leader*, a defender of traditional Protestantism, commented that the passage of radical statements at the Philadelphia meeting of Reform rabbis

> take everybody by surprise. It is known that there were exceptional rabbis, who in religious belief were undistinguishable from Unitarians. . . . Hebrew prayers are abolished as unintelligible, the law of Moses is declared to have had only a temporary authority, and the doctrines of the Messiah and of the restoration of Israel are spiritualized into vagueness, and by some, definitely abandoned.

> The "peculiar people" are giving up their greatest peculiarity, that of holding intact all their religious traditions. In the 19th century the sun of prosperity and religious toleration has shone on the Hebrews but a little while, and they are already throwing off their cloaks of their own free will. Pretty soon they will merge into the mass of their countrymen, and be no longer Jew and Gentile but only American citizens.[75]

Orthodox Protestants supposed that Jews would remain Orthodox.

With growing and prosperous membership housed in seemly edifices, Anshe Chesed and Tifereth Israel dominated Jewish religious and, indeed, communal life in Cleveland. More German than English was heard within their walls. Jews of Yiddish background, however, as well as some who desired the worship they had known in their youth and others who were unable or unwilling to meet the rising financial and social standards of Tifereth Israel and Anshe Chesed, opened small places of their own. "As though two congregations were not enough," Isaac Leeser found in 1857 "a third, a Polish one, just called into life."[76] In 1860, a group of Lithuanian Jews led by the Rosenblatt brothers founded the Beth Israel Chevra Kadisha Congregation, which met in a hall over a hardware store.[77] An announcement appeared in 1864 of "the consecration of the Chevra Kadisha Synagogue on Bank [West 6th] Street, over the Soldiers'

Aid Society rooms"; this was a Bohemian congregation.[78] During the High Holidays there were quite a number of "ephemeral Minjonim [prayer groups] where every nationality enjoys the service after its own taste and custom."[79] Out of such a *minyan* of Hungarian Jews grew one of Cleveland's major congregations, B'ne Jeshurun (later the Temple on the Heights). Originally its sixteen members met in two rooms in Herman Sampliner's home in California Alley. Later it met in other homes and in Gallagher's Hall, near Superior Street and Erie (East 9th) Street, then the center of the Jewish population.[80]

By about 1865 Anshe Chesed had 130 members and Tifereth Israel 80; three small synagogues may have had 60 altogether. Since the Cleveland Jewish population was reasonably estimated at 1,500 in 1864, there were perhaps 250 families and a considerable number of single adults. The 270 who were affiliated with the congregations thus represented a large majority of the city's male adult Jews.[81] Cleveland was indeed a synagogue-focused Jewish community, and its members became convinced that the religious ways of their fathers had to be altered. As they felt themselves swiftly becoming Americans in citizenship and business, they wanted their life as Jews to acquire the forms and decorum of other American religions. Isaac M. Wise's term "American Judaism" suggests what was sought. No external authority and hardly any philosophy or scholarship existed in Cleveland to restrain or direct their wish to change Judaism. True, there were ties of sentiment and memory, and several traditionalist laymen were able to slow down the pace of change, especially at Anshe Chesed. But this elder congregation lost members to the rapidly reforming Tifereth Israel. Few Cleveland Jews remained in 1870 to uphold Orthodox Judaism.

EDUCATION

The first generation of Cleveland Jewry sponsored the secular as well as the religious education of Jewish children. Since it was determined in Central Europe early in the nineteenth century that Jews should give their sons a basic general education, many immigrants had learned the common branches in local Jewish communal schools.[82] The public schools they

found in America in the 1840s and for some time thereafter
were poor places. Elijah Peet's *Business Directory* for 1846–
1847 counted thirteen public schools in Cleveland, where seventeen ill-paid teachers instructed 1,500 children (of whom 25
percent were absent daily). Private schools enrolled 500 pupils.
The law of 1851 that created the free public schools of Ohio
had as its author Harvey Rice, a Cleveland lawyer and businessman of enlightened interests who had been elected a state
Senator. Supported by taxes rather than voluntary contributions,
these public schools were meant to be "cheap enough for the
poorest and good enough for the richest,"[83] a slogan which implies that they were as yet neither cheap nor good. Over a
decade passed before public schools approximated this goal.

Meanwhile—unlike Milwaukee, for example—there was no
secular, liberal German school in which Jewish children who
grew up in a German environment might enroll.[84] Jews thus
had to open Jewish schools during the first decades of their life
in Cleveland. Cleveland's first Jewish school was opened by
Anshe Chesed when it seceded from the Israelitic Society late
in 1844. Asher Lehman, its teacher, was a native of Neustadt
near Unsleben. Twenty-two children, aged four to seven, studied
the three R's and were also "instructed in Hebrew and German
reading and writing, translating the prayers and the Torah, and
in Jewish writing and reading, together with exercises in the
catechism." In 1846 there were fifty-six children, by 1849 there
were sixty-eight. A record still exists of the curriculum and the
progress of the pupils,

> thirteen of whom have learned to translate Genesis, and eighteen
> others have made some progress in translating the principal
> parts of the prayers, and can answer a number of questions in
> *Ben Sev Yesoday. Haddath.* The five oldest boys know the
> principal rules of the Hebrew grammar, and are partially through
> with the verbs, not a mean thing in the acquisition of the sacred
> language. Lately, also, the congregation engaged an English
> teacher, to act in conjunction with Mr. Asher Lehman, the He-
> brew master; so that the children can now attend school regularly,
> as they need not go elsewhere to learn the necessary rudiments
> of education . . . . too much praise cannot be awarded to Mr.
> Asher Lehman for his perseverance in his ardous labors, amidst

all the discouragements of a very limited salary in the first place and other difficulties.[85]

An unusual attempt was being made to transplant the improved Jewish education of Germany to American soil. Lehman, who had studied under the "well-known Rabbi Hirsch of Gelnhausen" and had taught in Hanover, served at the school until 1849, and again from 1853 until 1861.[86] The use of the catechism by the Polish-German *maskil* Judah Ben-Zev (1764–1811) and the systematic instruction in Hebrew grammar reflect the eighteenth century Hebrew Enlightenment ideas of Moses Mendelssohn and his disciples.[87] That such a program could continue was probably due to the cohesion of the Unsleben group, the undeveloped state of public education, and, not least, the devotion of Asher Lehman.

German Jewish parents venerated German culture and wanted their children fluent in that language.[88] Isaac Leeser opposed this, maintaining that "a mixed language at school" was "a great wrong." He insisted that "perseverance in this course will keep up a wide breach between the natives and those who speak English on the one side, and the exclusive Germans on the other." All should "unite in the use of English. . . ."[89] But Leeser's counsel was not followed during these early years.

Jewish educational efforts received a rather sugary compliment from the *Daily True Democrat*:

> Our friends, the Jews of this city, have shown their devotion to education and the good of their race by establishing schools here. We cannot but compliment our Hebrew friends on the zeal and energy with which they act in their educational efforts. . . . The thought uppermost in their mind is, that good citizenship requires a good education, and, therefore, they are zealous. So united, so wise.[90]

Favorable comment also followed the public examination which was conducted in 1850 and was attended by the Mayor, City Council, and other dignitaries. The children exhibited their skill in "reading in Hebrew and translating into German. . . ." The Bible and prayer book were the texts; "in German, the mother tongue, the pupils seemed to be perfectly at home."

English included "reading, writing and speaking the language, Geography and Grammar. . . ." Music was taught by "Professor" Adam, a recent arrival from Prague. The lengthy exhibition concluded in the evening with dialogues and declamations by the boys. The school then enrolled about eighty-five boys and girls, "not exceeding 10 or 12 years of age," and its annual budget was about $800. The *Plain Dealer* was impressed:

> These examinations evinced the perseverance of the teacher and the industry and docility of the pupils. If we consider that these children are learning to read and speak two languages quite dissimilar to their mother tongue . . . we cannot but admire the proficiency which has been made in the mastery of what seems to us insurmountable difficulties.[91]

Anshe Chesed's school was "in a highly prosperous condition" in 1855 with "more than 60 pupils,"[92] while Tifereth Israel was making little educational effort. A public examination is mentioned in 1851[93] and there was talk in 1856 of opening a day school,[94] but the little congregation was preoccupied with erecting a synagogue, and their children probably went to the Anshe Chesed school.

In 1858 Anshe Chesed discontinued its school. The reason given was the depression which had begun in 1857, making the congregation unable to bear the financial burden of a free school. Other reasons were also influential. The Cleveland public school system was larger and better and now included a good high school, twenty-three school buildings, and 5,750 pupils. Zeal for German language and culture must have been balanced by an appreciation of the moral and material value of public school education. However, there was still a Protestant evangelical tone in the schools. Thus, during the religious revival of 1858, fervent prayer meetings were held in schoolrooms after school hours, and teachers joined ministers in leading them.[95] "Without a school, Judaism has but a gloomy future," was Isaac Wise's comment on the closing.[96]

Tifereth Israel resumed Jewish education in Cleveland when the congregation's dynamic Benjamin Peixotto set up a "Hebrew Sunday School" and became its volunteer principal. The 20 children who started the Sunday school soon increased to 100, with two men and four women as volunteer teachers. The Sunday school remained Peixotto's enterprise and closed when he resigned from Tifereth Israel.[97] Peixotto's efforts in Jewish education as well as in Tifereth Israel, B'nai B'rith, the Mercantile Library Association, and as a *Plain Dealer* editorialist truly entitled him to reminisce "without egotism . . . that it was my happiness to have contributed something towards the early intellectual growth which has ever marked [Cleveland's] life."[98]

Anshe Chesed reopened its day school in 1861 with 150 children, most of the town's Jewish children of elementary school age.[99] Asher Lehman had moved to St. Joseph, Missouri, and could not be enticed back.[100] The school taught English, Hebrew, and German,[101] but English instruction was by now primary. Superintendent of Schools Luther Oviatt accepted the Board's invitation to visit "and assist as much as possible in bringing it to such a standard in the English branches, as will favourably compare with any in the state."[102] However, the school closed permanently in 1865.

When Peixotto rejoined Tifereth Israel in 1864 he reestablished its school. Without the school, he observed, "parents are obliged to look for opportunities for private teaching at perhaps great expense, or to let their children grow up without any or with insufficient Hebrew and religious education. . . ." In the new school a code of regulations was exhibited in each schoolroom, and in 1870 the name was changed from "Sabbath and Sunday School" to "School of Religious Instruction." The curriculum was rudimentary Hebrew, moralistic Bible stories, and catechism.[103] The focus of education for Jewish children now shifted to the public schools, where it was to remain.

Over 500 children, most of native Cleveland Jewry before 1900, were educated in Anshe Chesed's day school between 1844 and its final closing in 1865. The two main teachers during those years, Gustavus M. Cohen and Asher Lehman, were trained pedagogues—true rarities among nineteenth century American Jewry. The curriculum, though modernized, was strongly traditional. It is a sobering thought that all this effort had no significant impact; not even a fond recollection remains. In this respect the Jewish cultural level and religious devotion of Cleveland Jewry seem no different from those of other American Jewish communities where day schools, if they existed at all, had brief and puny careers. That the day school continued a full decade after adequate public school education became available was probably because the German elements were as important as the Jewish in its curriculum. As German declined in relation to English, the school lost its attraction. Jewish studies could be taught after public school hours. Stronger forces were indeed shaping American Judaism than the educational efforts of conscientious men.[104]

Of Jewish education beyond the elementary level there was none. The learned Joseph Levy announced in 1852 that since his sons were now conducting his grocery business, he was at leisure to instruct qualified boys gratis in Talmud and Jewish law codes. No response came, but Levy did deliver "edifying lectures in the German and Hebrew languages" every Saturday afternoon. These were probably Talmud discourses, the continuation of a traditional practice.[105]

CHARITY AND ITS INSTITUTIONS

Burial in the Jewish manner was performed before a congregation existed and became a service every congregation gave its members. Tifereth Israel originally wanted to share the existing Willett Street cemetery by sharing its costs, but it later purchased cemetery land adjoining Anshe Chesed's. Burial plots were first offered at public sale to the highest bidders, then sold to members at thirty dollars and non-members at fifty. Funerary monuments and inscriptions were required to conform with Jewish law and usage, and even when the congregation was moving towards Reform, it followed Jewish tradition in refusing to permit the removal of a body. A picket fence separated Anshe Chesed's dead from Tifereth Israel's, and an attempt in 1869 to consolidate the cemeteries was no more successful than proposals to amalgamate the congregations.[106]

Aid to the distressed was another deep-rooted Jewish tradition, and establishing charitable societies came as naturally as the organization of a synagogue and a cemetery. Synagogues or other societies sometimes contributed to out-of-town or over-

seas appeals from their treasuries. Thus, Sir Moses Montefiore's appeal of 1853–1854 for aid to famine victims in the Holy
Land, which raised about $5,000 in the United States and in-
spired the founding of the North American Relief Society, received $25 from Anshe Chesed. In addition, individuals sent $57
through George A. Davis.[107] About 1855, a society for local
charitable purposes was established under the typical name of
Hebrew Benevolent Society. Davis was its president, Benjamin
Peixotto was secretary, and sixty members were enrolled. Joseph
Hays, who came to Cleveland in 1856, recalled his efforts for
this society:

> Every member was to pay $4.00 per year. We started with 120
> members, and at the annual meeting the year following, we
> found we only had 20 members left. I realized that we not only
> needed more members, but more money also. I began to solicit
> funds, and called on people to pay into the fund. It gave me con-
> siderable trouble, however, to get them to give. When we had
> 120 members and were getting from each $4.00 a year, we gave
> an annual ball to help the fund along. I was much opposed to
> this ball, as I did not believe we should dance at the expense of
> the poor. I suggested that everyone give as much as they felt
> able, and that we discontinue having a ball. This brought in con-
> siderable more money. . . . I was such a persistent collector
> that after a while when they saw me coming they would not ar-
> gue, but reached for their pocketbooks.[108]

The annual ball raised about $200 in 1860, "far more than has
ever been made." In 1861, Joseph Hays' brother Kaufman became president of the Hebrew Benevolent Society. It must later
have been reorganized or revived, for the Reverend G. M. Cohen
was said to have "founded" it in 1863. In 1866 there were
about 150 members.[109]

Charity was by no means confined to these societies. Thus the
body of a poor, friendless young store clerk who died was
claimed by "the Polish congregation" and interred in their burial
ground. A certain Jackson who performed these *mitzvot* was officially thanked by the local B'nai B'rith and had his expenses
refunded.[110]

A Jewish Ladies' Benevolent Society was established in 1860
with sixty-five members, to care for the needy among "the

gentler sex of our persuasion." Three men were appointed "to give a permanent organization to the society during the first six months." In 1863 it raised $190 at its second Purim ball. As in other communities, non-Jews as well as Jews attended the event—Clevelanders had few respectable social functions to attend. The Jewish Ladies' Benevolent Society became Lodge No. 1 of the Daughters of Israel, aiding both needy members and outsiders.[111] Like congregations, charitable societies were to some extent based upon land or religion of origin. The Hungarian Aid Society was organized in 1863, with all its twenty-one charter officers and members being Jewish.[112] A Hungarian Ladies' Aid Society was established in 1868.[113]

In fact, the early societies were not of great importance in the Jewish community, where charitable activity for local needs did not assume a major role until the 1890s. The ambition and confidence of the city's Jewish communal leaders, however, made Cleveland the site of the first regional Jewish charitable institution, the Jewish Orphan Asylum of B'nai B'rith's western division (District Grand Lodge Number 2). The seed of the insitution was planted, improbably enough, by the guerilla depredations of the Confederate raider General Morgan in 1863. The District Grand Lodge No. 2 delegates assembled in Cincinnati found that he had made the railroad route to their St. Louis destination unsafe, so they adjourned northward to Cleveland, where, as on previous occasions, Benjamin Peixotto came to the fore. He persuaded the assemblage to adopt an annual capitation tax of one dollar to finance the proposed asylum and inspired the ladies of nine cities to form societies to build up the fund. These ladies' groups "met with considerable opposition," Isaac Wise reported. Very likely, many felt that they should devote themselves to their local poor rather than to an unrealized project in a distant city.

The Civil War, while delaying the orphan asylum's establishment, also promoted it by tragically increasing the number of fatherless children. No more than $3,000 of the $12,000 raised by 1867 represented donations of $25 and more; the balance was collected "almost exclusively from the small gifts of the many."[114] In the summer of that year, with the war and the postwar depression concluded, a Board of Trustees was established and authorized to choose a site. It found a ready-made asylum in Cleveland: four improved acres occupied by a large building known as Dr. Seelye's Water Cure, with the facilities needed for a residential institution. Located at Sawtell Avenue (later East 51st Street) south of Kinsman Street (later Woodlawn Avenue), it was an attractive buy at $31,000.[115] Wise grew lyrical over the property's "beautiful grove of native timber . . . a natural ravine which has been and still is being skillfully terraced and from the banks of which several copious and never-failing springs are gushing . . . the crystal milk from mother earth's bosom. . . . A cupola crowns this noble sanctuary of simple humanity and from it one can overlook [*sic*!] the truly beautiful city presenting almost a microcosm of modern active civilization. . . ."[116]

An elaborate dedication took place on July 14, 1868. A parade including flags, floats, bands, and civic dignitaries and B'nai B'rith officials marched to the grounds, where they were treated to a program of oratory. The entrance was covered with a white canvas festooned with leaves which proclaimed:

Seid gegrusst!
Vater und Mutter den Waisen sein,
Bringt der Liebe lehnend Streben,
Selbst ein rechter Mensch zu sein,
Und der Menschlichkeit zu lieben.

(Greetings!
Be mother and father to the orphan
Striving to bring love
To be a just man oneself
And to love humanity.)

From his seat on the platform Wise gazed upon "a vast audience" of 2,000 persons or more—more than the Jewish population of the city. No doubt many Christians, curious or sympathetic, came to the proceedings.[117]

Two months later the Jewish Orphan Asylum gathered in its orphans:

We left Louisville, with 12 orphans adopted there. On Sunday, Sept. 27th, previous to our departure, 5 orphans from Vicksburg, and two from Evansville, had arrived, who started with our party. The parting scene of their relatives and acquaintances on the mail-boat was heart-rending, yet they all soon cheered up and were all very happy on the voyage. In Cincinnati we met the orphans from that place, 12 in number. . . .

When the train arrived in Columbus, we were met by the noble ladies and gentlemen of that city, and a sumptuous lunch was given by them to the little ones. . . . At five o'clock we safely arrived in Cleveland, three omnibuses were awaiting [sic] and took our precious load to its destination, where already the children from St. Louis, Chicago, Indianapolis, Detroit, and other places, had arrived. . . .

The following day . . . in the afternoon the children from Memphis arrived also; by this time there were already 65 orphans in the house. At six o'cock, P.M. . . . all the children were officially received by the worthy president of the Asylum, A. Aub, Esq., who made some very touching remarks to the little ones, who seemed all so affected, that every little child in the room was crying. [Four speakers followed. Then] Mr. L. Aufrecht, the Superintendent, was introduced to the children by the president; he spoke so feelingly, and the scene was so affecting, that not a person of the sterner sex even could withhold from giving vent to his feelings—it was beyond description.[118]

At the close of that year, the asylum was home to forty-six boys aged three to fourteen and thirty-five girls aged five to fourteen.[119] Treasurer Kriegshaber reported "heavy responsibilities and an empty treasury" to start, but the institution speedily stabilized its finances during the boom times. By mid-1869, two years after the asylum had started with $12,000, the building had been substantially improved and $61,000 of the $77,000 debt paid. Annual expenses of $20,000 were readily covered by prosperous trustees, B'nai B'rith lodges, and ladies' aid societies throughout the Middle West.[120] Nothing came from the government in that period. The institution valued its real estate in 1876 at $125,000, and a sinking fund and other assets were worth another $100,000. The standard of the Jewish Orphan Asylum far surpassed the local Protestant Orphan Home.[121] Cleveland Jewry felt deeply tied to these children, who were regarded as precious wards of the community.[122]

Their synagogues, societies, and now the great orphan asylum showed that these prospering immigrants had come far indeed in thirty years.

PART TWO

Ascending to Importance, 1870–1920

III

Native Jewry in the Industrial City, 1870–1920

IN the half-century which followed the founding decades of the Jewish community, Cleveland occupied a focal position in America's industrial growth. Its population grew from 92,829 in 1870 to 381,768 in 1900, when it at last passed its old rival, Cincinnati, which had a population of 325,902. The Lake Erie city more than doubled during the first two decades of the twentieth century, reaching 796,841 in 1920. Cleveland, now sixth in population among the nation's cities, was a United States and world center of heavy industry. Here the coal, oil, and iron extracted in the Northeast converged, brought by four major and several minor railroads, and by steamboats and barges plying the Great Lakes. Industrial plants were concentrated the length of the city's befouled Cuyahoga River and along the ubiquitous railroad tracks, and took up much of the Lake Erie frontage as well. Oil refineries, iron and steel mills, foundries, and machine shops sprawled about the city. A visitor from New England during the 1890s observed that Cleveland

> leaves a confused impression of ringing hammers, the heavy smell of the moulding room, the swing of cranes, the hot breath of furnaces, the red gush of molten metal. . . . Or approach the city from the lake. It is first a long, brown cloud; then a score of dim smokestacks appear; then the sunlit face of a tall building; then the sun is obscured. . . . You have a mezzotint collar, and your fingernails are reduced to half mourning. . . . So Clevelanders smile and endure: smoke means money and money is the principal thing.[1]

The masters of these enterprises dominated the city's economic, and, for a long time, its political life. The civic and political affairs were refined and humanized, especially during the administrations of the city's matchless Mayor Tom L. Johnson (1901–1911) and his immediate successors.

65

Near the mighty, smoke-belching industries were comparatively modest factories producing shirts, coats, suits, knitwear, and kindred goods. Rarely were Jews to be found in the heavy industries, but they were numerous in the production of these soft goods. Jewish representation in trade and commerce and among the city's doctors, lawyers, and other professional men was also quite conspicuous. Within dynamically expanding Cleveland, its Jews held a distinctive place, just as did the other ethnic and religious groups of the city. In 1910 the Jewish economic position was summed up:

> The Jews of Cleveland are engaged in many different commercial pursuits, being important factors in industrial and commercial enterprises, particularly in the manufacture of cloaks and clothing and all kindred garment industries. They control the chief brass industries and that of making agricultural implements. They conduct the leading department stores and are among the most skillful garment workers. The more recently arrived immigrants are mechanics, such as bricklayers, plumbers, electricians, etc.[2]

Jewish occupations, formerly concentrated in retail trade, had thus greatly diversified.

Tradesmen and Merchants

The average Clevelander was likeliest to meet his Jewish fellow townsman in a store. The number of stores greatly increased with the vast growth of population and production. In 1881 the annual police census counted 2,070 "retail dealers." Next year there were 3,064. Even allowing for numerous failures, this was a substantial gain. Wholesale firms, not so readily established, increased at the same time from 312 to 364.[3]

Meanwhile existing retail businesses considerably expanded. Thus, I. L. Fuldheim opened a shoe store on Public Square in 1880, doubled its size in a Superior Street location seven years later, and in 1904 attained "the highest point yet reached in [his] career as a shoe dealer in Cleveland." This was an elaborate store at the premier location of Euclid Avenue and Colonial Arcade.[4]

Cleveland's new masses required garments, and Jews figured prominently among both their makers and their sellers. Competition among rivals could be fierce, as the retail clothing trade demonstrated. At the brothers Jacob and Joseph Steinfeld's large Superior Street store, men's suits were sold together with "a fine assortment of hats and caps;" the prosperous shop's "only drawback laying in the danger of it becoming too small to meet the requirements of a rapidly growing business."[5] But it was the coming of Stein, August, and Garson, "extensive clothing dealers and manufacturers of Buffalo, Rochester and New York City," which inaugurated the predicted "new era in the clothing business in Cleveland."[6] The members of the partnership later changed to Nathan Stein, A. N. Stein, L. N. Stein, and Leo Bloch, also of Stein, Bloch and Co. of Rochester, New York. Garson and August bought out Henry Beckman and launched the new enterprise with "a great slaughter sale."[7] Their Excelsior Clothing Store opened in March, 1883, with brass bands and a costumed parade which led to a store equipped with

> the most magnificent chandeliers with electric lights burning in them . . . fountains running cologne and other perfume; great masses of flowers . . . ornamented pillars of different colored marble . . . the orchestra rehearsing delightful music . . . [a] never ending procession of people. . . . not in Philadelphia, Chicago, New York, or even in London or Paris, can be found a similar establishment exceeding in . . . extent and beauty [the new Excelsior].[8]

Excelsior advertised aggressively, employing not only "hard sell" claims that they sold at wholesale prices,[9] but freak methods like a wedding performed in the show window. "The couple consented to this public marriage in consideration of value received from the clothing company."[10]

Another aggressive retailer opened just after Excelsior, the Cleveland Clothing Company. Originating with the H. Michaels family of Rochester, the new firm acquired Moses Koch as a local partner and became Michaels, Koch and Stern.[11]

All these firms conducted cutthroat, nearly slanderous advertising competition in the daily press.[12] Steinfeld took the lofty pose of the Old Reliable, disdaining the "humbugging gift schemers."[13] When Stein, Bloch and Co. gave up on Excelsior[14] and sold out to the rising Detroit clothier, J. L. Hudson,[15] the Old Reliable clucked that "the people of the state are rapidly opening their eyes . . . the public are on to the swindlers now. . . ."[16] (A later account had it that Excelsior, with its big store and corresponding overhead, was doing only $90,000 yearly business when it sold out.)[17] The Cleveland Clothing Company and Steinfeld kept up the abusive competition, although the former divided into East Side and West Side stores and in 1887 the Old Reliable brothers, Jacob and Joseph Steinfeld, also divided when Joseph established his own Famous One Price Clothing Store.[18]

Still it was more common to form and reform partnerships quietly than to indulge in noisy mutual bombardment. A newcomer from Madison, Indiana, Martin A. Marks, well connected by virtue of his marriage to a daughter of Kaufman Hays, entered the Klein and Lehman men's clothing firm and soon made it Klein, Marks and Co.[19] Joseph and Kaufman Hays, who as Hays Brothers conducted a retail clothing business for twenty-five years, sold out in 1883 to H. F. Klein and S. J. Lichtenstadter, and the new firm continued in business into the twentieth century.[20] Kaufman Hays went on to greater things, as we shall see.

Business failure also appears to have been common. Ambitious businessmen might readily overextend themselves—Excelsior is a conspicuous example—and competition was fierce. An economic downturn which began around 1888 brought the downfall of several firms. A proprietor of record, Mrs. Yetta Marx on Ontario Street opposite the market, was foreclosed by nervous creditors when her assets were merely $1,000. "Mrs. Marx's business has been carried on by her husband and no books have been kept," but the couple may have been allowed to come to terms with their creditors and resume business.[21] More complicated was the failure of Lehman and Richman. One bank went to court to collect $19,000 from the firm and another did so for $14,000, and an array of creditors followed.[22]

Jewish predominance in the clothing trade is suggested by the Jewish names of firms going through receivership and most of their commercial creditors as well.[23] The *Plain Dealer* recognized this when it observed in 1892 that "the Hebrew holidays cause the usual decrease in sales of textile goods. . . ."[24] Not only was the sale of clothing Jewish, but, as we shall see, its manufacture also.

The law of the State of Ohio was considerate of Sabbath-observing Jewish merchants after Judge Thurman's 1853 decision that Saturday closing might substitute for Sunday within the terms of the Sabbath law. Complaints reached the Mayor from aggrieved clothiers, however, that "several others in the same business keep open on Sunday on the plea of closing Saturday, but that they do sell on Saturday and every other day. The subject was referred to the superintendent of police."[25] Very likely it was pressures within the trade which led to the prosecution and conviction of men like Louis Leon for selling clothing on a Sunday.[26] It was also reported that small Jewish merchants, eager to get ahead quickly, disregarded and thus nullified early closing agreements among their fellow-shopkeepers.[27]

Sharp business competition led to the use of demeaning expressions, not excluding religious slurs. One abusive postal card to Excelsior asked, "Don't you know that little Jew up the street [Steinfeld?] is selling goods for less than you paid for yours?"[28] The year before, E. R. Hull, Excelsior's non-Jewish arch-rival, had—with equally dubious form—published cards accusing him: "You open your Doors CHRISTMAS DAY this Infidel Work will Bring Curses on your INFIDEL HEAD you vagabond. . . ."[29] On another occasion an advertisement invited the public to contrast Hull's Sunday closing with the conduct of Old Reliable. Steinfeld, who "attempts to increase his gains by keeping his store open on Sunday, a day when all respectable dealers close their doors."[30] Even in the calmer days which followed the bitter competition and bankruptcies clothing was an exacting business.

Clothing and its accessories far from exhausted Jewish participation in the city's retail trade. At the bottom of the commercial ladder stood the peddler, eagerly awaited in the countryside but scorned and bedevilled on city streets. Complaints arose from residents of streets bordering Scovill Avenue "of the many insolent peddlers who infest the neighborhood." Many allegedly "walk abruptly in houses and if they are not patronized frighten women with oaths and abuse."[31] They were often annoyed in the streets as they scavenged for rags and scrap metal or when they attempted to sell their wares.[32]

In 1896 the Jewish peddlers formed a protective society for the purpose of prosecuting those who molested them on the streets. This Cleveland Jewish Peddlers Protective Society with its membership of 92 charged that the police saw no harm in having "a little fun with the Jews." Mayor McKisson expressed sympathy, while police officials promised to speak to the principals of schools and to sift charges against policemen who would not protect peddlers.[33] In 1910 the Peddlers' Self-Defense Association was established, and quickly enrolled 180 members. With the rising lawyer Alfred A. Benesch as its counsel, its "purpose of self-protection from loafers and rowdies" was promised "every assistance possible" by the police.[34] In contrast, Adolf Daube (or Dalby), a rural peddler, "successfully carried on business. . . . He travelled about the country with horse and wagon and managed to lay by something for a rainy day."[35]

Slightly better off than the peddlers were the hucksters, itinerants who sold foodstuffs from their horse-drawn wagons. Of such men we also hear little except when they were haled into court for short-weighting a customer, selling bad merchandise, or violating some local ordinance whose purpose was to handicap them in relation to shopkeepers. On occasion they were bothered when they struck back at children who pestered them.[36]

Far above these little entrepreneurs ranked Cleveland's well-established Jewish mercantile upper class, stalwarts of the Chamber of Commerce and the Retail Merchants' Protective Association and of the Reform temples.[37] The city's merchant class was by no means predominantly Jewish, however. Of thirty "well-known business houses" on the Superior Street shopping thoroughfare in 1896, six were identifiably Jewish (Nussbaum and Strauss, J. Wolf, Solomonson Optical Co., J. Steinfeld, Henry Baker, Louis Leon), and the names of three were opaque (Standard Shoe Co., Ohio Rubber Co., Six Little Tailors); the rest were Christian.[38]

Several Jewish enterprises were sketched by the *Plain Dealer* in a general survey of Cleveland business taken in 1892. There were Guggenheim Brothers, founded around 1870, Einstein

Brothers, dating to 1865, and Ulman, Einstein and Co., established in 1866—all wholesale liquor jobbers and distillers. Jewish tobacco dealers and manufacturers included two of the three firms mentioned in the survey. In 1878 H. J. Cohen was functioning as a builder and contractor.[39] Mahrum Mittelberger bought out Simon Newmark's hide business in 1871, had I. Allringer as a partner from 1878, and occupied three stories and a basement on Michigan Street.

Among commission merchants Abraham Wiener (1840-1921) was outstanding.[40] He had been brought to Cleveland in 1841 as an infant, and he left school when his father died in 1852 to assist his mother in their little grocery. He also had a delivery route for the *Plain Dealer*. The youngster learned the commission business through operating the grocery, and in his early twenties he set up A. Wiener and Co. on River Street. For thirty-five years the "boy commission merchant of Cleveland" throve in his business, into which he brought his younger brothers. By 1892 Wiener Brothers and Co. had a large premises and a storage warehouse, and did a big business on the Great Lakes and in "all the principal cities in the country," while Abraham Wiener was a pillar of civic and Jewish life. He was vice president of the Cleveland Board of Trade and a director of the Cleveland Board of Industry and of the Walker Manufacturing Company. Of his many offices in the Jewish community, Wiener's favorite was the presidency of the Jewish Orphan Asylum, in which he succeeded his father-in-law Abraham Aub of Cincinnati. Rabbi Louis Wolsey became Wiener's son-in-law in 1908.[41]

As in many other big cities, Jewish merchants were prominent in founding large department stores. The Bailey Company, opened in 1881 and incorporated in 1890, was taken over in 1899 by Louis Black and an associate.[42] The May Company, third unit of a national organization originating in Denver in 1888, was established in Cleveland ten years later when David May and his associates bought out the E. R. Hull and Dutton Company. In 1902 it was Ohio's largest retail business.[43] One of Cleveland's best known stores was Halle Brothers, founded by Moses Halle's two sons, Salmon and Samuel. In 1891 they bought out the stock of Captain T. S. Paddock's store on Superior, and in 1902 they opened their first store on Euclid Avenue. Today's imposing store on that main street served its first customers in 1910.[44]

Nothing significantly distinguished Jewish merchants among the merchant class of Cleveland. The only trade they dominated was clothing, while they were prominent in dry goods, liquor, and tobacco. Their ethos did not differ markedly from that of other Cleveland merchants during America's Age of Enterprise and Cleveland's greatest age of growth. Hard work, diligent attention to detail, and payment of debts in full were the recognized virtues; indeed, they were the ones cited when a deceased businessman was to be praised. What may distinguish the Jews is that the economic virtues of their numerous businessmen were widely supposed to be traits of the Jewish group as a whole.

MANUFACTURERS

Iron, steel, oil, and machinery made Cleveland's fame and wealth as a city of industry, but these were not usually the businesses which attracted the Jews. None, for example, were among the associates of John D. Rockefeller—Harkness, Flagler, and others—whose colossal fortunes were started in the Lake Erie city.[45] There were, however, two Jewish foundry owners, and the Cleveland Brazed Fork and Tubing Co. was owned by three Rosenfelds, H. De Fraque, and A. I. Newman.[46] Simon Fischel (1846–1917), who started as a grain dealer, became one of Cleveland's and the Middle West's foremost brewers, heading first the Bohemian Brewing Co. and then the Cleveland and Sandusky Brewing Co.[47] Nevertheless, the Jews were more prominent in manufacturing those goods they were most active in selling, mainly clothing and textiles. A business survey by the Plain Dealer in 1892 summarized:

> The manufacture of ready made clothing is carried on very extensively, there being twenty-two large manufacturing and wholesale houses. . . . There are six houses engaged in the manufacture and jobbing of hats, two large hosiery manufactories and the capital invested in the manufacture of ladies' cloaks and wearing apparel will probably exceed $1,000,000.[48]

Every clothing firm mentioned in the survey was Jewish, and most of them had been founded during the 1870s or later. One firm, Alt and Willner, made pants and vests in a large establishment on St. Clair Street. They employed 400 workers, and three travelling salesmen sold their products in northern Ohio and neighboring states. Another, Kastriner and Eisenman, was already known as K. and E., later to become Kaynee; it was well on the way to national prominence in the shirt and blouse business. K. and E. had 250 workers; the variety of their production is suggested by its wholesale price range of $1.75 to $27.00 per dozen. Cleveland was also known for the manufacture of men's clothing. Thus the brothers Simon and David Rosenblatt made pants, overalls, and shirts beginning in 1876. In the three floors and basement of the long, narrow building they occupied on St. Clair Street twenty workers, probably cutters, were employed; 250 to 300 more worked for sub-contractors outside.

Cleveland's importance in clothing manufacture was further exemplified by such large firms as H. Black and Co., Landesman-Hirschheimer Co., Joseph, Feiss and Co., and Printz, Biederman Co. Black started in the wholesale dry goods business and then began to make linen "dusters" and "evening coats." This was the start of the cloak industry in Cleveland, led by Black until his death in 1880.[49] His nephews (one of whom became Black's son-in-law) inherited the firm and transferred it to New York in 1893, but by that time it appears to have declined in standing.[50] One of Black's partners was his Cracow-born brother-in-law, James Horwitz, who became a physician at the University of Vienna and practiced medicine for some years after coming to the United States in 1853. Horwitz then joined the Black firm, while keeping active in Jewish and general cultural and charitable affairs.[51]

Jacob Landesman, a native of Hungary who arrived in the United States in 1874, entered business in 1880 with Felix Hirschheimer, an 1865 immigrant from Württemburg. Their company, incorporated in 1896, became one of the city's foremost cloak and dress firms.[52]

Joseph, Feiss and Co. was the outgrowth of an older firm that passed through several changes during this period. The firm, established during the 1860s by Kaufman Koch and continued by his son, became Koch, Goldsmith; when Moritz Joseph bought in upon his arrival in Cleveland in 1873, Koch, Goldsmith, Joseph and Co. was formed. The departure of the two senior partners through death and retirement, respectively, and the entry of a new partner finally brought about the change of name to Joseph, Feiss and Co. Old Moritz Joseph (1835–1917) remained active in his firm until just before his death; the company by then was one of the country's largest men's clothing manufacturers.[53]

Printz, Biederman Co., established in the bleak depression year of 1894 by Moritz, Michael, and Alex Printz and Joe Biederman, survived into better days and prospered in manufacturing "Ladies', Misses' and Children's cloaks, suits, and skirts. . . ." By 1902 their original 75 employees had increased to 300, and the premises grew proportionately.[54]

By the second decade of the twentieth century garments ranked among Cleveland's foremost industries. Women's clothing produced in 1909 was valued at $12,788,000, more than twice its value in 1904, while men's clothing was valued at $5,953,000 and hosiery and knit goods at $2,957,000.[55] During the second decade of the twentieth century, their value multiplied to the 1919 figures of $35,308,000 and $19,433,000 for women's and men's clothing, respectively, and $10,003,000 for hosiery and knit goods.[56] These values were approximately eight times higher than in 1899.[57] Not only was entrepreneurship in the booming industry predominantly Jewish, but so was a considerable proportion of the labor. The conditions thus existed for the Jewish labor movement to take root in Cleveland.

CAPITALISTS AND PHILANTHROPISTS

A few of Cleveland's Jewish merchants and manufacturers did not enlarge their firms but gradually turned to the commerce in money as such—a prominent occupation among European Jewry since the High Middle Ages, but less so among American Jews outside New York City and San Francisco. Here the foremost figure, once again, was Kaufman Hays. He had been an organizer of the Teutonia Insurance Company as early as

1867, but it was a casualty of the Great Chicago Fire of 1871. Hays became a director of the Citizens Savings and Loan Company in 1875 after having been a stockholder there and in the City National Bank. His major role began in 1886, when he was among the organizers of the Euclid Avenue National Bank. In 1903 it merged with Park National Bank to form the Euclid-Park National Bank; ultimately, as the First National Bank of Cleveland, it became the city's largest banking institution. As founder, lifelong director, member of the Finance Committee, and vice president, Hays from 1893 to 1905 collaborated with men like the future governor and ambassador Myron T. Herrick, C. F. Brush, and Solon L. Severance. This versatile man also took over a bankrupt worsted mill as bank trustee and built it up as the Cleveland Worsted Mills.[58] Among Cleveland's other banks in 1886, when the Euclid Avenue Bank was organized, the Union National Bank had the highest Jewish representation among its stockholders: three Halles held $25,000 in capital stock, followed by the rich clothing merchant S. Mann with $18,750, and eight others. All were merchants and manufacturers, but it was only Kaufman Hays who was shifting into finance.[59] In 1902 five leading Cleveland banks[60] had only five Jewish directors among them.[61] On the other hand, the Mutual Building and Investment had mostly Jewish officers,[62] and the German-American Savings Bank had Max Levi as its long-time treasurer as well as other Jews among its officers and directors.[63]

In 1883 Solomon Ulmer had only $300 left after losing his money in business. With that sum he opened a little office in a back room, furnished it with a kitchen table and two chairs, and became a mortgage broker, finding money in exchange for mortgages. By 1904 he was important enough in the field to advertise widely, and in 1924 his firm became S. Ulmer & Sons, Inc., dealing in mortgages and other investments. The firm had offices in most of Ohio's cities.[64]

The Bank of Henry Spira had quite a different beginning; the twenty-eight-year-old Hungarian immigrant shopkeeper turned in 1891 to the business of steamship tickets and currency exchange. By 1916 Spira was engaged in general banking while still pursuing his specialties. These were particularly important to immigrants in contact with the old country, and through their patronage the Bank of Henry Spira could open substantial headquarters at Woodland Avenue and East 31st Street.[65]

While Kaufman Hays remained the only important financial figure among these prosperous gentlemen, it was his son-in-law Martin A. Marks (1853–1916) who played a far more major role as civic and Jewish leader.[66] Marks left the clothing trade to become northwest Ohio manager and later general manager of the Equitable Life Assurance Society, and from 1906 was identified with Hays' worsted mill and banking interests.

Like Marks, Edward M. Baker (1875–1957) combined financial and civic, as well as Jewish communal prominence. A grandson of the Reform pioneer, Rabbi David Einhorn, and descended from other Reform leaders, he had been a Reform rabbinical student until he turned to business. Shortly after settling in Cleveland in 1901 as a stockbroker, he rose to prominence in public life. Baker was president of the Cleveland Stock Exchange, four of whose thirty-five members were Jews, for a period of fifteen years.[67] A founder and for five decades a trustee of the Federation of Jewish Charities, sometime president of the City Club, member of the Cleveland Community Fund Council, and the Jewish community's representative on the elite American Jewish Committee, Edward M. Baker was one of Cleveland Jewry's most representative personages.[68]

Two local Jews were prominent in public utilities. Of Maurice J. Mandelbaum, whose father Jacob (1834–1915) was already a man of wealth, "it is said that he owns more miles of [street] railways than any other man in the State of Ohio." As a principal owner of the Southern Ohio Traction Company, he had ambitious plans for getting control of the banks of old state canals to lay interurban trolley railway tracks.[69] Barnet Mahler, who had an adventurous career in local politics, was "a commission merchant on a modest scale" until 1894. Seven years later he was "one of the principal financial advisers of one of the strongest street railroad syndicates that has ever been formed" and a pioneer of the then-flourishing interurban trolley lines. The extent of Mahler's interests is suggested by his single order of 50,000 tons of steel for rails.[70]

Still more adventurous was the career of Augustus F. (Gus) Hartz (1843-1929), for a generation manager and lessee of a different sort of public utility—the Euclid Avenue Opera House. Hartz left his native Liverpool, England, at the age of twelve and became a touring magician with his elder brother until he performed in Cleveland in 1879. Here he remained, enjoying the trust and friendship of the Opera House owner, Marcus A. Hanna, while shifting to a more stable and highly successful career as a respectable impresario. Hartz's interests ultimately extended to oil and banking.[71] Abraham L. Erlanger (1860-1929), who lived in Cleveland during his youth and young manhood before moving to New York and acquiring national power in theatrical management, bought an interest in the Euclid Avenue Opera House, while leaving Hartz in full control[72]

The Progressive reformer Frederic C. Howe, who gathered abundant experience of Cleveland political and economic affairs as Mayor Tom Johnson's lieutenant, divided wealthy Clevelanders into those "easily and permanently rich," and those "equally well-to-do, [who] have an uncertain status." The former group possessed economic power and were prominent in the general community; the latter were not. The upper elite had their money from local land long held in their families, and from mines, iron and steel, banks, and public utilities. Those who were also rich but less powerful and assured were owners of competitive manufacturing plants and retail and wholesale businesses, brokers, members of the professions, and businessmen without banking connections.[73] Obviously the second group was far larger than the first, and all Cleveland Jews who attained any economic success or importance belonged in it. Even Kaufman Hays, who came closest to the first group, seems to have been more active as clothier and textile manufacturer than as banker.

Jewish businessmen were not economic or social philosophers. Men like Abraham Wiener acted out their social impulses in civic and charitable activity. During the Progressive Era, however, when unrestricted business enterprise and many of its practices underwent widespread criticism, more reflective businessmen's voices were heard. By that time the Jewish businessman of German stock was likely to be American-born

and well-educated. Paul L. Feiss, of the Joseph and Feiss clothing firm, was a civic leader and a national figure in the scientific
management movement. Edward M.

Baker and Charles Eisen-
man (1865–1923), shirt manufacturer, were leaders of the Federation of Jewish Charities who expressed the enlightened
businessman's credo. "How a man has accumulated his means
and how he expends them—here lies the test," said Baker, for
"surplus [of wealth] as such is not a legitimate object of attack."
Every man of means was obliged to "ask each of himself, to what
extent shall I help save human life? To what degree shall I contribute towards the education, the comfort or the health of those
who have been denied what has come to me?"[74] Eisenman
emphasized the "good business principle" to "make . . . employees comfortable and content, happy and healthy . . . because it pays" in better production and in a succeeding generation of the skilled workmen needed by industry.[75] Such a bald
appeal to self-interest was probably what Eisenman believed
would persuade his fellow-businessmen to donate money. His
truer feelings were expressed a year later, in 1911, when he asked
a more radical question:

> What are the fundamental causes that make and keep the people
> so poor? Why is it that in normal times people cannot earn their
> bread?

On this occasion he implied that diseases from slum housing
conditions caused life-long debility and poverty:

> But where are the houses of the poor? Who knows them? Who
> rears structures for them? . . . It is a shameful waste of God's
> good free gifts to let little children pale and sicken and die in
> the poor, crowded homes of this big city. . . .[76]

His own experience as employer and philanthropist also convinced him that

> unemployment, more than low wage, is the besetting sin of
> society. . . . More, perhaps, than any single cause, involuntary
> idleness is responsible for the economic injury and mental bit-
> terness of self-respecting toilers. . . . The employer of labor
> fully recognizes the evil and is working toward its eradication.[77]

Incisive as was his critique, he depended on enlightened capitalists who would strive to cure these social ills. Not all capitalists did so:

> But so long as in modern industry men refuse to recognize the oneness of business and social interests, so long as they continue to promote efficiency in production chiefly in the direction of their own goals, without respect to their responsibilities to the community, just so long and in such increasing proportion will communities be compelled to administer privately to the cause of charity and philanthropy.[78]

Thus, enlightened private business will care properly for its employees. Until all businessmen treat their workers fairly, philanthropy will be necessary.

With their breadth of view and humane sentiments, men like Feiss, Baker, and Eisenman assumed that as entrepreneurs they would benefit their workers in the same way that, as philanthropists, they benefited their clients. They did not foresee that their own workers would organize strong trade unions to discharge functions which they, as entrepreneurs, regarded as their own. Indeed, Eisenman and men like him fought trade unions for years as an infringement upon their rights as businessmen and employers.

PROFESSIONALS

Cleveland's Jewish businessmen were joined by a slowly increasing number of professionals, principally in law, medicine, teaching, and journalism.

The Cleveland public schools annually published lists of the teachers whose employment had been renewed for the following year—the concept of tenure lay well in the future. A large majority of the teachers were women, some of them daughters of well-known local families—Halle, Weidenthal, and others.[79] Few men's names reappeared more than twice or three times, while quite a few of the women continued for many years.

Civil service of a different sort was rendered by Police Sergeant Jacob Stein, who served from 1866 twenty years or more.[80] "Cleveland's most celebrated 'Hawkshaw' " was Jacob

Mintz of the Mintz Detective Agency. He even became president in 1914 of the Ohio Chiefs of Police Association, although he was not a public official.[81]

Limited scientific development took place mainly around the colleges, with little Jewish participation. There was, however, a dazzling exception in the austere physicist at Case School of Applied Science, Albert A. Michelson (1852–1931). In 1907 he became the first American to win the Nobel Prize, after having worked at Case from 1882 until 1889. There were also a few architects;[82] L. A. Dreyfos was an analytical chemist in private business;[83] and Jewish pharmacists were numerous enough for the local delegation to the American Pharmaceutical Association meeting to be composed of four Jews.[84]

A few Jews shone in the arts. Louis Rohrheimer, of a well-known local family, resettled in town in 1895 after European study and travel. A designer and interior decorator, he was also one of the three teachers at the Cleveland Art Club's school and later became a successful photographer.[85] The prominent academic painter and illustrator Louis Loeb (1866–1909) received his first instruction at that school. By 1895 Loeb had illustrated Mark Twain's *Pudd'nhead Wilson* and was supported by his publisher, the Century Company, while polishing his talent in Berlin.[86] The art of photography had an elderly exponent in David Kline, a native of Germany who had travelled and photographed in Siberia, China, Alaska, American Indian territory, and elsewhere before settling into the more conventional pursuit of his profession.[87]

Evidence of Jewish participation in musical activities could be found in the press, which periodically reported recitals by promising young singers and instrumentalists and sometimes noted their departure for study in New York or abroad.[88] The leading violinist residing in the city was Sol Marcosson, whose long career included playing first violin in fine local string quartets and functioning as the original concertmaster of the Cleveland Symphony Orchestra.[89] Marcosson once purchased a Stradivarius violin for a reported $4.000.[90]

Cleveland Jewry could also claim two writers. Martha Wolfenstein (1869–1906) was the eldest daughter of Dr. Samuel Wolfenstein, Superintendent of the Jewish Orphan Asylum, and was his housekeeper after the death of her mother in 1885. She first produced mainly translations from German. Two original works later made her well known: *The Renegade and Other Tales* (1905), and a novel from the Austrian ghetto, *The Idylls of the Gass* (1901). She was mortally ill of tuberculosis when she wrote a play; so far as is known, it was never produced.[91] Ezra Brudno (1877–1936), brought from Lithuania as a child with his family, attended Harvard Law School and was practicing as a lawyer when he wrote *The Fugitive, The Tether,* and *The Little Conscript.* Unlike Martha Wolfenstein's sentimental writings, these novels by a son of the new immigration had an obsessive bitterness. Their portrayal of an immigrant father's attempt to retain control of his child and to remove him altogether from all influence of America annoyed many Cleveland Jews. It does not seem to correspond to Brudno's personal experiences. Throughout his life he advocated the total assimilation of the Jews into Western culture, and only "prejudice and violence" had prevented this end from being achieved. Brudno saw nothing in Judaism which deserved the effort of preservation.[92]

There were several Jewish journalists in Cleveland. Vienna-born Felix Rosenberg (1844–1916) served first in the Confederate and later in the United States Army and succeeded in being commissioned as a rather elderly Major during the Spanish-American War. However, most of his years in Cleveland after 1876 were spent in journalism.[93] Rosenberg, whose wife was not Jewish, edited *Town Topics,* a strongly conservative weekly of and for local high society. A family of journalists could be found among the nine children of the pioneer Emanuel Weidenthal (1828–1897). Two daughters, unmarried, were teachers. Maurice Weidenthal (1856–1917) was city editor of the *Recorder,* besides serving as a local drama critic and then as publisher of the *Jewish Independent.* Henry Weidenthal, another son, was city editor of the *Press,* sports editor of the *Plain Dealer,* and a feature writer, while son Leo (1878–1967) had a long career not only in journalism but in civic affairs and public relations.[94]

The classic professions of law and medicine had growing numbers of Jewish practitioners. At least one physician attained eminence, Dr. Marcus Rosenwasser (1846–1910), one of the eight immigrant children, mentioned earlier, of whom some became Rosewater. After high school he returned to his native Prague to pursue medical studies and went on to the universities of Vienna and Würzburg before returning home to establish practice in 1868. His service as obstetrician at St. Ann's Maternity on Woodland Avenue "was arduous and laborious, for the large foreign population in his neighborhood came to rely almost exclusively upon him." Dr. Rosenwasser became one of the city's leading gynecologists, a specialty which he studied in Boston. He taught that subject at Cleveland's two medical schools, was for some time Dean of the Cleveland College of Physicians and Surgeons, and served a term as President of the Cuyahoga County Medical Society. Consultant, surgeon, family physician, life-long volunteer physician to the Jewish Orphan Home, Dr. Rosenwasser had enjoyed an honored, fully-realized career by the time of his death in 1910.[95] An equally notable career seemed to await Dr. Julius Wolfenstein, also trained abroad and a rapidly rising otolaryngologist, but the tuberculosis which afflicted several of Dr. Samuel Wolfenstein's children carried him off in 1894, aged twenty-eight.[96] Dr. Ignatz Friedman, born and trained in Hungary, established himself in 1886 as an internist and practiced until his accidental death in 1905.[97]

The Cleveland bar had few Jews before the 1890s. One of the first, Peter Zucker (b. 1856), was active in politics and sat on the Board of Education. After he was exonerated by a Bar Association committee of charges of misconduct connected with a bankruptcy in 1893, Zucker and his brother, also a lawyer, moved to New York.[98] Emil Joseph (b. 1857), related to pioneer Jewish families, was a businessman's lawyer who was active in civic and philanthropic affairs.[99] Nathan Loeser and Edgar A. Hahn, sons of native Jewry, established themselves as leading lawyers around the turn of the century. At the same time Alfred A. Benesch (1879–1974) was beginning his career in the profession; it was to form the basis of his long and outstanding service as City Councilman and then as Director of Public Safety under Mayor Newton D. Baker beginning in 1913. The role of merchant and businessman no longer typified as a matter of course Jewish participation in the city's economy. Nineteenth century Jews not only raised sons or accepted sons-in-law to inherit their firms, but also provided Cleveland with many of the doctors, lawyers, and public servants already needed in the complex industrial metropolis.

THE LIMITS OF SOCIAL ACCEPTANCE

The city's life was thus open to Jewish talent. The limitations which gradually crept in were not yet noticeable in 1877, when the *Cleveland Leader* joined in the nation-wide reprobation of Henry Hilton, who had turned away the leading Jewish banker Joseph Seligman from the Grand Union Hotel in Saratoga:

> [W]hen he assumes to ascribe to the great body of the American people the sentiments of bigotry, prejudice and intolerance, which are necessarily impelled in the statement that the admission of Hebrew families will injure the [Grand] Union Hotel or any Hotel he makes a mistake of the character of those blunders which are said to be worse than crimes. Here and there a vulgar beggar of yesterday suddenly mounted on horseback by virtue of shoddy or petroleum may side with Judge Hilton. . . . [Hilton's act] will cause a blush of shame to mantle the cheek of every true liberal-minded American. It is insulting to the popular feeling of right and justice to all men of whatever race who continue themselves as gentlemen to say nothing of the public sense of courtesy and politeness due to a people, at least the chosen of God, and not merely the arbiters almost of the world's destinies by reason of their wealth be honored throughout the world, for the sterling worth and acquirements and the true gentility of many of their members.[100]

The incorporation of the myth of world Jewish economic dominance into an article meant to assuage and compliment the Jews, published in the city whose citizen John D. Rockefeller was just then rounding out his oil monopoly, suggests latent ideas which in time emerged to be codified in social exclusion and the denial of equal opportunities.

The partisan Democratic *Plain Dealer* appeared more alert

to the political advantage which lay in exposing anti-Semitism on the part of Republicans than to the disreputability of anti-Semitism itself. Two attempts by Lewis Seasongood of Cincinnati to secure the Republican nomination for lieutenant governor were "cruelly sat down upon" as party conventions "remorselessly slaughtered" this Jewish hopeful. The newspaper alleged that "a majority of the delegates said they could not go before their people and ask them to support a Hebrew," while the Western Reserve Republicans announced they "would not vote for a d--d Jew."[101] These highly colored reports may indeed contain truth, but Ohio Democrats no less than Republicans did not place a Jew on their state tickets until the twentieth century was well advanced. When the New York Republican Club as well as the Ohio Society of New York blackballed the former Clevelander Benjamin F. Peixotto in 1889, the burden of the *Plain Dealer* was again political: "the fact that he is a Hebrew tells against him with his Republican fellows."[102] Yet it should be noticed that at least in politics the existence of anti-Semitism was furtive and touched with guilt. It was the opposition which would gleefully reveal the truth.

Outside the sphere of partisan politics, an anti-Semitic novel of 1888 was roundly chastised in the *Plain Dealer* as "a specimen of blind, brutal bigotry. . . ." A visit to Alaska was recommended for anti-Semitic and anti-Catholic bigots, "where their blood might become cooler" and where they might be able to assail only one another.[103] Hostility to Jews and to Catholics might not have been coupled in the *Leader*, however, for that daily itself displayed an anti-Catholic tone.

Hardly less than Cleveland's upper class Protestant churches, its temples provided much of the city's civic leadership, especially after 1900. But Jewish participation in the life of the general community did not mean whole-hearted acceptance into it. The example of Martin A. Marks seems instructive. Banker and insurance executive, long-time President of Tifereth Israel (which became The Temple during his incumbency), he was a pillar of civic endeavor, particularly of the Chamber of Commerce. As chairman of the Chamber's Committee on Benevolent Associations, he was the prime mover in founding the Federation for Charity and Philanthropy in 1913—first in the nation, but ten years younger than the city's Federation of Jewish Charities. (John Anisfield, clothing manufacturer and philanthropist, was the other Jew among the twenty-two members of the committee.)[104]

And yet, for all this civic eminence, Marks was not really confident of his acceptance, to judge, at least, from his exhortations to fellow Jews. The activities of Rabbi Gries, later his brother-in-law, drew Marks' highest praise when he declared that "the better feeling that exists between Jew and Gentile in the community is due to his efforts."[105] They were invaluable indeed, for now "a more exalted opinion is held of the Jews and Judaism."[106] Marks "knew that all are pleased at the great interest taken by our Christian fellow citizens who have been attending our services in large numbers."[107] A Christian-Jewish gathering at the newly completed temple, at which liberal Protestant clergy spoke, moved him to think "that the difference between the Jew and the Gentile is not so great after all, is worth to our people the price that our Temple has cost."[108] Good order at religious services was also important in favorably influencing Gentile opinion. Marks warned that "no matter what one Jew does all Jews are blamed for it," so it was for them "to overcome this prejudice . . . by becoming part of the country itself. . . ."[109] All this was not the thinking or the rhetoric of a man genuinely confident of his place in the general community. Alfred Benesch, himself for years the leading Cleveland Jew in public life, recalled no instance of anti-Semitism in his experience of politics and the educational system; but so hermetically was the Union Club closed to Jews that the endorsement of Mayor Baker and John H. Clarke, future U.S. Supreme Court Justice, could not gain him membership.[110]

If Jews were prominent in business organizations and philanthropic effort, they were seldom found in more honorific positions—for example, as trustees of the Cleveland Symphony Orchestra and its predecessors (where there were numerous Jewish musicians, however), the Museum of Art, and the Western Reserve Historical Society. To be sure, the Cleveland Council of Sociology, a group of leading businessmen, lawyers, and clergymen who met regularly between 1893 and 1914 for luncheon addresses and discussions on major social issues, included about fifteen Jews in its invited membership of 124.[111] That hub of left-wing reformism, philosophical anarchism, and free thought called the Franklin Club appears, however, to have had no Jewish member during its career between 1895 and 1901.[112] Jewish families appeared in no negligible numbers in the *Cleveland Social Directory* in 1885–1886.[113] The *Cleveland Blue Book*, likewise started in 1885, was at first distinctly a Yankee listing which subsequently broadened itself. Four of the Jewish family names in the 1885–1886 *Social Directory* did not appear in the Blue Book and two—Rabbi Gries and A. F. Hartz—were added. On the other hand, Catholics and "non-English," including Jews, were reportedly kept out of social clubs and fashionable benevolent societies.[114]

For some time Jews retained their prominence in Cleveland's shrinking Germanic sphere. The Gesangverein membership roster of 1883 showed a large contingent of both singing and supporting Jewish members.[115] True, in the early 1880s a few members of the Gesangverein systematically blackballed Jewish applicants. However, the large majority of the society saw this with mounting displeasure. The identity of the blackballers was discovered and their practice ceased. This form of social exclusion was at that time considered reprehensible and had to be carried on furtively.[116]

Jacob Mandelbaum and Abraham Wiener, who was not of German birth, were prominent investors in the local German press.[117] But it was Samuel Wolfenstein, rabbi and director of the Jewish Orphan Home, who came to be "regarded as a representative German of our city, having always taken a great interest in the welfare of our German citizens. . . ."[118] He presided over the North American Saengerfest of 1893 which was held in Cleveland, and other Jews were prominent among its organizers and participants and in the audience.[119] In his opening speech, Wolfenstein declared that the "German-American has become conscious of his new and well loved fatherland. . . ." To fulfill the glorious destiny of America, "the German-American must lend to the American genius the mightiest force and the finest product of his own, the German genius," of which he pronounced music the supreme expression.[120] It is truly noteworthy that this address included no reference to Germany itself. Quite possibly, Wolfenstein, like many liberal German-Americans, regarded with profound disillusion the authoritarian regime which had unified and now ruled Germany. The German anti-Semitic revival of the 1880s must also have dampened enthusiasm for the native land, especially among Jews.[121] What was treasured in the German heritage was therefore spiritualized, detached from German soil and government, and adapted philosophically to American life. Wolfenstein's speech suggests such a mode of thought. Negative developments in Germany, the American trend towards cultural assimilation, and the coming of non-Germanic Jews from Eastern Europe made this Saengerfest of 1893 the farewell song of Jewish Germanism in Cleveland.

Cleveland sheltered an abundance of German and other fraternal secret orders which provided death benefits and social pleasure to thousands of townspeople. It was estimated in 1904 that 50,000 persons belonged to some order, in addition to an uncounted number of Masons.[122] One of the larger orders in 1889 was the Knights of Pythias, which had thirteen local lodges. To join, it was necessary only "to recognize the fatherhood of God and the brotherhood of man, to be sound in health and of good moral character."[123] However, forty Jewish applicants set about organizing their own Deak Lodge, allegedly because "in several of the branches. . . . [they] were blackballed simply on account of their religion. . . . It has been done in numerous instances. . . ."[124] Denials followed, but they were usually qualified, like that of one Deak member: "There is just enough truth in your article to give the *Plain Dealer* an excuse to publish it, but that's all."[125] Louis Black, a Pythian and leader of Cleveland's Hungarians, who, like himself, were then almost all Jews, reluctantly observed "that Deak lodge consisted almost entirely of Jewish members and was chartered for their benefit."[126] Rabbi Machol advised Jews to "go where they are wanted," but felt confident that the blackballing at the Pythian lodges, like that at the Gesangverein, was the furtive act of a few hostile individuals.[127] The official *Pythian Knight* also repudiated anti-Semitic exclusion,[128] and there the matter appeared to rest—official policy versus individual lodge action and Jewish reaction. Quite different was the advice of Supreme President Wheeler to

The Perry Street Theater, home of Yiddish drama and vaudeville. In the car
(l. to r.) are Alex, Barney and Charles Bernstein, 1905 (Mrs. David Schulman)

Cleveland Jewish Band, I. J. Masten, director, gave its first concert in January,
1915 (Mrs. Esther Berman)

Dedication ceremony of Camp Wise, 1907 (Western Reserve Historical Society)

Children boarding the Woodland Avenue Interurban en route to Hiram House Camp, ca. 1905 (Western Reserve Historical Society)

Montefiore Home for Aged, established in 1882 at E. 55th Street and Woodland Avenue. ca. 1910. (Cleveland Trust Co.)

The Jewish Orthodox Home for Aged with a new brick facade, 5912 Scovill Avenue, 1911-1921 (Western Reserve Historical Society)

Olam Katan ("Small World"), December 14, 1906, a newspaper produced by the children of Garber and Floch's Hebrew School. The photograph shows the young writers and editors (Western Reserve Historical Society)

Sewing Room of L. M. Weiss' and J. A. Randell's Cleveland Skirt Factory, 227 St. Clair Avenue, ca. 1905 (Jewish Community Federation)

Congregation Anshe Chesed's (Fairmount Temple) Scovill Avenue Temple at East 25th Street, occupied from 1887 to 1912 (Fairmount Temple)

Congregation Anshe Chesed's (Fairmount Temple) Euclid Avenue Temple, dedicated in 1912 (Fairmount Temple)

Congregation Anshe Chesed's (Fairmount Temple) synagogue on Eagle Street, occupied from 1846 to 1887. Congregation B'nai Jeshurun (Temple on the Heights) occupied it from 1887 to 1906. (Fairmount Temple)

Gustavus M. Cohen (1820-1902), cantor and composer, rabbi at Congregations Anshe Chesed and Tifereth Israel from 1861 to 1867 (Fairmount Temple)

Rabbi Michael Machol (1846-1912) of Congregation Anshe Chesed, 1876-1906 (Fairmount Temple)

Rabbi Barnett R. Brickner (1892-1958) of Congregation Anshe Chesed, 1925-1958 (Jewish Community Federation)

Rabbi Louis Wolsey (1877-1959) of Congregation Anshe Chesed—Euclid Avenue Temple, 1907-1924 (Mrs. James Elsoffer)

the Chicago lodges of his small Order of Tonti—again in 1889—
advising them to keep out Jews, who were dangerous dynamit-
ers and communists. Trouble was expected from Jewish members of Cleveland lodges, outraged by Wheeler's canard.[129]

Jews continued to socialize with other Jews. Yet the old fa-
miliarity was disappearing as the Jewish community grew
numerically larger and socially differentiated. Thus the custom of
young ladies holding open house to all callers on New Year's
Day was "becoming more of a farce each year" because of unknown visitors, and its cessation was "near at hand" in 1885.[130]
Jewish social clubs sprang up to organize and stratify Jewish
social life, and passed from the scene with equal regularity.
What brought such clubs to social success or failure is implied
by a report on the dissolution of one of them:

> The discord arose at the time when the officials grew over-con-
> fident of their success and admitted all grades of Hebrews, Ger-
> man, Hungarian, Bohemian and Polish, in the Society. . . .
> One of the main features which will bring about discord among
> the Hebrews, is allowing all grades to associate together. It is an
> essential point here that all factions associate separately. . . .
> Harmony was broken.[131]

At the summit of Jewish clubs stood the Excelsior. "Club opening is Brilliant Event," the *Plain Dealer* reported to its readers
about the Excelsior Club's ball which ushered in 1909. "Cleveland has seen few, if any, displays of handsomer gowns or more
magnificent jewels than those worn by the women in attendance
at this affair,"[132] which inaugurated the opulent new clubhouse.
The Excelsior Club, which had existed since 1872 in progres-
sively more luxurious quarters, was the scene of prosperous
German[133] Jews' social affairs.[134] However, it is likely that none
of the Excelsior's 300 members forgot even during the New
Year's Eve splendor how fellow upper-class citizens had devious-
ly sought to prevent them from building in the fashionable environs of Western Reserve University. "The so-called aristocracy
of the East End object to a Jewish Club in their neighborhood.
. . . There is only one reason and that is, the Excelsior Club
is a Jewish organisation!"[135] President Thwing sought to buy
the land for his university's alleged needs and declined to prom-

ise an adjacent site as a substitute. Then the board of the Museum of Art sought Mayor Johnson's aid in condemning the land for still another approach to its proposed building—a necessity it had just discovered. The Mayor "positively refused to become a partner in the conspiracy" and told Excelsior to build its clubhouse.[136]

The bitterness which accompanied building the new home on Euclid Avenue served notice that wealth and culture and civic activity would not admit Jews to the company of their Gentile social and economic equals, a condition which was then becoming the common experience of American Jews. A policy of polite self-exclusion came to be generally followed by Jews, although Alfred Benesch possessed the prestige and determination to embarrass the exclusionist Union Club by preventing a dinner of his fellow Harvard alumni from being held there.[137]

Lower down the social stepladder, Jews became uncomfortably familiar during the 1890s and the first decade of the twentieth century with manifestations of hostility. Molesting Jewish peddlers on city streets (mentioned elsewhere) was probably an old story. However, Jews were disturbed to see derogatory stories appear in high school publications, even if they were suppressed after Jewish protests.[138] On one occasion, High Holiday worshippers leaving B'ne Jeshurun were assaulted by a band of about forty youths from a high school nearby.[139]

It was not only "a sudden outburst of some petty prejudice," as the Young Men's Hebrew Association interpreted such occurrences, that inspired some Gentile house owners to refuse to rent to Jews.[140] Thirteen years earlier, in 1895, an unnamed "prominent Jewish family" rented a house on Kensington Street, only to find their landlord attempting to renege on the lease after hostile neighbors threatened "they would make it unpleasant for them in every way." Reportedly, the matter was "amicably arranged." The *Hebrew Observer* was uncharacteristically fervent, however:

> We would say emphatically that the streets of Cleveland are not devoted to the exclusive use or benefit of any religious sect. The Jews do not intend to limit themselves to any one street, district or any special location.[141]

The same organization appealed to Jews to boycott theatres which presented "Hebrew comedians"—vaudeville performers whose stock in trade featured offensive characterizations of Jews.[142] Some of these manifestations may have been common for years, and the militancy of Y.M.H.A. members was just then making them public. This increased hostility may well have been partly due to the aspirations of the new Jewish masses of Cleveland, many of whom were energetically seeking education and housing and jobs outside the confines of the immigrant Jewish quarter, and were encountering segments of the population unaccustomed and unwilling to accept them on an equal social level.

THE POLITICAL ARENA

Not many Jews, obviously, could expect a listing in a society book or a place on the board of a civic institution. Most Jews' acceptance by society was indirect, through the distinction which their individual representative figures might attain; this was especially true in politics. The level of municipal political leadership was rather low in 1888, when Jewish participation in political and professional life was set forth:

> There is an unusually large number of Jewish physicians, a number of attorneys who have well earned reputations and a few journalists. The Board of Education is composed of twenty members, and four of them are coreligionists, Peter Zucker, Esq., the President, Mr. Barney Mahler [a former president], Mr. Joseph Goodheart, and Mr. Frederick Gunzenhauser. The Hon. Joseph Black is now in Buda Pesth, representing the United States as Consul at that point. His brother, Louis Black, is a member of the Board of Fire Commissioners and Colonel in the Uniform Rank of Knights of Pythias. . . . Mr. Kaufman Hays is the Vice President of the City Council; Mr. Jacob Mandelbaum is a member of the Board of Equalization, and Felix Rosenberg is a member of the Board of Health.[143]

Most of these were patronage appointments. Few members of the Board of Health, for example, could have been more modestly equipped for their duties than Felix Rosenberg, faithful

Republican editor. Mandelbaum had the successful business-man's and real estate operator's knowledge for his position. Kaufman Hays capably saved the city's credit after City Treasurer Axworthy defalcated. The most conspicuous service rendered by Jews was their membership on the Board of Education, a phenomenon in other American cities as well.[144] These were all appointive, not elective, offices. Jewish citizens could reasonably feel that their group had not been slighted or disregarded by the holders of political power.

It has been noted that Cleveland's early Yankee stock tended after approximately 1873 to withdraw from the political domination it had held since the city's founding, and to concentrate in business and civic endeavor.[145] Although they would not have minded seeing fellow Jews in honorific political positions, the Jewish pioneers generally stayed away from politics; Mahler and Mandelbaum, who did mix, were involved in public utilities. One of the few who sought elective office, Joseph C. Bloch, a lawyer active in Cleveland Hungarian affairs, ran successfully as a Republican for the State Legislature and later became a municipal judge. The *American Israelite*'s local correspondent, piously disclaiming political partisanship, noticed Bloch as "the only Jew on that massive ticket" and recommended that he "should receive the hearty support of the Jewish population in Cleveland, which will go a great ways toward his success."[146]

Next year the local *Hebrew Observer* sought to mobilize Cleveland Jews for a contrary purpose—to defeat John I. Nunn for a City Council seat. Nunn was accused of tricking a Jewish candidate to quit the race for the party's nomination, of tolerating someone in his retinue who declared he "wouldn't support a Jew for any office," and of having unfairly connived to defeat Abraham Wiener on Election Day: "Need more be said? We have nothing to say against Mr. Nunn's record as a councilman, but we are satisfied that his opponent will make, at least, as able a representative as Mr. Nunn. . . . Liberal Gentiles or Israelites, what say you? What action should you take at the polls?"[147] Nunn lost. The untoward remark by one of his confidants, together with unfair tactics against candidates who were Jews, persuaded the well-informed editor that Jews who wished to attain elective office still had to be protected through group

solidarity, and that an incumbent with a relatively satisfactory
record had to be defeated to make the lesson plain. The next
year Nunn nominated Aaron Hahn for representative in the Legislature, one of the former rabbi's several unsuccessful political
forays.[148] Politics offered various ways to make amends.

The politics of Cleveland during the last three decades of
the nineteenth century were those of large American cities in
general. Businessmen interested in little more than public
order and low taxes, men who sought municipal charters which
granted monopoly rights to provide public utilities, particularly
streetcars, helped to debase public life in order to acquire and
hold these lucrative franchises. Maurice Maudelbaum and Barnet Mahler ranked among the city's utilities magnates. The new
immigrant masses were managed politically by political func-
tionaries, "bosses" frequently from their own people, who gave
them simple favors and guidance in return for their votes on
Election Day. One of Cleveland's best known was Harry Bernstein (1856-1920), a Jew of Polish descent, whose total control
over the largely Jewish Fifteenth Ward downtown earned him the
sobriquet of "Czar" Bernstein. Bernstein had conspicuous business interests in his district including a theatre, restaurant,
saloon, and hotel, but his main interest, from which the others
derived, was in procuring a large Republican majority on Election Day. Bernstein was rough-and-tumble and hardly capable
of functioning outside the sphere he ruled. However, his young
lieutenant of the 1890s, Maurice Maschke (1870-1936), was a
man of different quality who soon surpassed his mentor. Maschke, born in Cleveland of German-Jewish stock, had been educated at Harvard Law School. By 1899 he controlled the downtown wards, including Bernstein's. Maschke was eclipsed politically during Mayor Tom Johnson's years, but as head of the
Republican party organization in Cuyahoga County from 1909 to
1932, he was one of Ohio's most potent Republicans, attaining
importance in the national councils of his party.[149]

Now and then a political dissenter or reformer appeared on
the scene. One was Morris Black, of the pioneer Hungarian
Jewish family of clothing manufacturers and occasional politi-
cians. Like Maschke, Black graduated from Harvard Law School
and returned to Cleveland—not to rise to power within a function-

ing political machine, however, but to rebel against its dominance. Young Black won election to the shabby City Council
and promptly began to air embarrassing questions effectively.
In 1896, however, he suddenly died before reaching the age of
thirty.[150] Four years later, the reform of which he was a harbinger came to maturity in the person of Mayor Tom L. Johnson, America's greatest metropolitan mayor of the Progressive
Era.

Johnson was a traction magnate converted to Henry George's
single-tax program, who became a formidable warrior for the
public interest. He possessed dramatic flair and tenacity and
intimate knowledge of public issues, and "influenced people
because he knew how they felt . . . ditch digger and president
of a bank," as Alfred A. Benesch expressed it.[151] The style of
his administration somewhat resembled that of New York City's
Fiorello H. LaGuardia during the age of the New Deal. The accommodations and deals of earlier decades were swept aside as
Johnson, like his able but more staid successor, Newton D.
Baker, succeeded in drawing the loyalty of immigrants from
their bosses and led Cleveland to become the model Progressive city administration.[152]

The rhetoric of Jewish communal leaders during the Johnson
years suggests their sympathy with his ideals. The conception
that responsible civic bodies were obliged to act upon the problems of poverty and immigration became widely accepted in
Cleveland and may well have influenced the established Jews
of the city to organize more effectively as a community than
almost anywhere else. Jews appeared in Mayor Johnson's official circle. Benesch, who, like Maschke and Black, had gone
to Harvard Law School, served under Johnson, calling him "the
greatest influence in my life." Under Mayor Baker, whom he
regarded as "not in the same class" with Johnson, Benesch
became Director of Public Safety in 1914, responsible for Cleveland's police, fire, housing, and smoke inspection. Maurice
Bernstein, the son of Polish immigrants, was a Progressive state
legislator from Cleveland and a committee chairman responsible
for key Progressive legislation. Joseph Lustig, like Benesch of
Bohemian Jewish stock, also sat in the legislature as a Progressive.[153] American Progressivism, a highly diverse movement,

varied considerably in its responses to immigrants. Progressive leaders met with varying success in attracting immigrant votes, but the record of Johnson's municipal Progressivism was notable. Cleveland's established Jews also found the Progressive atmosphere an attractive one,[154] and the increasing number of new immigrants could count on Progressive sympathy.

IV

East European Immigration

NEAR the end of 1879 "quite a number of emigrants, mostly Bohemians, [were] expected in Cleveland" shortly. "They have with hardly a single exception, relatives here. The Bohemians, as a class, are hardworking, industrious and peaceable."[1] Some of them must have been Jews, for Bohemian Jews, like those from Germany and Hungary, had been coming to Cleveland for thirty years. Immigrants from these lands, together with Irish and English, continued to constitute most of Cleveland's immigration for years to come.[2]

Jewish immigrants, however, now began coming to Cleveland from a new source and in unprecedented numbers. There had been earlier arrivals from Polish lands during the 1850s and 1860s, but Russian, Polish, and Rumanian Jews arrived in substantial numbers only after 1881, and in flood tide after 1904. These newer Jewish immigrants arrived in Cleveland from Eastern cities, travelling in the same railroad cars as immigrants from Italy, Poland, Greece, Serbia, and Hungary. All were to contribute to the vast population growth of their adopted city; the Jews, who were about 3,500 of the 159,404 residents of 1880, numbered around 75,000 of 796,841 in 1920. Nevertheless, the reasons for massive Jewish immigration to the United States, and to Cleveland, differed substantially from those of their immigrant contemporaries, and even from those of the earlier German Jews.

East European Jews emigrated mainly for economic reasons. Their numbers had risen by an amazing natural increase from perhaps 1,250,000 around 1800 to approximately 6,300,000 in 1900—the latter number not including the very large emigration which had already taken place. The Jews of Eastern Europe constituted two-thirds to three-quarters of world Jewry. The great majority of them were confined within the Russian Pale of Settlement and the provinces of Russian Poland, and, within

101

these, to the small cities and villages, and to traditional crafts and petty commerce. Their wretched economic plight was thus linked to the restrictions upon domicile which kept them off the land and out of the newer Russian industrial cities. Their numbers multiplied, but they were unable to improve their rickety economic basis. They were victims not only of Russia's economic backwardness, but also of the radically hostile policies of the Czar's government, which mistreated them with endless administrative chicanery and winked broadly at pogroms. During the same period the economic backwardness and poverty of Galicia (Austrian Poland) greatly reduced the effects of Jewish emancipation in that Hapsburg land. Rumanian Jews could hardly enjoy their relative prosperity because they were treated—contrary to international treaty—as rightless aliens, liable to physical attack and summary expulsion in a strongly anti-Semitic atmosphere.[3]

Pogroms and edicts lent urgency to the massive East European Jewish exodus, though its basis was essentially economic. The largest voluntary international migration of Jews in history took place between 1881 and the coming into force of the Johnson Act of 1925, as some 2,350,000 East European Jews exchanged oppressive regimes and impoverished lands for freedom and economic opportunity in the fastest-growing economy on earth. The proportion which reached Cleveland was obviously small, yet the numbers were still large enough to transform the city's sedate Germanic Jewry into a pulsating, economically diverse Jewish community where Yiddish overwhelmed the vanishing German tongue and existed alongside English for decades. East European Jewish immigration and its effects make the decades between 1890 and 1940 the most varied and interesting in the history of Cleveland Jewry; the same can be said of most other American Jewish communities.

FLOW AND RECEPTION

Early in 1881 the local press wrote indignantly against "Germany's Persecution of the Jews," referring to a disturbance in Berlin which was inspired by one of Court Preacher Stöcker's anti-Semitic speeches. Declaring that "those in authority not only know of these outrages, but secretly approve of them," the *Plain Dealer* denounced Bismarck and the German regime in vigorous terms. "Let those maltreated people come to this country. . . . [We are] not hesitating for a moment to trust to their excellent qualities as good citizens. . . ."[4]

As the newspaper wrote of these troubles of German Jews it was at the same time publishing news of much more serious anti-Jewish outbreaks further to the east in Europe. The notorious Russian pogroms which began around Easter, 1881, and continued with intervals until 1884 were first reported in Cleveland on May 13, 1881.[5] The local response to Russian brutality was severe. After reporting the murder of a Jewish family in 1882, the *Plain Dealer* said:

> After all the years that have elapsed we are yet very near the Dark Ages. The cruelty, fiendishness and bigotry of these butchers have never been surpassed in the world's history. How much moral aid and comfort the butchers received from the intellectual and social crusade against the Jews in Germany we leave our readers to guess.[6]

Reported plans to emigrate to the United States were welcomed. "This is the material for good citizenship. The new comers help to hurry along the settlement of our waste places which goes far to justify the great increase in railroad building."[7]

Later in that eventful year of 1882 the newspaper learned that "the Russian refugees have now abandoned the attempt to settle here." Probably referring to the proto-Zionist Hovevei Zion colonists, it found that instead, "their thoughts turn to Palestine, the land to which every Hebrew feels that all Israel is ultimately to be gathered. . . . Stranger things are recorded in history" than a mass movement of Russian Jews to Palestine.[8] (True, but not many.) Ohio Republicans that year included in their campaign platform a clause extending sympathy to Russian Jewry. This combination of vote-catching and humanitarian sentiment did not go unremarked by opponents:

> the Republicans of Ohio have only sympathy with the Russian exiles, and none at all for the workingmen and the oppressed of other countries. . . . The Republican Party has plainly an-

nounced that it does not want the votes of the workingmen, German, Irish, or of anybody but fanatics, hypocrites and Russian exiles.[9]

These assertions were intended to be hostile to Republicans, and not to Russian Jews, as later *Plain Dealer* comments were to prove.

A few Russian Jews who arrived by the end of 1881 received assistance from individual Cleveland Jews, but it was becoming clear that substantial immigration might be expected, requiring concerted effort. Local Jews at a mass meeting in January, 1882, heard facts and exhortation. The clothing manufacturer Siegmund Mann, presiding, "in the course of a lengthy address, made use of the following words":

> Brethren, the truly benevolent and charitable will give—must give to all, not consider race or nationality. . . . At the present time the Russian exiles need our sympathy, our help, our assistance, more than any other class. . . . Money is plenty in our land. We are rich. Our land is blessed with peace and plenty. None are poor amongst us but those who are too hard-hearted, hard-fisted and miserly to feel for their fellow-man and relieve suffering.

Cracow-born Dr. James Horwitz likewise "hoped that all invidious distinctions might be obliterated, that it did not matter from whence a Jew came. . . ." Clearly, both Mann and Horwitz realized that difference in geographic origin was indeed an "invidious distinction" in Cleveland Jewry. At any rate, $341 was raised at the meeting.[10]

During the first half of 1882 Russian Jews continued to arrive:

> Among the Russian refugees just arrived and ready to go to work are a carpenter, a tailor, a pocketbook maker, a saddler, a tinsmith, two locksmiths, and three laborers. They may be employed on application to Mr. S. Mann, No. 78 Water St.[11]

By mid-summer, "many Hebrew refugees from Russia [were] settling in Cleveland. They tell terrible stories of the cruelty of the Russians toward them. Many of them have considerable property."[12] In the autumn there arrived a large group without warning: "Forty-seven Russian refugees arrived in the Union Depot this morning. They were entirely destitute and helpless."[13] Like other groups which arrived similarly in other cities, this one may have been sent in haste by the Hebrew Emigrant Aid Society to prevent the increasing concentration of immigrants in New York as unprecedented numbers kept arriving at Castle Garden. Certainly, no one in Cleveland was ready for them. David Black, the pioneer Hungarian Jewish settler, thought of appealing to the Austro-Hungarian Consul in Pittsburgh for aid—probably because the new arrivals had been forwarded from the Austro-Polish city of Brody—but no help arrived from that improbable source. Somehow or other these new immigrants also settled in.

By this time, the number of Russian Jews must have far exceeded Siegmund Mann's capacity to find jobs for them. Early in 1883, perhaps fifteen months after the arrival of the first Russian refugees, there were complaints that "about two hundred and fifty . . . are not merely a great burden to the Cleveland Hebrew Relief Society, but they give great trouble also to the Distributing Committee." These refugees' insistent demands had continued "ever since the 'immigration trouble' commenced."[14] The Hebrew Relief Society somewhat later recalled that,

> it is mostly due to [President] Mr. Jacob Mandelbaum that we had here in Cleveland no scandal with the several hundred Russian refugees residing here. This Russian affair is a very difficult problem.

"Tramps, lazy fellows, vagabonds" were turned away, and it was "the poor man that may expect relief, but not the pauper. . . ." Thus,

> we succeed with the Russian question, so far that of the several hundred Russians who received assistance last year about two-thirds will not apply for assistance this year. They need not apply; they get along nicely and independently.[15]

Still, "over three hundred Russian families" lived in Cleveland in 1884, of whom "a great many receive relief all the year round."[16] The struggle to establish themselves was a harsh one.

Solomon Fuchs, by way of example, was allowed by Superior Street merchants, most of them Jewish, to set up a curbstone stand to peddle notions, while Philip Weis sold pocketbooks and combs on Superior Street and Monumental Park. We hear of them molested by "college boys and young clerks" and street children.[17] On the other hand, some were assisted to move on to the short-lived Jewish agricultural colony at Painted Woods, North Dakota.[18]

The Russian Jewish newcomers took their first steps as a group by founding the "Berg Street Kehillah," a frame synagogue built "on reasonable terms, so that in a few years they will own it."[19] Worship was probably not the only activity within the synagogue. There was study of sacred literature, charitable effort, and possibly weddings, funerals, and circumcisions as well. The gamut of traditional socio-religious events must have taken place: hence the term kehillah (community) was attached.

After two or three years of Jewish communal preoccupation with the "immigration trouble," attention to the matter decreased strikingly. Even the reports from the Emigrant Detective at the railroad depot made no reference to Russians among the Germans, Italians, Bohemians, Irish, and Scandinavians who passed through or settled in large numbers. Local Hungarians continued to show concern for their brethren in the old country, especially during menacing times such as the Tisza-Eszlar blood libel in 1883.[20] Virtually all Hungarians in Cleveland before 1900 were Jews; they even conducted an elaborate Hungarian festival in 1887.[21]

Little is known of the interval between an immigrant's arrival in the United States, which in the vast majority of cases meant New York City, and his coming to a western city like Cleveland. As we have seen, the immigrants of 1882–1883 were dispatched by the Hebrew Emigrant Aid Society in New York, but such shipments ceased once that organization terminated in 1883.[22] Dispersed, these earlier arrivals were a magnet for later ones. The difficulty to be overcome was that of raising ten or fifteen dollars for the cheapest train ride to the Middle West. When the Pennsylvania Railroad briefly lowered its fares from New York to Chicago and to St. Louis in 1885, and the Baltimore & Ohio did likewise for its Baltimore-Chicago route, many immigrants seized the opportunity to travel the distance for a nominal one dollar.[23]

The polyglot arrivals at the local railway depot were tense, weary, yet deeply hopeful foreigners:

> A car load of immigrants arrived on the Lake Shore [railroad] yesterday afternoon—Italians, Hungarians, and Scotch. The [police] immigrant officer conducted them from the car to their waiting room, where they were furnished with bread, bologna, sausage and coffee at half the regular price. One German woman among them has been a cripple six years. . . . One Italian, whose wife arrived the night before, was in a state of the greatest excitement: first, on account of his wife, and, secondly, on account of his trunk. . . .[24]

Most of these immigrants travelled on separate coaches of the train and were looked after by a policeman while they were changing trains at Cleveland.[25]

PROBLEMS OF SETTLEMENT AND ADJUSTMENT

As the location of the synagogue suggests, new immigrants' dwellings were concentrated in and around Berg Street. We also have the lurid evidence of a fire in December, 1886, which destroyed four houses occupied by twenty-six families including over one hundred persons, who lost their belongings as well. They were "mostly Bohemians, Poles and Russians, with a few Hungarians. . . ."[26] Yet aside from such misfortunes the city, and the Jewish community within it, appears to have taken little notice of its new arrivals, at least until 1890, when the decree expelling thousands of Jews from Moscow stirred Cleveland Jewry.[27] The expulsion was cruelly carried out during the Russian winter, as protests rang forth. Rabbi Machol's Sabbath sermon aptly noted that the week's Biblical reading commenced, "They moved"—by the Czar's edict; it continued, however, "they settled"—but where? "Let the influential men of our city take the matter in hand, call a meeting of all the Israelites in the city, and see what plan could be adopted, what course could be pursued for the benefit of these poor sufferers."[28]

Seven hundred did attend such a meeting, at which a local branch of the American Committee for the Ameliorating of the Russian Refugees (later the Jewish Alliance of America) was established.[29] Martin A. Marks, the rapidly rising businessman and civic leader, was chairman of its executive committee of seven, of which such prominent personages as Abraham Wiener, Joseph Metzenbaum, and M. Sampliner were also members. Meanwhile, the city's Democratic Party convention uttered words of sympathy:

> The persecution of the Jewish people by the Russian government justly deserves and receives our unqualified censure. . . . this government, in connection with the enlightened governments of Europe disposed to unite with us, should take proper steps to alleviate the wrongs thus inflicted on this long-suffering and oppressed people.[30]

Political statements aside, it is from this point that Jewish immigrants actually became the continuous concern of Cleveland Jewry, the principal item on the Jewish community's agenda for forty years to come. The first steps taken in 1891 were the solicitation of wearable old clothes and usable household goods, and the establishment of a Russian Refugee Society for new arrivals, a Hebrew Temporary Home, and a Ladies Auxiliary Society to teach housekeeping to immigrant girls.[31] Not all these were efforts of native Jews. In 1897 the Hebrew Shelter Home was "started in this city by the Russian Hebrews. . . . The aim and purpose of this organization is to protect poor people—strangers, as well as residents of the city, who are worthy of support." Three days of free lodging were to be given in this transplantation of the traditional "guest house" (*hakhnassat orhim*) of European Jewry.[32] In its building, opened in 1905, it accommodated 883 persons in 1910, describing itself as "the only institution in town which asks no questions of its clients.[33]

Jewish immigration thus stimulated Jewish communal endeavor. The Russian Relief soon merged with the invigorated Hebrew Relief Society,[34] while rudimentary classes established by the ladies became within a few years a branch of the National Council of Jewish Women and its Council Educational Alliance.

This generosity of effort, however, contained a degree of misunderstanding which was bound to provoke irritation and, in time, a hostile reaction. Martin A. Marks' words at a mass meeting of Russian Jews in December, 1891, exemplify some of these attitudes:

A large number of Russian refugees has come into our midst, and we have endeavored to provide for their wants. Our object now is to make them feel that they are part of this great country. We want to teach them the customs of the land and to prepare them for citizenship, and to conduct themselves as citizens. It is a well-known fact, no matter what one Jew does all Jews are blamed for it. The only way for you to overcome this prejudice is by becoming part of the country itself and to do this you must become supporters of its institutions. We cannot carry on this work unless your hearts are with us. We will be aided by many of our friends in Israel, and the rest remains with yourselves.[35]

The mingling of benevolence with condescension, and of altruism with enlightened self-interest, would long characterize the many activities which Cleveland Jewry conducted for its immigrants.

No attempt was made to keep records of new Jewish arrivals. How little the older segment of the Jewish community knew the newer may be partially inferred from the vagaries of Jewish population estimates from about 1880 until 1905. In the former year, the number of Cleveland Jews had been estimated at 800 men and 700 women over 21, and "about 2000" were noted as minors, for a total of 3,500.[36] The local reporter Uncle Sam [Oppenheimer] mentioned 20,000 Jews in 1888,[37] where three years earlier he had spoken of only 2,000 families[38]—and there is no hint of Cleveland Jewry's doubling in that interim. In 1895 the *Plain Dealer* repeated the estimate of 20,000 given for 1888,[39] while later in the same year Uncle Sam mentioned 3,400 to 4,000 families.[40] An 1897 estimate was 25,000.[41] Writing on Cleveland in 1903 for the *Jewish Encyclopedia*, Dr. Samuel Wolfenstein practically gave up and merely estimated 15,000 to 25,000. By 1905, when the concluding Volume XII of that great project was written, the Jewish population of Cleveland was set at 25,000.[42] It is obvious that no one had any remotely accurate notion of the correct figure, at least before 1905.

There was no doubt, however, that the number of Cleveland Jews was greatly increasing due to the flow of immigration, and there was uncomfortable awareness that it constituted a social and communal problem. Emma C. Davis, a Jewish public school teacher, in 1895 published an evaluation of the Russian Jews, who were "among the most distinctly foreign of all the races represented in Cleveland, amalgamating themselves most reluctantly with our American progressiveness." She thought little of "these bigoted followers of the orthodox rabbinical law . . . uneducated paupers . . . whose minds are stunted, whose characters are warped and who have become adepts and who have grown wily in the evasions of law and in their struggles for existence. . . ." Turning to their homes, Miss Davis was repelled by "the filthy squalor of these crowded hovels where deprivation, hunger, cold, darkness, disease, and many times intemperance can but develop selfishness, sensuality, cruelty and brutality." The litany proceeded, but a saving excuse could be provided for all the faults: "the pangs of starvation . . . absolute, abject, poverty . . . terrible adversity . . . only one benumbing tragedy of oppression and tyranny." It was the aim of Emma Davis and public school teachers like herself to bestow upon immigrant children "evaluation of character and development of intelligence," yet these efforts were undone when the pupils "return to their homes, where all the conditions of their life drag them down again to the lowest levels." The Progressive Mission social settlement then being planned by young Jewish women to counteract the efforts of the Hebrew Mission could improve Russian Jews, particularly children, by exemplifying "higher, purer planes of living."[43]

There is no record of protest from the immigrants against this extremely invidious characterization of their life and beliefs; such silence suggests their social and cultural isolation. Miss Davis viewed Jewish immigrant life from a height of moral arrogance which she attained by her faith in the public education of her day. The wide gap between children's homes and public schools meant simply that "the poor oppressed Russian outcasts" were morally and socially degraded. Not more than a decade later, sentiments like these would be altered, or at least muted. Were they then expressed, the storm of immigrant protest would be matched by native Jews' disavowals.

More moderate than Miss Davis but still unfavorable to the new Jewry of Cleveland was another contemporary editorial view expressed in the Jewish press:

> Those recent arrivals have not elevated the standard of Judaism in this city; in fact they have been a stumbling block. Jews generally are gauged by the action and appearance of their brethren, and in both instances there is ample cause for criticism.

Within their "ghetto," the article continued, corrupt elections redound "to the disgrace of the Jewish people. . . ." Shady practices in the Jewish ward were "advertised throughout the state, giving out the impression that the ballot, which every intelligent Jew holds most sacred, can be bartered for a mess of pottage."[44]

The Woodland Avenue district where new immigrants dwelled had come under the political domination of Harry Bernstein (1856–1920), a Polish immigrant of 1869 who acquired an unsavory reputation. From the restaurant-bar he operated, Czar Bernstein, as he was called, secured the Republican political allegiance of several thousand recent Jewish immigrants. His Sixteenth (later Twelfth) Ward unfailingly returned near-unanimous votes for Bernstein's candidates. It was "common report . . . that there are a few men in the cultured sixteenth who may be persuaded for a consideration to cast an almost solid vote for any man. The common, vulgar term for it is bought."[45] The "Bernstein gang" regularly tampered with voting, so that "majorities in the sixteenth ward [were] made to order. . . ."[46] The domination of Bernstein as political boss of the immigrant Jewish district, and the notoriety it achieved, scandalized the respectable Jewry of Cleveland. In March, 1899, over a thousand Jews attended a meeting in the ward at which Bernstein and his methods were roundly denounced as a dishonor to Judaism.[47] Yet the "czar" held his stronghold, expanding his business interests by the erection of a hotel and a theater, and later embarking on banking. Bernstein built his power upon his hospitality and generosity in small things and his facility in arranging favors; such skills confirmed the loyalty to him of poor foreign immigrants who often sorely needed such help. The decline of Bernstein's power began with the shift of Jews from his district and the Cleveland municipal progressivism which attracted immigrant support. Knowing his constituents' mind, Bernstein as a city councilman declared his support of Mayor Tom Johnson. Not quite a czar any more, Bernstein still remained wealthy and politically important until he died in 1920.[48] Immigrants knew him as their friend.

Complaints in the general press about the new Jewish arrivals were mild, nevertheless. The *Plain Dealer*, when considering "The Future of Emigration" as it appeared in 1887, rejected suggestions that immigrants lacking means be excluded. It invoked instead "the widespread feeling that a limit should be put to foreign immigration, or that it should be put under greater restriction. . . ." Only immigrants coming to live from charity or by their wits, or imported strikebreakers, should be kept out. To bold-hearted Europeans on the move, it recommended "in case they are shut out of America" to settle "in the south seas, besides Africa with its vast realm of undeveloped possibilities."[49] By no means did this leading newspaper oppose Jewish or other immigration, however. True, it reacted to reports a few years later of a fresh surge of newcomers by grumbling that "we can do without a large increase of population by way of New York harbor for some time yet,"[50] but, as the concluding "yet" implies, this was probably a temporary view in the aftermath of the disastrous panic of 1893. About a decade later the *Plain Dealer* noticed "remarkable changes" in the sources of immigration, as Italy, Russia, and Austria-Hungary became the main lands of emigration. The statistics "suggest serious reflection," since the newcomers settled in cities; "the probable influence of the new element on the character and social and industrial interests of our urban population cannot be ignored."[51]

Such a hairsbreadth balancing of views tends to show that in general Cleveland was an unlikely center of anti-immigration feelings. Hardly any American city had higher proportions of foreign-born and foreign-stock population. In 1900 32.6 percent were foreign-born, and 42.9 percent more were native-born with one or two foreign-born parents; in 1920, with a population which more than doubled to 796,000, 30.0 percent were foreign-born and 38.9 percent had one or two foreign-born parents. Nativism had a dim political future, even the sort which stirred the earlier immigration against the later. Yankee industrialists—and Jews of earlier, Germanic stock as well—built their enterprises on immigrant labor. The Progressive Mayor Johnson based much of his political power upon solicitude for the newcomers, and such successors as Newton D. Baker (1914–1917) also provided sympathetic leadership.

THE PEAK YEARS

The late nineteenth century wave of Jewish immigration had been impressive, but the great Jewish increase in Cleveland came between 1905 and World War I. After the confused and unreliable population estimates of the previous decades, one finds a rough but clear increase recorded:

Year	Estimate	Source
1905	25,000	*Jewish Encyclopedia*, XII, x.v. "United States"
1906	35,000	Industrial Removal Office correspondence (MS)
1907	40,000	*JR&O*, October 11, 1907; *AJYB, 1907*–1908
1910	45,000	*AJYB, 1911–1912*; obtained from Industrial Removal Office
1911	50,000	Nathan Loeser, President, Mount Sinai Hospital, in *JR&O*, January 27, 1911
1912	60,000	*AJYB, 1917–1918*, p. 412; obtained from Industrial Removal Office
1917	75,000	*loc. cit.*; obtained from Bureau of Jewish Statistics and Research, American Jewish Committee

During these years the American Jewish population ascended sharply from about 1,000,000 in 1900 to about 3,700,000 in 1915. The growth of Cleveland Jewry more than matched that of American Jewry during this period, and considerably exceeded that of Cleveland itself. In their city they constituted two percent of the population in 1880, five percent to six percent in 1900, and over nine percent twenty years later.

There was good reason for the decisive upward turn in Jewish immigration during the opening years of the twentieth century. Not only did the Cleveland economy greatly expand in the fields where Jews were apt to seek their livelihood, but events in the Empire of the Czars were driving vast numbers of Jews and others to more secure and promising lands. The iron chain of disaster began with the Kishinev pogrom of Easter, 1903, which disturbed the world not merely for its ferocity and destructiveness but also because of the all-too-obvious complicity of the government in the killing of 43 Jews and the maiming of 500. Cleveland, like other cities, held a large protest meeting. Jacob Furth, an organizer of the Industrial Removal Office (see below), reminded the audience that "a vast immigration from Russia" could be expected, and "naturally, they will come to America in large numbers."[52] Indeed, three refugee families from Kishinev who reached Cleveland in January, 1904, told horrifying stories of barbarism and butchery. Arriving "in utter destitution" they were provided with relief and jobs.[53] A few short weeks earlier, a headline read: "FRIENDS SLAIN; HOMES LOOTED; Jewish Refugees From Blood-Stained Gomel Reach City." Moses Baillen hid his family in a village from the Gomel pogrom of September, 1903—which was marked, incidentally, by the first manifestation of armed Jewish defence. "Then he secured a little money, bribed an official at the frontier and turned his face toward America."[54] Hundreds of thousands of Russian Jews were deciding to do likewise as Russia plunged into its disastrous war with Japan in 1904, passed through revolution in 1905, and ended with a pogrom-ridden counterrevolution and economic depression in 1906–1907. In Rumania a blood-stained peasant uprising in 1907 also drove Jews out of that land. A small Rumanian Philanthropic Society first sought to aid these immigrants, and a Rumanian Relief Committee took up the work in 1907.[55]

When the Russo-Japanese War broke out, Superintendent Isaac Spectorsky of the Council Educational Alliance expressed what many Russian Jews like himself must have felt:

And yet in proportion to their loyalty to the [Russian] people, is their hatred for the tyrannical government which makes of Russia one immense prison house. Therefore, in the present emergency, the Jews certainly hope that Russia will see her downfall. Many Jews will pray that Japan may sound the death knell of that government which has denied them religious freedom.[56]

Indeed, Jacob H. Schiff, who for years had employed his influence as the nation's foremost foreign banker to keep Russian securities off the American financial market, now actively aided the placing of the Japanese war loan.[57] Some Jews, on the other hand, feared that such expressions and activities would make things still worse for Russian Jewry. To Sol Rotkovitz, "a well known orthodox Jew," reports of Jews siding with the Japanese "instead of ameliorating the conditions of our people in Russian territory, will only make matters worse."[58] The Zionist Abraham Kolinsky announced that "Zionists as an organization, while sympathizing with Japan, are opposed to any organized effort on the part of the Jews of this country to lend material aid to Japan."[59] Meanwhile, the *Plain Dealer* speculated on the "significant migratory movement" of conscripts fleeing military service for their Czar in eastern Siberia. It "threatens to make trouble for Russia and possibly for this country" because "their hurried flight" made it likely that "the proportion of destitute among them will be unduly large." Yet the newspaper felt sure of "the world's sympathy and generosity" towards these refugees.[60]

Cleveland Jewry reacted fervently to these disasters, and the general community also participated. As word reached the city of the wave of pogroms instigated by Russian Czardom in November, 1905, a series of protest meetings was held. The City Pastors' Union convened one at historic Old Stone Church, at which "a large and enthusiastic audience of all denominations united in the cause of humanity to give hearty expression of sympathy for the suffering and persecuted Jews of Russia. . . ." Many political, religious, and civic leaders heard denunciations of Russia oppression, combined with assurances that the march of human progress yet continued—as proved by the rarity of such atrocities and the vigorous protest against them by civilized men. Three meetings were held by the Jewish community. At Tifereth Israel Rabbi Gries presided over the demonstration of native Cleveland Jewry. Immigrant Jews who filled Beth Hamidrash Hagodol synagogue were addressed by Rabbi Moses Z. Margolies of New York; "convulsive sobs shook the frames of many" when he finished, and again after the prayer for the dead. Perhaps this traditional, emotional style of memorial no longer suited Westernized immigrants, since the Zionist association called "a mass meeting especially for the younger Jews of Cleveland" at Anshe Emeth Synagogue.[61] Besides taking up collections for Russian Jewry, these meetings urged President Theodore Roosevelt, as mediator between Russia and Japan, to intercede with the Czar's government to aid the Jews. The Federation of Jewish Charities, established two years earlier solely for local needs, nevertheless responded to an appeal from Oscar S. Straus and managed the city's campaign for the nationwide Russian Relief Fund. When it concluded two months later, there was $19,000 for remittance to the Fund, and $654.91 remained to be turned over to the Russian Emigration Society of Cleveland, which was lending money to local immigrants to bring their families out of Russia.[62] Gregory Maxim, a visiting revolutionist about to return to the struggle in Russia, received a generous response to his appeal for aid to the Jewish Socialist Bund. But nothing came of predictions that many would join him and return to Russia.[63]

The actual outcome of the disasters in Russia was the greatest movement of Jewish emigration ever seen. From 1903 through 1914, 1,271,676 immigrants recorded as "Hebrews" entered the United States; less than fifteen percent of that number settled in such other developing lands as Canada, Argentina, Brazil, South Africa, and, significant for the future, Palestine.[64] These Jews formed approximately ten percent of net immigration to the United States during this period. Together with their fellow immigrants who also settled in Cleveland, they utterly changed the ethnic composition of the city. The Cleveland of Western Reserve Yankees, with its Germans and Irish, was submerged by these new masses of Poles, Rumanians, Slovenes, Italians, Magyars, Greeks, and still others who tripled its population from 261,000 in 1890 to 796,000 in 1920.[65] Thus, the Jews were not an isolated foreign group but were one of the great manufacturing metroplis' numerous immigrant communities. Among these, they were the only one that possessed a native wing which could provide social and philanthropic leadership. This position was not lacking inner complexities and tensions, but was one which nevertheless was of great benefit to the rapidly expanding Jewish community.

Much of Cleveland's "most steady increase" in Jewish population was due to "the prosperity of those who came" before 1897. These earlier immigrants, "after saving a little money, persuaded all [!] their relatives to emigrate. This, coupled with the persecutions of 1892 [1890?] and the natural increase, has made Cleveland a great center of Judaism."[65a]

The family of Ezra Shapiro, in his maturity prominent in politics and the Zionist movement, may exemplify this process. His father, a non-practicing rabbi educated at the great Volozhin yeshiva, and an elder brother preceded him to America. Mrs. Shapiro and her other children arrived in 1907. Prosperous Uncle Brudno, a cigar manufacturer in whose factory "nearly every Jew" newly arrived found work as a start, helped them during their first days.[66]

The unpolished memoirs of Max Sandin (1889–1970), who was to have a stormy life as an anarchist-socialist, depict the journey thousands of Jews took to reach Cleveland. Sandin waited until his formal induction into the Russian army before escaping, thus relieving his impoverished parents of legal responsibility for their son's act:

About October 21, 1910, a few days after I was officially accepted in the Czarist army and given the loyalty oath, I left Dvinsk, the place where I was born, raised, went to *cheder*, and started my schooling in the Socialism of Karl Marx. . . . For two days we, a group of 12, 9 men and three girls, were in the hands of an agent who led us out of Russia to the German border. We slept in day time or sometimes crawled on all fours until we arrived at the city Grayevo and crossed the German border at 2 o'clock in the morning.

For 3 days we were fenced in in a two story building under quarantine. Then one morning we were told to board the boat Brandenburg at Bremen. We were 14 days on the ocean, It was what we were told "an oxen ship." I am sure that the oxen had a more enjoyable trip than the passengers.

We arrived in Baltimore, Md., on November 12, 1910. The next day I came to Cleveland, Ohio.

Max Sandin's family in Dvinsk dwelled in a house each of whose six rooms sheltered a family, with one kitchen serving for all. In Cleveland he found his brother living on Scovill Avenue

in a four room suite and a wall paper and paint store in front. . . . There were a living room, 2 bed rooms, and a large kitchen, all for one family and gas, electric too.

Here was opulence! Sandin discharged a duty which perhaps made him, the newly confirmed atheist, uncomfortable; he

brought a pair of silver candlesticks a present from my mother to her daughter-in-law to pray on Friday nights when they lighted the candles and met the Sabbath. In my travel box I had my phylactery to pray a gift from my pious Father but I never used them.

"A few days after my welcome as a guest," American realities were faced:

My brother asked me, "What are you going to do?" I said, "I would like to start at the painting trade temporarily and will go to night school to take up a profession, dentist, or a lawyer," etc.

My brother and sister-in-law said no. "We don't advise you to become a painter. You better go into peddlery." I said I did not like the idea to sell or to buy. "I want to be a worker not a business man."

The next day my brother took me to a 5 and 10 cent store, bought a suit case for 65 cents, 5 gas mantles, 1 dozen shoe strings, a dozen soaps, 6 wash cloths, and several more house articles. Told me that tomorrow you will start working. The next day I packed my suitcase with all the 5 and 10 cents merchandise. Was told to board a Scoville Ave. streetcar and ride to the last stop. It will be West 73 St. and Clark Ave. a Polish and Russian neighborhood that I shall go from house to house and sell my wares. I worked till 4 P.M. I made profit in six hours working $1.65. The union wages of a painter was $2 a day, or 25 cents an hour. In the first day as a peddler I made more than an experienced painter [!] but I did not like it. The next day I went out about 9 in the morning and about 4 P.M. I came home. I had profit $2.25. I almost sold all my wares.

This was a promising start. At this point, however, Sandin's career began to diverge from those of thousands of his fellow Jewish immigrants:

I said "no more" and threw away my suit case and the remaining shoe laces, soaps and needles. This was the second and last day as a business man.

I became an apprentice as painter and paper hanger. A week later I became a member in the Painters Union Jewish local 123. . . . [67]

Not all immigrant peddlers were as tough-fibred as Max Sandin. Most of those who peddled stuck to it and made the best of their hard lot, stimulated by the many examples of prosperous shopkeepers and even merchant princes who had started where they were now starting. An unfortunate few, sensitive and lonely, could not endure their psychic and physical hardships. "Struggle in New World Too Hard" was the newspaper epitaph for the suicide of a former student in Russia who had to peddle after failing to make a living as a private tutor. His note read, "I am Israel Goldman of No. 47 Scovill Avenue. That's all. Goodby all."[68] Another despondent young man, Nathan Giser, received assistance from a Jewish charity to find a job helping a locksmith. Three weeks later he hung himself, leaving behind letters to his betrothed in New York.[69]

INDUSTRIAL REMOVAL

In addition to voluntary immigration, a smaller stream of immigrants arrived in Cleveland through the efforts of the Industrial Removal Office. The latter was a branch of the Baron de Hirsch Fund, heavily endowed in 1891 by the philanthropist who also sponsored Jewish colonization in Argentina. After none-too-satisfactory experiences with agricultural colonies, the American trustees decided to devote much of the Fund's income to dispersing Jews away from the fearfully congested immigrant neighborhoods of New York City, and, to a minor extent, Boston and Philadelphia as well. The Industrial Removal Office aided employable Jewish immigrant workmen to move to such other large cities as Buffalo, Detroit, Indianapolis, Pittsburgh, and Milwaukee, as well as Cleveland.[70] While it was usually B'nai B'rith lodges in the respective cities which functioned as the local agents, in Cleveland the Council Educational Alliance, Cleveland Council of Jewish Women, B'nai B'rith, and the Hebrew Relief Association officially collaborated, with the last-named body actually supervising the work.[71] Local expenses were borne by the Baron de Hirsch Fund. There were 72,526 immigrants distributed by the Industrial Removal Office from 1901 through 1917, of whom 9,784 were sent to points in Ohio; of the latter, 2,671 came to Cleveland from the time it became part of the network in 1904[72] through 1913. The movement reached its peak in 1906 and 1907, when 716 arrived, and then dropped sharply during the depressed years of 1908 until late in 1909. Then it gradually rose to a new peak in 1913, when 329 were sent.[73]

The local agent of the I.R.O. sought jobs for immigrants before inviting the New York office to send suitable candidates, and met the arrivals and assisted them to settle. He also attempted to find members of their families or good friends who might act as their temporary local hosts. A typical beginning at the New York end was an inquiry such as the following:

> January 2, 1905
> We have before us the application of Louis Schwartz, a clothing cutter by trade, twelve years here. He is used to both knife and shear. He worked in several large houses here and has brought a reference from the last place he worked at. He has a wife and three children. Will you kindly inform us whether there is any likelihood of obtaining work for him at his trade and whether we may send him and his family.[74]

Schwartz could come, but he probably was told to leave his family in New York until he was reasonably established in Cleveland. Later in the same year of 1905, a tailor four months in the country wrote gratefully to New York:

Your agent got work for me on the second day. I get $10 a week and am very grateful to the office. I have this week sent $20 to my family, which I never could have done in New York.[75]

To be sure, not all was success. Of 249 persons sent to Cleveland in 1907, 15 percent quit the city. This was considered a gain, since it appears that 25 percent of the approximately 150 carefully selected persons sent the previous year had failed to remain. The 1907 group was classified as:

one hundred and fifty-three consisting of 87 single men and 17 families, who were sent to the care of this office, and 96 people, consisting of 21 families and 17 single men, who were sent to friends or relatives.[76]

It sometimes occurred that, notwithstanding earlier correspondence, work in their own trades would not be found for removal cases. Thus, five men who arrived in November, 1909, found no work at their skilled specialties within the tailoring trade. Following the rule, "they were plainly informed before they left [New York], as all our applicants are told that they must be willing, in case of necessity, to accept any employment offered them, should no work at their trade be available."[77] This was well and good, but hardly held against the detested reality of coming to a strange city merely to undertake inferior and worse-paid labor than New York City had offered:

Men with such trades are always reluctant to accept factory work, claiming they are physically unfit to do manual labor. Four of the men mentioned were absolutely ignorant of the [English] language. . . . they refused to accept [manual labor], and there has been much dissatisfaction all around.[78]

Much more frequent, fortunately, was the request of the Cleveland agent to send from New York the family of a removal client, who

is now working and has good prospects before him. I also recommend that you send the furniture right along with them, otherwise they will surely be in distress upon their arrival here.[79]

During the nation-wide depression from late 1907 to the end of 1909, when removal work throughout the United States had to be drastically curtailed, it was suggested that the local I.R.O. agent "make daily trips to nearby places, say within a radius of fifty miles, and endeavor to find positions in the factories of the towns he visits.[80] The Clevelanders, while doubtful, thought

> this experiment might meet with more or less success in spite of conditions. ·. . . some of our local Jewish business men who visit towns in Ohio on matters of their own business may incidentally be able to accomplish some good.[81]

The I.R.O. might sometimes find itself collaborating in the process of immigration. Thus, Harry Caplan, "who was sent here to [Cleveland] some months ago," was now requesting that his brother, for whom he had "paid for his ticket from Europe," might receive I.R.O. help to proceed to Cleveland. The brothers were skilled workers, to judge from the fifteen dollars' worth of tools each needed. Harry promised that "he will supply [his brother] with work and assist him otherwise."[82] We do not learn the decision in this case, however.

The varieties of removal work are aptly illustrated in a 1908 letter from Cleveland to the New York headquarters:

> Regarding Oscher Drescher, I wish to say that we can not find him at 501-3 Central Ave (at neither 501 nor at 5013).
> In regard to Ike Cohen and family, I have interviewed L. Sobolovits of 3621 Orange av., who is himself only a poor workingman unrelated to the Cohens, and both unwilling and unable to receive the family.
> In reference to Israel Horwitz and family, I believe it is adviseable to have them come here to join the father who is working and can care for them.[83]

The 2,671 self-supporting immigrant workers, besides their families, who reached Cleveland through the Industrial Office constituted a significant addition to the Jewish population. The sponsors hoped for more:

> . . . have any families, relatives, or friends joined removals independent of our assistance, since upon the extent of such inde-

pendent attraction the ultimate success of the movement very largely hinges.[84]

It does not seem unreasonable to suggest one person coming to Cleveland for every one sent by the I.R.O. However, as we have noted, a significant minority did not remain in Cleveland; the letter which inquired about "independent attraction" also wondered why only forty-three of the last seventy-seven cases sent to the city were still residing there.[85] Yet 5,000 to 6,000 persons constituted a substantial addition to Cleveland Jewry.

HOMES AND WORK

During the late 1890's East European immigrants were found "largely settled in the district contiguous to Broadway, and that neighborhood is a veritable ghetto. Hill, Orange, Cross, Berg streets and lower Woodland avenue is their mecca." Property values in the district suffered "a noticeable decrease," allegedly on these immigrants' account. "In many cases a household occupies two rooms scantily furnished, in which they cook, eat and sleep." Their children filled those streets in warm weather, "while their elders lie around in dishabille, apparently at peace with all the world. . . ." A "foul and tepid atmosphere [was] naturally caused by being housed so close together without proper sanitary arrangements. The odor of old rags and decayed vegetables" was redolent of many inhabitants' livelihoods. The reporter noted, however, that these people were "frugal, and in many instances accumulate much money, at which time they quickly move to more commodious quarters."[86]

About a decade later, late in 1908, investigators of the United States Commission on Immigration visited Cleveland, among other major cities, to scrutinize housing and labor conditions among immigrants. Dividing immigrants by nationality, and classifying Jews as "Hebrews, Russian" and "Hebrews, other," they surveyed the length of time in the United States, age strata, income, and housing conditions of 115 households of the former and 30 of the latter group who were living around East 26th Street. This district was "70.9% Hebrew." The houses which the Jewish immigrants inhabited were originally built as one-family houses by the Germans but the Hebrews have converted them into three and four family houses. They are one or two story frame dwellings situated directly on the street or behind small yards of varying depths. . . . Rear houses are commonly used as rag shops.[87]

Among the 5,622 Cleveland immigrants studied by the Comission, 834 were Jews, of whom 521 were foreign-born; the American-born were probably to be found among the 357 children under 14. Forty-five percent of the foreign-born had come to the United States after 1903, another 32 percent had arrived during the decade preceding 1903, and the remainder had come still earlier.[88]

The 834 Hebrews lived, as mentioned, in 145 households, of which 41, relatively few for immigrant communities, took in boarders. The "Hebrews, Russian" around East 26th Street averaged 5.70 persons per household of 4.17 rooms, paying $8.95 monthly rent; "Hebrews, other" were slightly better off on the average, with 5.32 per household of 4.24 rooms paying rent of $9.31. Altogether, Cleveland's immigrant groups had households averaging 5.18 persons (with many lodgers) cramped into 3.59 rooms; their rent of $6.89 was far beneath that paid by immigrant Jews. Native-born Clevelanders, by way of contrast, had 3.88 persons in 4.28 rooms. Nearly all the Jewish houses studied for the purpose (144 of 148) had private water supply, but only three-eighths (53 of 145) had indoor toilets; in these respects also they were somewhat above the immigrant average.[89] Jewish immigrants were thus paying much higher rents for larger and better appointed apartments than did other immigrant groups. Rents may have been higher partly on account of proximity to the expanding downtown district; other immigrants tended to live further out, near the large factories where they worked. Five years after the Immigration Commission's studies, in 1913, the square mile near East 26th Street was inhabited by 3,397 families comprising 21,480 persons, mainly Italians and Russian Jews, and reportedly contained "some of the worst housing conditions of the city." Here 1,619 of the 1,732 buildings had only one or two stories, but 58 percent of all of them were "in a bad or only fair state of repair." Yet rents averaged $6.75 for three sorry rooms and $9.00 for four, noticeably higher than in better districts.[90]

The 141 Jewish immigrants whose occupations were recorded were represented in many trades, but concentrated in a few. No less than 39 were independent peddlers, and 10 were in the kindred trade of rag and metal junk dealers and sorters. Twenty were employed as tailors, with 4 more working for themselves in that trade. After these 73, there were 7 carpenters, 5 grocers, 4 teamsters and drivers, and merely 4 (of 506 among all immigrants studied) laborers; the rest were widely scattered. The average annual earnings of males eighteen and over were $406 for "Hebrews, Russian," and their family income was $501; for "Hebrews, other" the respective figures were $440 and $620. This was well above the general average for the foreign-born, which was a much poorer $350 for males eighteen and over, and $486 for families.[91] A final feature invites attention, the differences between "Hebrews, Russian" and "Hebrews, other." Whenever perceptible, they show the latter in a more flourishing condition. They lived in larger quarters for which they paid higher rent, and their men earned 8 percent more in a year. The most telling differences lies between family earnings of $501 and $620. One may speculate that the "Hebrews, Russian" were the more recent and younger arrivals, with younger families which could contribute less to the household than the "other" Jewish immigrants; these were the earlier arrivals with older children who helped to raise annual household income by $180—from $440 to $620.

The small sample taken along one street during the depression year of 1908 only partly reflected the economic reality of immigrant life. There was nothing unusual in the distinctive Jewish occupational distribution. Nearly every immigrant group had its peculiar economic stratification. Thus, the Czechs were mostly skilled workmen, many of them tailors and cigarmakers, while an estimated 90 percent of Polish immigrants were engaged in "exhausting physical labor," some at Jewish-owned Kaynee and Cleveland Worsted; the Letts were mainly factory workers.[92] As we have seen, a prime Jewish occupation was peddling, and scavenging was connected with it. It was a trade which had to be conducted in poor neighborhoods. One novice recalled his first experiences with horse and wagon:

[I]nstead of heading toward the isolated farms away from the city, where the farmers were eager to receive peddlars amicably, my uncle, who was the manager of our business, rode out only a mile or so from our house. He began to "huckster" at the top of his voice: "Paper! Rags! Paper! Rags!" But the only immediate response to this announcement was the jeering cries of the street-urchins: "God-damn-Jew-Sheeny!" These insults cut me to the heart and their bitter taste was more than I could bear.[93]

When his uncle insouciantly picked junk out of backyards, the youngster protested. His uncle retorted:

That's business! That's the business of peddling! Everything goes into the wagon. If you're too finicky you'll never make a living.[94]

Every peddler soon learned the real difficulties of business. Physical assault was a frequent problem, and peddlers might suffer "ugly wounds, inflicted upon them by street loafers or other vicious persons." The police helped very little, at least until 180 peddlers united in the Peddlers Protective Association and, led by their counsel Alfred A. Benesch, demanded and secured "a more conscientious handling of such cases." Jewish peddlers ceased at last being "the sport of the corner tough," but theirs remained a harsh livelihood.[95] With the Association's cooperation, the Council Educational Alliance offered "instruction in peddling. . . . the correct methods are taught and as a result there have been fewer arrests for violation of peddling ordinances. . . ."[96] Repeated attempts to impose a license fee on peddlers were supported by large hucksters desiring to squeeze out small ones, by retail merchants, or by those who wanted quiet, neat streets. In 1910, when Commissioner of Licenses Daniel E. Morgan (later City Manager) proposed a stiff twenty-five dollar peddling fee, a protest meeting was held. This issue, which hundreds of poor Jews saw as threatening their livelihood, brought a tumultuous delegation to the City Council, led by Czar Bernstein's ally, ex-Councilman Harry Adelstein. Councilman Alex Bernstein succeeded in having the measure tabled, but it was later enacted.[97]

Peddlers aspired to leave their grueling routine for the life of a storekeeper. Not that their hours were shorter than those of peddlers; in fact, they were probably longer. The Jewish area was checkered with innumerable stores. On main streets like Woodland Avenue and its principal cross streets, retail business went on from early morning until the small hours. By the time the last grocery or candy store shut its doors and its proprietor joined his family living in back, bakers were arriving to start their day. Most stores retailed what they bought at wholesale, while others, like bakers and some dairymen, and perhaps a few jewelers, sold what they produced themselves. The *City Directory* of 1912, in the district of Woodland and East 55th street (originally Willson Avenue), listed no less than eight jewelers, ten bakers, twenty-five barbers, six barrelmakers, three bicycle dealers, twenty-one shoe stores, seven bottlers and bottle dealers, thirty tobacconists (many of them petty manufacturers), five clothiers, fifty-five candy stores, sixteen druggists, eleven furniture stores, and nine saloons; groceries were perhaps beyond counting. Aside from a drugstore with three branches, all the stores were individually owned. Only two or three of these shopkeepers were not Jewish.[98] A great many of the stores were puny and marginal, set up from the shopkeeper's accumulated savings, perhaps as a tailor or peddler, and the savings of his family. Small stores were entering and abandoning business all the time.

For the newly arrived immigrant, labor in a workshop was likely. Little Rose Pastor (later Stokes, 1879–1933), later a socialist and trade union leader, arrived in Cleveland with her family in 1890 and had to go directly to work to help support her overburdened parents. With an older girl, she approached a cigar workshop in a street under the viaduct:

> Timidly, we push open a heavy metal door. The suffocating effluvia of tobacco dust strikes us in the face. . . . There are many workers here and work benches all of new wood. A row each, facing the two long walls of the narrow loft, two rows in the middle built as of one piece, facing each other. The bodies move in short sharp rhythm, as the arms roll dark brown sticks on a board, or cut dark brown leaves into patterned pieces or chop the ends off the sticks with a small cutting tool.[99]

The makers of better cigars had a well-established union which provided relatively good wages and working conditions.

Their union label on cigars was valuable enough for non-union manfacturers to try occasionally to appropriate. In 1880, and again in 1890, the cigar-makers won strikes. To judge from the names mentioned, one-quarter to one-third of manufacturers and workers were Jewish.[100]

Years later, another newly arrived youngster found work at Brudno's cigar factory. Like Rose Pastor, he had to work two weeks for nothing as a learner and at half pay for a few weeks more before regular wages came in.

> The most you could make was ten dollars a week. We worked piecework—$3 a thousand. The most any worker could turn out was between 700 and 800 cigars, and only very few could do that. The average worker made only about 500 a day, which meant a dollar-and-a-half a day.[101]

Like the youthful Samuel Gompers in London and New York cigar-making shops during the 1860s, the impressionable youth found intellectual compensation for his poor wages.

> Only Jews were employed in Brudno's factory. We were given Saturday off but worked on Sunday. All the employees were either members of his family or just plain *landsleit* who knew somebody in the family. There were a few young men who had [been] ordained as rabbis and also some "genteel" young men who in the old country had never done a stitch of work. Here, having no other means of making a living, they became cigar workers. . . . I really enjoyed the spiritual life at Brudno's factory. . . . At one of the tables sat dignified, pious Jews with handsome beards and discussed Torah. They tossed about quotations from Scripture and argued about learned matters. Opposite them sat young people discussing the problems of the world with fervor and passion.[102]

Jewish immigrants practiced a variety of trades. Thus, the membership of one society of immigrant Lithuanian Jews included those of carpenter, presser, painter, teamster, peddler, paperhanger, stogiemaker, shoemaker, electrician, bricklayer, butcher, cabinetmaker, tinner, brass worker, huckster, varnisher, cloakmaker, salesman, photographer, rag peddler, blacksmith, and dentist; amongst all these, carpenters and painters

seemed to predominate.[103] The needle trades, that "great immigrant metier" in New York, by no means dominated the Jewish
immigrant economy in Cleveland. Unlike the conditions ob-
taining in New York and most other cities, garments in Cleveland tended to be made in substantial modern factories, well
capitalized and employing modern methods and machinery. As
has been noted, some of the city's leading Jewish names—Joseph,
Eisenman, Black, Feiss—were found in the trade. In 1910 the
8,377 workers in fifty garment establishments constituted four-
fifths of those in the trade—a striking contrast to New York City,
where 78 percent of the Manhattan shops employed five persons or less.[104]

Cleveland was second only to New York in cloakmaking (the
manufacture of ladies' coats), and this major branch of the
industry was concentrated in factories. Immigrants could learn
the advanced skills and the use of power machinery at the
Council Educational Alliance.[105] Most men's clothing shops
were small, but in the women's garment trade a dozen factories employed 200 to 1,000 workers.[106] Their owners sometimes found themselves in annoying competition with small
workshops; one larger manufacturer, John Anisfield,

> was in the store and if you heard him talk it would have taken
> all the thought of going into that business out of your mind. He
> complained bitterly of the business and wished himself out of it.
> I told him that that was only on account of the backward and
> unfavorable season, but he believes it will never come back to
> where it was, owing mainly to the Competition of the East side
> ki ki cloak makers who are not only ruining the cheap cloak trade
> but also copy fine goods and kill living profits.[107]

Who were the "ki ki"?[108] These were the small workshops where
Jews could be found working under poor conditions, ambitious
to be in business for themselves. An unofficial inspector was disturbed by the conditions he witnessed:

> *42 Henry St.* Clothing shop. No. in shop 18; No. of women 7; No.
> of hrs. from 7 till 8 or 9. Paid by the piece, 25¢ a garment. Three
> of the girls say that when they work rapidly they can make 14
> garments a day between them. The place was comparatively
> well lighted, but had absolutely no ventilation. . . . One toilet

was used by both men and women and no place afforded for a cloak room . . . the whole appearance of the place unsanitary.[109]

Workshops were established further from downtown as well:

If one will take a Broadway car into the southeast part of the city, alight from the car on any street in or near the 50's, and walk for a few minutes he will see a bunch of wires leading to the back of some substantial looking house, and if he follows this guide, he will usually find a home workshop. The home workshop generally employs from 10 to 30 people, occasionally as many as 75. The employers are usually foreign born tailors who hire their own countrymen as workers. Women sometimes engage in this kind of small contracting. Often husband and wife control the shop together, working with their employees.[110]

Some factories maintained a system of "inside contracting," by which workers within the factory had their employees next to them, whom they provided with work, supervised, and paid. In economic terms this made the factory a series of workshops. When these "inside contractors" struck at the large M. T. Silver firm in 1896, President Vicha of the city's Central Labor Union withdrew his support upon finding that the strikers did not intend to include their own workers in the union.[111]

Cleveland's garment industry had a long history and a complex ethnic pattern among its workers. Four-fifths of male employees, and two-fifths of women, were foreign born.[112] Nowhere was this ethnic diversity more apparent than in the clothing workers' unions. A cloakmakers' union of 1894 found that "some spoke English, others only Bohemian [sic], a few German and the balance Jewish. Every motion that was made had to be translated into each of these languages."[113] Some of the Bohemians were probably Jewish.[114] It was the Bohemian tailors, strongly supported by the clergy and press of their community, who were the mainstay of garment unionism.[115]

Yet unionism in the years before World War I was generally ineffective. The strike against Silver, which included a violent clash between police and strikers, failed; so did an attempt to unionize John Anisfield & Co., where a union negotiator was accused of betraying the striking workers.[116] There was another major, unsuccessful cloakmakers' strike in 1904 which included "250 cloakmakers who work for Jewish contractors in the Perry and Orange street district."[117] In 1907 "nearly a thousand cloak-makers" founded a union. Altogether there were 1,700 in that trade, and "all of them are Jews."[118] The supreme union effort came in 1911, under the impact of the great New York cloak-makers' strike of 1910 and the surge of Jewish trade unionism. The newly powerful International Ladies Garment Workers Union called a general strike on June 6, 1911, of approximately 5,000 workers. Notwithstanding $325,000 in financial aid to the strikers received from other unions and progressive groups, the large manufacturers, who were well-organized and willing to endure large losses, kept out the union. For years to come, gar-ment unionism in Cleveland was feeble, as the manufacturers improved the efficiency of their large plants, minimized seasonal work, and employed women as much as possible. Meyer Perl-stein, the able ILGWU organizer who arrived in 1914, organ-ized nationality branches for Jewish and other workers, but until World War I introduced the Federal Government into la-bor relations workers generally feared and avoided unionism.[119]

In mid-1918, with wartime prosperity and rapid inflation, the union was again ready to strike for recognition and a large wage increase. Once more the large, well-financed clothing manu-facturers refused any dealings with trade unionism. Of ap-proximately 6,000 employees in the trade, about 2,500, mainly from small shops and H. Black & Co., left work. Their number was increasing and the strike was becoming another protracted struggle when Federal authorities, who wanted no interruption in the production of military uniforms, intervened. Former Mayor Newton D. Baker, now Secretary of War, secured the agree-ment of both sides to a Board of Referees, and this panel presently awarded the workers a large wage increase. From this point began a new era in labor relations within the Cleveland ladies' garment industry, which later drew nation-wide atten-tion.[120]

Clothing was a massive industry, and its labor movement pro-fessed socialist, internationalist ideals. The ethnic diversity in the Cleveland clothing industry, together with trade union ideals, made ethnic and religious attachment a secondary matter. Some trades were strongly Jewish, however, and their trade unions were unabashedly Jewish in membership as well as in self-definition.

Jews employed in smaller, mainly Jewish trades could organize readily, especially in the few which were entirely Jewish. Thus, the six Jewish bakeries, whose thirty-five men made the breads preferred by Jews and were "the exclusive makers of pumpernickel in Cleveland," dealt readily with their bosses in union fashion.[121] In 1912, the twenty-five drivers and bottlers of seltzer, the carbonated drink sometimes called the Jewish "workingman's champagne," also struck for a six-day, sixty-hour week and a $15 weekly minimum wage.[122]

The case of Jewish building workers was more complex. In the winter of 1902–1903 there were only about twenty Jewish carpenters in Cleveland. They worked twelve to fourteen hours daily for wages ranging from six to nine dollars a week. Wages, always low, were lowest in winter because days were short and the weather was severe, so less work could be done. Now a group of New York carpenters arrived, among them a certain Abba Huttenson. His first job was with a company of nine workers who used to take jobs and do the work themselves, but who occasionally hired other workers. Huttenson tried to unionize the workers but those in Cleveland were "of the old school" and "not radically inclined." In the spring of 1903, however, the first meeting to organize a carpenters' union was held in the home of one of them, Joe Bandel, who had been influenced by Huttenson and had circulars printed at his own expense. About twelve came to the meeting, and eighteen or twenty were finally organized in a union. This was the foundation of the Jewish Carpenters Union of Cleveland.[123]

The union succeeded in being chartered as Local 1750 of the United Brotherhood of Carpenters and Joiners. When the carpenters of Cleveland struck for higher wages in May, 1904, only the Jewish local, demanding 27 1/2¢ and 32 1/2¢ an hour, won; the Gentile local, which sought 45¢ an hour, lost. Local 1750's membership promptly tripled. Late in 1910 it numbered 156 members, and more were expected.[124] The business agent did not disdain old-fashioned methods. When informed that a union man was working below the union scale, he would take prayer book and phylacteries to the man and compel him to swear on them how much he was being paid.[125] In 1912 Local 1750 won the hourly 45¢ rate and "Jewish members belonging to other locals are asked to affiliate with this local." It enrolled almost all eligible Jewish carpenters and was one of Cleveland's strong unions. A perverse attempt was made by DeLeonite socialists in 1912 to break a strike of the conservative Jewish carpenters. Establishing a branch of the Industrial Workers of the World, they secured recognition from the struck businessmen. The carpenters overcame the peculiar alliance, aided "by the allied unions of bricklayers, painters, plumbers, and other Jewish workers, and their little scheme will cost them a fine bunch before they are through with it."[126]

Stalwarts of Local 1750 were also pillars of the Synagogue of the Government [Province] of Grodno, whose members were pledged "to strictly refrain from labor on Saturdays and Jewish holidays."[127] Jewish tradition and American craft unionism were the foundation of this modestly successful union, rather than the secularist, socialist internationalism of the far larger industrial unions in the garment trade. It waged "an aggressive campaign to make a fair [i.e., union] job" of the Euclid Avenue Temple, then under construction.

> The Jewish workers say that it does not look well for the religious folks to erect a house of worship with unfair labor. No. 1750 is receiving the hearty cooperation of the cloak and garment makers, bakers and other organized trades, as well as one of the local Jewish newspapers. The indications are that the temple will be an empty sort of affair after it is finished unless union labor receives a square deal.[128]

Rabbi Wolsey would not (and probably could not) change his congregation's policy.

> Perhaps that is what the wealthy attendants want. They don't care about coming into contact with the poor Jews unless they can use them to work like a lot of slaves for next to nothing.[129]

Unlike the usual practice among secularist, radical trade

unionists, the criticism was not extended to Judaism and religion in general. Perhaps it was the influence in their community of the Jewish carpenters, many of whom were observant Jews, that impelled Rabbis Liebowitz and Eryen to endorse union labor for their new Orthodox synagogue. Their declaration earned the public thanks of Local 1750, and scored a point for immigrant Orthodoxy against the Reform Jews.

In 1909 a Jewish Bricklayers Union emerged, striking against the open shop. Two years later it struck again, for higher wages and better treatment. The *Jewish Independent*, reporting this, remarked that a Jewish bricklayers' strike was "a news item, that's all." Had this story been printed "twenty or even ten years ago . . . it would [have been] regarded as a joke and the 'Yiddishe bricklayer' humor was one of those early stunts of the 'Hebrew comedian.' "[130] Little is known about these strikes, but the Jewish union's acceptance in 1912 of an invitation from the leftist Cleveland Federation of Labor to join the local Building Trades Council antagonized the conservative 1,000-member Local 5 of the International Bricklayers and Stone Masons Union, which had refused to join.

A few months later, when Local 5 struck because the Building Trades Council awarded a job to the tile-layers rather than to them, the Jewish union sent its men to the jobs at the Council's insistence. Negotiations between Jewish and Gentile bricklayers ensued, with the Jews willing to accept any suggestion but the proffered one, that they give up their own local. The Jews claimed they had special problems, and that so much anti-Jewish feeling existed in Local 5 that Jewish bricklayers would get no work. They would accept Local 5's jurisdiction but would not give up their own local. To the smiles of all those on Local 5's committee, its president said, "You Jews will create such a situation here that we will have to treat you as they do your brothers in Russia." The Jewish delegation rose and left the hall. At the next election to the Building Trades Council those who sympathized with the Jews were not re-elected, and the local of Jewish bricklayers was ousted from the Council for not belonging to the American Federation of Labor—though Local 5 also did not belong.

The Jewish Bricklayers Union then turned to the immigrant

community in the Yiddish press, telling their story and asking those needing brickwork to call on them and to use only contractors employing Jewish labor. The success of this appeal is problematical. At any rate, in September of that year (1913) the Jewish bricklayers joined Local 5 and gave up their union after ten years of separate existence. Within Local 5, however, they retained a separate organization to care for their special problems.[131]

The 1912 *City Directory* showed a variety of Jewish unions. There were Bakers Union No. 50 (Jewish); Building Laborers No. 184; Cap Makers Union No. 18; Carpenters and Joiners Brotherhood No. 1750; Cloak and Skirt Pressers Union No. 37; Cloak Cutters Union No. 42; Cloak Makers' Union No. 26; Newsboys and Bootblacks Protective Union; Painters and Paperhangers Union No. 123; Skirtmakers Union No. 27; and the Garment Workers Joint Examining Board, which seems to have examined candidates for the cutters union.[132] The garment unions were then at low ebb after their disastrous strike the previous year.

The complexity of East European Jewish immigrants is well illustrated by their unionism. The garment unions represented the secular, internationalist, socialist ideals for which the Jewish labor movement gained fame. On the other hand, the well-established small unions were avowedly traditional in their craft unionism and also, to some extent, in their Judaism. These contrasting aspects of union organization among Jews exhibit their universalism and idealism, as well as their pragmatism and traditionalism.

It was a harsh, sometimes embittering life for Jewish and other immigrants. Hopefulness was what sweetened its hardships.

Congregation Tifereth Israel's (The Temple) synagogue on Huron and East 6th Streets, occupied from 1856 to 1894 (The Temple)

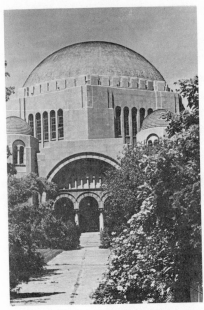

The Temple, University Circle at Silver Park, occupied by Congregation Tifereth Israel since 1924 (Richard Karberg)

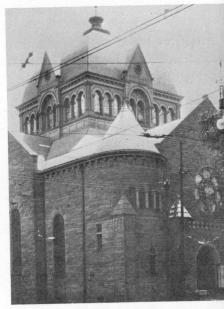

Congregation Tifereth Israel's (The Temple) Willson Avenue Temple, 2301 East 6th Street, occupied from 1894 to 1924 (Cleveland Public Library)

Rabbi Isidor Kalisch (1816-1886) of Congregations Anshe Chesed and Tifereth Israel, 1850-1855 (The Temple)

Rabbi Aaron Hahn (1846-1932) of Congregation Tifereth Israel, 1874-1892 (The Temple)

Rabbi Abba Hillel Silver (1893-1963) of Congregation Tifereth Israel—The Temple, 1917-1963 (The Temple)

Rabbi Moses J. Gries (1868-1918) of Congregation Tifereth Israel—The Temple, 1892-1917 (Western Reserve Historical Society)

Congregation B'nai Jeshurun's (Temple on the Heights) Synagogue on Scovill Avenue at East 55th Street, occupied from 1906 to 1925 (Cleveland Public Library)

Temple on the Heights, 3130 Mayfield Road, as it appeared shortly after its dedication in 1925 (Temple on the Heights)

Rabbi Israel Porath (1886-1974) of Congregations Oheb Zedek and Heights Jewish Center, 1925-1974 (Jewish Community Federation)

Rabbi Sigmund Drechsler (1843-1908) of Congregation B'nai Jeshurun, 1887-1905 (Temple on the Heights)

The Jewish Center of Congregation Anshe Emeth (Park Synagogue), East 105th Street and Grantwood Avenue, dedicated in 1920 (Park Synagogue)

Rabbi Solomon Goldman (1893-1952) of Congregations B'nai Jeshurun and Anshe Emeth, 1922-1929 (Park Synagogue)

Rabbi Samuel Margolies (1880-1917) of Congregation Anshe Emeth, 1904-1917 (Park Synagogue)

First Officers and Trustees, Federation of Jewish Philanthropies, 1904 (Jewish Community Federation)

V

Temples, Rabbis, and Reform 1870–1920

WHILE Jewish immigrants, who were mostly traditional in religion, reached Cleveland in ever increasing numbers, Jews of the earlier settlement were crystallizing a form of Judaism they found appropriate to their life and beliefs. Five of Cleveland's 164 churches in 1880 were Jewish.[1] Fifteen years later, the city's total of 275 congregations and religious bodies included eleven synagogues.[2] By 1920 the total grew to 410, while a 1923 enumeration mentioned sixteen Jewish congregations of which some were mergers.[3] Jewish population growth by immigration and natural increase was thus paralleled by the founding of congregations and, as we shall see, the expansion of existing ones. Yet the social hierarchy of the synagogues hardly changed. Between 1870 and 1920 the Reform congregations Anshe Chesed (Euclid Avenue Temple, after its establishment on that premier throughfare in 1912) and Tifereth Israel (already being called The Temple around 1910) held their status as the foremost synagogues in the city by virtue of age, their members' prosperity, and their elaborate structures. Tifereth Israel was Reform by 1870, while Anshe Chesed arrived there by a more gradual process.

One of the three small congregations of 1870, B'ne Jeshurun, founded by Hungarian Jews, moved through changing decades ultimately to become the city's first Conservative congregation. The other two, and all the newcomers, were founded by immigrants on a home-town or native region basis. They all remained Orthodox before 1920, even while some of them were discarding their East European characteristics.

The high proportion of synagogue affiliation which existed during the first thirty years of Cleveland Jewish life ended. Among the estimated 800 males over twenty-one in 1876, Tifereth Israel members numbered 75 and Anshe Chesed 124; the three little congregations probably did not exceed 50 members altogether.[4]

OBSERVANCES AND BELIEFS

Congregations grew, but Jewish religious life and the beliefs which sustained it became weakened and diluted among Cleveland Jews of early stock. Thus, Anshe Chesed's Rabbi Michael Machol, who became more forthright and attached to Jewish tradition as his years of service lengthened, depicted in 1898 the vanishing observance of the Sabbath:

> I look around in my own congregation. . . . everyone of our trustees is to be held responsible, who has an hour to spend on Friday evening and spends it anywhere else outside of the house of worship. I hold every merchant responsible, who can easily make it possible to attend the service for an hour on Sabbath morning, but lets it go out of mere convenience. I hold every woman responsible, who attends to her marketing on a Sabbath morning and goes to the matinee in the afternoon, but has no time to visit the temple for an hour and impress the child with the sanctity of the day. I hold our daughters responsible, who have six days in the week to attend to their purchases, but prefer the seventh day, though everybody knows it is their Sabbath, to do their shopping.[5]

Actually, disregard of the traditional Sabbath was already widespread by 1882.[6] The press, which had once announced categorically that all Jewish firms would be closed on Rosh Hashanah and Yom Kippur, and some every Saturday, now merely noted "a great many places of business owned by Hebrews are closed in honor of" Yom Kippur only.[7] A difference was observed between "Jüdische merchants," evidently recent immigrants, with whom "Ontario Street is fairly strewn," and "our large establishments" on Superior Street, "where business is done on a large scale." The Ontario Street merchants closed on Rosh Hashanah. Those on Superior Street, however, "were forced to keep open Monday [the single day of the Reform Rosh Hashanah] so as to enable their employees to put in full time for what little salary they receive, otherwise these houses would go to the wall."[8] Though Rosh Hashanah was ignored, downtown Jewish merchants were chided and exhorted to observe Yom Kippur "by attending divine service all day Monday, to keep your place of business closed and to have a good attendance at the houses of worship." Another argument, often potent, was openly employed, probably for the first time: "If the Jews would observe their most important holidays a little more there would probably not exist so much prejudice among our Christian people. They see that you treat your legal holidays with contempt, and for that reason, if no other, they have very little regard for the Jewish race."[9]

The traditional Passover Seder was also "rapidly declining from notice," Rabbi Machol lamented.[10] He observed with concern the seeming break in generational continuity. "Parental indifference cannot promote the piety of the young; the absence of the parents from the house of worship will not teach the children to attend the service, the source of devotion springs forth from the domestic sanctuary."[11] Machol's annual series of Friday evening lectures was meant "to bring the young generation to the synagogue once a week, whereas heretofore they only put in an appearance in the house of worship on Rosh Hashana [sic] and Yom Kippur. . . . They cannot suggest the slightest excuse for not attending Friday evening services." The "young people, who constituted the larger part of the audience" of Jews and Gentiles, "listened attentively . . . to some good words of advice" addressed to them "and many coincided with the views of the reverend gentleman."[12] The lectures were "of a religious nature, which most of the young generation have failed to study in their earlier days."[13] One week, attendance

was very small owing to . . . a masque ball at the Germania Hall. It may be well and good to stay away from the temple once in a while, but to attend a ball on a Friday evening, when your presence is desired at the synagogue, is dull of comprehension. There is undoubtedly good, real enjoyment to be had at the ballroom, which the temple does not promote, but to be enlightened on the religious topics of the day was preferable.[14]

Prosperity held perils for Judaism, Rabbi Hahn sighed.

How is it that the larger the church edifice, the smaller the attendance, and with the height of the towers comes a corresponding decrease in religious enthusiasm. Our temples are filled two or three times a year to suffocation and throughout the remainder of the year they are deserted.[15]

There are glimpses of non-Jewish forms of religion among Cleveland Jews during the 1890s and early 1900s, a period notable in the history of American religion for the impact of secularization and the rising awareness of social problems among the urban churches of the upper middle class. There were members of congregations who were seeking "varieties of religious experience." In 1889, Frederick Muhlhauser, a substantial manufacturer of shoddy and former member of the Board of Education, published a sharp-toned pamphlet entitled *Spiritualism* replying to Rabbi Machol's sermonic attack on that movement. Muhlhauser, an inactive member of Tifereth Israel,[16] replied to the rabbi's apparent criticism of spiritualism as a superstition by citing Biblical heroes who supposedly communed with "the spirit world." Coming closer to home, Muhlhauser asserted:

> Your congregation comes to the synagogue week after week and year after year, and where is there a sign of progress? They mechanically read page after page of a prayer in the Hebrew language, which they do not understand. The method of the past has developed a lot of materialists, who will proclaim to your face that they do not believe in a God. . . .[17]

At Anshe Chesed, too, "a few members . . . have recently been heard to express views favorable to Spiritualism, some of them going so far as to lean in that direction."[18]

On the other hand, conversions to Judaism are recorded. Two men, both already married to Jewish women, became Jews in 1880 and 1888, respectively. This was of "rare occurrence."[19] Rabbi Machol had converted five women by 1889, all of whom "make good Jewish wives."[20]

The rising young lawyer, Peter Zucker, spoke with self-deprecating candor on the condition of Judaism among his contemporaries. Addressing them directly at Anshe Chesed's cornerstone-laying ceremony, he warned that

> your dislike of religious customs—impatience of religious forms and almost entire disbelief of religious worship—must in the course of time inevitably lead to that bitter end [assimilation and disappearance]. The men, and perhaps too often the women of Israel, can for a large part (barring the infidels) be grouped

into three classes—agnostics, materialists and know-nothings. The first are not very numerous, for the average Israelite is of too impatient a nature to remain long poised on the ridge of indecision. The second and third classes group together, since every know-nothing is a materialist. The last classification is peculiarly my own and in it I include that great number of our youth who sweepingly deride laws, customs, tenets and principles, the origin of which they do not remember. . . . Every manly and honorable man hates an apostate, despises a coward. . . . No one better than myself knows the faults of my people—knows that many of my race are filled with mean characteristics, are frightfully commonplace in their nature and lowly in their desires. But it is not because of their religion. . . .[21]

Years later, that congregation's Rabbi Louis Wolsey, newly arrived from Little Rock, Arkansas, found to his dismay:

There seems to be not the slightest qualm of conscience about changing from Judaism to Christian Science, Unitarianism, Comptism, Ethical Culture, Atheism and Christianity. To change gods is with them like changing clothes. . . . The Ethical Culture Society furnishes a morning's instruction, and commands no difficult observance. . . . It is a convenient, easy, vest-pocket edition—and hence a rushing of Israel to this bargain-counter. And yet more steep their senses in the lotus gardens of pleasure. . . .[22]

Still other non-believers in traditional theism sought neither "the spirit world" nor "lotus gardens" but turned to thoroughgoing secularism. Young Morris Black, grandson of the pioneer Hungarian, went to Harvard and became the first political reformer in Cleveland. When he suddenly died in 1896, there were no religious exercises, and his friend, Frederick C. Howe, delivered a funeral address.[23]

Nevertheless, most Jews remained members, whether passive or active, of the two large congregations, Anshe Chesed and Tifereth Israel. They probably accepted in a general way the dictum of the Jewish weekly that both church and synagogue

must be broad and liberal in their views. They must conform to present conditions. They cannot afford to cling too closely to the doctrines that had a firm stronghold upon past generations, but give to the people those religious principles that will fit adequately with things as they are today.[24]

CITADELS OF GERMANIC REFORM

Cleveland's two early congregations embraced Reform at different rates of speed between 1870 and 1920. Tifereth Israel, Reform by 1870, remained so with Rabbis Jacob Mayer (1867–1874) and Aaron Hahn (1874–1892)[25] and reached its furthest departure from Jewish tradition during the incumbency of Rabbi Moses J. Gries (1892–1917). During Gries' rabbinate, the congregation expanded greatly, building a fine edifice on Willson Avenue in 1897 and increasing its membership past 800 by 1917. Anshe Chesed shifted slowly towards Reform under the leadership of Rabbi Michael Machol (1876–1906). After 1890, however, Machol seems to have drawn the line at further reforms. While Machol was much liked and continued to serve until his retirement in 1906, Anshe Chesed's material growth lagged behind Tifereth Israel's, and it had only 186 members in 1907. The congregation became fully Reform under the rabbinate of Louis Wolsey (1907–1924), and by 1916 its membership had increased to 711.[26] After 1912 it was known as the Euclid Avenue Temple, thanks to the splendid structure it built there at a cost of $260,000.

With the standard of Orthodoxy abandoned, the rabbis possessed broad freedom to interpret Judaism for themselves and their congregations. After the period of the founders ended, the life of the congregations indeed centered upon the rabbis' views and activities. The passive role assigned to the congregation and laity, one of paying dues, coming to a membership meeting once yearly, and attending services essentially as spectators, enhanced the "rabbinocentric" quality of the temples. Little besides worship and Sunday school took place in them until the coming of Rabbis Gries and Wolsey in 1892 and 1907, respectively. These American-educated young rabbis initiated the congregational groups and activities which were then also becoming common in upper-class urban Protestant churches.[27]

Jacob Mayer served as Tifereth Israel's rabbi until he resigned in 1874 to become rabbi of Baltimore's Har Sinai Congregation, where David Einhorn's radical Reform Judaism had made an indelible impression. Mayer was idolized by Tifereth Israel for "his liberal views regarding the Jewish religion, as he so masterly expounded them from the pulpit and nobly defended them outside of it . . . ; he elevated Judaism in the eyes of our Christian fellow citizens and removed, to a great extent, the barriers of prejudice." However, his fervid teachings, garbed in facile rhetoric, also earned the hostility of traditional Christians and Jews, as we have seen. His Cleveland congregation upheld him, as did Har Sinai in Baltimore until the astounding denouement of Mayer's career. Shortly after his induction into Har Sinai's pulpit, rumors began to spread in Baltimore that before coming to the United States Mayer had been converted to Christianity and had served as a missionary in Glasgow. When he could no longer ignore the rumors, Mayer fiercely denied them, then desperately fabricated alibis, and even invented a wayward twin brother. The rumors, however, turned to truth. Late in 1876 he left his congregation and Baltimore, and was heard from no more until his death in St. Louis in 1890.[28]

Aaron Hahn (1846–1932) shortly succeeded Mayer in Cleveland. His youth was passed in the yeshivot of his native Bohemia, where he acquired rabbinic ordination of the traditional type from rabbinic authorities.[29] Biographical details beyond that point are rather scanty, but it appears that he pursued Hebraic and Oriental studies at German universities and by 1869 was in New York as rabbi of the Orthodox Rodef Sholom Congregation. To it he dedicated his German book, "The Conception of God in the Talmud and Zohar and in the Principal Theosophical Systems."[30] This was an attempt to demonstrate the Jewish belief in God as the world-soul, and thus to link rabbinic and mystic theology with the main currents of Western theological thought down to Spinoza, Leibniz, and Schleiermacher. It appears to have drawn no attention and soon disappeared into the oblivion where derivative, hasty works of scholarship are heaped. If the businessmen who conducted the affairs of temples and employed Hahn had read his first book attentively, they might have surmised the direction their rabbi would follow in years to come. During his incumbency at Tifereth Israel, Hahn also produced a technical study of the Talmudic forms of argu- mentation[31] and a *History of Arguments for the Existence of God* (Cincinnati, 1885). Both these books were learned, but they failed to probe deeply or to exhibit critical independence, and were essentially superficial resumes of large, complex sub- jects. For a mid-western city of the Gilded Age lacking books, other Jewish scholars, or appreciative laymen, they were still an unusual accomplishment. They were Aaron Hahn's private efforts, however, neither noticed nor honored by his congrega- tion. Hahn delivered the former work as lectures at Hebrew Union College; the latter was his doctoral dissertation at that institution, with lengthy and complimentary quotations from Isaac M. Wise's *Cosmic God*. Was Hahn hoping to quit the routine and the mounting irritations at Tifereth Israel by being appointed to the Hebrew Union College faculty by Wise? If he did hope, he was disappointed.

Hahn came to be a frequent lecturer in secular, liberal cir- cles. He gave a series of well-attended Sunday afternoon lec- tures before the Cleveland Liberal League, a society for "free thought," on topics which included "Voltaire," "Rousseau," "Spinoza," and "Shaftesbury and English Deism." To Tifereth Israel it was an "honor for Dr. Hahn to give such satisfaction to a society consisting of exclusively English-speaking people." He also lectured in the synagogue on Sunday morning beginning in 1886, without any worship. Here Hahn's subjects ranged from Napoleon to Humboldt, to Buddha and Jesus, and over foreign cities and countries. The lecture on the Christian savior, highly interesting to local Christians but requiring due caution, was based on contemporary scholarship by D. F. Strauss and Ernest Renan. It emphasized Jesus as a Jew, and concluded that "Jesus was crucified, not on account of any religious teach- ing, but because he was suspected by the Roman governor of being a religious agitator."[32]

In Hahn's day Tifereth Israel pursued Reform consistently. It appointed a committee of three in 1874 to speak with those members "who still persist in keeping their hats on" under the option granted to old members from 1869. Next year, by a close congregational vote, all were required to remove their hats dur- ing services. Rabbi Hahn was dogmatic on this point. An invitation to speak at the dedication of B'ne Jeshurun's synagogue in 1887 became a public issue when he made clear he would address that semi-Orthodox body bare-headed. A funeral prevented his attendance and avoided a stormy scene.[33] Worship in the Reform manner was well arranged and decorous. Thus, in 1888, as in earlier years, programs "stating in full the exercises of the day" were distributed at the outset of the Day of Atonement. No one was allowed to leave or enter except at fixed times, and "the only obnoxious element" was the "old-time habit" of a "large bouquet of flowers which is brought into the temple of the parents. . . ."[34] President Martin A. Marks in 1895 praised warmly "the excellent deportment within and without the Temple in marked contrast to the noisy and disorderly conduct in some of our sister congregations, particularly the gathering of crowds on the outside. . . ."[35]

Hahn was meanwhile becoming more interested in religion in general than Judaism in particular, and in the bearing of the new social science of anthropology upon man's religions. At the same time opposition to him[36] increased with each reelection to a three-year term. Sensitive to this rising antagonism, Hahn, addressing his colleagues at the Central Conference of American Rabbis, gave what was in effect his apologia:

> If a rabbi is disliked it may be because he is too dutiful, too conscientious, too anxious to see his fold living and doing right.
> It is not always a shame to have enemies. Very often a rabbi may be proud of having them. It always depends upon the cause of the enmity and the character of the enemy.[37]

In 1891 the president observed that "now in the very prime of his usefulness to us, we hear mutterings of his incapacity." There was "lack of harmony in our congregation. . . . that our honorable rabbi should be the cause is indeed to be regretted."[38] The unanimity of his reelection to a five-year term in 1892 was so deceptive that Hahn resigned, even rejecting the congregation's complimentary resolutions and its decision to pay his life insurance premiums.[39] A group of his admirers established the Sunday Lecture Society of Cleveland in 1892 to hear the former rabbi's talks, which would "serve the cause of knowledge, enlightment, education and progress . . . from a liberal, rational historical and empirical standpoint."[40] The short-lived group was "said to be practically an ethical culture movement," all but one of whose officials were Jews.[41] Hahn, meanwhile, pursued his plan of studying law. Although he entered that profession when almost fifty years of age he became quite successful, particularly as counsellor to real estate investors.[42] Until his death in 1932 at the age of eighty-six, Hahn rarely appeared again in Cleveland Jewish affairs.

Contemporary with Hahn, but more consistent and happier in his rabbinic career, was Michael Machol (1845–1912), who came to Anshe Chesed after Gustavus Cohen was politely dropped. A native of Prussian Poland, Machol received his rabbinic training at the Jüdisches Theologisches Seminar in Breslau and earned a doctoral degree at the university in the same city, both in 1869. He then emigrated to the United States, where he served briefly in Leavenworth, Kansas, and as assistant rabbi at Kehillath Anshe Maariv in Chicago until he came to Cleveland. Although his Germanic culture and personal religious beliefs drew him ever further from the views of the congregation, he was personally well loved. When the Machol family visited his parents in Germany in 1886, the congregation as a body escorted him to the railway station and during his absence built him a home.[43]

Anshe Chesed, known as the Eagle Street Synagogue until it moved to Scovill Avenue in 1887, was considered as of "a moderate reform tendency." Shortly after Rabbi Machol came, it ceased observing the second day of festivals, and in 1878 it installed a new organ to accompany its choir, among whom Mrs. Moses Halle was apparently the only Jewish chorister. Sermons, called lectures, were usually delivered in German; they were given in English about once a month. The quasi-Conservative Jastrow prayer book was used. When a motion to uncover heads during services was presented in 1889, "the greatest excitement prevailed for a period of fifteen minutes. . . ." In 1891, however, only a direct personal request by Rabbi Machol restrained several members from uncovering their heads at Yom Kippur services, and a few weeks later a large majority decided that heads would be uncovered thenceforward; old-timers might continue to be covered if they wished. The same decision had been taken by Tifereth Israel twenty-two years earlier.[44] Sermons became the focus of the service: "the audience commences to assemble shortly before [Rabbi Machol] steps forward to deliver his discourse. . . ." Anshe Chesed's rabbi found it "rather difficult to impress our age with the necessity of prayer, since we have commenced to reason in regard to its value, certainly in a manner which is always advanced with the object in view to discard an obligation. . . . Modern worship lacks enthusiasm," without which "all our improved prayer books and all our changes of the service will be of little avail. . . ."[45]

Machol was deeply skeptical of the direction of the changes he accepted, but he kept his peace, usually avoiding polemics with his radical contemporaries at Tifereth Israel, Rabbis Hahn and Gries. He did not turn to the immigrant community for spiritual warmth, nor to the Zionism which took root there. In March, 1912, six years after his retirement and six months before he died, Machol delivered a parting word:

> Conservatism has a way of its own; and for the man who clings to and represents the conservative party, religion is not merely a matter of mind and reason but also, and very much so, an object of the heart. Conservatism, as I always understood it, and tried to impress it upon my audiences, means not to ridicule the Bible, not to sneer at faith, not to destroy every ceremony, not to annihilate every Jewish peculiarity, not to dwell exclusively on the negative but to uphold the positive side of Judaism; not to cater to the applause of the masses, nor to the compliments of the so-called enlightened. . . .[46]

Michael Machol's conservatism was an individual outlook, unaffiliated with the Conservative movement arising around Solomon Schechter and the Jewish Theological Seminary. He outlived the age of moderate, Germanic reform in Cleveland.[47]

REFORM JUDAISM IN THE AMERICAN MODE

Aaron Hahn's resignation in 1892 made way for Cleveland's first native born, Hebrew Union College-trained rabbi, Moses J.

Gries (1868-1918). A native of Newark, New Jersey, Gries came from a family of Germanized Hungarian immigrants.[48] Following his graduation in 1889 from Hebrew Union College and the University of Cincinnati, he served in Chattanooga, Tennessee, until he moved to Cleveland three years later. Rabbi Gries was then only twenty-four years old, and he served Tifereth Israel for twenty-five years. His election in 1892 came at a strategically important time. The generation of founders, the immigrants of pre-Civil War days, was aging and dying away, and their heirs were not seeking Reform Judaism expressed in the German tongue and the rhetoric of Hegelian idealism, nor did they require it justified with reference to Jewish tradition. Their Judaism was now to derive and find justification from their American experience.

Edward M. Baker admirably expressed the faith that the basic tenets of "Judaism and the American Spirit" were in harmony. He noted the Anglo-American anti-Semitic intellectual Goldwin Smith's allegation that Judaism was "tribal" and "a vast relic of ancient barbarism," and admitted that even less prejudiced men "fail to see that Judaism has life or function." Writing in 1904, Baker set himself the task of replying to these opinions and answering the question "whether my Judaism is in harmony or in conflict with my Americanism." The young financier defined the principles of Americanism as "man's dignity and worth," "that all men are equal in point of humanity," "justice," "a sense of human brotherhood," "alertness, ambition, activity," "optimism . . . hopefulness," and "patriotism." Turning to Jewish sources—mainly the Biblical prophets—the former Reform rabbinical student found each principle

> in accord with the principles of Americanism. Throughout the ages Judaism quivers with the passion of liberty. . . . This I know, that our age stands more in need of the words of the prophets than the voice of the apostles. . . . there is that in the spirit of Judaism which if applied to our American life would make our civilization better, deeper, stronger! . . . Let, then, a knowledge of Judaism and a consistent practice of its precepts be the Jews' contribution to American life. . . . the signs are multiplying that Judaism, in perhaps a different form and under a different name, will be the religion of the future.[49]

The earlier Reform Jewish conception of a mission to propagate ethical monotheism among all nations was subtly changed here to a Jewish obligation to guarantee and enhance American liberal idealism—a conception which became widespread in twentieth century Reform Judaism and was also expressed by Rabbi Gries throughout his ministry.

Gries' conception of his office, as he declared in his inaugural sermon, was that of "the leading, speaking, seeing, and judging conscience . . . the living prophet of righteousness. . . . His is the mission to fulfill human ideals, to lead man to God and to bring God into human lives."[50] Unsatisfied only "to invoke the blessings of religion upon births and marriages and deaths," Gries conceived of the rabbi as the one who "stands in the place of the prophet of old" in his "absolute fearlessness, his plain truth speaking and his moving earnestness."[51] These brave words of a young man differed from the traditional rabbinic role of expounder of the Law and its meaning, and rather resembled the sentiments of a growing group of middle-class urban Protestant ministers. As law and theology waned in the religious life of the urban middle class, personal and social ethics and rudimentary psychology began to predominate as sermonic subjects. Throughout Rabbi Gries' long ministry, the center of which lay in the Progressive era, his closest ties were among the liberal wing of Protestant clergy. In the radical positions he took on Judaism, Gries enjoyed strong support from his senior colleague and fellow radical in Chicago, the scholar and orator Emil G. Hirsch (1851–1923). But Gries' venerable mentor, Isaac M. Wise, disavowed his former student's act of shifting the Sabbath to Sunday.[52]

Rabbi Gries' first eight years, more or less, were devoted largely to remodeling Tifereth Israel. German was discarded. The Union Prayer Book was adopted upon its publication in 1894, but Gries prepared another one the following year.[53] The synagogue on Huron Street was now small, antiquated, and in the center of a business district. To replace it the congregation, at a cost of $99,000, built a splendid edifice on Willson Avenue which seated 1,200 in its sanctuary. It was a square building of buff sandstone in the Romanesque style, surmounted by an arched dome with a square cupola with eight stained-glass windows.[54] During the new temple's construction, Rabbi Gries emphasized a point he long continued to make:

> We have chosen to omit symbols which proclaim the oriental and the foreign. Our temple is none the less Jewish. . . . Let then the appearance of our temple proclaim to all, that we are not a people in the midst of the nation, that we are not foreigners, nor children of the East, but that we are Americans . . . and all our hopes and happiness in the occident.[55]

Even the construction of an Ark for the Torah scrolls came in question. Rabbi Gries, mantaining that the Torah reading was "a custom," "not . . . a law divine," led the congregation to abandon the Torah reading from Hebrew scrolls. Thenceforward the Bible was read in English from a book. The Ark, however, was retained.[56]

A storm burst over transferring the observance of the Sabbath altogether from Saturday to Sunday and abolishing Saturday services. Reform leaders had long wrestled with the Sabbath problem but generally avoided so radical a step. Thus, at Tifereth Israel and elsewhere in the country, Sunday lectures, with some worship, had been supplementing Saturday's Sabbath worship since the mid-1880s. President Martin Marks argued in 1893 "that no matter what the attraction may be on Saturday, business cares have and will interfere with our attendance which has gradually drifted so that our Saturday service only attracts a few of the regulars and those desiring to say Kaddish. Our Sunday service has drawn large crowds. . . ."[57] Marks later admitted, however, that the "greater portion" of the increase on Sunday was "due to the attendance of non-Jews and non-members." It was true that contemporary churches found it "an especial accolade," in Robert Cross' words, "if ceremony and sermon were so distinguished that prominent visitors to the city regarded a visit to the church as 'one of the things to be done.'" However, it was embarrassing to have visitors see so few members, a condition which undermined the raison d'être of Sunday services. A committee was delegated "to induce our merchants to abstain from going to their places of business on Sunday" and attend services in company with their families.[58] When Saturday services were abandoned in 1898, they were already nearly extinct in point of attendance.[59]

Rabbi Gries defended the proposal on practical grounds. "I have never favored Sunday as against Saturday as long as there seemed any chance of preserving the Jewish Sabbath, but the conditions of the day are such that the Sabbath is no longer a Sabbath. . . ."[60] However, success in restoring the Sabbath by the shift to Sunday was only mixed. By 1904, Gries argued:

> The Temple believes in Sunday Sabbath. Let us put forth an effort to make our day of rest, our day of worship, a real Sabbath for ourselves and our children. It is not now a true Sabbath. It brings only partial rest. Only half the day is holy, the other half, too often devoted to pleasures and pursuits not uplifting.[61]

Despite such disappointments, and notwithstanding the general refusal of Reform Jewry in the United States to adopt Sabbath on Sunday instead of Saturday, The Temple has retained this extreme break with tradition to the present day. This trend did not pass without sharp local criticism. When Anshe Chesed described its belief "in a reform which is of a purely progressive nature, and eschewing all which savors of Nihilism and destructiveness," it was pointing at its fellow Reform congregation.[62]

By the beginning of the twentieth century, Tifereth Israel, now known as The Temple, held a place among the leading houses of worship in Cleveland. Its 1871 membership of 96 became 286 by 1894; there were 340 members in 1898 and 595 in 1910.[63] The Temple Society, founded in the new Willson Avenue edifice in 1896, was open to Gentiles and non-members as well as members and offered lectures, concerts, and theatricals. There was a full round of activity at The Temple. A typical week in 1914 included a meeting of the Sewing Circle of The Temple Women's Association, rehearsals of the volunteer choir, preparations for an operetta, and meetings of Boy Scouts and Camp Fire Girls. Euclid Avenue Temple offered similar activities. Such programs attracted middle class Jews, but not immigrants. The temple was the first institutional synagogue in the

United States, typifying the self-conscious "integration" of its congregation with the Jewish and general community.[64]

Rabbi Gries was a respected member of Cleveland's fraternity of liberal, mostly Protestant clergymen. He often appeared before non-Jewish civic and religious bodies, and spoke for Jewry at the Cleveland Centennial celebration of 1896.[65] Ministerial colleagues paid him tribute on the fifteenth anniversary of his tenure. The Methodist Reverend Worth M. Tippy, at the dedication of whose church Gries had spoken, declared that "three-fourths of what I say at Epworth [Church] are identical with what Rabbi Gries says at the Temple. Gradually we will find that the other fourth will be wiped out and we will find ourselves co-workers under the blessing of one heavenly Father." An Episcopalian speaker paid tribute to the rabbi's broadmindedness. The Reverend Paul F. Sutphen of neighboring Second Presbyterian Church admired the character of children when Rabbi Gries "had the privilege of moulding their young lives."[66] It was no wonder Martin Marks, The Temple's president, claimed that "the better feeling that exists between Jew and Gentile in the community is due to [Rabbi Gries'] efforts."[67] By praising Gries Marks and the ministers were also lauding the classical Reform, as it was later called, which he represented. The rabbi exemplified the effort to gain the recognition of Judaism, or at least Reform Judaism, as an American religion. Gries minimized the differences in belief and practice between Judaism and the other religions of America.

In 1898, in a large and elaborate wedding, Rabbi Gries took as his bride Fannie Hays, daughter of Kaufman Hays.[68] He thus became son-in-law of perhaps the richest Jew of Cleveland, and also brother-in-law of Martin Marks (whose request to relinquish the congregation's presidency on that account was declined). Needless to say, Gries' already firm position in the congregation was made even stronger.

Rabbi Gries also spoke on social problems. An address delivered in 1897, when Progressivism was hardly a cloud on the city's political horizon, was bold indeed for its day. After asserting that the absence of a city hall, public library, art museum, or public auditorium were signs of deficient public spirit, the rabbi became sharper:

The successful have a solemn duty to perform—to help redeem the failures in life. Our cities are the plague spots of the world. We need a reform in the commercial and industrial system. Unless we get it blood may flow. We must reach the poor and wretched who think they are oppressed, and sympathize with them and aid them and encourage them or they will be a menace to the peace of society. We must not discharge men when times are hard. If the times are hard for us they are harder for the poor toilers who live from hand to mouth. Don't give them charity and alms, but only do them justice and give them an opportunity to earn money to buy food, for the self-respecting toiler asks for no more. Thousands in the large cities toil in hovels which they call home. Such a home! We are criminally careless, for we suffer the penalty, for the clothing manufactured in those disease breeding places spread contagion.

Trusts, corporations, and syndicates need restraint. They are too much interested in legislation. During the recent fight in the City Council the street railway officials said the fight was thrust upon them. I say that so long as the threat of a fifty-year franchise is hanging over our heads the fight is thrust upon us. We want no government by injunction but justice to all men. If a corporation dares to influence legislation for its own good, the members of it are not good citizens, but a menace to free institutions. . . . [69]

His oft-repeated theme, adumbrated in this early sermon, was that the better classes had to cleanse their hearts and establish civic virtue by removing corrupt officials and installing honest ones:[70]

Voters, be independent and rebuke the nominations [of the] unfit and unworthy. Get good men by refusing to vote for bad men. Compel the parties to make their appeal to the best by the best. Be independent. Break the party yokes and shackles. . . . Those are the best citizens who share most fully and bear most successfully the duties of citizenship. I appeal to all men of character, of intelligence and of power.[71]

Reading between the lines of these sermons, it seems apparent that Gries was endorsing Mayor Tom L. Johnson.

In common with the mildest of the social gospelers, Rabbi

Gries found the basic fault in "avarice and greed and the money-getting spirit, and the selfishness and ambition of the world today."[72] Altogether the social concerns of Judaism as expounded by the rabbi of The Temple were those of the civically active, respectable, enlightened bourgeois. They were benevolent towards, but remote from, the poor and the immigrant, as was Rabbi Gries himself.

Fourteen years after Moses Gries first entered The Temple's pulpit, Rabbi Louis Wolsey began his eighteen-year incumbency at Anshe Chesed. Born in Midland, Michigan, in 1877, he was trained at Hebrew Union College and, from his graduation in 1899 until he came to Cleveland, was rabbi in Little Rock, Arkansas.[73] In 1912 Wolsey married Florence Wiener, daughter of the wealthy civic and business leader, Abraham Wiener.[74]

Under Rabbi Wolsey's guidance, the last of German was discarded and the Union Prayer Book introduced. It also appears that Wolsey was less hostile to Zionism than Gries.[75] Shortly after the publication of Ezra Brudno's controversial novel, *The Tether*, in 1908, Rabbi Wolsey discussed it in a sermon which opened fiercely:

> This pulpit belongs to me, and I shall allow no dictation or superintendence on the part of the congregation. . . . I stand here for the independence of the Jewish pulpit. I shall speak upon the subjects that accord with my own judgment of the congregation's needs, and I shall invite into my pulpit whomsoever I please. I shall speak out of my conviction as to the truth, and I shall not be biased by any fear of summary action upon the part of the congregation. . . .[76]

Unlike his colleague at The Temple, Wolsey was given to rather sweeping declarations. Soon after he came, he preached on "The Failure of Reform Judaism," a title which tended to conceal a thoughtful analysis of the subject. Wolsey defined Reform's "original meaning" as an attempt "to reconcile the Jewish religion to the Jew's life after he had emerged from his narrow ghetto." It intended to "vitalize formalized Judaism" by declaring its "religious outlooks and its moral system as of greater importance than its ceremonial institutions and its ritual observances. . . ." Reform, therefore, "severed many a dead branch from the tree of Judaism." Contemporary Reform, however,

> attempted to equate Judaism with all universal religions, and by thus destroying the uniqueness of the Jew and the Jewish religion, has prepared the way for the assimilation of the Jew . . . that the Jew is a member of a race, a family of people who are the bearers of these truths—was rejected by Reform. . . . *The time has come to emphasize the specially Jewish aspect* of our religion. . . .[77]

Such phrases as "uniqueness of Israel," "Jewish feelings," "our own traditions" studded his sermons. These statements suggest that Wolsey, at this stage of his career, was attempting what such prominent younger Reform rabbis as Stephen S. Wise and Judah L. Magnes were doing: to reassert the distinctive religious and ethnic qualities of Judaism as well as its universality.[78]

These strong words nettled the austerely Reform Rabbi Gries, who challenged Wolsey to state his program for the reform of Reform, and reproved his colleague's "fling at the 'superior rich' and the 'German aristocrat' " as "unwarranted and uncalled for."[79] Rabbi Wolsey would attempt to "awaken Jewish feeling and stimulate Jewish enthusiasms if we clothe our eternal principles with those old forms which still retain their old-time poetry," like the *kiddush* over wine on Friday evening at home.[80] The debate of the rabbis quickly turned personal. Wolsey made the revealing observation that he would "work and preach along the lines of a conservative interpretation of Judaism," and if that failed he was "convinced that we must then accept either assimilation or Zionism."[81]

This debate, quite apart from its personal tone, tended to reflect the far-reaching changes in Cleveland and American Jewry arising from the vast immigration of East European Jews. Members of the Reform temples were, of course, the pillars of charitable service to the immigrants, and Rabbis Gries' and Wolsey's sermons on occasion dealt with their problems. Rabbi Gries warmly defended Russian Jewry while declaring that there was no solution for their plight in emigration or in Zionism, but that "emancipation is the only remedy."[82] However, he was remote from the East European immigrants and could have little effect upon them. To him their Orthodoxy, socialism, Zionism, and Yiddish were alien and distasteful, just as his extreme Reform could not attract them. In 1917, in the prime of his years, Moses Gries marked his silver anniversary in The Temple's pulpit by announcing his retirement. He died suddenly a year later. Congregational leaders led by Benjamin Lowenstein, the president, sought as their new rabbi one who knew and could attract the East European Jewish stock, now the large majority of Cleveland Jewry. Such a successor was found, twenty-four years of age, who was serving as the Reform rabbi in Wheeling, West Virginia. He was Abba Hillel Silver.

VI

From Immigrant Piety
to American Traditionalism, 1870–1920

HARDLY had the Jewish year of 5648 begun in September, 1887, when "a well-known Hebrew citizen" arranged to take a willing reporter on a tour of the local synagogues. They began at Hill Street, near the Haymarket, where the guide pointed to "two synagogues that will illustrate to you the dark side of the European ghetto." These were Beth Israel Chevra Kadisha (Household of Israel, Holy [Burial] Society) and Ohavei Emuna Anshe Russia (Lovers of the Faith, Men of Russia). One of them was visited on the Day of Atonement, in its "rather small" upstairs room "which was densely packed with men, most of whom wore their shrouds" (*kittel* worn on Yom Kippur) and prayed peripatetically in their stocking feet. The women were crowded into a small gallery above. "Candles were burning brightly, and the entire surroundings bore the air of scenes in the ghetto during the Middle Ages."[1]

The next synagogue to be visited was also "considered among the ultra-orthodox." This was Anshe Emeth, the Polish congregation in existence probably thirty years. Here the reporter noticed "a certain air of refinement;" ushers met the two visitors and "everything was orderly and quiet." He saw "little distinction in the mode of worship as a whole," between this synagogue and the previous one. The cantor led the people, who prayed and sang in a softer tone. All men wore prayer shawls, but not all wore white shrouds. Most of the women sat in a gallery, but some were seated on the men's level.

Nearby was "the temple on Eagle Street," just vacated by Anshe Chesed, "where the Hungarian congregation B'ne Jeshurun worships."

Unlike the other two places, men and women occupied the same pews, and only one man wore his shroud and he occupied a seat in the gallery. The men wore their "talith," but a few here and there could be seen without it. . . . . there was no sound of an organ, but the "chazan" was surrounded by a quartet of boys, who chimed in with him, and every now and then the congregation would join and repeat the prayers and chants in a loud tone of voice.

The differences among these three congregations seemed petty once the two men entered Anshe Chesed. "Compared with the others it could scarcely be recognized as a place of worship of the same denomination." Less traditional still was worship at Tifereth Israel. "While the prayers in all the other synagogues were chanted by the 'Chazan,' Dr. Hahn simply read them in Hebrew, German, or English and the choir in the gallery, accompanied by a beautiful sounding organ, took up the refrain and chanted the prayers."

Said the guide to the reporter, "You have seen all the shades of belief and modes of worship. The rest are orthodox, most of them only open for the great holidays of New Year's day and the Day of Atonement."

The stages of this synagogue tour illustrated the mingling of forces—religious beliefs, European regional origins, length of time in America, and social standing—which shaped Jewish religious life in 1887, and indeed at most times. Thus, there were two Russian congregations. One, Beth Israel, existed by 1860,[2] while the other, Ohavei Emuna, was founded by some of the numerous Russian Jews who immigrated during the 1880s and who still worshipped in the manner of the innumerable little prayer houses of the East European Pale. The Polish congregation, Anshe Emeth, was probably the same one mentioned in 1857 by Isaac Leeser,[3] and its full generation of experience showed in the comparative decorum of the worship. The Hungarian congregation, B'ne Jeshurun, stood midway between these new immigrant conventicles and the august Reform temples of the German Jews, just as Hungary itself lay between Russia and Poland and the West. The same could be said of the Bohemian synagogue, also called Chevra Kadisha, which existed by the 1870s, slightly off the beaten track at Case Avenue and Orange Street. Finally, there were the two Germanic

Reform temples towering over the little synagogues. Germany, to Hungary and Bohemia, to Poland and Russia—by the late nineteenth century the synagogues and their dates of founding speak much of the history of Cleveland Jewry.

Eight congregations conducted services on Saturday morning, and

> compared with how the service is attended in some Western cities the Cleveland places of Jewish worship are well attended. . . . The [Reform] Radicals, the Conservatives, the Polish, the Russian, the Hungarian, the Bohemian, the Lithwaks, the Herzogtuemer [Prussian Poles] have places of worship of their own.

In the chapel within the recently opened home for the aged, services could not be held:

> Some would be in favor of the old Polish Minhag, others again in favor of the old Minhag Ashkenaz, and again others would like [Reform] Minhag America. The consequence is that they go out of the precincts of the Home and attend the service where it pleases them.[4]

These regional divisions were recognized and often deplored. Rabbi Machol inquired,

> Wherein lies the justification in establishing German congregations, Hungarian congregations, Bohemian congregations, Polish congregations and Russian congregations, and these very same congregations sub-divided again in their religious societies with peculiar names—when we all take pride in being called Americans? . . . there is many a synagogue in this country[5] the first impulse of its [sic] erection was strife and quarrel and ill feeling. . . .[6]

The Jewish newspaper likewise found it,

> deplorable that there is not only social distinction among the various nationalities of Jews, but this discrimination is carried on to congregational life and we have Hungarian, Russian and German congregations. These different congregations have certain grievances against one another. . . . There is no reason why the

German, Hungarian or Russian Jews should form different congregations.[7]

Notwithstanding such deprecations, Orthodox Cleveland synagogues founded before 1920 were based in almost all cases on
their members' European territory of origin.[8]

Russian and Polish immigrants' religious outlook sought
primarily the literal preservation of the Judaism they knew
rather than its adjustment or adaptation, so the recreating of
the old country's religious forms was necessary and profoundly
satisfying. That this could not really be done underlay many
of the tensions and conflicts which were a commonplace among
these congregations.

BOHEMIANS, HUNGARIANS, AND POLES

Many Jews of Bohemian extraction joined the Reform temples, but some of them maintained the Chevra Kadisha for
about fifty years. It became a permanent congregation on the
Day of Atonement, 1873. With about 100 families, "of whom the
majority had shortly come from their native country," the Chevra
Kadisha devoted its first years to acquiring a cemetery.[9] In
1884 they dedicated their own synagogue on Case Avenue, a
"very nice structure, not very large, but cozy and temple-
like."[10] The Bohemians altered the service somewhat, and introduced family pews. "Their chasanim [sic; cantors] are old
members, who used to be readers, teachers and shochtim in
the old country, but now they think of engaging a graduate of
the Hebrew Union College."[11] Actually their rabbi was Carl
Ballenberg (1815–1895), who emigrated about 1885 and was
"all his life-time [a] Rabbi . . . but of liberal views and broad
principles. . . ."[12] When he retired in 1890 Solomon Beckerman
(1860–1909) succeeded him as hazan and part-time preacher.

Chevra Kadisha's membership was "composed mostly of
people who work hard for their daily bread" and showed "sacri-
ficial spirit." Unlike other congregations, the little synagogue
did not become grander or move with its wealthier members,
but pursued a quiet existence on Case Avenue. That street
"and all the little streets in the neighborhood, such as Burwell

and Croton, harbored most of the Jews who came from Bohemia. Gradually the children of these pioneers moved away, the old people alone remained and many of them joined the silent majority, but the old House of God, the landmark of a generation, still remained and somehow managed to eke out an existence."[13] In 1916, however, young Rabbi Adolph Steiner was brought from Cedar Rapids, Iowa, the congregation renamed itself Chevra Kadisha Temple Israel, and "the children and grandchildren of the pioneers who had long since joined some uptown temple, agreed to help the mother congregation where their parents and grandparents worshipped to give it a new start in life."[14] But the plans came to naught, and not long after the little synagogue closed permanently and its membership was absorbed into The Temple.

In contrast, the annals of the Bohemian congregation's two contemporaries, the Hungarian B'ne Jeshurun and the Polish Anshe Emeth, were often stormy, and both grew to substantial size. B'ne Jeshurun reached importance by 1890, although it underwent numerous internal quarrels over its religious orientation. Anshe Emeth adhered to Orthodoxy and advanced more slowly, becoming a major religious institution around 1905. It, too, was not spared schisms and controversy.

"Is there any particular need for a Hungarian synagogue in Cleveland?" the *American Israelite* sniffed in 1880, but "Hungarian B'ne Yeshurun synagogue" (one of the early forms of transliteration) retained its territorial designation into the twentieth century.[15] B'ne Jeshurun's early history followed a familiar pattern. It had been founded in October, 1866:

Twenty members constituted the congregation at that time, and being unable to build a place of worship or even rent a hall, Mr. [Herman] Sampliner, who then lived in California Street, gave the use of two of his rooms for religious meetings every Friday evening, Saturday morning and the minor holidays. For the High Holidays a large hall was rented, then known as Gallagher's hall, located opposite the cathedral on the northwest corner of Superior and Erie Streets. The congregation worshipped in California Street for six months, after which it rented small rooms on St. Clair Street and Oregon Street. The first step in advance was made when the congregation rented Halle's hall on

Superior Street, now known as Frohsinn Hall. On Sabbath days its members met in the small room on the second floor and on holidays the large upper hall was used. In October, 1878, with a membership of sixty, a permanent place for a synagogue was leased and fitted up on Michigan Street, Rev. Mr. Klein being engaged as the rabbi and leader. Recently the congregation grew in number and influence. . . .[16]

Around 1886 land for a building was acquired at Ohio and Allen Streets, but instead the Eagle Street synagogue was purchased for $15,000 from Anshe Chesed, which was moving to Scovill Avenue.[17] A cemetery was also laid out in Glenville.

As a congregation of prospering immigrants with a somewhat Germanic cast, B'ne Jeshurun no longer adhered to Orthodoxy in its European form. An American traditional style did not yet exist during the 1880s and 1890s; Conservative Judaism, for which they might be said to have been groping, was hardly born. A probably short-lived congregation, Beth-El, appeared in 1884 "to consist of Hungarians and to be conducted upon a conservative reform plan." Its officers featured prominently in B'ne Jeshurun's later annals, so Beth-El might have been absorbed into the larger congregation.[18]

In 1886 Rabbi Sigmund Drechsler (1843–1908), a native of Hungary who had been educated at the yeshivot of his native land and in the Orthodox ("Hildesheimer") rabbinical seminary of Berlin, began his twenty years' service. He showed much ability to glide through the congregation's religious and political tempests and became a well-loved figure.

B'ne Jeshurun's dedication of the synagogue it acquired from Anshe Chesed in 1886 was a discordant event. Rabbi Aaron Hahn, who had balked over the insistence that he cover his head when present, could not come after all; nor could the more pacific Rabbi Machol. The speakers were Dr. Adolf Friedman, superintendent of the local home for the aged, Rabbi Heinrich Zirndorf of Hebrew Union college, and no less a personage than Isaac Mayer Wise.

All the sermons were preached in German, and peculiar sermons they were for such an occasion. Most of them were of a missionary nature, advising the congregation to change its mode of worship

from Orthodox to what is called Reform. Several of the influential members of the B'ne Yeshurun congregation felt rather provoked to be talked to so plainly regarding and against the ancient
ceremonies of their faith. . . .[19]

The famous Reformer expressed his life's conviction that American Judaism was synonymous with Reform, and that the quasi-
Orthodox B'ne Jeshurun, once in a synagogue of its own, was
morally obligated to adopt that form of Judaism. Despite American freedom, Wise chided the congregation, "you persist in
clinging to your old prejudices, your old customs. From your
country you have imported customs, supposed to be religious,
that have never been taught in the Torah or in any of our sacred
writings." He challenged them to produce proof from Jewish
law of the requirement to be covered or to face east during
worship, or to observe a second day of holidays.

> You persist in clinging to the traditions of the long forgotten dead
> and buried past instead of searching after noble truths and
> knowledge to gain the esteem and confidence of your fellow-
> men. . . . American habits and American life clash not only
> with Jewish orthodoxy, but with Christian orthodoxy as well.
> Judaism is in great danger today owing to uncalled for orthodoxy.
> We will not get the following of our youth; the second generation
> will desert Judaism. . . .[20]

Nothing better expressed the annoyance of Reform Jews with
immigrant Orthodoxy, and their confidence that Reform had to
prevail, than these words by Reform's foremost exponent.
During Wise's astounding address, Rabbi Drechsler held his
peace. Next week he blandly cautioned his congregation that
moving day always held danger that furniture might break;
B'ne Jeshurun had to take care not to "damage" their religion
in moving to Eagle Street.[21]

B'ne Jeshurun maintained its modified Orthodoxy until 1904,
when a quarrel erupted over the mixed seating of men and
women. Since this had long been the practice, the dissension
may have originated among recent Hungarian arrivals of firmer
Orthodoxy. A reported eighty-five men, most of them B'ne
Jeshurun dissenters, established the new Oheb Zedek congre-

gation. B'ne Jeshurun was then engaged in selling its Eagle Street building and moving, and matters almost came to court over the disposition of its cash assets; however, a settlement was apparently reached.[22] Oheb Zedek developed as an Orthodox congregation and purchased a former church building on Scovill Avenue.[23] Rabbi H. A. Liebovitz (b. 1873), of Hungarian birth and education, was brought from New Haven and began an active leadership.[24]

B'ne Jeshurun "has passed through many struggles, differences and divisions, but has survived them all." Emptied of its Orthodox group, it erected an impressive structure at Scovill Avenue and East 55th Street[25] and had 454 members in 1910.[26] Its religious orientation was uncertain, as could be seen in the case of Rabbi Drechsler's successors. Young Rabbi Abraham E. Dobrin, the first alumnus of the Jewish Theological Seminary to serve in Cleveland, stayed merely two years.[27] Next came Rabbi Samuel Schwartz (b. 1881), a graduate of the rabbinical seminary of Budapest who also graduated from Hebrew Union College. As he recalled long after, "The congregation was definitely opposed to Reform. But they heard about me having been a Yeshiva Bocher [student] in Hungary and concluded that I could not possibly be an out and out reformer." Rather to the young rabbi's surprise the congregation engaged him, supposing, as he thought, "that I would revert to my orthodox type." He found B'ne Jeshurun "orthodox with a touch of liberalism, family pews, late Friday evening services, modern orthodox prayerbook, English sermon, Saturday morning regular orthodox service, the chanting of the entire weekly torah portion, etc." Close to orthodoxy as it was, with members who "still had a taste for a 'droshe' [homiletical sermon]," B'ne Jeshurun at the same time had members who also belonged to Reform temples. Rabbi Schwartz found himself unable to behave in the Orthodox manner.[28] He won praise as "an able German talker [who] can deliver sermons in English almost entirely free from foreign accent."[29] (Schwartz recalled that preaching in German "was real torture.") After three years of outward congregational prosperity, Schwartz announced his resignation because "the undercurrent of dissension [was] so strong." From the pulpit he complained of "a species of bossism" by unnamed persons who demanded that "you will work and be my obedient servant" or suffer unpleasant consequences.[30]

He was succeeded by Rabbi Jacob Klein, whose background was entirely European.[31] Serving from 1912 to 1918, Rabbi Klein saw the membership increase from 500 to 725. Less and less did B'ne Jeshurun stress its Hungarian background, although the occasional use of German and the backgrounds of older members and most of its rabbis maintained this national character. The arrival of Rabbi Solomon Goldman (1893–1952) in 1919 presaged a stormy period during which B'ne Jeshurun was to become a Conservative congregation.[32]

Anshe Emeth, originally Polish, became a congregation of East European Jews. After wandering among meeting halls for some years the congregation purchased the Erie Street Methodist Church in 1880 and made it a synagogue.[33] Before the arrival en masse of their countrymen they thus had acquired a home which "although not large in size, is the finest synagogue in the city."[34] Its dedication in a sense marked the civic debut of this congregation, and was attended by Mayor Gardner, judges, and "the fair daughters of Israel arrayed in costly robes and costumes and a rich display of gold and diamonds." The city's two rabbis and Dr. Simon Wolfenstein spoke, Rabbi Hahn without a hat. "All three ministers dwelt upon the progress of Judaism and, while they professed esteem for a congregation which adheres to orthodox rites," they advised them also to behave well towards their fellow men.[35] Besides Orthodox worship and perhaps traditional sacred study, Anshe Emeth conducted numerous balls, usually for Purim and Simhat Torah.[36]

The congregation's religious leadership was a stormy issue. Evidently they did not desire a rabbi of the East European type, nor could they find a satisfactory person to serve as cantor and occasional preacher.

During the five years of its existence [on Erie Street] the congregation has had four pastors, the last one taking his leave yesterday [August 13, 1885]. Rev. Mr. Paltrovich, the first pastor, displeased his flock by interfering and meddling with matters that did not concern him. Rev. Mr. Leon [Lane?] was not satisfied with the duties of his office and insisted on carrying on the business of a "shochet". . . . Rev. Mr. Rappaport was not orthodox enough to suit the congregation, and the last on the list, Rev. Mr. Ettinger, has just tendered his resignation in keeping with the demand of the trustees of the temple.[37]

Ettinger was sent on his way after his fiancee's family learned that he had left behind a wife and children in Bucharest.[38] Next came Solomon Philo, who "conducted services" and pleased his hearers "by his excellent reading and interesting lectures."[39] Early in 1888 he too departed, his unexpired contract bought out.[40] Probably during the 1890s Solomon Beckerman served as rabbi for a few years.[41]

Anshe Emeth endured a time of troubles in the late 1880s. From the time it occupied its building, the attentive *Plain Dealer* commented, "that religious society has been divided against itself, resulting in constant quarreling and bickering between the two factions, known as the orthodox and reform parties."[42] The "reform" wing comprised the officers of the congregation, who avowed that for Anshe Emeth "reform" meant not Reform Judaism but merely the seating of men and women together and the robing of the cantor. After a tangle of elections and counter-elections, riotous scenes, near-secessions and money settlements made and unmade, the outcome was a victory for the Orthodox. They won out probably because they were steadily reinforced by newcomers still attached to the unaltered mode of worship.[43] Its orthodoxy confirmed, the congregation merged with a smaller one and erected a large building on Forest Avenue in 1904.[44]

Anshe Emeth reached its full stature under the rabbinic leadership of Samuel Margolies (1878–1917). He was the son of Rabbi Moses Zebulon Margolies (1851–1937), then of Boston and later of New York, who had come to the United States in 1882. In 1890 the boy returned alone to Eastern Europe to study at the yeshiva of Telz (which years later resettled in Margolies' adopted city). Once back in America, Margolies enrolled in Harvard, from which he graduated in 1902. Combining a deep education in Talmudic learning with a secular education in the arts and sciences, and as the scion of a rabbinic line, Rabbi Margolies brought to his office a background probably un-

matched by any Orthodox rabbi in the land. He won recognition as the representative figure of Cleveland's East European Jewish immigrants in the native Jewish as well as in the general community. Anshe Emeth's rabbi was an effective preacher in both English and Yiddish—a rarity at the time—and also a vigorous Zionist and Hebraist[45] who became a founder of modern Hebrew education in the city.

Rabbi Margolies was the first articulate Orthodox spokesman in Cleveland. He amply fulfilled his congregation's expectations "that he will serve as a strong connecting link between the children of the members of the synagogue and the older features of the Jewish faith."[46] Soon after he arrived he replied cogently to the *Jewish Review and Observer's* complaint that "Orthodoxy took the shell and left the kernel of our beautiful faith" and its suggestion that worship be held in English:

> The vernacular cannot be substituted for Hebrew, not because it is not permissible to pray in any other language, but for another reason. Orthodox Jewry insists on Hebrew, because by this Judaism will be saved from being a religion understood only by its clergy. . . . Orthodoxy, therefore demands from every Jew that he should teach his children Hebrew. . . . Now as to the *drosho* [homiletic discourse] of the *maggid* [preacher] . . . in some orthodox congregations it is not necessary to have English sermons, because the majority are newcomers, and do not understand the language. They need spiritual advice and guidance as well as the young people, and therefore the *maggid* with his Yiddish sermon is just as much needed as some modern rabbis with their German sermons.[47]

Samuel Margolies served as Anshe Emeth's rabbi for twelve years until he unexpectedly resigned in 1916 to enter business.[48] One year later he was killed in an automobile accident. His was the largest Jewish funeral in the city's history until that day, as many thousands followed in the procession after his coffin.[49] Rabbi Margolies left Anshe Emeth as Cleveland's largest Orthodox congregation with many more worshippers and a wider influence than its membership of 300 suggests.[50] Soon thereafter it went through another stormy transition, to a near-Orthodox form of Conservative Judaism.

IMMIGRANT CONGREGATIONS

There were other immigrant congregations in which the question of religious orientation never consciously arose because they sought only to transplant faithfully the ways of Judaism as they knew it from their native towns and regions. This did not mean that immigrants were all Orthodox in their personal lives, notwithstanding the shorthand semantic equation of "Orthodox" with "East European immigrant." Many were indifferent observers of the Sabbath and visited a synagogue only on High Holidays.

While congregations had more seats than members or even regular worshippers, on the Jewish New Year and Day of Atonement demand for seating far exceeded the synagogues' supply. As early as 1893 the New Benevolent Association was formed to hold services at the YMCA.[51] Beth Hamidrosh Hagodol, whose synagogue, once a German church, was too small, rented the same place a few years later, after ascertaining formally that no Christian symbols were obtrusive.[52] Other "congregations" were founded simply for the purpose of High Holiday observance; this was "usually a commercial exploitation of holiday piety upon the part of some individuals of varying degrees of religious worth" who catered to "vast numbers of 'unaffiliated' in the community." Services were sometimes held "in any hall or room obtainable. Some of them are places connected with saloons, with dance halls, theatres of questionable character. . . ."[53] Beginning in 1909, the Council Educational Alliance attacked these practices by means of its High Holiday Orthodox Peoples' Synagogue. In its first year 479 seats were leased at rates below $1 and 48 were distributed gratis to the poor.[54] One theatre proprietor, his synagogue business now gone, announced his conviction that "it is not proper to convert a theatre or hall into a house of God."[55] In 1914 the recently founded Council of Cleveland Rabbis, to which all local rabbis belonged, assumed responsibility for the Peoples' Synagogue.[56]

The existence of High Holiday synagogues, whether more or less reputable, demonstrates the extent of religious sentiment which would well up periodically. As another indication of popular religiosity, "about 200,000 pounds" of matzot were con-

sumed during Passover.[57] Immigrant synagogues carried on religious life at other times as well. Lithuanians, more than other Jews in Eastern Europe, had retained the traditional forms of local communal structure with recognized rabbinic direction in halakhic matters, and it was usually the Lithuanian (popularly, Litvak) congregations which sought out a rabbi who could transplant some of this function to America. In 1890 a rabbi recognized as Chief Rabbi by several of these congregations stayed briefly in Cleveland. His name was not recorded, but he reportedly came from Pittsburgh. After several Talmudic discourses and, apparently, an attack on the local Hebraists of the Ahavas Sfas Ibri society, the "Chief Rabbi" chose not to remain.[58]

Later in the same year, however, the Litvaks attained their goal when Rabbi Benjamin Gittelsohn (1853–1932) accepted an invitation to leave the rabbinate of Trashkun (Troschkunay) and settle in Cleveland. The new rabbi was the scion of a rabbinic line, but his childhood and youth were impoverished. His mother was widowed and the boy was a wandering, hungry yeshiva student until his marriage. In 1878 he became town rabbi of Avanta, where he remained until he moved to Trashkun in 1883. The latter town had 779 Jews in 1897, who constituted 78 percent of its population, and they were almost all poor. Rabbi Gittelsohn suffered material want in these honorific positions until "friends and acquaintances" in Cleveland extended their invitation. The large American city, and the immigrant Jewish community within it, differed by far from the small towns he had known, but his reactions were restrained. "Here too I found no ease or repose, nor did I have joy and pleasure, [but] thank God who brought me here I have just a little bit"— enough, at least, to enable him to publish two learned works.[59] Rabbi Gittelsohn was at first rabbi of Beth Israel—Beth Hamidrash Hagodol[60] and gradually became the rabbinic authority for several other congregations. He did not play the representative role taken by his junior, Rabbi Margolies, and appears to have been a quiet, scholarly figure.

Cleveland congregations continued to attract Lithuanian rabbis after the turn of the century. Rabbi Gershon Ravinson came to Beth Hamidrosh Hagodol about 1903, but his four years' tenure erupted in a quarrel which ended in court,[61] and the unfortunate man died soon after. Ohavei Emuna Anshe Russia, like many of its type, either did not desire or could not afford a rabbi, at least until 1909. Then, long after its move from Hill Street to Scovill Avenue and East 37th Street, it secured Nachman H. Ebin (1884–1942) as its rabbi. He, too, was Lithuanian; he possessed ordination from notable rabbinic authorities and also acquired an American education after his arrival in the United States in 1904. As was typical of Orthodox rabbinic modernists, Rabbi Ebin was an active Zionist, and the scope of his activity extended throughout the Jewish community.[62] He thus resembled his older contemporary, Rabbi Margolies, until he departed for a Brooklyn, New York congregation in 1924.

A matter of deep importance to immigrant Jews was reflected in the founding of the Chesed Shel Emeth [True Kindness] Cemetery Association early in 1903.[63] The first interment in its tract on Ridge Avenue took place at the end of 1904.[64] Besides burying the indigent, the Association served a dues-paying membership estimated at 500 in 1909. During the first seven months of 1914 it conducted sixty-four burials; dues were then $1.20 per annum.[65] Various larger congregations also had their cemeteries.[66] The imminence of death brought serious reflection and sometimes moving spiritual expression. Thus, Adolph Fisch, a retail businessman until his death on February 20, 1904, left behind an ethical testament to his wife and family. While citing the Talmudic dictum that death atones for all sins, he nevertheless begged pardon for having provided so meagerly for them during his life. He actually left about $15,000 for his widow, son, and three daughters.

First and above all, I want to be buried according to Hebrew rites. I want to be placed in a plain, wooden coffin, without polish or glass. Take the braid off my prayer shawl. No sermon shall be preached over my corpse, as I do not want anyone to say falsehoods over me. Under no circumstances shall there be any flowers on my casket or on my grave. Mourning week, also, you need not keep, because each of you has to seek his daily bread. Do not deprive the children of any enjoyment or amusement. Let them continue their music lessons. If you wish to have a stone set on my grave, get a cheap one. . . .[67]

Many immigrant Jews satisfied their religious wishes not through congregational membership and its benefits, but by resorting to different places for specific needs. The immigrant might be a regular worshipper at a congregation of which he was not a member, or attend the Peoples' Synagogue on the High Holidays; the event of death was provided for by membership in the Chesed Shel Emeth; several benevolent societies existed to protect him somewhat against the costs of illness. Any congregation would allow him to have the Bar Mitzvah of his son, who would have been instructed at an independent communal Hebrew school or by a private tutor. Kosher meat and provisions, including matzot, were of course on the commercial market, and so were such religious supplies as prayer books, prayer shawls, and phylacteries. (In 1906 angry housewives, supported by Jewish trade unions, conducted a consumer strike against the rising price of kosher meat.)[68] Congregational rabbis served all who might turn to them to perform marriages and funerals, or to give responsa to questions in Jewish law. The religious life of immigrant Jews thus resembled that of Eastern Europe by its diffusion among independent and sometimes rival organizations, with congregations playing the leading but by no means dominant role.

This looseness had obvious disadvantages. In the absence of communal responsibility ignorant or unscrupulous men could perform a Jewish religious marriage, or, what was worse, a divorce, without a civil one, heedless of the vital distinction between the public status of Jewish law in Russia and the United States. Chatzkel Busch, who performed such a marriage in 1893, was arrested.[69] The kosher meat trade was a frequent offender because it had the difficult task of balancing religious law with commercial interest; no communal group successfully regulated this trade. In 1892 Judeh Berman, the main *shohet* for about ten years at the John J. Flick slaughterhouse where Cleveland's kosher meat was produced, and which slaughtered fowl and about 100 steers weekly, claimed that not only Jews but some Gentiles, including physicians, ate kosher meat for sanitary reasons.[70] Uncontrolled enterprise in the trade readily brought about public recriminations between retail butchers, each alleging the other was *treif* (not kosher).[71] No disinterested body could adjudicate; only Orthodox rabbis, whose sole sanction was their personal prestige, could perform this function.

Not all the immigrants were pious, but Christian attempts to proselytize among them failed. A cry of anger arose when the Josephine Mission, a branch of the Euclid Avenue Baptist Church, opened its doors in the midst of the Jewish immigrant district and enticed Jewish children to its classes with candy and sewing instruction. The Christian clergy in charge did not conceal their intentions. "Hands Off Our Children" headlined the *Jewish Independent*,[72] as synagogues, Zionists, and the Council Educational Alliance, in a rare display of unity, organized a mass meeting and an effective boycott which ended the Josephine Mission's threat.[73]

A 1907 survey located twenty-three synagogues in Cleveland.[74] There was a "Synagogue of the Government [Province] of Grodno," whose members were not only "natives of that Russian state, but all the organizers [were] members of the Jewish Carpenters' Union." They pledged "to strictly refrain from labor on Saturdays and Jewish holidays."[75] In 1906 a Hungarian congregation appeared bearing this principle in its name: Shomre Shabbos (Observers of the Sabbath), "the orthodox of the orthodox"; they had a "stringent rule" that only Sabbath observers could be admitted to membership.[76] They acquired a frame house on East 37th Street, and from 1912 to 1915 I. Lefkowitz, also from Hungary, was their rabbi.[77] There was Nusach Ari congregation of Hasidic Jews, "a sect entirely new to Cleveland Judaism," which made its appearance in 1906.[78] It could have been identical with the Zemach Zedek congregation, reportedly founded in 1903, probably by Hasidim of the Lubavich persuasion.[79] A bare ten families on the West Side, where very few Jews ever lived, founded B'nai Israel in 1910. They worshipped in a rented hall until 1925.[80]

These and the other East European immigrant synagogues originated close to one another. During the 1880s they clustered near Hill Street where Agudath Achim and two others, probably Kenesseth Israel and Ohavei Emuna Anshe Russia, were situated. Shaarei Torah was known informally from 1897 as Crystal's shul because it met in Isaac Crystal's house on Orange Avenue. After 1900 Woodland Avenue was the street of synagogues. As the locus of immigrant life shifted eastward, new congregations were founded in the new areas. Thus, Agudath Bnai Israel Anshe Sfarad established itself in 1914 on East 51st Street near Woodland Avenue, close to the Ahavath Zion (Zionist) congregation founded the year before; not far away was the synagogue of Jews from Tetiev, Russia, standing on Case Avenue between Woodland and Scovill.[81] Furthest east was Bes Tfilo (with variant spellings, for example, Beth Tefilah), founded in 1913 with Rabbi Margolies' strong encouragement. Enjoying rapid growth, by 1915 it possessed an attractive, remodeled house.[82] The foresight of Anshe Emeth's rabbi was realized afterwards. Beth Tfilo and Anshe Emeth merged in 1916, providing the congregational basis for the huge Cleveland Jewish Center erected between 1919 and 1922.

The number of Orthodox congregations was twenty-four in 1918, when a Union of Orthodox Congregations (Agudas Hakehillos) of Cleveland was formed. It took the ambitious step of electing Chief Rabbi Maier Jung of the Federation of Synagogues in London as its chief rabbi, and secured his acceptance.[83] Rabbi Jung did not come, but his son Rabbi Leo Jung came to Kenesseth Israel in 1920 and served two years.

Gradually the natives' dislike of immigrant orthodoxy softened. There was still annoyance with foreign ways, but Cleveland was so crowded with foreign-language religious bodies that Jews could hardly be disturbed about "foreign" Jewish houses of worship. The "religious societies with peculiar names" deplored by Rabbi Machol,[84] it was slowly realized, were serving a deeply significant purpose:

> We Jews who have been born and reared in America frequently become impatient with the immigrants coming to this country. We look with disfavor upon their quaint customs, particularly in many instances as far as their religious observances are concerned.
> We seem to forget that it is their intense loyalty to their ancestral faith that is largely responsible for much of the misery they

endure in their native land, and in order to escape it they have come to these shores. . . .

The immigrants regard their Judaism as one of the most precious possessions and are willing to make any sacrifice for it.

Judaism will never be eradicated here, for these people will not give up that which has cost them such a great sacrifice.

If immigration has brought with it a Jewish problem, it has also brought much good, and one is the preservation of Jewish ideals.[85]

It was by no means clear during the second decade of the twentieth century how the religious zeal brought by Russian and Polish immigrants would be perpetuated in the secular, urban, open life of America and of Cleveland. Then the Temples of Cleveland began to influence the immigrants more than either side suspected, as the effects of American education and culture became apparent within Jewish life.

Alfred A. Benesch, 1879-1973
(Western Reserve Historical Society)

Abraham H. Friedland, Hebrew poet
and author, director of the Bureau of
Jewish Education, 1924-1939 (Bureau
of Jewish Education)

"Czar" Harry Bernstein, 1856-
1920 (Mrs. David Schulman)

Mrs. Siegmund Herzog, president,
Jewish Community Federation, 1924-
1927 (Jewish Community Federation)

The northern end of the Glenville district, the intersection of E. 105th Street and St. Clair Avenue, ca. 1925 (Cleveland Board of Zoning Appeals)

Community leaders at the laying of the cornerstone for Mt. Sinai Hospital, 1916, (Mt. Sinai Hospital)

President Philmore Haber presides at a meeting of the Executive Committee of the Jewish Community Council, ca. 1942 (Jewish Community Federation)

Torah scroll being moved for the dedication of Congregation Bene Ya'acov Kol Israel (Kinsman Jewish Center). Pinhas Newman is bearing the scroll, 1932 (Joseph Newman)

The Jewish Carpenters Hall, E. 135th Street and Kinsman Road, home of Local 1750, ca. 1935 (Western Reserve Historical Society)

Headline in the *Jewish World* announcing the Palestine Mandate, 1921 (Western Reserve Historical Society)

Nahum Sokolow, Hebrew writer and Zionist leader, planting a tree at the Hebrew Cultural Garden; standing to his left are Rabbi Israel Porath and Ezra Shapiro, 1930 (Bureau of Jewish Education)

Jewish War Veterans parade in protest against pogroms in Eastern Europe, June 6, 1919 (The Jewish Independent)

Winter view of Coventry Road business district, Cleveland Heights, 1924 (Fraser Realty Co.)

VII

Education and Culture

THE day school connected with Anshe Chesed congregation closed in 1865. Afterwards, Jewish children attended the public schools of Cleveland, and few if any were found in the private "classical academies" and other upper-class schools. In the public schools, little was said about Jews as pupils or teachers, probably because they enjoyed equality of treatment and of opportunity. Only in the twentieth century, when public attention to immigrants and their children became widespread, did ethnic and religious groups within the public schools, including Jews, receive much notice. Jewish education also advanced conspicuously at this time, and the Cleveland Jewish community gained recognition as one of the educational pathfinders of American Jewry.

PUBLIC SCHOOLING

The question of religion in the public schools, which raised issues never completely settled, appeared in Cleveland as it had in other cities. Besides the expectations which all parents probably have of their children's schools, Jewish parents assumed in addition that their children's public schools would be free of religious exercises. Some earnest Christians, however, unwilling to reconcile themselves to the removal of distinctive religious expression from their children's schools, pressed for the inclusion of Psalms, the Lord's Prayer, Bible readings, or Easter and Christmas celebrations in the school schedule. Jews, who supported public schooling warmly, combatted such proposals.

One incident occurred in 1901, when the School Board decided to require each school day to commence with the reading of the Ten Commandments, the Lord's Prayer, and Psalm 23. Allegedly, this had long been the practice. Rabbi Machol's first reaction was by no means negative, for he contended even of

186

the Lord's Prayer that "every word in it is a Jewish word." Yet within the day he and other rabbis and a few lay leaders swung into action, soliciting individually each member of the School Board to cancel the decision.[1]

More moderate proposals, requiring only Bible reading, were likewise opposed by Cleveland Jewish spokesmen. A bill before the legislature in 1915, which would have accomplished this, leaving school boards throughout Ohio to select the passages, was roundly condemned. Addressing the Cleveland delegation to the legislature, Rabbi Gries expressed confidence that "the Jews of the entire state are absolutely opposed to any affiliation of church and state and to the introduction of religion in the public schools." Such a problem already existed, he added: "If I'd begin to tell you of the sectarian occurrences you would be amazed." Hitherto the Jewish community had taken "no action of protest," referring individual cases "to school officials and they take care of them quietly." Bible reading, he argued, required commentary to have meaning, and commentary could not but be sectarian. Rabbi Wolsey, supplementing his colleague, denounced "placing the religious instruction of my child in the hands of the School Board." This conclusion was that of Gries, of the American Reform rabbinate in particular, and of most American Jews at all periods.[2]

Even more sweeping was the local Jewish newspaper's view. It insisted that, contrary to the claims of apologists for Bible reading, "there are many ways of teaching morality without using the Bible."

> One of the fundamental principles of this great American Republic is the separation of church and state, and when we introduce Bible reading into our public schools we are acting contrary to this spirit.
>
> We strongly advocate the reading of the Bible in our homes, and parents who neglect to impress their children with the vast importance of this book are depriving them of a rich heritage in life.
>
> The mission of the public school is to provide our children with that secular education which will enable them to be a credit to the nation, and when they have done this they have accomplished their purpose.[3]

The issue of Bible reading was difficult because it conflicted with other, agreed moral values and with the contrary viewpoint which was held by important groups. It was easier to secure small changes in school practices which did not collide with other groups or with the school organization as a whole. Already, in the early days of Jewish settlement, permission had been obtained "for the Jewish scholars of this city, [to] be absent from school on the Day of Atonement without any detriment to them."[4] The school year opened on Rosh Hashanah, 1888, without any of the four Jewish members of the School Board requesting a change of schedule, but a recurrence was avoided in 1893 when a City Council resolution requested the School Board to shift the opening day.[5] When Jewish organizations protested that of all Shakespeare's plays "The Merchant of Venice" was studied in high school, the Superintendent of Schools, mindful of its place on reading lists for college entrance, "expressed himself in favor of allowing another of Shakespeare's plays to take precedence in the course in cases where the parents of Jewish children in a class object to the reading of this particular work."[6] Any prejudicial effects of the problematic masterpiece would of course continue in non-Jewish schools.

It should have been possible to promote Jewish day schools among pious immigrant Jews or cultural Zionists. Among Cleveland's contemporary immigrant groups, the religiously devout and ethnic nationalists were zealously establishing private, mostly Roman Catholic, schools for their children. However, one discerns no voice urging this for Jews.

Cleveland had fifty-two Roman Catholic schools which enrolled over 28,000 children, of whom 17,000 studied in schools where they learned their catechism in many native tongues, including Polish, German, Czech, Slovak, Slovenian, Magyar, Croatian, and Lithuanian. Indeed, German was long taught in the public schools to attract German children.[7] The Roman Catholic Church itself in Cleveland showed "no particular enthusiasm" for teaching these languages, which it undertook only to meet parental insistence.[8] The Catholics, under Irish episcopal leadership in most cities, although not in Cleveland, were being led vigorously towards Americanization.

On the other hand, many of the Protestant and Eastern rite

churches extensively represented in Cleveland were devoutly committed to the ancestral tongues. Moreover, strong secularist wings among such immigrant groups as the Bohemians fostered languages for non-religious, nationalist reasons.[9] The ethnic groups within Cleveland's newer immigration, who originated mainly in the empires of the Czars and the Hapsburgs, had often endured severe discrimination on account of the languages they spoke. With these obstacles removed in America they established a wide range of schools for their children, both ethnic parochial schools and afternoon and Sunday schools.[10]

Despite these precedents, there was no attempt to establish Jewish day schools in Cleveland. The education of Jewish children proceeded entirely within public schools, supplemented by a variety of afternoon and Sunday schools.[11] The readiness, indeed the alacrity, with which Jewish parents from Eastern Europe, who had resisted educational blandishments and coercion by European governments, sent their children to American public schools suggests trust in them, as well as the conviction that public schools were necessary for their children to advance in American society as they had not in Russia. "We do not favor parochial schools," declared the Orthodox Rabbi Samuel Margolies, "for this would separate the Jew from his neighbor. The Jew by nature is a cosmopolitan, and prefers to mingle among his fellowman."[12]

The 1,591 women who constituted over 99 percent of the elementary school teaching staff in 1908 included 61 Jews who were native Americans or native daughters of a foreign-born father, and 19 more who were born abroad. Of this total of 80, only 17 had East European origins, while the rest were of German and Hungarian stock.[13] Cleveland's teachers were mainly German and Irish women. Jewish women constituted only 5 percent elementary school teachers, a proportion, as we shall see, much beneath that of Jews among the pupils. Obviously, teaching was not an occupation favored by Jewish women, possibly on account of a Jewish social bias towards marriage and family for women. On the other hand, the annual lists of teachers who had been reappointed—security of tenure was still unknown— included Jewish women, sometimes bearing prominent Jewish family names.[14] It is suggestive of the future that of the 89 foreign-born teachers, as many as 19 were Jewish. Teaching as a career for men lay further in the future, mainly with the development of high schools.

In 1908 there were 23,822 children of native-born parents in the public schools, while 35,119 others were themselves born abroad or had at least one parent born abroad. Of the latter group, 4,819 were Jewish; there is no division for the former.[15] Adding the Jewish children of native stock, there were probably 5,500 Jewish public school children in 1908. Seven years later, after intensive immigration, there were 6,795 pupils who reported Yiddish-speaking homes and 5 to 10 percent more who, in the opinion of the sympathetic investigator, concealed the Yiddish spoken at home or reported English if it was even passively understood by their parents.[16] (To be sure, Yiddish was indeed unknown in many homes, especially of earlier Jewish stock.) Around 1915, therefore, probably 9,000 to 10,000 Jewish children attended Cleveland elementary and high schools, out of a total of 75,000 enrolled.

Neighborhood public schools rapidly acquired and lost a Jewish character as Jews moved, usually in an easterly direction:

> A school census taken in the Woodland Avenue section in 1908 showed 86 per cent Jewish children, a similar census taken in 1918 showed but 59 per cent; . . . a census taken in 1918 in schools of the Fifty-ninth to Seventy-ninth Street section showed 70 per cent Jewish children and . . . a census of the One Hundred and Fifth Street section in 1915 showed 20 per cent Jewish children, while in 1918 this percentage had increased to approximately 50 per cent.[17]

The 1915 Cleveland Education Survey found the city's schools tedious, overdisciplined places, with a narrowly traditional curriculum taught by a poorly paid staff supervised by pedantic, ill-trained principals. German, once taught throughout the elementary grades, had declined in importance and was a high school subject exclusively.[18] There was lingering prejudice against the foreign, probably of the sort expressed years earlier by Miss Davis (quoted in chapter 4). Teachers frequently assigned reading matter which was inappropriate for poor immigrant children.[19] Yet basic skills, the three Rs, were assiduously taught, and we possess definite indications of the academic success of Jewish children.[20] The following list shows the preponderantly Jewish public schools in the city and each school's score on the city-wide spelling test, which was regarded as an important indicator of reading ability and academic progress:

School	Total Enrollment	Children From Yiddish-Speaking Homes	Score in Spelling	Other Home Langs.
Case-Woodland	837	448	83	Czech, 132
Central	883	440	82	
Dike	1,063	659	79	
Kennard	1,196	847	77	
Longwood	651	427	84	
Mayflower	1,177	494	80	Italian, 184
Outhwaite	1,440	1,033	84	
South Case	960	638	75	
Woolridge	1,211	527	79	

All these "Jewish" schools surpassed the city-wide spelling average of 76, and two were tied for second place.[21] Yet among the Jewish schools were some of the city's "lowest per cent of children . . . who are both over-age for their grades and making slow progress."[22]

The scholarly investigators of 1915 found that Jewish immigrant schoolchildren were academically the most successful among all the immigrant stocks of the city. Professor Judd commented upon the success of the Jewish immigrant children in oral reading:

The children in Jewish [public] schools are distinctly ahead of the average Cleveland pupil. In spite of the fact that they are surrounded by poor economic conditions and that they often use a foreign tongue, these children seem to rise above their handicaps better than any nationalities under similar conditions.[23]

Professor Miller also attempted to explain high academic achievement by these children of "the most complex and variously regarded of all our immigrants. . . ." He interpreted the presence of "the commonly mentioned 'Jewish characteristics' " as the outcome of "conditions of economic and social life under which the Jew has been constrained to live for generations in every country." In general,

> Judaism is not so much a dogma as it is a progressive education. Jewish children are eager pupils, not because they are naturally brighter than others, but because the whole Jewish life develops mental alertness and the learned are traditionally respected.

He recommended that teachers acquaint themselves with such aspects of Judaism as its holidays, and even "some effort should be made to understand what the Talmud deals with."[24] Here was a far-reaching statement; it reflected the gradual increase of sympathy and understanding for immigrants in general which informed Miller's book and which he urged upon Cleveland schools.[25]

But schools did not change quickly. Neither was every Jewish child an attentive, capable student. For many, the routine of school was dull past endurance, and the promised rewards to be gained in later life a remote fable. Elementary school terminated the formal education of most children. The proportion of Jewish youth continuing to high school was higher than among the children of other groups, yet of all fifteen-year-olds, merely 77 boys and 132 girls were in school. Even of these, only 63 boys and 67 girls were in high school, while the others, probably recent immigrants, were learning rudimentary language skills.[26] The majority of fifteen-year-olds held jobs, attaining their maturity at work.

Even before the adolescent years, problems of child life were manifest. Around 1909 it was found that 98 of 282 newsboys investigated were Jewish, most of them under fourteen. They earned thirty to fifty cents daily, hawking newspapers.[27] The better element among these youngsters organized in a Newsboys and Bootblacks Protective Union, which met at the Council Educational Alliance and was chartered by the American Federation of Labor. The union even had its sickness and death fund and protected the "rights" of its members to the street corners where they worked. The newsboys and bootblacks made no distinction of race and color, but all their officers but one were Jewish.[28] During the same period a band of semi-delinquent boys who called themselves the Zookies roamed the streets. They came from very poor German, Negro, Jewish and Slavic homes, where during the harsh winter "the same tale would be told—no work, no money, hardly anything to eat, and no coal to keep the family warm."[29] Hardly different were the dirty, neglected Jewish boys, aged around twelve, who built a "clubhouse"—a cave in the railroad yards.[30] Rabbi Wolsey spoke of "the backroom gambling dens on Woodland Avenue in which Jewish young men are led on to destruction."[31] Several hundred Jewish children reached Juvenile Court yearly. Although most cases were minor, such as newsboys "staying out nights," the thought was worrisome to Jewish social workers.[32]

With the number attending high schools so limited, that in the colleges was bound to be paltry. Sons of the older Jewish stock went East, particularly to Harvard, and so did some of the brightest immigrant youth. Alfred A. Benesch, a poor Bohemian immigrant's son, recalled the encouragement to try for Harvard in 1896 from a sympathetic teacher at Central High School.[33] At the local Western Reserve University, only four "Hebrews" were counted in general academic studies and two or three more in its medical school. Law was the favored subject, perhaps because it could be studied at night. Baldwin University Law School had nine foreign-born and thirteen foreign-stock Jewish students among its enrollment of 108, and the similar figures at Western Reserve were seven foreign-born and seven foreign-stock out of an enrollment of 131. Undoubtedly there were also native-stock Jews whom the Immigration Commission did not count separately.[34] The age of the Jewish march to college lay in the future.

Public schools were not only for children. Many mature immigrants overcame their weariness at the close of a long day's work to attend night school. Cleveland's first night school had been opened by the Council of Jewish Women around 1897, and the city took it over in 1900.[35] By 1904 thirty-five elementary and three high schools conducted evening classes for 2,700 students. Like other ethnic groups, Jews tended to concentrate in the schools in the Jewish immigrant district, where the teachers also knew the Yiddish which was the native language of most students.[36] Like the Jewish children, the adults quickly won a reputation. The city's supervisor of the program said:

> The Russian Hebrews are probably our best students, not that they are any brighter than the others, but because they seem to be more desirous of getting a little education. They have been known to be able to write after only two months of study, and their writing would compare favorably with that done in the regular sixth and seventh grades.[37]

Night school met only from November until May, and the Council of Jewish Women continued the program during the summer. Its plans illustrate the problems of immigrants and the institutions which sought to serve them:

> For those who studied in the gymnasium or who have a higher European education special classes will be arranged, so that they will not be hindered by such as do not possess their training, and therefore must be taught more slowly.
>
> There will also be special classes for people who understand other languages, such as Russian, Hebrew, German and Hungarian, and who, therefore, can grasp English more rapidly than those who only know Yiddish. Pupils, however, who never learned any language, and who only understand Yiddish, will have teachers who will explain in Yiddish anything they cannot otherwise comprehend.
>
> A splendid new text book has been procured, which was written especially for foreigners. Also, people who cannot attend night school four times a week because of overtime work, will be accommodated in a special class that meets only twice a week— provided there is sufficient demand.
>
> We are going to open a day class in English . . . for those whose occupations do not permit them to attend night school . . . bakers, night watchmen, melamdim or teachers of Hebrew, etc.[38]

In time the summer classes were also transferred to the city, with the Council Educational Alliance cooperating in enrollment and curriculum.[39]

In 1915, when night school for immigrants was at the peak of its development, 1,976 of its 11,402 students were Jews.[40] The young adult immigrants who preponderated in night school were hopeful and ambitious, and knowledge of English was the key to many of the things they sought in America. Two aspiring young sculptors began in such schools. Max Kalish (1891–1945), who came to Cleveland as a child of three, was able to commence his art studies at the Cleveland School of Art, where he later taught, while William Zorach (originally Zorach Finkelstein; 1887–1966), son of impoverished immigrants, was enabled to leave Cleveland in 1903 for New York and the European study which brought him world renown.[41] The painter brothers Abel (1883–1962) and Alex Warshawsky (1887–1945) grew up and received their early art education in the same fashion as Zorach and Kalish. Rose Pastor, sweatshop worker and daughter of needy newcomers, began her career in poetry under the patronage of the more prosperous members of her Friendly Club.[42]

SUNDAY SCHOOLS AND TEMPLES

There is a photograph taken around 1909 which shows well-dressed boys and girls thronging down a temple's steps as they left Sunday school. They hardly look different from their parents and elders who descended the temples' steps at the conclusion of worship.[43] Indeed, this was the point. The Sunday schools were training children to take their place one day as members and participants. It was not piety and erudition that were sought, nor the mastery of Hebrew which they presupposed. Because Judaism was conceived as a universal moral code, Jewish education consisted of moral didacticism taught catechistically and by example from Biblical history.

Both Reform Temples conducted Sunday schools. In 1876 they enrolled 214 children who were taught by five teachers. Tifereth Israel

consists of 4 classes. The lowest class learns to read Hebrew, the rudiments of catechism and Bible history up to Moses. The second grade continue their studies as the lowest grade but add the translation of certain portions in the prayerbook. The upper grades continue as above including translations from the Pentateuch.[44]

Tifereth Israel had only two classes and fifty children in 1886. "Sessions are held every Saturday and Sunday morning in the basement of the synagogue."[45] Special events marked the year. There was an annual public examination, adorned with addresses by pupils and examiners and with prizes. Thus, in 1875:

> The scholars all gave proof that they had improved their time well, as they showed a proficiency in catechism, biblical history, Judaism, reading and translating [Hebrew] which far exceeded the expectations of every one present. Little Miss Esther Nusbaum spoke the closing speech, after which Master Goldner stepped upon the Almemmer, and with a few well-timed remarks presented to Dr. Hahn, in the name of his class-mates, a beautiful inkstand, with gold pen and pencil holder.[46]

During the summer there was a Sunday School picnic. The annual highlight, however, was confirmation on Shavuot, which was the graduation from Sunday school. This was an elaborate event in the beflowered synagogue, during which the children delivered prayers, confessions of faith, and hymns, underwent oral examination, and heard the sermon dedicated to them.[47] Much of this was in German. The Sunday school's library included "a choice lot of German books by the best authors, which are in daily use by the Sunday School children."[48] Lists of confirmands were published, and reveal a preponderance of girls. Probably some families still preferred the traditional boy's Bar Mitzvah to the group confirmation. Tifereth Israel, always the more Reform, still reported five Bar Mitzvah events in 1890, besides eighteen children in its confirmation class.[49] The Jewish Orphan Asylum also conducted a Sunday school, headed by Dr. Simon Wolfenstein, director of the institution and himself a rabbi.[50]

Until the 1890s Sunday school was a rather tiresome matter. A few teachers were paid two dollars per session, and parents were more than once reminded of the necessity that their children attend, and punctually.[51] Tifereth Israel's 50 in 1886 inched to 70 in 1892, while the 150 whom Anshe Chesed claimed in 1885 dwindled to 135 by 1908.[52]

By the early 1890s generational change and the arrival of Rabbi Gries brought the radicalizing of Reform at Tifereth

Israel and the de-Germanization of the congregation. The same changes brought the removal of Hebrew from the curriculum. Too little Hebrew was taught to learn it well, and too much to keep children interested. The *Hebrew Observer*, in raising the issue, could invoke clear, well-known certainties:

> We are not a nation and never will be one again. When we did exist as a nation, Hebrew was the national tongue. Its usefulness is now a thing of the past. It is but a memory which will have to be laid aside eventually. . . .[53]

Facts close to home could also be cited:

> We would be greatly surprised should it be found, upon examination, that there is *one single person* who attended the Sabbath Schools of Cleveland, who can translate a single verse from Hebrew into English.[54]

The journal pursued the matter and its viewpoint struck sympathetic chords at Tifereth Israel.[55]

Rabbi Gries discontinued the confirmation and substituted a combined examination and graduation ceremony.[56] Soon afterwards, the congregation discontinued the study of Hebrew, which had been pursued only by a small, optional class, mostly of non-members' children, on Saturday morning.[57] A new spirit infused the stale school; its practices and curriculum were harmonized with those of the congregation as the American-trained rabbi assumed charge. Its new edifice on Willson Avenue was much nearer the children's homes than the small former synagogue on Huron Street. President Martin Marks jubilantly reported:

> For the first time since I have been connected with the congregation and probably for the first time in the memory of our oldest members, our children are anxious and look forward with pleasure to their attendance at the Sunday School.[58]

There were 86 children on the rolls in 1893; in 1905 there were 880, making it the largest Jewish Sunday school in the land.[59]

The congregation now required parents to be members in order to enroll their children.[60] Most complied, but few parents took much interest in the Jewish education of their children, as the Temple noted.[61] The Sunday school, large and bustling as it was, was not an expensive item in the budget. In 1901–1902 the cost of instruction was $1,249.00, other expenses were $39.69, and an unspecified amount was required for overhead.[62]

Anshe Chesed's school, like the congregation itself, lay in the doldrums during Rabbi Machol's later years. When Rabbi Wolsey succeeded him, and a few years later the beautiful Euclid Avenue Temple was erected, the Sunday school underwent the boom which Tifereth Israel had enjoyed fifteen years before. Wolsey led the Euclid Avenue Temple to reintroduce Hebrew, bringing for the purpose one of the Talmud Torah teachers.[63] By 1916, 638 were enrolled, of whom 81 were in a unique high school program. There was a normal class for training prospective teachers.[64] Rabbi Wolsey's *Lessons in Judaism for the Confirmation Class*, which his congregation published in sixteen leaflets in 1919, provide a glimpse of the broad, liberal Judaism he sought to inculcate.

In 1920, Abba Hillel Silver, three years rabbi of The Temple, "made an earnest appeal [to the Board] that the teaching of Hebrew to children of the Temple be encouraged and urged."[65] The source of the appeal lay not only in Silver's Hebraism, but also in the worldwide Hebraic-Zionist revival. The new Hebrew education which had started in immigrant circles was spreading.

JUDAISM FOR THE IMMIGRANT CHILD

B'ne Jeshurun's teacher and cantor delivered an apologia before the commencement of the first public examination of its Sunday school pupils in 1885. He observed that

> in Europe . . . the children are compelled to study from morning till night, and here they are only permitted [!] to visit the Hebrew school twice every week, Saturday and Sunday, except during public school vacation, when they attend four times a week. Taking all these circumstances into consideration, . . . he felt positive that the result of the examination will prove satisfactory to the children's parents.[66]

Actually, some of the immigrant congregations conducted a

heder like that of East European Jewry, a room where the *melamed* (schoolmaster) taught each child in turn. The content of the teaching was rudimentary: prayers, basic Jewish law and practice, a bit of Pentateuch, and preparation for Bar Mitzvah. At the new Oheb Zedek in 1883, "the Rev. D. Feuerlicht is doing excellent work here. Besides his other duties he teaches thirty-four pupils four times every week in Hebrew, religion and history, and they succeed well."[67] No doubt this was more or less a *heder*. Immigrant parents knew little about American public schools, but they wanted their children's education as Jews to be the familiar one which they had themselves received. A boy's achievement of his religious majority at Bar Mitzvah assumed greater importance as it came to symbolize generational continuity to parents who had left their own parents in Europe and were gnawed by uncertainty over their "American children" (*amerikanishe kinder*). No educational program—even secularist—that failed to provide somehow for Bar Mitzvah could draw pupils. The *heder*, however, provided for little else.[68]

On the other hand, the immigrant congregations flattered the Reform Temples by imitation. Not only did B'ne Jeshurun conduct a Sunday school, but on Shavuot it conducted a confirmation, as did even Anshe Emeth.[69] Long after Anshe Emeth was supporting intensive afternoon education, it could report that its Sabbath school (meeting on Sunday) had 407 children enrolled.[70] B'ne Jeshurun's membership of Hungarian stock had now become quite acculturated, and the institution "was anxious to retain its children and to pattern its religious school after the example of the two Reform congregations . . ." whose Sunday schools some of the congregation's children attended. Rabbi Schwartz, of Reform training, worked hard at improving B'ne Jeshurun's Sunday school.[71] A change in schooling occurred, for we hear from Rabbi Jacob Klein, Rabbi Schwartz's successor, that 264 children were in the "daily Hebrew school, where the Jewish religion, the Jewish Torah, and Jewish lore are taught."[72] These more prosperous congregations, which were consciously trying to shed their immigrant character, tended to accept the Sunday school as the Jewish educational model. Behind it stood the wealth and prestige of the Reform Temples. More intensive Hebraic education came to be identified with poorer Jews, immigrant ways, and incapacity to become proper Americans.

In 1885 the *Plain Dealer* noticed a banquet and ball at a hall on Ontario Street, held by friends of the "free school in Hebrew" which had been established two years earlier, "known as the Talmud Torah."[73] One year later the institution, now called the Sir Moses Montefiore Hebrew School, was teaching fifty "children of poor parents in the rudiments of the Hebrew language and religion" in a building on Broadway near Cross Street, which its new patron, A. Goldsoll, helped it to acquire. "The establishing of this school is largely due to Mr. J. Nowinski, who began a year and a half ago, going from house to house and collecting small sums from 5 cents upward."[74] East European Jewish tradition did not aid American Jewish communal schools, since the child's education was considered a parental duty which the community assumed only in case of dire poverty or orphanhood. The emphasis upon children's poverty which American fund-raisers thought necessary helped to degrade such institutions socially. Another institution, called the Baron de Hirsch Free School, was opened in 1896, probably at Kenesseth Israel Synagogue. "The school is open to all Jewish children, whether or not their parents are in any way connected with the synagogue. Sessions will be held daily from 4:30 to 6 P.M."[75]

The newly founded Council of Jewish Women combined its social work with Jewish training given in its Sabbath School. Within two years it enrolled 250 children, two thirds of them girls, and at the close of 1907 the Council Sabbath School had an average attendance of 550. The ladies, who came from the Reform Temples, were careful about religious sensibilities:

> In the oral lessons mentioned, the children are taught Biblical history, from which the best moral lessons are drawn, free from anything which may lead to any superstitious belief, and still the most orthodox of our co-religionists could find no fault with our teachings.[76]

Besides, "these worthy poor" were treated to free clothing once yearly, mainly hand-me-downs from the ladies' families.[77] The school had sixteen classes under "a well qualified staff of trained teachers," and met at the Council Educational Alliance nine months of the year.[78]

One of the *hadarim*, that of Messrs. Garber and Floch, differed strikingly from the others. Rejecting the monotony of rote learning and translation, it taught its pupils by what came to be known as "the natural method." Hebrew was a living language, and a Hebrew-speaking environment was created in the classroom in which the Hebrew subject matter was taught. This was not merely a novel pedagogic technique. Modern Hebrew would become the language and symbol of the modern, humanistically religious culture which would arise in Palestine, and could be fostered in the American Diaspora. The Hebraist pedagogues pursued their goal despite poverty and the indifference of parents who trusted to *heder* education, and the resistance of school boards who shared the parents' attitudes and needed their patronage to maintain the schools.

The "improved heder" (*heder metukan*) of Floch and Garber drew to itself a group of youngsters possessing zeal and esprit. The journal *Olam Katan* [The Little World], which appeared in November, 1906, was "printed entirely in the Hebrew language and all its editors, correspondents, reporters and other writers are boys and girls" at the Garber and Floch school.[79] The ears atop the front page declared, "The rebirth of the people depends on the rebirth of the language; there is no people without a language," and "Hebrew youth, learn the Hebrew language; 'from out of the mouths of sucklings and babes, Thou hast founded might.' " On the front page appeared a photograph of the authors—two girls and seven boys, aged eleven to fourteen. Some of the teachers and school boards laboring with apathetic parents and indifferent children must have wondered whether this verve and creativity could not be brought into their schools.

Meanwhile the Talmud Torah, as the Montefiore Hebrew Free School was generally known, was eking out its existence on East 35th Street. It derived its 1904–1905 income of approximately $3,800 in roughly equal shares from tuition, contributions, seat rentals in its synagogue, and its unique matzah concession. Under the terms of the latter, the institution as early as 1901 had exclusive local distribution rights for the popular Manischewitz matzah. (One year, when Manischewitz denied them the exclusive right, they bought matzah from another firm and a "matzah war" followed over the 200,000 pounds to be sold to Cleveland Jewry).[80] Principals and teachers changed often, and the Board involved itself in the minutia of classroom attendance and instruction. Its teachers in 1902 were paid a paltry $20 monthly for working from 4 to 7 P.M., although a teacher-principal earned almost three times as much.

The Jewish educational scene was a gray one until 1907, when it underwent a revolutionary change of direction:

> [T]he Progressive Party was victorious in the election of officers of the Talmud Torah . . . and the platform of the Committee of Seven was adopted. The platform provides for a playground and kindergarten and the rearrangement of the building suitable for children. Modern methods will be introduced in the instruction of Hebrew.[81]

This was hardly the manner of change normally adopted in traditional Jewish life. Indeed, the terminology—"Progressive Party," "election," "platform," and "Committee of Seven"—was strikingly reminiscent of American, and Cleveland, Progressivism. Rapid change followed promptly. The building was renovated, and soon thereafter Messrs. Garber and Floch consolidated their school with the Talmud Torah and entered its employment.[82] The broadened communal appeal of the Talmud Torah was shown by the appearance at the reopening not only of Orthodox local rabbis, but of the rising leader Alfred Benesch for B'nai B'rith, and of Rabbi Louis Wolsey. It was perhaps Wolsey's first appearance before immigrant Cleveland Jewry, and he avowed, "I came here that you might regard me no more nor less a Jew than any who walks among you."[83]

The school's boys and girls studied five days a week, the first three grades one and half hours at a time, upper grades two and a half hours. The program was the "natural method." A child who passed through the entire program had "a very decent Hebrew education for those days," as Ezra Shapiro, one who did, expressed it.[84] Crowded homes, dingy streets, and poor weather much of the year assisted in bringing children to the Talmud Torah for long sessions after school hours. Classes met all day during the summer. The Talmud Torah won widespread recognition as a model Hebrew institution. Bible and Hebrew were studied simultaneously in "Hebrew and broken English," but never in Yiddish, as Shapiro recalled. Modern Hebrew literature, a true innovation, was also studied. Youthful graduates taught beginners.[85] The Palestinian educator Dr. Benzion Mossinsohn visited and complimented the Talmud Torah in 1916,[86] and Professor Miller was also impressed by what he saw:

> The rooms are crowded to capacity, the instructors are mostly young men who are students in high school or college and have been well instructed in Hebrew before coming to America. . . . many more desire to attend than can be accommodated. These schools are secular and while sympathetic with the orthodox religion, they are really nationalistic in purpose.[87]

Religion and ethnicity were so indissolubly related in the lives and minds of the Talmud Torah's teachers and leaders that these observations would have been rejected out of hand. A question publicly raised by the newly arrived Orthodox Rabbi Samuel Benjamin, who "was informed that this school is not conducted in a religious spirit," provided the opportunity for a comprehensive reply:

> The child who is sent to Hebrew School at the proper age and continues his studies there for a period of 7 or 8 years, when he graduates from the school, has acquired a fairly practical knowledge of the Hebrew language which enables him to read intelligently any Hebrew book. He has completed the entire Tanach [Hebrew Bible], and a large part of Chazal [Rabbinic literature], he has a fine understanding of the new Hebrew literature, and of Jewish history, customs and laws. And if he has attended regularly the children's school [synagogue], he is well acquainted with the Jewish Liturgy.
>
> But most of all, he leaves the school a Jew in every sense of the word. He knows the Jewish past and present, and he hopes and strives for the Jewish future, and he is proud of all that is Jewish.
>
> Any one who has a keen psychological observation can readily recognize the Talmud Torah student, even in his home life, because he is different, more refined and more intelligent than others.
>
> However, only those who complete the entire course can hope to fully enjoy the fruits of their studies and they can rightly be

called "Jewish Children" for they are truly worthy of the name.[88]

Obviously, the institution was handicapped by the enrollment of many who did not complete its ambitious program. Rabbi Benjamin, however, declared himself "perfectly satisfied with what is taught in this institution. . . ."[89]

The Cleveland Hebrew School, as the Talmud Torah was also known, flourished. In these years it did not experience much difficulty in raising its budget, which was $13,648 in 1916–1917. It was able to anticipate the drift of Jewish population by opening branches on East 55th and East 105th Streets. At its peak, about 1918, the school numbered 795 children from 520 homes. Of them, 229 were free; 277 paid one dollar monthly or less; and 289 paid more.[90] It was decided "to obtain teachers whose profession is teaching only," and to pay a large salary, $150 a month.[91] Indirectly acknowledging the Talmud Torah's success, Ohavei Emuna and Beth Tefilah synagogues also opened Hebrew schools of the Hebraist type.[92]

By the second decade of the twentieth century, when the various religious outlooks had thus established their stronger or weaker educational arms, the Zionist Hebraists moved to the forefront. In 1915 a new educational movement appeared in Cleveland, that of Yiddish education in a secularist spirit. The sponsors were the socialist Zionist organizations, and the curriculum made room not only for Hebrew but also for the Yiddish which secularist socialists advocated as the language of the Jewish masses. The Yehoash People's School claimed 200 children a year later.[93]

The mainspring of the Talmud Torah at this time was Rabbi Margolies, whose personal prestige and ability to raise needed funds were a valuable supplement to his skill at conveying the philosophical meaning of Hebraic education. When he died in 1917, the institution launched an appeal for $100,000 to create a Jewish Center of which the Talmud Torah would be the core, and his name was given to the school (the Montefiore had long been discarded).[94] The center was built within a few years, but in conjunction with Anshe Emeth, the rabbi's congregation.

Yet these institutions were far from educating all the Jewish children. In 1908 it was noted that the Talmud Torah and four other synagogue schools counted 1,850 children; 550 more were in the Council Sabbath School. There were an estimated 5,750 Jewish children in the public schools of the area.[95] Seven years later Professor Miller estimated that one-half to two-thirds of the children in one public school, nine-tenths of whose pupils were Jewish, "have this sort of private [i.e., not public school] instruction in Hebrew and Yiddish."[96] Jewish education was a matter of zealous concern to a few, but of slight interest to many more.

A NOTE ON THE CULTURAL SCENE

Among the immigrants an indefinite but significant number possessed Jewish learning in Bible, Talmud, and other spheres. Cleveland Jewry, like American Jewry in general, was uncongenial to the traditional ideal of study, including that of sources regarded as Divine relevation. The educational activity of native and immigrant Cleveland Jewry remained at the elementary level. Only in the last decade of our period was it possible to acquire slightly more than this at the Cleveland Hebrew School. Young men went elsewhere, generally to New York City, for a Talmudic education.

Cleveland's sole productive rabbinic scholar was Rabbi Benjamin Gittelsohn, whose writings are discussed elsewhere. Very little local attention was given to his learned accomplishments. Aside from Rabbi Gittelsohn, no Cleveland rabbi from the time of Rabbi Hahn until Rabbi Silver wrote in even a minor way on any field of Jewish scholarship or thought.

Among other Cleveland Jews, Edward M. Baker, the former Reform rabbinical student, wrote an able apologetic article on "Judaism and the American Spirit," quoted here. Not to be overlooked were Cleveland's two Jewish novelists, the short-lived Martha Wolfenstein, and Ezra Brudno, whose last significant novel was published in 1910 although he lived and practiced law until 1936. A local poetess was Debbie Horwitz Silver, (1854-1932), daughter of Dr. James Horwitz, whose style echoed Robert Browning. She published a volume of verse, *Scenario*, in 1925, written over several years. "The Suppliant at Our Gates" and "Sing, Israel!" exhorted Jews to be good, and blamed centuries of compulsory ghetto life for Jewish features Mrs. Silver found unattractive.

Cleveland was a regular stop for speakers. It was favored for conventions by such groups as the Central Conference of American Rabbis, Zionist organizations, and B'nai B'rith, and the oratorical harvest during these events was stimulating. The Zionist movement regularly sent lecturers and speakers. Rabbis Hildesheimer of Berlin and Wolkin of Warsaw stopped in Cleveland early in 1914 during their American tour on behalf of the recently founded Agudath Israel, an Orthodox organization. Reuben Brainin, the distinguished Hebrew author, appeared in 1909 to promote a federation of Hebraists.[97] The immensely popular Sholem Aleichem spoke and read from his writings one evening in May, 1915.[98]

Visitors also supplied Jewish entertainment. Anshe Chesed raised money for its new temple in 1887 when it imported a German theatrical troupe to perform the comedy *Ein Gluecklicher Familienvater* at Haltnorth's beer garden. "The garden was never more attractive or crowded as [sic] it was with the elite of our Jewish society."[99]

Yiddish theatre provided the favorite entertainment. The Yiddish troupes which set out on tour from New York found eager audiences in Cleveland for serious and light plays. The first Yiddish troupers arrived in 1894–1895, appearing in Germania Hall and the Metropolitan Theater, then the center of the Russian Jewish neighborhood. These visits continued until 1899 when "Czar" Harry Bernstein, with his eye for business and politics in combination, established the Perry Theatre for Yiddish shows. A resident company was installed, and I. Weinstock was the director. A contemporary reported:

> I don't know how much of a success the enterprise was from the financial point of view, but from the artistic, insofar as the Yiddish theatre had then developed, it was a complete success. The performers were talented people, almost all of whom had appeared successfully in New York. The plays they presented were not of the kind one sees today on the Yiddish stage, but what they were in those days. Goldfaden's operettas, Lateiner's "scenes from life," and Gordin's first plays were very nicely performed.[100]

The Perry Theatre was indeed not a commercial success. Jews

were leaving the neighborhood and Bernstein's standing declined, in part because of his political setbacks in Mayor Tom Johnson's day. The Perry ended its career as a Yiddish theatre, but visiting troupes continued to appear. When Jacob Adler, the premier Yiddish actor, brought his company from New York to perform the great playwright Jacob Gordin's *Stranger*, the *Jewish Review and Observer* declared, "The dramatic art of this company is something marvelous."[101] Such events were intermittent. At Bernstein's Perry Theatre, on three consecutive nights, audiences could see *Bar Kochba*, Abraham Goldfaden's dramatic musical out of Jewish history; *Chayim in America*, a comedy on the trials of a "green" immigrant; and *King Solomon*, an opera buffa first performed in New York, probably in the early 1890s.[102] Typical was a week's fare at I. R. Copperman's Coliseum Theatre, where eight performances went on in seven days. It included

> a Russian drama in three acts and four scenes, entitled "The Jew in the Czar Land," by M. Gable. Special costumes and scenery have been prepared for this production.
>
> Sunday evening, March 13th, "A Green Jew in America," by M. Gabel. A Yiddish drama in two acts showing the life of a typical old Jewish father in America.
>
> Saturday and Sunday matinees and Monday night, March 12, 13, 14, "The All-Rightniks," a comedy in two acts by Max Gabel. Comedy and pathos follow each other in rapid order during the run of this play, and lovers of good clean, comedy can expect enjoyment in witnessing this clean comedy.
>
> Tuesday, Wednesday and Thursday evenings, March 15, 16, and 17, a clean comedy in one act, "A Good Wine in a Bad Barrel."
>
> Mr. Simon Paskal, the well known tenor, in new Yiddish songs.
>
> Mr. Philip Singer, the well known Yiddish song writer, in Yiddish monologues and Yiddish comic songs.
>
> The latest moving pictures.[103]

General admission cost ten cents and a box seat, twenty cents.

"Forget about your troubles," urged impresario Relkin in 1918, and see "The Season's Greatest Musical Success," *Die Chazan'te* (*The Reverend and Lady*), which featured the great

star Boris Tomashefsky. The show offered twenty-one musical
numbers written by Joseph Rumshinsky. Prices were up: evening performances cost 35 ¢ to $1.50.[104]

The land of oppression, the problems of settling in America,
the flashy success of the "all-rightnik," traditions undergoing
change, family troubles—what crossed the Yiddish stage was the
experience and the troubles and hopes of its audience. These
could reach the English stage also, as witness *Rachel Goldstein*,
a comedy by Theodore Kremer about "a young Yiddish girl
who, in emigrating to America with her father, meets with many
startling adventures."[105] As early as 1913, the Yiddish theatre
was reported to be suffering from the competition of moving
pictures—more severely, so it was said, than the general theatres.
Americans still went to their local theatre besides seeing the
new film shows, but the Jews, "at least those of Cleveland,
appear to be satisfied with picture shows."[106] The new medium
would soon overwhelm theatrical entertainment. As its nemesis,
however, Yiddish theatre had not films but the declining use of
Yiddish itself. Songs and comic routines were in steady demand, and the newfangled moving pictures were also offered to
eager audiences. The popular arts were a form of education
for their immigrant audiences.

VIII

In Balanced Tension: Jewish Communal Life

THE leaders of Cleveland Jewry during the 1870s were successful immigrant businessmen. Most of them were merchants and a few were manufacturers, usually of clothing. Forty to fifty years later, their sons or grandsons would be solid businessmen who had aided and profited in the huge growth of their city. Living more opulently than they could have dreamed during their youth in Bavaria or Bohemia, the prosperous immigrants reformed their Judaism to conform to their realities and expectations. In its Reform version Judaism taught that they were no longer in exile awaiting merciful Divine redemption, but were permanently at home in free America of which they were fervent, patriotic citizens. Their Judaism was not a distinctive, segregated religious way of life. It was simply a religion like all the religions flourishing in America and constituted the sole division between them and other Americans. Those who professed Judaism could move freely in every sphere of life. By this optimistic, rational faith, Cleveland Jews of the Age of Energy lived and prospered.[1]

Yet there were sentiments and habits which did not fit this spiritual symmetry. Jews mingled mainly with other Jews, and with a gusto which proves that their social life was not merely a gathering of outcasts from the larger society. They sought news about Jews elsewhere in the United States and in other parts of the world. Their group consciousness much exceeded that of people who only worshipped together weekly.

During the half century from 1870 to 1920 the group expanded not only in size but also in activity. During the 1870s Cleveland Jews had little more to do as Jews than worship at the temples once weekly and send their children there for Sunday school. Very few took part in Jewish charity, and that was mainly represented by the Jewish Orphan Home, which received children, as well as donations, from the entire region. At B'nai

B'rith if their means were moderate, or at the Excelsior Club if they were well off, they might meet their friends. When their numbers were merely in the two thousands they could usually learn news of their community from one another, or read it in the local daily press or in the *American Israelite*, which was published in Cincinnati. Cleveland Jewry's interests were firmly focused on Cleveland. Calls from overseas were only occasional —often through the venerated Sir Moses Montefiore. The sole employees of the Jewish community—excluding janitorial workers —were the two rabbis at the temples and the director and staff of the Jewish Orphan Home. Teachers were part-time, and the few little immigrant congregations also had constant turnover of their part-time rabbis and cantors.

The situation toward the close of our period in 1920 was quite different. The Jewish population of Cleveland was then about 75,000; even by 1900, it exceeded the number who could communicate face-to-face. Family connections were still influential, but there were too many Jews and too great a diversity of ideas for a social oligarchy to dominate Jewish life. The ordinary Jew could not only attend synagogue and send his child to a daily Hebrew school, but might occupy himself with acts of charity to his neighbors through many organizations. Not only was he likely to work alongside other Jews or to be a businessman in a line where most of his competitors were Jews, but he might well belong to a Jewish trade union. If he had some Jewish knowledge, there were frequent classes to study Talmud or to discuss modern Hebrew literature. Zionists always held numerous meetings. All Jewish institutions were supported by voluntary effort and their maintenance, let alone improvement, therefore required constant attention. These affairs were certainly a continuing subject for discussion in thousands of households and among friends and neighbors.

Jews also dwelt near one another, and Jewish neighborhoods were clearly defined. For example:

> The center of Jewish population at that time [1888] was Woodland Avenue between Erie [Ninth] Street and Willson [East 55] Avenue and most of the side streets running south of Woodland to Central and Scovill Avenues. Orange Street and Broadway had many Jewish residents and some Jewish families were beginning

to move on Case, Kennard and Willson Avenues. When a few Jewish families moved to Willson Avenue it was thought they were a great distance out.[2]

Jewish institutions sought to shift with Jewish neighborhoods, especially those like synagogues and the Council Educational Alliance which depended on people flowing in.[3] A youthful participant recalled long after:

> Jewish cultural life in general stood at a very high level. Jewish Cleveland seethed and fermented—assemblies and meetings, almost every evening, all sorts of gatherings took place—debates, concerts, balls.[4]

The need for Jewish social communication was served by two substantial weekly newspapers in the English language and a third in Yiddish. Communication was also enhanced when the sheer volume of Jewish public life underwent manifold increase. At least fifteen congregations were as large as the two temples had been in 1870, and there were many more little ones. Moreover, there were schools, Zionist societies, trade unions, social clubs, and philanthropic institutions ranging in size from a little benevolent club to a full-scale general hospital, all affiliated in one way or another with the Jewish community. The employees of these institutions—rabbis, teachers, writers, social workers, and professional directors—helped to multiply social communication. The Jewish community, including all its institutions, probably spent about $20,000 in 1870, excluding the care of the children at the Jewish Orphan Home. Fifty years later, the Jewish communal bill, excluding the high cost of five custodial institutions and funds raised for overseas, was probably over $300,000. The tribulations of Russian Jewry since the 1880s had accustomed Cleveland Jews to contribute funds for their relief. However, contributions to aid stricken overseas Jews, mainly in Eastern Europe, were required on a far greater scale than ever beginning in 1914. A new kind of solicitation, for reborn Jewish Palestine, also began in earnest about this time. In 1920 the former overseas need still appeared temporary, and the latter was quite new; Jewish needs were still primarily local. Jewish population in Cleveland multiplied arithmetically between 1870 and 1920; however, were it possible to measure Jewish social communication and communal activity, multiplication would be exponential. This was the process which molded the Jewish community in Cleveland.

PRESS AND COMMUNITY

The affairs of the Jewish institutions and congregations in the city, not to mention Jewish individuals, drew abundant attention from the local press. Devoting little space to world affairs and not much to those of the nation, the newspapers focused on state and city affairs. As the reader will have noticed, the *Plain Dealer* published not only sermons and accounts of institutional meetings but eyewitness reports of interesting and occasionally controversial events. For example, difficulties between rabbis and congregations, decorously avoided by the Jewish press, were laid out for all to read. The *Plain Dealer* did not shun controversy. On the other hand, it was polite and respectful towards Judaism, and its accounts of Jewish ceremonies and festivals, given in terms of Jewish tradition, were detailed and accurate. News about Jews, including anti-Semitic incidents and courtroom proceedings which Jews probably preferred not to have aired, were ferreted out. But no instance of Jewish stereotyping, or of labelling malefactors as Jews, appears throughout thousands of Jewish references.

As the city's population vastly increased and national as well as international news likewise grew in volume and interest, attention to Cleveland Jewish life in the daily press was bound to decrease. Moreover, extensive and benign as was the attention to Jewish life in the *Plain Dealer*, it could not create the communal sense which a specifically Jewish journal could. In 1889 Cleveland's first Jewish newspaper, the *Hebrew Observer*, made its appearance. Its editors were Hiram Strauss and Samuel Oppenheimer, who as "Uncle Sam" had been the *American Israelite's* Cleveland correspondent. Four years later Oppenheimer joined Jack Machol (Rabbi Machol's son) to establish a second weekly, the *Jewish Review*.[5] In 1896 Dan S. Wertheimer, who published playbills and did other printing, entered the field by buying out the *Jewish Review*. Three years afterward

Wertheimer also bought out the *Hebrew Observer* and combined his two newspapers into one weekly, the *Jewish Review and Observer*, which was to have a long career as a Cleveland Jewish newspaper. Like its predecessors, this newspaper was aligned distinctly with Cleveland Jewry's older stock. It covered local news thoroughly, although more discreetly than the *Plain Dealer*, documenting the affairs of established institutions such as the Reform Temples, Jewish clubs, and philanthropic institutions connected with the Federation of Jewish Charities. Conscious of its role as the Jewish communal newspaper of record, it often provided official reports, budgets, and quite full (and historically valuable) obituaries. The immigrant sphere was remote from the *Jewish Review and Observer*, but a genuine effort was made to reach into it. It was extensive and objective in reporting about Zionism, of which it disapproved. Jewish trade unions were a conception harder to understand, and were frequently locked in combat with some of the leading Jews in the city. They were seldom mentioned. The many immigrant societies, as they acquired size and permanence and shifted to English, could also expect to be noticed in the *J.R.&O.*

A second Jewish newspaper, the *Jewish Independent*, began to appear in 1907. Its editor was the experienced journalist Maurice Weidenthal, and after his death in 1917, Leo Weidenthal, his brother, took over until his retirement and the paper's termination in 1964. The *Jewish Independent* also had a dignified appearance, but its style was more peppery and the impress of its editor was more visible. The independence expressed in its title implied freedom from the trammels of a social circle or a specific outlook, and suggested some of the vigor of Progressive Age journalism. The newspaper's public seems to have been centered in the newer Jewish community of Cleveland, children of East European immigrants. Yet there was really not much difference between the two publications. Both presented Jewish life in a favorable light and welcomed all Jewish activities they regarded as positive.

These weeklies generally stayed aloof from controversial public issues, contenting themselves with fervent expressions of American patriotism. The *Jewish Review and Observer* departed from its established policy when it declared in 1912:

> Socialism and discontent with social conditions will exist as the powerful kings of finance persist in retaining the lion's share of the wealth while those who have helped in securing the colossal fortunes are at the bottom of the financial ladder with little prospect of getting any higher. . . .
>
> It is not the accumulation of wealth that creates the socialist, but the lack on the part of the wealthy of their responsibility to society.[6]

Echoing Jewish communal leaders in Cleveland, the newspaper's answer to socialism was the social obligation of wealth—a conception not without nobility which was also flattering to those with wealth. And there were no "powerful kings of finance" among Cleveland Jews to take umbrage.

An early Yiddish newspaper was the *Jewish Reporter*, which I. Wold, a Woodland Avenue printer and bookseller, printed with M. Balogh in 1893. Nothing further is known of this effort, since no copy is known to survive.[7] It was Samuel Rocker, scholarly publisher of rabbinical education and Zionist convictions, who became the central figure in Cleveland Yiddish journalism. He was warmly recalled as "a great sage . . . a Yiddish Walter Lippmann."[8] The *Jewish Banner*, his first effort, was part English and part Yiddish. It was succeeded by the *Yiddishe Fahne*, all Yiddish, printed in New York with a large section on Cleveland.[9] In 1908, "backed by Cleveland business men," Rocker published the *Jewish Daily News*, probably in English and Yiddish. His most long-lived organ was the *Yiddishe Velt*, which commenced weekly publication in 1913 and deeply influenced Cleveland's immigrant Jewry.[10] Most of its space was devoted to general and Jewish news, and to the serialized novels which were a staple of the Yiddish press. Yet Rocker also wrote long, thoughtful articles on contemporary problems, drawing liberally on Jewish literature and folklore for illustration and proof. The *Yiddishe Velt* followed its declared principle that all Jews formed one great family who had to be united by a sense of pride and the demand that justice be done them.[11] The editor considered it "our highest duty in this country . . . not to drag Jewish questions into political life," where "we are first and last American citizens." This led him to conclude that "it is our highest duty as Jewish citizens so far as possible to place the best and ablest Jewish candidates in public office," exactly as other ethnic groups were doing.[12] Mass immigration had led in the development of the United States after 1880, and immigrants should promptly become citizens.[13] Having thus reconciled American citizenship with the desire for group recognition in political life, Rocker endorsed candidates before Election Day, a practice anathema to Anglo-Jewish newspapers. When Rocker discussed socialism, his perspective differed from that of the *Jewish Review and Observer*; the question for him was whether religious orthodoxy and socialism could be in harmony. Observing that Judaism and socialism both inculcated sympathy for human suffering, Rocker concluded, "every human being who is human must be stirred by everything humane." This included socialism, whose doctrinaire aspects, he implied, were not essential.[14] And if moderate socialism was acceptable, Jewish trade unionism could of course be endorsed;[15] equal rights for women also gained Rocker's approval.[16]

Sixteen years after its first appearance the *Jewish Review and Observer* offered its interpretation of the tasks of Jewish journalism. It regarded some of its value as being the "only medium of information concerning Jewish matters" for scattered Jews and those "not affiliated with congregations." It served all Jews by bringing them news from distant parts. Even Christians acquired Jewish news and information from Jewish newspapers. Moreover, claimed the *J. R. & O.*, "many difficult problems confronting our people have been solved," and "Jews have been saved from many cruelties" and "better treatment for the Jews in many countries" secured—all thanks to the publicity provided by the Jewish press.

> Through these papers publicity is given to important Jewish movements, and it is due to this fact that success crown [*sic*] these efforts, for nothing affecting communal welfare can be successful unless it has the cooperation of the public.[17]

These were general press functions applied to Jewish life. But the *Observer* also recognized the special function which a

Jewish newspaper served in multiplying the ties among Jews
which were the essence of a Jewish community:

> The social news contained in the Jewish papers also have [*sic*]
> its value. It is the means of keeping our co-religionists throughout
> the country in touch with one another, thus insuring a closer bond
> of union among them, though they may be separated by a dis-
> tance of many miles.[18]

The number and vigor of Jewish young people's clubs drew
editorial praise for similar reasons.[19] A Jewish Men's Association included "men from all grades of society, from the lowest
to the highest . . . connected with all the temples. . . ." It
proposed to establish "a meeting place that will centralize
Jewish activities. . . ."[20]

Reporting and commenting on the activities of Jewish groups
and individuals, Cleveland's Jewish press, like that throughout
the land, filled an important role by helping to define and
solidify the community to which it spoke.

CHARITY AND COMMUNITY

It was charitable activity which became the binding force in
making disparate sections into one conscious community. Charitable aid to other Jews was a function of the Jewish community, both from immemorial Jewish tradition and by virtue
of the American religious outlook. Before the 1890s, however,
charitable endeavor did not preoccupy the Jews of Cleveland.
The early Hebrew Benevolent Society of the 1850s and 1860s
seems to have expired some time after 1866, and its helpmate,
the Jewish Ladies' Benevolent Society, continued as a small,
prosperous mutual aid society which also granted charity.[21]

There were other similar societies. The Hungarian Benevolent Social Union had become mostly social. The Austro-
Hungarian Ladies Benevolent Society (Oesterreich-Ungarische
Frauen Unterstuetzungs-Verein) was organized in 1888, and by
1897 it had 250 to 300 members to whom it provided sick
benefits: forty-five or fifty dollars was disbursed monthly in
charity. Meetings at the Pythian Temple were probably social

occasions.[22] Another group, the First Galician Charitable Aid Society (Erste Galizianer Unterstuetzungs Verein), held its first annual ball in 1905, with the proceeds "used towards helping the poor."[23]

The continuous history of Jewish philanthropic activity in Cleveland opens with the founding of the Hebrew Relief Society in 1875. Its principal founder and leader for many years was James Horwitz, the Cracow-born physician turned clothing manufacturer; also among its founders were Jacob Mandelbaum, and Simon Sampliner. Until the establishment of the Federation of Jewish Charities in 1903, however, the Hebrew Relief Society "never collected more than about $6,000. . . ."[24] Typical of the H.R.S's rudimentary methods during its early years were the proceedings of December 20, 1880:

> The chairman stated that there was a destitute family in the city to whom relief should be afforded. The relief committee was thereupon instructed to look after the case.[25]

Relief was also dispensed to applicants, who told their stories at Sunday morning committee meetings.

During the 1890s there was talk of coordinating charitable efforts, at least to prevent duplication of assistance and to discourage wandering beggars. In 1882 a special Russian Relief Committee was organized alongside the Hebrew Relief Society, reflecting the contemporary belief that the immigration of 1882 from Russia was a unique episode. It continued its separate operations until 1894, when the two bodies merged.[26]

Meanwhile the H.R.S. continued in its accustomed way:

> During the past year [of 1904] 176 families were assisted, consisting of 288 adults, 474 children and 78 transients, and a total of 1,016, to whom 1,236 times assistance was given. Among these were 22 old couples, 16 widows with 35 children at home, 23 deserted women with 62 children, and 3 women with 14 children, whose husbands were temporarily absent; 26 families were constantly dependent, consisting of 48 adults and 77 children, received regular weekly or monthly allowances, as they were without any visible means of support or with such meagre and insufficient earnings.[27]

Of $10,329 spent by the Hebrew Relief Society in 1904, $3,091 was in cash for general relief; $2,091 was in rent payments; $1,281 went for fuel; clothing and furniture were supplied to the extent of $1,276; and only $336 was spent to transport clients, the larger part local consumptives sent to a Denver hospital.[28] More than any institution, the H.R.S. felt the local economic pulse. It foresaw the extreme distress which occurred during the depression winter of 1893–1894.[29] The year 1908 was reported "the hardest in the history of our organization" on account of "the ebb and flow of the recent financial depression" of 1907.[30] During the much improved year of 1909, the Society's budget, now risen to $16,000, was divided proportionately as follows: 35 percent, cases of sickness; 23 percent, effects of tuberculosis; 7 percent, desertion; 6 percent, old age and debility; 15 percent, insufficient earnings and temporary unemployment; 6 percent, insanity, intemperance, imprisonment, transients, and other causes. The remaining 8 percent presumably went to administration.[31]

Necessary as was this work of the Hebrew Relief Society in an era when public assistance to the destitute hardly existed, there was little about its scale or methods to inspire the Jews of Cleveland. "There is something wrong with some of our Jewish people from a standpoint of liberality in affairs of charity . . . ," the Jewish newspaper complained. It admitted that this was common "in all our thickly populated centers." Of approximately 25,000 Cleveland Jews, claimed the *Hebrew Observer*, "not over 350 people" supported local Jewish charities. Rather inconsistently it concluded, "The Jewish people of this city are well known for taking care of their poor, and are, we think, as liberal as [in] other cities of its class."[32] The Society was at pains to discourage itinerant Jewish beggars who sought a few days' free lodging and fare to the next city, where they repeated the operation. Local Jews were urged not to give money to "*professional schnorrers*" or indeed anyone else, but to refer them to the H.R.S., where they would be investigated properly.[33] To repel undeserving "lazy vagabonds," the Society established a labor test, asking able-bodied applicants to cut and saw wood for pay. It claimed that "worthy applicants, truly anxious for work, were always willing to saw and split some wood for a reasonable pay."[34] Little is heard after 1900 concerning the labor test or the vagabonds it was to repel. A nation-wide "Transportation Agreement" among local Jewish charities had effectively ended this evil.

Sigmund Shlesinger (1848–1929), who as a young Hungarian immigrant had been an Army Indian scout and fought in Indian wars, succeeded Horwitz as the pillar of the H.R.S.[35] Now a successful tobacconist, Shlesinger, like his predecessors, found little public interest in H.R.S. efforts.[36]

In 1904 the Society brought A. S. Newman from Chicago to begin a lengthy tenure as its first professional superintendent. Under Newman's direction the beginnings of case work were apparent:

> The applicants for relief had been obliged to appear at the weekly
> or bi-weekly meetings of the board of directors and to personally make their needs known to that body. Much of the aid
> was distributed then and there during the meetings. . . . The
> system was neither expedient nor fair. . . . [Now, in 1906] all
> applicants appear before the superintendent only.[37]

The Superintendent possessed discretionary powers, subject to the board's control. However, "applicants were not and are not prohibited from coming to the meetings of the board of directors, and in rare cases still do come. . . ."[38]

The H.R.S.'s new stress lay upon "investigation of the mental, moral and physical needs of each member of the family under consideration,"[39] and by no means commanded universal assent. Bitter altercations occurred; more than one applicant could not "understand that we form a comprehensive plan of action" for each case and saw no reason for "cooperating with us for his own good" before receiving any aid.[40] "Sometimes refusal . . . would exasperate the bolder ones to violence."[41] When President Shlesinger took pride that "every applicant's case is now studied from every angle," he was actually touching a raw nerve.[42] Not every "friendly visitor" (a volunteer who visited clients' households to aid and guide them) won an unfeignedly warm welcome.[43] One prospective donor to the Federation—and others may have done likewise—cited his own practice of giving cash to needy Jews he knew of, explaining that beneficiaries "claim there is too much red tape" at Federation charities. Citing the instance of a crippled, elderly Jew who earned less than one dollar daily selling newspapers downtown, he told the Federation solicitor, "If you can get your organization to help this man and help his family and do what is right by them, I will be too glad to give you $10 and join you."[44] In reaction to the investigative deliberateness of "official" Jewish charities, there was an Instant Aid Society to provide unquestioning emergency aid in small amounts.[45]

It was impulses more constructive than dissatisfaction with the Hebrew Relief Society that brought other institutions into existence, however. New needs sprang up and had to be met, and old needs had to be finally satisfied. Thus, when immigrants established the Jewish Relief Society in 1897, they sought to emphasize that they did "not necessarily conflict" with the H.R.S. They would "reach certain elements and make investigations where perhaps the Relief Society cannot."[46]

The Infant Orphan Mothers' Society, organized in 1898, scraped up $800 to open its asylum in 1901 for infants up to five years of age. Children above that age might enter the Jewish Orphan Home.[47] In 1907 it occupied a converted residence on East 40th Street and served also as a temporary shelter for the children of institutionalized parents. Besides receiving support from the Federation of Jewish Charities, the Home had behind it the Jewish Infant Orphan Home Society, 750 strong.[48] Several years later the Home was reorganized to remedy its internal shortcomings.[49]

Originating in 1905 in a somewhat similar manner, the Hebrew Free Loan Society (at first named Gemilath Chesed) lent small sums to temporarily embarrassed borrowers or to those seeking to start in business. This was "distinctly a Russian Jewish form of philanthropy," its promoters asserted. Actually, free loans had a long pedigree in Jewish communal life. In 1909 the Hebrew Free Loan Society granted 700 loans, amounting to $20,451; virtually every borrower paid back. Most loans were twenty-five and fifty dollars.[50]

The Legal Aid Society, a non-sectarian endeavor, was founded in 1905 by B'nai B'rith initiative.[51] What it sought to do for needy clients, the Immigrant Aid Societies sought to do for Jewish immigrants. There was an Immigrants' Aid Society of about 200 persons during the 1906 Russian pogroms which lent money in order to help in "rescuing families of some of the Cleveland Jews from the clutches of Russian murderers."[52] Manuel Levine and Ben Feniger, prominent young attorneys, led the Cleveland Immigration League, founded in 1914 to assist any immigrant of whatever origin "against flagrant abuses to which he has been subjected," mainly in the labor market. It also encouraged enrollment in citizenship classes.[53] Levine and Feniger were also leaders of the Cleveland Independent Aid Society, founded in Joe Folkman's kitchen in 1895 "to help afflicted members, to assist the worthy poor, and to aid charitable organizations and beneficent institutions."[54] Vigorously led, and numbering 500 members in 1915, the Independent Aid Society possessed broad civic interests. Thus, they mustered an impressive delegation to oppose a bill for compulsory Bible reading in the public schools.[55]

When the Hebrew Relief Society moved from simple material relief towards comprehensive social service, there were societies within the immigrant milieu to replace it. In addition, charitable groups among East European immigrants also identified new areas of service. In extreme contrast to the native groups, the difference between giver and recipient was not sharp. Mutual aid frequently helped outsiders as well. This characteristic made it easier for self-respecting persons to request and receive aid than to do so at the bureaucratized, official Hebrew Relief Society. Yet however philanthropy was administered, all participants recognized that there were ties of dependence and obligation.

If little about the Hebrew Relief Society could draw lay leaders into its service, far different was the case with the Council Educational Alliance. This institution was less stamped with poverty and suffering than was the H.R.S. In 1895 a Friendly Club was organized by young Jewish women who in the spirit of their time desired to establish a benevolent relationship between themselves and poor immigrant Jews. At the same time a branch of the National Council of Jewish Women was established in Cleveland which amalgamated the Ladies Benevolent Society, the Ladies Sewing Society, and the Personal Service Society. These middle-class Jewish women devoted themselves primarily to volunteer social work, and the

Cleveland branch became the largest of the N.C.J.W.[56] Their interests and the needs of Jewish immigrants led to the founding of the Council Educational Alliance in 1897, into which the Friendly Club, the Young Men's Jewish Association, and other small groups were absorbed. Its charter of incorporation declared its purpose "to engage in educational and philanthropic work". The name probably came from the Educational Alliance, which had recently been opened on New York's Lower East Side.

The incorporators constituted a group of local notables.[57] The Alliance commenced with a grandiose fair, which opened with messages from former President Harrison and Governor Asa S. Bushnell and closed with an impressive profit of $11,000. This start, and the donation of his house on lower Woodland Avenue by Moritz Joseph provided the wherewithal for the Council Educational Alliance.

The C.E.A. was preceded in the Jewish immigrant neighborhood by Hiram House, founded by George Bellamy in 1896 and supported by Samuel Mather and other wealthy men of old Cleveland stock. Hiram House was a social settlement, unlike the C.E.A., but it provided many of the services which were to come from the Jewish institution. Jews attended Hiram House, and it took particular pride in its star alumnus, the future judge Manuel Levine, whom it helped learn English when he was a new immigrant youth in 1897.[58] As an institution maintained by outsiders, Hiram House infused its social work with evangelical qualities but made no attempt at proselytizing. Many Jews went there, but it could not, obviously, become intimately part of the Jewish community as did the C.E.A.[59]

C.E.A. activities expanded. A city library branch was placed in the building, free legal aid was made available, and jobs were sought for applicants. A gymnasium and playground were set up, and the city's first public baths were opened.[60] Classes for English, gardening, cooking, embroidery, debating, sewing, dressmaking, and child care, as well as numerous youthful social clubs all carried on within the small building, which kept open from 8 A.M. to 10 P.M. In 1907 one of the C.E.A.'s most valuable and popular features was inaugurated with Samuel D. Wise's donation of a resort hotel—Stein on the Lake—and money to establish what was called Camp Wise. Hundreds of children attended for several weeks each summer, and for most of them it was their sole contact with nature.

In addition to all these activities at the C.E.A., there were entertainments and forum lectures whose speakers included Mayor Johnson and other notables of the day. The topics announced included the Trust Problem, Trade Unions and Socialism, Compulsory Arbitration, Municipal and National Ownership of Public Utilities, The New Municipal Code, The Smoke Evil, and The Dance Hall—a spectrum of questions agitating thoughtful Clevelanders and Americans. Physical security was assured on the occasion of one neighborhood dance by requesting the prominent private detective Jake Mintz "to inspect [the] crowds and see if [he] recognizes objectionable characters."[61] Issues of the day could also create sensitive situations within the C.E.A. Thus, the reaction to the distribution of a union broadside at the Alliance brought forth a Board resolution:

> Whereas this Alliance received its support from employees and employers and whereas it is desired that a continuance of this support be maintained; therefore be it Resolved that we deem it inexpedient that meetings favoring Unionism or Anti Unionism be held within the grounds or buildings of the Alliance; but nothing herein shall be construed as restricting the discussing of Economic or Social Problems.[62]

A Sunday school was carried on at the Council Educational Alliance. However, the Jewishness of the C.E.A., like that of its contemporaries in other American cities, was taken for granted rather than cultivated. Questions arose periodically concerning the use of the building on the Sabbath. For example, it was requested of "the Secretaries of Clubs and Teachers to refrain from writing on the Sabbath and doing such other things as are objectionable to the people of the neighborhood."[63] The matter of the Sabbath was dealt with in terms of appeasing local religious sentiment, rather than with a view toward devising a Sabbath program. At the outset the Council of Jewish Women expressed the aims of their project:

> In bygone times alms-giving served the purpose of rendering temporary relief, thus perpetrating [sic] poverty. A new awaken-

ing has come. . . . The moral and mental faculties must be
fostered as well as the body. . . . Men are born to see, hear, talk
and think. Lectures, music, by known artists and thinkers . . .
must be utilized to teach the lesson of universal love. Let us seek
to show self-respecting manhood and womanhood the true foundation to all higher life.[64]

To these blurry sentiments was added an attack on "conditions
which proceed from wrong legislation at the fountainhead."[65]

From 1900 to 1906 Isaac Spectorsky, who had received a
Russian education, served as director. To some extent he spoke
for immigrant Jews to the press. After his resignation (he later
became director of New York's Educational Alliance) directors
came and went until Walter Leo Solomon (1873–1934) took the
position in 1914. While his predecessors were deeply committed
to far-reaching social reform, Solomon, who had been active
in the Ethical Culture Society, was especially devoted to the
personal culture and social refinement of those whom he influenced. He emphasized "the bareness of life, the lack of a share
in the cultural heritage of the race, the meagerness of inspiration which constitutes poverty. . . ." Settlement workers "must
bring to those less fortunate some vitalizing portion of their
universal heritage."[66] It was a matter of regret to him that the
C.E.A.'s activities sought large numbers and tended to give
members what they wanted without significantly improving
their tastes or culture. He reiterated these beliefs throughout
his service from 1914 to 1920, and later from 1929 until his death
in 1934. At Rabbi Gries' urging, Miss Ida Schott (1874–1967)
left the school system in 1913 to begin a life-long association
with the C.E.A. and its auxiliaries and successors.

Rabbi Moses J. Gries, prominent in C.E.A. affairs throughout
his life, expressed the reality of the Alliance's efforts:

The Alliance is the natural center for the people of the neighborhood. It interests itself in all the interests of the neighborhood. It exercises also a public influence—all the public movements for the benefit of the city . . . in the establishment of
the public Bath House and Gymnasium on Orange Street, in the
investigation of the housing conditions of the poor, in the development of the public parks and playgrounds and skating
rinks and the like.[67]

Gries observed that some established Jews were still unsympathetic to the Alliance, considering aid to the newcomers in exclusive terms of material aid:

> The emphasis of our work is educational. The work of the Alliance is not fully understood and appreciated by our community. I do not doubt there are still some who believe our work, with all our classes and clubs, to be a fad and unnecessary. We do not relieve poverty or alleviate physical want, but no want is more distressing than the deprivation of opportunity.[68]

Was it symbolic that the Council Educational Alliance took over the building which the Excelsior Club quit in 1908? True to Walter Solomon's view, the C.E.A. was "a cultural and inspirational center for the people of *its* [author's italics] neighborhood and a civic force in all vital problems."[69] The institution was not, however, a common ground for all elements of the Jewish population. Nor was it a settlement house where educated, devoted members of the native Jewish community might live among the newcomers and share their lives with them.[70] It was rather a contribution to the welfare of immigrant Jews from their benevolent native patrons.

Public expression was given at last to the inevitable tension between the C.E.A.'s benefactors and the recipients. At the 1911 annual meeting, "Rabbi N. H. Ebin delivered an address in Yiddish, demanding that the Orthodox element of the comity be more numerously represented upon the Board." Then followed addresses by Rabbi Gries as President and by Charles Eisenman, President of the Federation of Jewish Charities. Samuel Rocker, the Yiddish editor, took the floor, "protesting against the characterization of the Alliance as a charitable institution," presumably in the foregoing speeches.[71]

When the Federation of Jewish Charities claimed in 1912 that "the number [of Jews] . . . who need help of some form has increased to 20,000" since 1903, the Yiddish newspaper exploded with anger at the inclusion of self-supporting C.E.A. participants among them. Angrily writing to Federation President Charles Eisenman, Samuel Rocker declared that

> we shall be under great obligation to you if you will inform us

how you reached your figure. Do you include in the 20,000 the children of the Council Educational Alliance Sabbath School? Do you include the Peddlers Association, the Citizenship Class and the other classes . . . ? Do you include in your 20,000 the borrowers from the Hebrew Free Loan Association? Do you include in the 20,000 the worshippers in the Peoples Synagogue . . ? Do you include also the people who draw books from the Branch [public] Library in the Council Educational Alliance Building?[72]

This attack on the ill-chosen words of the native philanthropists, following the previous year's stormy annual meeting, suggested that it was desirable to seat representative immigrants on the C.E.A. Board. Rocker himself, together with Rabbis Ebin and Margolies and the young lawyer and Hebraist Aaron Garber, were chosen. "With some of the former fault-finding sidetracked," snapped the *Jewish Independent*, "nothing now stands in the way of increasing in every way the usefulness of the Alliance."[73]

The philanthropists, somewhat chastened, were on notice that their relation with immigrants could not be one of alms-giving. Ultimately, however, these conflicts could only be solved by the social and cultural developments that would come with time. The social and economic gulf between Woodland Avenue and the East End was still too wide to be bridged by the most tactful of words or the most valuable of institutions.

CHARITY, FEDERATION, AND COMMUNITY

Philanthropic effort was one sphere in which native Jewry could all share, whether as officers and committee members, as donors, or as volunteers. Immigrants and their children did not always embrace this proffered assistance. They were bound to learn, however, that the money and experience of the native Jews, and their extensive connections with the city's life, enabled them to conduct institutions of far greater scope and variety than any of the immigrants could maintain.

Jewish charity grew most rapidly during the 1890s. New bodies were emerging: the Hebrew Free Loan Society, the Infant Mothers Society for children too young to be accepted in the Jewish Orphan Home, and others. The Kesher Montefiore Home for the aged was established in 1884 by the Kesher shel Barzel (Bond of Iron) fraternal order in honor of the Anglo-Jewish philanthropist's centennial birthday. Immigrant congregations carried on various charitable activities. Finally, in 1897, Rabbi Gries advocated a general federation of Cleveland charities.[74]

The stirrings of a Jewish communal approach to Jewish social problems were perceptible throughout the land. To be sure, the religious affairs of American Jews were and remained congregational with loose denominational federations; educational activities around 1900 were nearly negligible, and the defense of nationwide Jewish interests was directed by the New York patrician leadership. Yet local social problems required not only money in large amounts, but money judiciously spent. Large centers like Boston and Cincinnati federated their Jewish charities in 1895 and 1896, and other cities followed suit. Several cities' charities combined in a National Conference of Jewish Charities which worked out a useful Transportation Agreement, already mentioned, to control the expensive nuisance of wandering Jewish beggars. This rising superstructure was based upon an important reality—Jewish immigration was huge, with no end in sight, and almost all immigrants were poor and could use some sort of assistance. Philanthropy, better organized and planned, was in the air among American Jews; humane, efficient, de-politicized government was being practiced in Cleveland.

The Progressive Era of the early twentieth century, it has been noted, was also an age of extensive businessmen's organizations and combined efforts for legislative as well as economic ends.[75] The leaders of coordinated Jewish charities were often prominent in organized business as well.

Cleveland Jews were thus ripe for organizing their charities before the first steps were actually taken. On May 30, 1903, nine prominent men met as a committee to begin the process of legal incorporation. They represented the older stock's outlook and vocations as well as any nine men could. Young Edward M. Baker was a fast-rising stockbroker, scion of notable Reform rabbis. Charles Eisenman was a shirt manufacturer, and Julius Feiss was also in that business; Emil Joseph, attorney, came from a garment manufacturing family. There was the tobacconist Sigmund Shlesinger, pillar of the Hebrew Relief Society, and Jacob Furth, important in B'nai B'rith; Martin A. Marks was President of The Temple and an insurance leader. Also present were Meyer Weil and Sol M. Hexter. Baker, Shlesinger, Marks, and Eisenman had come to Cleveland as young men from other parts of the country.

The group had already been active, for a Committee on Subscriptions had secured 77 pledges of $17,000.[76] Early in 1904, the amount was $38,168 from 835 persons. This was still 55 less than the number of individuals who had been contributing to the charities when there were separate campaigns.[77] Clearly, the ground had been prepared by private meetings and discussions among the nine men and others. Their first recorded meeting, in fact, had been held on November 20, 1902.

The constitution, adopted on November 20, 1903, defined the Federation's purpose as "the collection and apportionment of contributions, donations and legacies among Jewish charities and Jewish philanthropic organizations, and to promote education, science and art." Article IV, Section 4, contained the teeth:

> No aid shall be extended to any organization which shall, after January 1st, 1904, without the consent in writing of the Board of Trustees, give any ball, bazaar, fair or other entertainment for which tickets are offered for sale, or solicit advertisements or contributions, other than permanent endowments or membership fees, which latter, shall not exceed $3.00 per annum.

This clause was soon supplemented by a lordly statement of policy:

> The Board of Trustees of the Federation will look with disfavor upon any new Jewish charitable or philanthropic organization which may come into existence without the consent of the Board.[78]

As we shall see, quite a few institutions, not deterred by fear of the Board's disfavor, came into existence unsanctioned.

The idea underlying the Federation was to spare contributors to Jewish charities the nuisance and waste of rival solicitations by persuading or even coercing these charities to participate in a single campaign. Had this been its full purpose, the Federation would have remained merely an instrument for the convenience of contributors. Its founders had far-reaching intentions, however, which were partly presaged by a decision in November, 1903,

> that each beneficiary institution be requested to forward to this Board a memorandum of their cash contributions for the last two years, their expenditures and also an estimate of the amount needed for their work for the coming year.[79]

Thus began the Federation's regulation of its beneficiaries. This slow imposition of controls hardly went unrecognized and unchallenged by institutions proud of their independence. Elderly Abraham Wiener, after a lifetime of charitable endeavor for numerous institutions, took no part in the Federation. He did appear once to protest the alleged inadequacy of the appropriation to his beloved Orphan Home.[80] It seems probable that Barnet Mahler, that veteran individualist, resigned as C.E.A. president because his board decided to come under the Federation and to alter its by-laws accordingly.[81] There was no suggestion of his dissension in C.E.A. affairs. He returned to the Federation at a later date.

The most basic decisions lay in the allocation of funds raised. The $35,400 distributed in 1904 slowly rose to $46,450 in 1911 and then jumped to $106,315 for 1916. The period of U.S. participation in World War I saw the greatest increase, and by 1920 allocations reached $276,475. As to salaries, rent, and general expenses, the Board did not hold with expensive administrative habits; in 1916, they cost merely $4,987.

To receive an allocation from the Federation of Jewish Charities, a charity had to campaign actively among its supporters for contributions to the Federation rather than to itself. The Federation's leaders firmly prevented their constituents from conducting separate fund-raising activities in whatever guise. As one such enjoinder was phrased, "any other action would be inconsistent with the fundamental proposition on which the

Federation was based."[82] The Federation, for its part, was reluctant to accept as constituents poorer organizations—for example, the Hebrew Free Loan Society[83] and the Hebrew Shelter Home[84]—whose requirements were likely to be much higher than the funds their supporters could provide. When the Talmud Torah (Hebrew Free School) applied for aid, "there was some discussion as to the necessity of such a school." Charles Eisenman opposed the application, wearily declaring that the Federation "had on various occasions taken in institutions as beneficiaries with the promise of much additional money to the Federation, but unfortunately the returns in each case were very small in comparison with the expense incurred."[85] Requests for emergency appropriations, however justified, usually had to be denied. However, $500 was granted in 1915 to assist the newcomers' Jewish Relief Society to distribute free matzot for Passover. This was done "because the long periods of unemployment had reduced many families to a state of dependence."[86]

Early in 1904, the Federation of Jewish Charities allocated its first year's receipts:[87]

Jewish Orphan Asylum	$ 6,000	
Montefiore Home (for the aged)	3,200	
Denver Hospital (for consumptives)	1,000	
Council Educational Alliance	7,000	
Infant Orphans' Mothers Society	2,500	
Council of Jewish Women	2,500	
Mount Sinai Hospital	3,800	
Hebrew Relief Association	2,400	(part of 1903)
	7,000	(1904)
Total	$35,400	

The appropriation to the Jewish Orphan Asylum represented a contribution towards the care of local children in that regional institution. With extensive support reaching the Home from other sources, its allocation rose comparatively little, attaining only $15,000 of $276,000 allocated in 1920.[88] On the other hand, the Hebrew Relief Association, applying a slowly rising standard of aid to the much greater number of cases generated by a far larger Jewish population, had its appropriation increased to $50,000.

Charles Eisenman stood at the head of the Federation until his death in 1923, aged fifty-eight. Of substantial wealth though by no means the richest of Federation leaders, he and his wife (they had no children) lived in a downtown hotel from which he devoted himself intensively to business and philanthropy. His addresses to Federation audiences, quoted elsewhere, show his clear awareness of the ills of an industrial city and his reliance on the conscience of the enlightened rich to ease them. Eisenman appeared to recognize the limitations of philanthropy, once urging those who gave money also to devote "serious thought and attention to social action by which the causes that make philanthropy necessary, may be eradicated."[89] He conceived social action as a bourgeois obligation; trade unionism, the industrial worker's social action, was fought vehemently by Eisenman and his fellow employers who dominated the Board of Trustees. Unidentified with any individual institution, Eisenman brought to his presidency of the Federation a broad view of Jewish welfare needs. Like most Federation leaders of his generation, he had little to say of any specifically Jewish mission of the Federation. It is possible to discern, however, his determination that immigrant Jewish charities which matured be brought into the Federation network. This design began to be realized during the 1920s. The Federation's secretary, Edward M. Baker, somewhat younger than the rest of the founders, alone possessed the ability to couch philanthropy in terms of Judaism.

The leaders of the Federation of Jewish Charities, active businessmen who closely directed the daily affairs of their firms, did likewise with the Federation they built. Samuel Goldhammer began his service in 1907 as clerk and served until 1949 as executive, but virtually all significant matters were decided by the officers and Board. Whatever the limitations in their conception of Jews and of philanthropy, they were prudent and able in handling money, and impeccably honest. Building institutions was their forte.

Early in the Federation's history $2,500 was received from

the estate of Mrs. H. Black as an endowment to aid deserving students in their higher education.[90] This was the first of the Federation's restricted endowments for which it served as trustee. By 1912, when endowments were becoming relatively numerous, donors began to be urged that their bequests not be in perpetuity but that the principal be at least partly expendable. The Federation also attempted to persuade "a considerable number who gave in the hope that their memory might endure" not to bind their money to a specific institution or purpose which might wither, but to bequeath to the Federation itself with some discretion in allocating the money.[91] The early Board also debated whether a reserve fund ought to be amassed. The obvious point in favor was "that the safe, conservative thing to do was to build up a surplus fund against any emergency that might arise." Yet others maintained that money was given "for . . . immediate use," and a reserve fund "would tend to made the Board more or less indifferent and also have a bad effect upon the subscribers."[92] As it was, they complained that subscribers did no more than send money, taking no interest in what was done with it.[93] The later decision in favor of a fund reflected not only financial prudence but the Federation's establishment of an institutional identity.[94] Towards the same goals of permanence, it was also decided to establish an advisory council of two members from each of the constituent institutions, and to publish an annual brochure listing all contributors and describing the beneficiaries.[95] Several years later, each Federation institution was allowed to nominate a representative Trustee to serve alongside the fifteen Trustees at large. The latter were nominally elected by the contributors but tended to be self-perpetuating during this period.[96]

It was only a small step from supporting institutions to monitoring their financial practices. One which failed to provide an accurate accounting was directly informed that it would be expelled from the Federation if it did not comply.[97] Central bookkeeping was installed at Federation offices in 1914, and affiliated institutions were expected to submit monthly statements and invoices.[98]

From such administrative centralization of existing institutions it was again a simple—yet momentous—step for the Federation of Jewish Charities to endorse the establishment of a new institution. This occurred first with the Council of Jewish Women's proposal for a residence "where good girls who for one reason or another were without a home or proper home environment might be given a decent place to live." Such homes already existed in other American Jewish communities. The Board gave the proposal its "hearty support," especially because the home already had a building on Kennard Street and was expected to become self-supporting.[99] Thus began Martha House, named after the prematurely deceased novelist Martha Wolfenstein, Dr. Samuel Wolfenstein's daughter. When "the great influx of Negro population" made it "imperative for the Council [of Jewish Women] to consider at once . . . locating elsewhere. . . ," a quiet collection of funds was tacitly endorsed by the Federation and a new Martha House opened.[100] Camp Wise, operated through the C.E.A., was another new project encouraged and subsidized by the Federation.

These modest, useful undertakings were dwarfed by the constantly growing plans for a new Mount Sinai Hospital. The Federation of Jewish Charities had always supported Mount Sinai. It was a small institution in a converted house on Forest Street whose origins went back to 1892. Until the small Cleveland General Hospital opened in 1894, all the city's hospitals were private and most had a religious affiliation. These were the conditions when Rabbi Aaron Hahn set forth a rationale for a Jewish hospital in Cleveland:

> Because there are so many Jews in the community, some of them poor. There is a propriety in the Jews being in position to afford accommodations for their own indigent sick, no matter how accommodating the management of Gentile hospitals have been in the premises.
>
> Because orthodox Jews cling to their religious observances and orthodox dietary regulations. These are matters it cannot be expected can be attended to in a Gentile hospital, but can readily be regulated in a Hebrew hospital. There is no need that the agony of sick and suffering orthodox Jews should be increased by the thought that they cannot keep their religious observances.
>
> Because there is nothing more important than the relief of the sick.
>
> Because the wealth of the Jews in Cleveland permits it.
>
> Because the hospital would be the first absolutely local Jew-

ish institution in the city. The orphan asylum and the Montefiore home [for the aged] belong to the entire west. The hospital would belong solely to Cleveland.

Somewhat heavy-handedly, Hahn observed in conclusion "that as the doors of the Gentile hospitals of Cleveland had always been open to the sick Jews so should the Jewish hospital always be open to the Gentiles."[101] The rabbi's own daughter, Dr. Pearl Hahn, was to have a notable medical career and was one of the city's first woman physicians.

The little hospital was opened on Forest Street in 1903 by the Jewish Women's Hospital Society and served a small clientele for some years.[102] When it requested Federation aid in 1907 in raising $15,000 for needed improvements, Mount Sinai met a negative reception. Its President, Nathan Loeser, argued that Jewish charity patients were costing non-Jewish hospitals "all out of proportion to the funds which these hospitals received from Jewish contributors." The cost was $10,000, against Jewish contributions of merely $565. Moreover, declared Loeser, "Jewish physicians were discriminated against at the various hospitals," thus denying them required training and experience.[103] However, Federation trustees pronounced the hospital's plan "altogether inadequate . . . merely patchwork . . . $15,000 would not be sufficient or their present location suitable." The trustees were compelled to consider alternatives. "To build and equip a new hospital would be a tremendous undertaking," one declared. "St. Louis, which has a larger and richer Jewish community than Cleveland find their hospital an immense burden. . . ." Postpone the matter "for a number of years," he urged. Evidence from Cincinnati suggested that a new Jewish hospital might cost $200,000, besides the contribution from Jewish charity which might have to be $14,000 yearly—and the Federation had allocated only $38,000 to all its beneficiaries. Yet one trustee roundly declared "that it was up to this community to raise a sufficient amount of money to give the Jews of Cleveland a high grade hospital in every respect." But his colleagues, while rejecting a puny $15,000 improvement, hesitated before the vastness of a full-scale hospital. They decided only to investigate.[104]

In 1910, when prosperity returned after two bad years, Eisenman heard "much favorable talk in the Community regarding the building of a new hospital"; he even knew of some who "expressed a desire to contribute in a large way" for the purpose.[105] It was decided to raise $150,000 for a seventy-five-bed hospital, since "there was need in the Community for additional hospital facilities." In the committee's opinion, "the logical institution would be a Cleveland Jewish Hospital, built and supported by Jews, and non-sectarian in character." Before undertaking this project, a preliminary canvass would determine whether $75,000 in advance pledges could be secured.[106] The existing Mount Sinai now permitted itself to be absorbed into the new. The Jewish hospital movement officially separated itself from the Federation, but with the Federation a party to every major structural and financial decision the new hospital was really its child. The Federation of Jewish Charities accepted from the outset that it would have to make good Mount Sinai's expected annual deficits,[107] and in 1913 the public campaign for funds began.

Meanwhile, a movement for a kosher hospital spearheaded by Rabbi Samuel Margolies caused some concern.[108] Eisenman, seeking to conciliate Margolies, wrote to the rabbi that

the Hospital shall be a Jewish Hospital insofar that it is supported by the Jews of the Community and is intended primarily to take care of the Jewish sick of the city. . . .

As to Jewish physicians for Mount Sinai's staff,

the Committee will of course be favorable to them, as one of the incidental objects of the Hospital will be to provide opportunity to deserving Jewish physicians for practice and clinical experience. . . . the best men, irrespective of religion, will be selected [for the staff]. . . . If the choice lies between a Jewish and a non-Jewish doctor of equal merit and training, the preference will be given to the Jewish doctor.

Rabbi Margolies and his committee were raising the question of what, apart from the source of its money, made the planned hospital Jewish. Kosher food was one of the issues, and Eisenman declared:

I am in favor of a Kosher department in the new Hospital. . . .
I shall spare no effort to procure its installation.

The Federation's leader concluded with a direct plea:

It seems a pity that two movements of this kind should go on
simultaneously, working in opposite directions when perhaps a
little cooperation might bring all interests into one big movement, making it a splendid and successful institution for all the
Jews, and all of the city of Cleveland.[109]

Perhaps mollified, and probably realizing his group could not
build a substantial hospital, Rabbi Margolies withdrew. (A
kosher kitchen existed for one year, but after "it was found
impossible to secure competent cooks," the service was discontinued.)[110]

As the very large sums required flowed in, the Board of the
Federation could agree that the flexible pavilion type of hospital was preferable, even though it would probably cost
$100,000 more than the $400,000 needed for a fixed type.[111] By
1915 the Board set an upper limit for $600,000 for Mount Sinai
Hospital in its location at East 105th Street.[112] When the proud
new institution opened in 1916—incorporating a Jewish Free Dis-
pensary on East 55th Street[113]—Cleveland possessed one of its
finest medical facilities, the poor Jews of the city were provided
with another institution serving their welfare, and the communal authority and financial skill of the Federation of Jewish
Charities were triumphantly displayed.

Cleveland Jewry was later than most American Jewish communities in undertaking large-scale health services (Cincinnati's
Jewish Hospital was founded in 1859), but its hospital rapidly
assumed a notable position. It was, of course, non-sectarian.
President Paul L. Feiss declared at the cornerstone laying that
it was "our offering to suffering humanity of all creeds and of all
nationalities, but we must not be satisfied unless we can say
when we finally open the doors of this great institution to all
of the people of Cleveland, that it has been built by the Jews
of Cleveland."[114] To be sure, the Federation was dismayed at
the $181,000 operating deficit incurred in the first twenty-seven
months of Mount Sinai's work. Even allowing for wartime inflation, the amount was vast, but it was covered.[115]

Ten years after declining to endorse a $15,000 project to improve an inadequate little hospital, the Federation of Jewish Charities was the force behind a first-rate $600,000 medical institution. The Cleveland Federation was elevated from a prudent disburser of funds it gathered to the nerve center of philanthropy, the most important Jewish activity in the city. The Federation had yet to come to terms with those for whom its services had largely been meant. But when it did so, it proceeded from a position of power and experience.

Largely occupied though it was with philanthropic effort, the Federation of Jewish Charities found that it was representing Cleveland Jewry in other, broader Jewish matters. The Russian pogroms of 1905–1906 called forth its ready response; before the drive, opened $5,000 was advanced privately by Board members to the national treasurer, Jacob H. Schiff. Charles Eisenman observed that "the Federation had the only effective organization for the proper handling of the matter in the City of Cleveland."[116] Several years later when Schiff spoke to the Federation's annual meeting, the princely banker's high praise of his hosts must have been sweet music in their ears.[117] At other times the Federation also forwarded donations to Jewish victims of the San Francisco earthquake and fire, the Dayton flood, and the Balkan War.[118]

After several years of quiescence, legislation to restrict immigration was again proposed in Congress in 1906.[119] The Federation undertook to speak for Cleveland Jews in opposing the bill before Ohio's senators and the two Congressmen from Cleveland constituencies.[120] The more important of these two, Theodore E. Burton, heard frequently from these prominent Jewish constituents. The 1906 immigration bill contained a literacy test whose stringent application would have endangered immigration at exactly the period of severe pogroms in Russia. To be sure, other religious and ethnic groups would have suffered even more than the Jews from a literacy test. Telegrams were sent to Speaker of the House Cannon and Congressman Burton:

> The Federation of Jewish Charities representing the Jewish community of Cleveland earnestly request that you use your influence for the defeat of the immigration bill at present before

Congress. We are opposed to any literacy test, property qualifi-
cation or increase in head tax. We furthermore deem essential
and just that no bill be passed that does not contain an exemption
clause similar to that contained in the British Aliens Bill.[121]

No reply exists from Speaker Cannon, but Burton, writing to
Rabbi Gries, expressed his general opposition to the bill.[122] By
way of reply, the Federation reiterated its opposition to the
bill, which was finally passed with an increase in the capitation
tax as its main provision.[123] Rabbi Gries, Martin A. Marks, and
Edward M. Baker became a Federation committee to watch over
immigration bills.[124] Marks, Cleveland's member of the newly
founded American Jewish Committee, and his two collaborators
thus assumed a representative Jewish function under Federation auspices.[125]

The East European immigrant segment did not readily regard
the Federation of Jewish Charities as "representing the Jewish
community" of Cleveland, however it needed their aid. The
ties between immigrants and Federation magnates were those
of patron-client, and, not infrequently, employer-employee. The
gulf was wide and deep. Twice the newcomers attempted to
establish their own communal organs. While the older segment
of the Jewish community was organized upon the basis of
charity federation, though the process might conceivably have
been accomplished through the two Reform Temples, the newcomers sought to build from their rich organizational life of
clubs, synagogues, and societies.

In 1906 one hundred delegates from forty-five societies
founded the Union of Jewish Organizations; an equal number of
societies could not be reached to be included. The Union proposed "to advocate and promulgate general unity and harmony
among all the Jews in the city," and "to act as a central body
wherein the various organizations may, through their delegates,
interchange views and opinions regarding matters of general
importance to the Jewish community." A "Jewish Institute"
was also to be erected.[126] Prominent figures in the new organization were Rabbi Margolies, Abraham Kolinsky, Adolph J.
Haas, Max E. Katz, and Max E. Meisel. Perhaps hoping to be
recognized as local representative, the Union welcomed the
establishment of the patrician American Jewish Committee.[127]

The U.J.O. devoted itself to matters which disturbed many local Jews: a municipal bond referendum scheduled on Rosh Hashanah was postponed; protests to the police improved the plight of Jewish street peddlers; *The Merchant of Venice* was no longer required reading in high school; a hostile high school publication was officially suppressed; the singing of Christmas carols in "Jewish" public schools ceased.[128] A mass meeting and relief collection was undertaken for Rumanian Jews suffering during the peasant uprising of 1907.[129]

Having an effective record before the public authorities, who were mindful of the large numbers of voting Jews, must have been a heady experience for U.J.O. leaders. However, the Union of Jewish Organizations had foundations of sand—dozens of little organizations, each immersed in its own problems, and thousands of poor immigrant Jews with little time and less money to give. The Federation's claim to speak for all Cleveland Jews may have been rejected, but Union leaders hardly felt ready to assume that role themselves. The U.J.O. possessed little power in Jewish communal life. It had not even invited the Reform Temples to affiliate, while B'nai B'rith quit at the outset.[130] The Union had no success in providing kosher food at the Montefiore Home for the Aged. Nor was it successful when, objecting to the Federation's haughty resolution that all Jewish charities should first be investigated and approved by itself, the U.J.O. cited active, non-approved immigrant charities and urged the Federation to make them beneficiaries.[131] By 1908 its weaknesses were all too obvious. It invited practically everyone to attend its executive meetings "and introduce subjects of Jewish communal interest."[132] Its "period of inactivity" the next year presaged the U.J.O.'s demise.[133]

The example of the thriving Kehillah of New York City, headed by Judah L. Magnes, inspired an attempt at a Cleveland Kehillah in 1913–1914. The provisional officers' names were familiar from the U.J.O.—Rabbi Margolies, President; Max Kolinsky, Vice-President; Aaron Garber, Corresponding Secretary. It was Garber who wrote to Magnes:

Having united a considerable number of the existing in Cleveland [*sic*] Jewish Congregations, Lodges, Societies and Unions in one Community for the purposes and along the lines of The

New York Jewish Community, we wish, if possible, to avail ourselves of the experience you have acquired in organizing and heading The New York Community [sic].

Magnes, replying, urged that "representatives from all sections" be drawn in. They must avoid "political aggrandizement of any person or party" and exercise "great caution and restraint in giving publicity to their efforts."[134] Early in 1914 sixty-four organizations sent some 300 delegates to a Kehillah convention. They were greeted by Mayor Baker, who welcomed their fostering of "the community spirit . . . [which] helps to clear up misunderstandings that exist among various peoples and groups in a large city like Cleveland." Speakers dealt with "Religious Problems," "Educational Problems," and "Workingmen's Problems," and the program proposed included most of the activities of the former Union of Jewish Organizations.[135] Very little came of this Kehillah, however.

These immigrant attempts failed because Jewish wealth and prestige resided elsewhere, and neither side could yet establish constructive relations with the other. Nor was there any personality willing to lead both sides and acceptable to both. Cleveland Jewry had no Magnes, nor a Jacob H. Schiff, nor a Louis Marshall. True, a rising political figure like Alfred A. Benesch, aware of increasing East European power at the polls, was able to work effectively with immigrant Jewry. His own Progressivism contained social programs and legislation to protect the laboring foreign born. When Mayor Baker appointed Benesch Director of Public Safety (in charge of police, fire, and housing), the Yiddish newspaper hailed this as the mayor's "most popular act" for the Jews.[136] On the other hand, Rabbi Samuel Margolies' attempts to rival the established Reform rabbis in the Jewish community did not succeed. The Federation of Jewish Charities, possessing financial prowess, good connections with the city's political and business life, and confidence in its own right and ability, became the representative body of Cleveland Jewry. Only the Jewish masses were missing. The Federation cautiously sought ways of bringing in representative newcomers as junior partners, but this process had hardly begun before it was interrupted by the stresses and demands of World War I.

Charles Eisenman in 1919 was able to stress the Federation's function as a communal organ rather than a charitable group:

> Plans for the development of new activities or the development of the old in the scheme of philanthropic work, and movements of a general communal nature, have been submitted and have received the best judgment of the board of trustees. Each has been viewed in the light of its importance and the community's ability to meet those needs.[137]

On the eve of a major—and more successful—attempt at cooperation in 1922, Eisenman reviewed past attempts, "all of which had met with failure." This, he found, was "due largely to the fact that these elements had differed so widely from the Federation in their administration."[138] Eisenman's gloom was excessive.

THE CONTEST OVER ZIONISM

From time to time local newspapers published apocryphal stories about the acquisition of Palestine by the Jews. Rothschild, Montefiore, Disraeli, and the Turkish Sultan cropped up constantly in these fillers, which might interest readers. The schemes for the Jewish colonization of Palestine promoted by the English visionary Laurence Oliphant were also reported in the *Plain Dealer*.[139] Yet none of this provoked any recorded reaction from Cleveland Jews. The Blackstone Petition of 1891, drafted by William E. Blackstone and signed by several hundred notable Americans, urged upon President Harrison and Secretary of State Blaine the idea of an international conference to negotiate for the establishment of a Jewish State in Palestine. Such an idea was bound to irritate or offend most Cleveland Jews, who professed to Reform Judaism. Yet the *Hebrew Observer* was very moderate, perhaps because a document to which the Chief Justice of the United States and the Speaker of the House of Representatives, among others, put their names could not readily be waved aside:

> Whilst it is undoubtedly true that we of America, under the generous treatment here received, will look with thoughts of

ridicule upon this subject at first glance, nevertheless it is one deserving of serious consideration. . . . the question as to what shall be done with [Oriental Jews] has become such a burning one, that it would, in the light of the policy of the various countries, which deny admission to certain classes of emigrants, be a question worthy of debate as to whether or not the wisest plan would be to establish such a State. . . .[140]

Yet they fervently believed that the hope for all persecuted Jews was the emancipation they enjoyed in America and other Jews possessed in Western Europe. With emancipation, the millenial dream of restoration to Zion rightly vanished. It would be indeed undesirable and suggest a lack of national allegiance to speak of Jews as a nation, a nationality, or a people desiring an independent state. Jewish group life existed solely on the basis of religion and charity; the Jewish social clubs were never mentioned in this context.

In 1895 the *Cleveland Leader's* reply to a question, "Are the Jews a nationality or a sect?" stirred an interesting discussion.[141] The *Leader* replied, "A nationality. They have no country of their own, nor is there any Jewish government, but they are essentially a nationality, nevertheless." Whereupon "a well known and much respected citizen" protested:

> Kindly review the above, and see the error of your way. The writer is a Jew, born in this city forty-five years ago and because I am a believer in Judaism you would term me an alien. The Christians believe in the Old Testament as well as the Jews. Are they a nationality or a sect? I would invite you to visit the Jewish Temple next Sunday and determine for yourself if the Jews there assembled are Americans or aliens.
>
> Respectfully yours,
An American Jew

The *Leader*, taken aback by the letter, insisted that "nothing was more foreign to our thought and purpose than to deny to any Jew in Cleveland all the devotion to the government and institutions of the United States that he might cherish." Yet the Poles, with their state extinct and divided under three regimes, are still a nationality; thus,

> the Jews the world over still deserve the distinction of maintaining their individuality, a separate existence, such as can be

ascribed neither to religion, race, nor any other cause than a wonderfully preserved nationality. . . . The lines which bound sects and the ties which unite them do not cover the kinship, the deep, underlying and marvelously preserved national unity of the Jews.

Nationality remained unaffected by citizenship; here the example of the American Irish was cited.

It is not essential to the existence of a nationality that it should possess an independent government . . . or that the persons who compose it should be lacking in loyalty to whatever state they may be subject.

The *Hebrew Observer* found this remarkable analysis somewhat disturbing.

The query, whether the Jews are a nationality or a religious sect, is one of many questions on which the Jews themselves disagree. The great majority of Jews, however, rightly disclaim a nationality, holding Judaism to be strictly a religious belief and nothing more.

Disregarding the term "nationality," the *Hebrew Observer* declared that "nation" was only "a body of individuals gathered together for the purposes of self-government." Even the Poles and the Irish were not nations. This position left open a large middle ground between nation-state and religion which Irish, Poles, and also Jews could occupy.

The Zionist challenge to Cleveland Jews lay in this realm of ideas. The Zionists lacked the power and the means, and perhaps the inclination, to rival the leadership of the Reform Jewish philanthropists. Yet to the latter, Zionism was the most disturbing of the ideas found among the East Europeans. Not Orthodoxy, even though they might be embarrassed by its foreignness; anyhow, it appeared to be declining rapidly. Not socialism, even though its radical critique and vehemence were upsetting: Jewish socialism was quite ambivalent about its Jewishness. Zionism was active, gained adherents particularly among the children of immigrants, and was wholeheartedly Jewish. Opponents felt the Zionist vision of a Jewish state challenged their status in American life and raised questions about their loyalty to the United States. Their feeling was not set to rest by editorials like that in the *Leader*, nor by Mayor Baker's appearance at Zionist meetings; it arose from the Zionist view that Jews were in exile, *galut*. Even though Zionists in Cleveland, like those elsewhere in the United States, qualified their analysis, saying that Jewish exile meant lands where Jews were physically oppressed, and that Palestine would be a refuge for them only, the anti-Zionists were unappeased.[142]

We know little of Zionism in Cleveland before the first Zionist Congress, called by Theodor Herzl in 1897.[143] This historic Congress served to solidify the opposition to Zionism which abated very little until World War I. The *Jewish Review*, rather beside the point, found "enough poverty in our own country to relieve without sending contributions to a cause which has little need for encouragement. It is our humble opinion that the Zionistic movement would be a detriment instead of a benefit to our co-religionists in Palestine."[144] The *Hebrew Observer* was displeased at the *Plain Dealer*'s interviews with local rabbis on the subject of Zionism. It admonished the newspaper that European and American Jews, "excepting a few religious fanatics, are not in sympathy, and discountenance the movement." Munich was abandoned as the site of the first Zionist Congress, with the result that many Zionists "see the error they have made and are quickly deserting the sinking ship. Zionism 'On to Palestine' is dead."[145] In the wake of that Congress, held instead in Basel, the same weekly doubted that the funds for Herzl's plans could be raised, since "the better element of Jewry throughout the world" opposed them. No doubt both Herzl and Nordau "would be averse to settling in Palestine."

> There is plenty of room in the world to scatter the persecuted Russian Jews; why house them together again? We want no new ghettos.
> A body of Jews comprised mostly of Russian refugees with a scattering addition of idealists and zealots would indeed make poor timber upon which to found an empire, and prudent people will hesitate to give money or their influence to further such a cause.[146]

To these and other assaults upon the nascent Zionist movement no effective reply came from Cleveland's early Zionists.

The "oldest [Zionist] society in Cleveland" was reputedly the Ezras Chovevei Zion (Lovers of Zion Aid).[147] Its name suggests that it was founded to aid the early Lovers of Zion colonists of the 1880s. It still existed in 1913. After the revolutionary change wrought by Herzl's appearance on the scene in 1895, the first known group was organized in a synagogue on October 31, 1897. This was the Young American B'nai Zion Association. Reporting this event, the *Hebrew Observer* was "confident" that none "are representative Jews of this community, nor does any one of them wish to live himself in the Holy Land."[148] The Association had a clubroom on Orange Street, where their small library was open every Friday evening. On one occasion, addresses were delivered by G. Laufman, Rabbi H. Werner, L. Ginsburg, and R. Gittelsohn.[149] It was a major Zionist event when the "Russian orator" Zvi Hirsch Masliansky, the "Nationalist Preacher" who discoursed on Zionism in the traditional homiletic fashion, appeared at the Ohavei Emuna Anshe Russia synagogue. There he "pleaded with the Jewish people of Cleveland to advocate Zionism to its full extent and true meaning" and succeeded in "enrolling over one hundred members at annual dues of $1.00."[150] The magnetic Yiddish preacher-orator was later prevailed upon to speak once more.[151] Next year, the *Hebrew Observer* printed Nordau's address to the Third Zionist Congress but, it added, "we fail to see any direct progress" in the movement.[152] Yet the newspaper had just injected an altogether new note:

> We sincerely hope the Congress will succeed in purchasing Palestine. Not on account of forming a Jewish State, but because it would, in a measure, divert emigration of Jews in that direction, necessarily reducing the present large influx into the United States.[153]

Was it possible that some far-sighted native Jews, while remaining antagonistic to Zionism as an ideology, were beginning to murmur that the acquisition of Palestine would ultimately lessen their burden in Cleveland? If so, the thought passed. Herzl's efforts were bearing no fruit, and the Jewish influx to the United States, and to Cleveland, was becoming more massive yearly, as were the problems accompanying it. For this greatest concern of Cleveland Jews, Zionism appeared to offer nothing. In fact, Zionism might be a hindrance. Immigrant Jews, rather than devote themselves to becoming proper Americans in the mold which Reform Jews had cast, were thinking of a distant Jewish State to be created. Were Zionists loyal Americans? The charge embarrassed and irritated the Zionists.

Young Abraham Kolinsky (later Kollin; 1879–1968), a law student who later became a State Senator, delivered the first written defense of Zionism in Cleveland. He refuted the allegation that the Jews were too restless and individualistic to form a self-governing state. Kolinsky declared that the Zionist movement "aims to regenerate the national spirit of the Jews, and it also aims to establish a center to which Jews, who are enjoying only temporary immunity from persecution, may go when they are tightly pressed." As to Reform Judaism's conception of a Jewish mission to be scattered throughout the world in order to spread ethical monotheism, it showed no results after nineteen centuries. A territorial basis was required for a Jewish mission. Zionism will bring Jewish wanderings to an end, and Jews will "become revered and respected by all nations."[154]

The debate continued when Professor Richard J. H. Gottheil of Columbia University, then a leading Zionist, delivered an address in the city which, in the *Jewish Review and Observer*'s opinion, "would not do very much to converting anti-Zionists to his way of thinking." The newspaper insisted that "Palestine is not the place" on account of its geographic and physical conditions. True, every nation had its national home and "this might hold good were the Jews a nation, but they are not; they are simply a religious sect, as the Catholic and Protestant. . . ." The Jew underwent anti-Semitism in Europe and social ostracism in America.

> . . . but is that the reason he should seclude himself from the nations of the earth and live in his own country? No, the solution for this problem is that he mingle with his fellowmen and live such a life that his oppressors will soon see that their ignominious course toward him is unjust and will endeavor to retrieve it.[155]

The terms of the debate over Zionism slowly shifted, with Zionists emphasizing Palestine's role as a potential refuge for persecuted Jews. American Jews, fortunate in their country, should help to achieve it. They defined their "sole object and aim" as "the freeing of the persecuted and suffering Hebrew race all over the world."[156] More direct participation, such as by emigration to the Jewish State, was not contemplated; anti-Zionists in fact taunted Zionists that they would avoid living in the State of their dreams.[157]

Zionism continued to provide a subject for polemics while local Zionist activity increased steadily. B'nai Zion conducted an active social and philanthropic program, and in 1902 it established a young women's branch, the Roses of Zion.[158] Young Rose Pastor was president, and Celia Hahn, vice president. In 1904 there were twelve Zionist societies in Cleveland with a reported 900 members.[159] A year later, one hears of ten groups with 1,000 members.[160] The variety of their activity may be illustrated by the Tiphereth Zion Association's programs for May and June, 1910: Dan Sugerman spoke on "The Role of the Jews in the World of Art" and refuted derogations of Jewish artistic ability, then "concluded his lecture with several violin solos;" Max Simon treated the "Theory of Zionism;" arrangements for a convention were discussed; the members went to a beach party.[161] Cleveland Zionists rented a building on Forest Street in 1903, and a larger one in 1905, to be the Zion Institute.[162] By 1904 a Cleveland Zionist Council existed, associating all the small societies and representing them in public affairs.[163]

The character of Herzl's Zionist work did not permit early Cleveland Zionism to be political, and slender means made their philanthropy a matter of many little sums. On the other hand, the cultural emphasis was noticeable. Many of the Zionist movement's roots were in the Hebraic revival. A Hebrew and English library and reading room was set up. The C.E.A.'s Isaac Spectorsky, a sympathizer, spoke on one occasion on the "Study of Hebrew History and Literature," meaning "the need of the Jewish American youth of acquiring more fully the knowledge of his own history."[164] Local Hebraists, organized in Ivriah, were closely connected with the Talmud Torah. Ivriah meetings were conducted solely in Hebrew, and each of the eighty to one hundred members was expected to give a talk in Hebrew when his turn came. In 1908 Ivriah sponsored an all-Hebrew mass meeting with children from the Talmud Torah participating.[165]

This cultural endeavor, as well as fund-raising by means of balls and bazaars and flag days, Jewish education in a Zionist-related school, and continuous meetings and rallies and demonstrations, made Zionism a major presence in immigrant life.

Hundreds of Jewish households found in Zionism a focus for active idealism. Thus, Dr. S. P. Burstein, a Russian Jewish physician, and his wife were constantly active among Hebraists and Talmud Torah leaders, in the Union of Jewish Organizations and Kehillah efforts, and in Zionist endeavor. Each complemented the other. (The doctor and his wife were the parents, grandparents, and in-laws of several Conservative rabbis.) To plan meetings, and then to attend them, to give and raise money, to read and distribute Zionist literature: this was a deeply satisfying Jewish response to the demands of modern times. To strive towards a Jewish State in remote Palestine and to cultivate modernized Jewish culture in the American Diaspora also constituted a form of adjustment to American life. The American historian Timothy L. Smith sums it up:

> The cultivation of the sense of nationality through church and fraternal educational programs in America thus fulfilled two divergent purposes, though the immigrants themselves did not find them contradictory. America was in their eyes a land of many cultural traditions. Freedom, for men who had long struggled for it in the Austro-Hungarian and Russian empires, meant not only opportunity for personal advancement but liberty to maintain the cultural life of their ethnic group as well—in short, cultural pluralism. Nationalism in the sense of a political commitment to establish an independent homeland for their people, was focused almost entirely on the Old World. Native Americans and Jews who disclaimed Zionism rarely understood the capacity of religion to hold in balanced tension these two diverging goals of immigrant ethnic groups.[166]

With other immigrant groups also furthering their national aspirations in Cleveland, the climate was hospitable for Zionism.[167] In 1904 the Federation of American Zionists held its annual convention in the city—one of the important conventions of the F.A.Z.'s history, as it happened. While the proceedings belong to the general history of American Zionism, playing host to the F.A.Z. was a great event to Cleveland Zionists.

Upon the front of [Zion Institute] and for three miles up and down Woodland Avenue and Orange Street are banners bearing the legend, "Welcome Zionists," and with them are hung the beautiful emblem of the Jewish national movement—a blue and white flag bearing the symbolic shield of David. Portraits of Dr. Theodore [*sic*] Herzl, the originator of the Zion idea, are also in windows and on the front of dwellings surrounded by the Zion and American flags.[168]

The F.A.Z. convention was given detailed attention in the *Plain Dealer*.[169] A convention rally drew an estimated 2,500 people. Cleveland's Jewish judge, J. C. Bloch, previously unconnected with Zionism, presided.

Through every one of the twelve [!] addresses rang a note of defiance to oppression, and the determination to form a state which should become the national home of the Hebrews of the world.[170]

Commissioner Harris R. Cooley and City Solicitor (later Mayor) Newton D. Baker addressed the assemblage. Though the established Jewish community apparently ignored the proceedings, local political leaders could hardly disregard a movement which could bedeck several miles of street with flags and pictures, bring national figures to town, and attract 2,500 inhabitants of Cleveland to a rally.

Hardly a month later the Zionist movement was stunned by the death of Herzl.[171] Anshe Emeth synagogue was filled for a memorial meeting at which most of the speakers were rabbis. One of them was Aaron Hahn, sometime radical Reform rabbi at Tifereth Israel.[172]

Before 1905 Cleveland's Zionists had only the native Jews and Reform Judaism as their rivals. The immigrant synagogues and their related benevolent societies were in general passively sympathetic. Although the Zionist movement touched some of the most profound chords in Jewish tradition, these societies' and congregations' interests were focused on their immediate affairs. However, the city's Orthodox rabbis were Zionists, and several were active in the movement.

From about 1905 socialism appeared as a force among Cleveland Jews. A Jewish Branch of the city's Socialist Party was reported holding open-air meetings in the Jewish district by 1904,[173] and one of their expected speakers was the New York Yiddish oratorical firebrand Benjamin Feigenbaum.[174] In 1907 "Branch 5 (Jewish)," as it was then known, had a hall with a library-reading room of socialist literature.[175] Most of the books in this "free circulating library" were Yiddish, and "the public in the neighborhood [were] invited to avail themselves of the privileges of the library,"[176] which, in addition to indoor and outdoor propaganda meetings, constituted the Jewish Socialists' principal activity.[177]

> The library [in 1912] occupies five rooms, one for books, two for committees, a reading room and a reception room and 1,045 persons are regular readers who draw books, besides scores of others who drop in occasionally between the hours of 7 A.M. to 9 P.M. There are no dues charged and the library is supported wholly by voluntary contributions.[178]

Supporting the library, as well as causes like strikes, gave the Jewish Socialists their opportunity for social affairs such as a grand masquerade to benefit the library.[179] In 1914 a Jewish branch of the Young People's Socialist League was established.[180] All these activities had a common purpose: to bring to Jews the message of socialism.

There was a common aim to Zionism, which envisioned a Jewish State in Palestine, and the Jewish socialist movement, which sought to introduce the Jews into the mainstream of revolutionary movements. Both wished to align the Jews as a people with historical trends which would shape the future of mankind. Zionism looked to the rights of nations, while socialism forecast the coming victory of industrial workers. There was little interest on the part of socialists in Jewish matters as such. Zionism was regarded as an illusion. The socialists' deepest desire was effective trade unionism among Jewish workers; twice they sponsored short-lived local federations of Jewish workers.[181] It was the weakness of Jewish unionism in Cleveland, and its relative success only in the traditional, conservative Jewish craft unions, which forestalled the rise to importance in Jewish life of socialist movements, a development which did occur in New York.[182]

Jewish socialism was strong, not in trade unions, but at its fraternal base in the Arbeiter Ring (Workmen's Circle). Founded in 1900, this organization sought to provide for its members in a secular manner what traditional religious bodies customarily afforded: cemetery rights and death benefits, sick aid, charity, and cultural activity. Cleveland's Branch 79, founded in 1904 with 20 men, rose to 321 in 1925, while Branch 430, which had 25 founders in 1910, could count 105 members fifteen years later.[183] In 1920 Karl Marx Branch 559 was founded as a "pure Socialist Workmen's Circle Branch" and was active in the Socialist Party.[184]

Socialism also appeared in the Zionist movement, with its program of a socialist Jewish State to be built by the Jewish proletariat. By 1906 a Poale Zion ("Workers of Zion") branch of Socialist Zionists was active in Cleveland. Public debates with opponents were one of its favorite endeavors. Thus, "What Will Zionism Give to the Jewish Workingman?" was a subject it debated with the B'nai Zion society.[185] Somewhat later, the Herzl Association had "a large and enthusiastic audience" which heard "Resolved, that Socialism is Practicable" debated.[186] By 1913 two local branches of the Zionist Socialist fraternal order, the Jewish National Workers' Alliance, also existed in Cleveland.[187] The non-socialist Zionists maintained a fraternal order, the Sons of Zion, which had Judah Maccabee Camp No. 51 as its local branch.[188]

Poale Zion divided sharply among themselves on Territorialism, the question whether a Jewish State could be founded elsewhere but Palestine. The Territorialist Socialist Zionist, S. Danieli (Joseph Chernikoff), delivered three lengthy Yiddish addresses on the subject in 1907, drawing 500 to 800 persons to each one. He had "a poetic make-up and attracted attention in the streets and in the halls where he spoke." Upon his departure, Danieli pronounced Cleveland the leading Territorialist center, an honor it was said to share with Czestochowa in Poland.[189] A Socialist Zionist Territorialists' convention was held in Cleveland in 1908, featuring Dr. Nahman Syrkin and an array of noteworthy Yiddish speakers and ideologists.[190]

These Zionist intramural debates were friendly differences. However, Rabbi Moses J. Gries' renewed attack in 1907, provocatively entitled "Zionism and American Patriotism," stirred resentment. He denounced Zionist statements that Jews were insecure in the Diaspora and that they were a nation, charging that such talk prejudiced the position of American Jews. Gries assailed "political," as distinct from "sentimental" and "spiritual," Zionism for supposedly stirring up questions of Jewish loyalty.[191] On the other hand, Rabbi Louis Wolsey delivered a warmly pro-Zionist sermon soon after coming to Anshe Chesed. Rabbi Gries' fellow Reform rabbi praised Zionism "because it has already stemmed the tide of assimilation and reclaimed many an indifferent Jewish soul." He sympathized with Zionist idealism and respected its realism about the condition of the Jewish people, yet preferred the distant millenial hopes of Reform Judaism.[192] Ten years later, as Reform Judaism edged towards pro-Zionism, Wolsey veered to anti-Zionism.

Several new Zionist associations appeared on the scene before 1914. In 1913 fourteen women attended the first meeting of the Daughters of Zion; next year, their name became Hadassah. Thus began the city's branch of the famous women's Zionist organization, led by Henrietta Szold, which specialized in medical and social work in Palestine. Two years later Cleveland Hadassah had 150 members.[193] Much less successful was the Palestine Industrial Alliance, founded by Rabbi N. H. Ebin in 1911 to assist Palestinian economic and cultural institutions and encourage Orthodox Judaism in the reborn homeland.[194] Jews who yeared for more than remote participation in building the Jewish National Home organized the Cleveland Achuzah No. 1, a branch of the Palestine Land Development Company. Each member undertook to pay $200 within ten years for the land in Palestine which would become his to farm. By 1914 Achuzah's 45 members had $5,000 on deposit in the Anglo-Palestine Bank (today's Bank Leumi) and were corresponding with the head office in Jaffa about the tract of land they might purchase. They were wary of swampy areas; some members had lived in Palestine about 1902 and remembered the dreaded diseases. The membership included mechanics and skilled workmen, and all were planning early settlement. That was in February, 1914. The disaster of war put an end to the brave plans, and what happened to their painfully gathered funds is not known.[195]

Cleveland Zionists brought notable figures to their city. The Zionist leader and Russian Duma deputy Dr. Shmarya Levin appeared in 1906. The Reform leaders came, and the meeting dealt with Russian Jewry rather than Zionism.[196] Martin Marks' remarks on this occasion were dense enough to merit repetition: "He was glad to welcome a man of the type of Dr. Levin. . . . there is plenty of room in this country for Russian Jews who, after a short stay here, are satisfied with their condition. They make good American citizens. . . ." Dr. Nathan Birnbaum lectured eloquently in 1908 for the rentention of Jewish culture in its traditional manner and for the study of Yiddish.[197] Some of this was too much for Rabbi Margolies. He replied that "Jewish immigrants should drop the foreign attire and other things regarded in this country as odd and become Americanized as quickly as possible." Dr. Benzion Mossinsohn, pioneer of Hebrew secondary education in Israel, also came to Cleveland. Again, the Reform notables appeared, but little money could be raised for Mossinsohn's Jaffa High School.[198] In 1913 the Farband, socialist Zionists, were the sponsors of a rally denouncing the blood libel trial of Mendel Beilis in Russia. About 2,000 people heard political and religious leaders excoriate the accusations.[199]

The most important visit was that paid by Louis D. Brandeis during his Zionist speaking tour of the country in October, 1914, just after he assumed leadership of the movement. The Yiddish orator Masliansky was also there, but it was Brandeis' day. There was standing room only at the huge armory when the People's Lawyer, close advisor of President Wilson and famed opponent of vested privilege, was introduced by Rabbi Wolsey as "the next president of the Zion Republic." "Men and women stood up on the floor and on chairs and shouted until they could shout no more." Zionists might well render this ovation for their new leader, a man of impressive prestige and moral authority in American life, who could represent them in the highest places. Besides requesting funds to aid war-stricken Jews in Palestine, Brandeis spoke of Zionism in general. His speech emphasized the modernity and practicality of the Zionist idea and its value to Diaspora Jews as a shield against radical assimilation and social demoralization.[200] Brandeis agreed that "the meeting in Cleveland was excellent in quality," although the funds promised by local Zionists failed to flow in the amount promised. To his amanuensis Jacob de Haas he expressed the belief that "we have made a distinct impression on the non-Zionists—particularly at a small luncheon in which professed Zionists did not participate."[201] The new head of the movement spoke as the shadow of World War I began gradually to reach towards America.

WAR AND COMMUNITY

The European catastrophe of World War I, which continued almost three years before the United States entered it in 1917, had important effects upon Cleveland Jewry. Not only was there patriotic unity in time of war, but immigrant movements and those of old-stock philanthropists cooperated and even merged their objectives. The immigrants appreciated the financial prowess and organizational skill of the old stock, and the latter in turn came to understand the fervor and imagination of the newcomers.

As German armies began the war with their strike at France through Belgium, the editor of the *Jewish Independent* expressed his disgust with the European alignment: "It is inconceivable how France, a republic, and England, the most liberal monarchy in Europe, can ally themselves with brutal Russia, the most despotic government in all the world."[202] Indeed, hatred of Russian Czarism was the strongest feeling shaping Jewish opinion about the great conflict. When Turkey joined the Entente later in 1914, the spectre was invoked of the Czar defeating the Sultan and occupying Palestine: "Palestine under Cossack rule would be far worse than in Russia itself."[203] The desire to see Czarism crushed dominated the thoughts of American Jews during the early phase of the war. Germany, the ancestral land of most old-stock Jews, was widely respected. Most Jews, however, preferred to avoid committing themselves; Israel Zangwill's call from England to support the Allied side met a cold reception.[204]

The Jews quickly realized what war meant in Europe, for a great proportion of them had come from the very areas being bombed and overrun by German, Austrian, and Russian arms. They watched impotently as brothers, sisters, fathers, and mothers were stricken by hunger and disease, and were mercilessly deported into Russia before the advancing Germans and Austrians or fled west before oncoming Russians. Meanwhile, the new Jewish settlement in Palestine, the focus of great hopes, was being atrociously treated by the Turks.

Urgent appeals flowed in from Europe and Palestine, and landsmanshaften and synagogues and societies were already active when the principal organizations assembled at the call of the Federation of Jewish Charities on November 9, 1914, to consider how these efforts could be coordinated.[205] For B'nai B'rith, S. J. Kornhauser urged that his organization be entrusted with raising and distributing funds. However, merger of funds so raised into a general local collection was impermissible. Rabbi Margolies, that articulate opponent of Federation dominance, offered on the other hand to merge the local efforts of the East European Jews' Central Relief Committee into a combined campaign. Others present

> expressed the opinion that the Federation of Jewish Charities represented the authorized agents of the Local Community in the matter of raising funds for any general philanthropic purposes. . . . it was unanimously resolved that it was the sense of the meeting that the Federation of Jewish Charities shall undertake the solicitation of funds in this Community for the relief of sufferers in Europe and Palestine. . . ."[206]

The Kehillah promptly turned to the work, and so did the new War Relief Association, composed mainly of Hungarian Jews closely linked with B'nai Jeshurun.[207] However, it was the action of the Federation in taking charge of Jewish overseas war relief which was the supremely important communal precedent. By raising funds for overseas long before most of its contemporaries throughout the country did so, the Federation touched the deepest interests of the East European immigrant group and gained respect and support. The old-stock constituency of the Federation of Jewish Charities expanded their concerns from local charities to world problems, becoming familiar with the plight of European Jewry as they provided it with relief. Appeals for the same purpose sponsored solely by the immigrants would have received very little money from old-stock Jews. Early in 1915, the F.J.C. set $25,000 as the goal of its local campaign. The foresighted Edward M. Baker spoke in his moving plea not only of a "gigantic" task at hand, "to relieve present distress, but perhaps throughout a period of years to assist in the work of rehabilitation and reconstruction."[208] The nationwide People's Relief Committee, whose local branch was called the Jewish National Relief Committee, exemplified the zeal and self-sacrificing spirit of the campaigns conducted in the immigrant neighborhoods. Representing the Jewish community's secular, Yiddish-speaking left, the Relief Committee tirelessly carried on door-to-door collections, tag days, flower days, and bazaars. Rallies and conferences were often held to renew enthusiasm for the cause. From its inception until November 1, 1919, the People's Relief Committee raised $100,825.10 in Cleveland.[209] The Federation remitted funds to the newly founded Joint Distribution Committee, while other organizations sent the money they collected to the People's Relief Committee and other bodies which also had working arrangements with the J.D.C.

By February, 1916, $40,000 had been sent through the Federation of Jewish Charities, exclusive of private remittances, but "the Federation believes that sum to be insufficient" for a city of Cleveland's size, and set a goal of $100,000.[210] "For the first time in the history of the Jewish community of Cleveland we Jews have applied to all classes of people, irrespective of creed or religion, to assist us. . . ."[211] Local Zionists also continued their efforts for war-stricken Palestinian Jewry.[212] The Federation's drive was only moderately successful: early in 1917, it reported a total of $82,326, $2,600 of it from non-Jews.[213]

The disaster of war and the effort to raise funds quickened Jewish life. "Even though you have contributed to the [Jewish war relief] fund add to your contribution as there are no other people in the world that can do for these poor people . . . ," demanded a Jewish newspaper.[214] Zionists and other organizations conducted house-to-house collections, tag days, and synagogue appeals. However, opinion in Cleveland was still far from favorable to the Allies throughout 1915. The large German community, although much eroded by cultural assimilation, was of course the most prominent in demanding American neutrality and an embargo on munition shipments abroad. The Allied blockade against shipping foodstuffs to Germany stirred humanitarian protests, even from Mayor Newton D. Baker.[215] Similar notes were sounded in the Jewish press:

England's present alliance with Russia is doing her very little good for that country [sic]. Instead of England producing a beneficial influence upon the Russian government she is dominated to some extent by the policy of the Czar's government. . . . Thousands of tons of ammunition are being sent over to the warring countries from here. . . . If America would cease shipping the ammunitions [sic] the war would soon come to an end.[216]

The American Jewish position was described tendentiously:

The sound of wailing Poland awakens in the American Jew his dormant nationality. It is the call of his kin of old. Other races in America have felt other calls, but he alone of them all can respond and remain purely and truly American.

Among American Jews are many Jews so recently come from the fighting countries that their attitude towards the war is largely influenced by their personal experience. It is significant to observe in the refugees from Russia joy at the German victories. The former citizens of Germany are found on the side of the allies. The Russian Jew knows what Russian despotism, brutality, corruptibility, ignorance and drunkenness are. The German Jew has experienced German militarism, anti-Semitism, arrogance and restriction.[217]

France, "which crushed the devil of anti-Semitism" in the Dreyfus case, and England, are "fair lands of justice and liberty [which] receive the honor and reverence of German Jew, of Russian Jew and American Jew alike."[218] With Germany and Russia thus neutralizing each other morally (Austria-Hungary rarely entered any discussion), England and France could fairly claim the support of American Jews. No practical consequences were yet drawn from this interpretation. It is doubtful that American Jews of German descent really felt alienated and hostile towards their ancestral land, as Russian Jews generally felt towards theirs.

Rabbi Gries and Rabbi Wolsey both opposed President Wilson's first preparedness proposals. Wolsey's sermon denouncing them was entitled, "The Battle Cry of Fear," while Gries believed that preparedness was playing on a fictitious "German peril" which would arouse the spirit of hatred and divert America from her true ideals.[219] A Jewish newspaper found "no reason why fear should exist in this country." The martial spirit prevailed only because "some leaders . . . fear that this country will be invaded by an enemy . . . [an] imaginary invasion. . . ."[220]

Early in the war thoughtful Cleveland Jews realized that there would be fundamental political changes in Europe and the Middle East. The possible downfall of the Czars might end Jewish persecution and bring emancipation to Russian Jews. The possibility existed of minority rights for Jews along with other ethnic groups of Eastern Europe. There were also bound to be radical changes in the Ottoman Empire, and Zionists especially thought of a political settlement which might give Palestine to the Jews. America would be involved in these high affairs when the time arrived for decisions even if it did not enter the war. While the emancipation of East European Jews was universally desired, clear differences existed over minority rights and the future of Palestine. Unwilling to rely upon established American Jewish leadership to achieve these ends, Zionists led by Brandeis launched the movement for a democratically elected congress of American Jews to decide on post-war overseas policy.[221] Shmarya Levin quickly won the support of Cleveland Zionists,[222] but intricate negotiations proceeded at length in New York before the congress idea in modified form was reluctantly accepted by the established American Jewish leadership. By then the United States was at war.

The approach of war brought little increase in enthusiasm. To a Black observer in March, 1917, Cleveland was "a foreign city, about every nationality under the Sun." Yet he believed "that the foreigners, if put to the acid test, will stand by the President. . . . Many of the foreign societies and organizations have come out and pledged their allegiance; but whether this was done by persuasion on the part of the leaders or of their own volition, there is no means to determine."[223] For the Jews, the abdication of the Czar and the establishment of a democratic provisional government in Russia, which promptly repealed all anti-Jewish legislation, ended reluctance about supporting the Allied powers. The Ohio State Zionist Convention congratulated the Russian people, and Rabbi Margolies, speaking there, observed that the revolution emphasized the need for smaller peoples, like the Jews, as well as greater peoples to secure self-determination.[224] Yet Rabbi Gries remained unreconciled to the probability of America at war. "America will do more for humanity by not entering the war and leading the warring nations to a permanent peace, for war is a method of madness and does not decide who is right."[225]

When war was declared upon Germany, the *Jewish Independent* noted the occasion:

War!!
We all know what the word signifies. For nearly three years the nations of the world have been at each other's throats. It is our turn now.[226]

It reproved American Jews who issued gratuitous statements that American Jews would be loyal.

Fervid declarations of the war's moral meaning began to flow. Two days following the declaration of war, Judge Manuel Levine told a meeting at the Young Men's Christian Association that "America is entering upon the war with the battle cry of humanity." The foreign born have "a great opportunity . . . . to show they are not exploiters, seeking advantages in this country without returning to America the best that is in them. . . . America is seeking to mold the great brotherhood of all the peoples of the world and it will be a positive success if the foreign born will enlist in the war for humanity's sake."[227] Rabbi Abba Hillel Silver had just settled in Cleveland when he too struck a similar note at a reunion of young Jews expecting soon to join the army. "America has entered this struggle with a spotless record, and through this dreadful war, with its suffering . . . is seen the dawn of redemption. The battles of America, Judaism and humanity are one and the same."[228] Not only were there the armed forces of the United States to join. Cleveland had recruiting stations for the British-Canadian forces, the Polish Legion, yet-to-be-born Czechoslovakia, and Italy. There was a Jewish Battalion desk at the British-Canadian office and another in the center of the Jewish district,[229] where seventy-five young men volunteered for service in the British Army in Palestine.[230] At the war's end 2,914 were reported to have worn an Army or Navy uniform.[231]

Early in 1918, the Jewish Welfare Board, which conducted welfare work among Jewish soldiers and sailors, established a branch in Cleveland.[232] Wartime civic solidarity, in fact, extended into the field of philanthropy. The Federation of Jewish Charities thus became a constituent of the Cleveland War Chest, which financed its local and overseas Jewish requirements.[233] Civic and philanthropic leaders utilized this wartime success to establish a permanent Community Fund (later Chest). At first the Fund proposed to continue overseas Jewish relief, but this was not agreeable to the Jewish immigrant sector, nor could the vast sums required have been drawn through a nonsectarian local fund.[234]

The depressing story of the suppression of dissent during the war involved Jews only slightly. As late as May 20, 1917, a peace meeting was held in Public Square, and the Socialist Party openly held to its antiwar position.[235] At the later trial of Eugene Debs, Morris H. Wolfe of Cleveland was one of Debs' lawyers, while A. W. Mowshowitz was a bondsman.[236] The Cleveland representatives in the Ohio legislature were only lukewarm supporters of bills purporting to promote "100% Americanism."[237] The main sufferers from repression were the city's Germans. Numerous incidents of suppressing their press and institutions occurred, and coercive demands for patriotic behavior intimidated them.[238] A brief but serious incident was the riotous attack by a group of soldiers standing nearby upon a street corner Zionist meeting in September, 1917, which was mistaken for an antiwar gathering. Several persons suffered serious injury. Proper apologies were made, but the excitement over opposition to the war continued to produce serious tensions.[239] The municipal administration, however, did not seek the compulsory conformity of "100% Americanism." The Mayor's War Board set up a Cleveland Americanization Committee which, among other activities, published an informative series of pamphlets on the various ethnic groups in the city. Indeed, *Americanization in Cleveland*, a pamphlet published around 1920 during anti-alien and nativist near-hysteria, defined its subject in terms of immigrant contributions to the cultural and political enrichment of America, mutual respect among the immigrants and natives, and learning English. Such an enlightened public policy in Cleveland no doubt reflected years of civic education as well as, by this time, the well-developed voting power of naturalized immigrants and their native-born sons.[240] Jews, however, were unrepresented on this committee and unmentioned in its publications, suggesting that Jewish spokesmen preferred identification by religion, paralleling Catholics and Protestants, rather than as an ethnic minority like the Italians, Greeks, Slovaks, and many others. They probably kept apart intentionally from these activities.

Contrary to the fearful caution which was to prevail during World War II, American Jews generally, and those of Cleveland in particular, pushed ahead with their bold postwar planning for European Jewry. The 1917 goal of Jewish war relief in Cleveland was $150,000, but it was anticipated that $200,000 would be raised.[241] Nominations were presented for the city's five delegates to the American Jewish Congress, to be held in September, 1917. At a meeting of seventy-seven organizations' delegates, Rabbi Gries admitted that he had "seriously doubted" the congress movement, but "the time . . . has arrived when it becomes necessary to discover some means for uniting the various factions in Jewry" which "may make it possible . . . to solve the great Jewish problems."[242] At the session Gries was himself nominated, together with Rabbi Margolies, Aaron Garber, Dr. I. Milcoff, Mrs. I. J. Biskind, Mrs. J. K. Zwick, M. Friedman, I. Resnick, A. Simon, and G. Auerbach. "The coming election . . . begins to have the appearance of real politics" as two "independent candidates," Abraham Kolinsky and J. Chertoff, joined the field.[243] On Sunday, June 10, 1917, "about 6,000 men and women" voted in an early demonstration of women's suffrage. The results were:

Rabbi Samuel Margolies	4,706
Mrs. Jennie K. Zwick	4,309

Aaron Garber	4,217
G. Auerbach	3,945
Abraham Kolinsky	3,859

Not elected were Dr. I. Milcoff (2,739), Joseph Chertoff (1,685), and Alfred A. Benesch (1,285). (Since there is no record of his nomination, Benesch may have been a write-in.) Evidently Rabbi Gries withdrew, as did four other nominees.[244] Unlike the experience in other Jewish communities, there was no one, aside from Rabbi Gries' brief candidacy, who represented the old-stock Cleveland Jewry;[245] all the winners were active Zionists. The closeness of the vote for the three leaders strongly suggests that the Zionists, who organized the Congress movement, acted in united fashion to make certain that all delegates represented their views. As it happened, the meeting of the Congress was delayed until the war ended. Rabbi Margolies had died, and Dr. Milcoff was his replacement. When the American Jewish Congress met in December, 1918, most of the contested issues were settled, as it then seemed, on the international scene.

As the war advanced, the thrilling news arrived that Great Britain was "giving" Palestine to the Jews in the Balfour Declaration of November 2, 1917. A Zionist meeting soon after, and many more to follow, expressed gratitude for the great act and called upon Jews to give large donations.[246] Early in the next year a Palestine Restoration Fund was established, and at a vast rally in Gray's Armory Abba Hillel Silver delivered the first of his fund-raising orations in Cleveland for the Zionist cause.[247] The dimensions of Zionist activity were greatly broadened; Mayor Davis was Honorary Chairman, a British M.P. spoke, and former District Attorney Sullivan addressed the assembly. A professional fund-raiser was engaged.[248] Rabbi Silver's counterpart at Euclid Avenue Temple, Rabbi Louis Wolsey, pro-Zionist in earlier years, meanwhile turned anti-Zionist and took an active role in a short-lived, anti-Zionist association which was composed mainly of classical Reform rabbis. He avoided signing the anti-Zionist petition to President Wilson, however, pleading that the Jewish Reform laymen were failing to support their rabbis' anti-Zionist efforts.[249]

The hopes for a world made safe for democracy stirred by the overthrow of the Czar and the emanicipation of Russian Jewry as well as by the Balfour Declaration, were rapidly deflated. Before 1917 ended, Rabbi Silver found it necessary to denounce the canard already in circulation that the Bolshevik regime just come to power was Jewish, and that Jews-Bosheviks were German agents.[250] Terrifying reports were arriving of Jews massacred in Poland and the Ukraine. In addition to resolutions of protest,[251] Cleveland Jewry conducted the first protest parade in its history on June 2, 1919. Led by 500 returned Jewish soldiers, an estimated 15,000 to 20,000 persons marched. That evening, Gray's Armory was crowded beyond capacity as speeches on the subject were delivered by Mayor Davis, Father Francis T. Moran, the Reverend Joel Hayden, and Rabbi Silver. Letters from eminent public figures were also read to the agitated assemblage.[252] The worsening of the Ukrainian pogroms was marked by a day of mourning on November 24 of that year. Once again Gray's Armory was filled to overflowing as an array of speakers denounced the perpetrators and urged aid for the victims.[253] The tide of reactionary nativist, "100% Americanism" was also rising. Judge Bradley Hull was joined by Rabbi Silver in pressing the influential City Club to include this danger among the subjects of its forums.[254]

With the political future of Palestine seemingly assured, Zionists turned to large-scale fund-raising. Early in 1919 President Charles Eisenman of the Federation of Jewish Charities cautioned against fund-raising appeals "without consultation, without those who have been selected by the public to consider these very essential matters." He urged "the need of enhanced cooperation among the elements that make up our social body."[255] This appeal met little response at the time. The development of Palestine, however, required the formation of policies concerning the control and application of the funds raised. and this led to irreconcilable differences between two great Zionist leaders, Chaim Weizmann and Louis D. Brandeis. The open rupture between the two camps occurred at the Zionist Organization of America's convention which was held in Cleveland in June, 1921. When Weizmann, President of the World Zionist Organization and a noted chemist, accompanied by Albert Einstein, arrived in Cleveland in May, 1921, the Mayor and other notables greeted them in the City Council Chamber, and there followed a parade into the Jewish neighborhood. Case Institute of Technology was host to Einstein.[256] The convention which followed this triumphant reception, however, was the occasion for the public break between the Weizmann and the Brandeis forces.[257]

During the period of World War I, the Jews of Cleveland advanced far towards becoming a single community united by ties of common interest and social communication. Wartime prosperity narrowed the economic gulf between the newcomers and the more affluent old stock. Sons who served in the armed forces underwent a superlative acculturative experience. The general civic atmosphere in Cleveland, one of friendship for immigrant ethnic cultures, made Jewish ethnic expressions part of an acceptable social pattern, not foreign or menacing in public opinion. Immigrant ethnic life reached its peak during World War I years. All groups were urgently interested in the destinies of their native lands once the political structure of Central and Eastern Europe began to collapse. The 1920 U.S. Census also showed foreign languages at their peak in Cleveland. Yiddish, with 30,383 listing it as their native tongue, ranked behind German (120,000), Polish (65,000), Czech (43,000), Magyar (42,000), and Italian (35,000).[258] Old-stock Jews led in fund-raising for overseas Jewry, with the newcomers meanwhile putting heart and soul into efforts for their families and old townsmen. However, it was the newcomers who had the plans for the future of the Jews of Eastern Europe and of Palestine, and the old-stock followed with reluctance. The old relationship of patronage and philanthropy was ending, although equality and communal integration were not to be achieved before the 1940s, and not completely until the 1950s. The generation which followed was creative but restless during an age of unparalleled crisis that included the Depression and World War II.

PART THREE

Stormy Decades and Communal Order, 1920–1945

IX

Between War and Depression

THE 1920s were years of continued development for Cleveland. Population increased, if at a somewhat slower pace, as the 796,841 residents of 1920 were counted at 901,482 in 1930. More significant still, metropolitan Cleveland's population showed a massive increase; population growth beyond the city line had first become noticeable only in the 1910–1920 decade.[1] The city's residents were supplemented in 1930 by 301,356 living in the suburban belt, for a metropolitan total of 1,202,838. Only New York, Chicago, Philadelphia, Los Angeles, and Detroit had larger populations.[2] Economic growth continued apace. The banks of Cleveland, which held deposits of $675,000,000 in 1920, saw them rise to $958,000,000 in 1929, as bank clearings, another important indicator of economic activity, stood at $6,877,000,000 in 1920 and at $7,964,000,000 nine years later. Net tons of freightage arriving in Cleveland by lake and rail, most of it for heavy industry, increased from 21,992,000 to 35,015,000 during the same span of time.[3] Thus, Cleveland strengthened its position as one of the world's foremost industrial cities. Yet the industrial wage-earner's pay remained unduly low, a shortcoming which had much to do with the onset of the Great Depression.

Cleveland's Progressive heritage from the era of Tom L. Johnson and his successors and disciples had dwindled. True, the city offered excellent municipal services, and impressive parks were laid out and civic and educational centers built. An array of privately built downtown buildings dominated the Lake Erie skyline.[4] On the other hand, voting tendencies were markedly conservative. Cleveland gave Warren G. Harding an overwhelming majority in 1920, and in 1924 Calvin Coolidge carried the city—though by a small margin—over the Progressive Robert M. LaFollette. Even Alfred E. Smith, the Irish Catholic from the sidewalks of New York, who should have drawn the vote of the masses of new-stock immigrants by then composing most of the population, lost decisively to Herbert Hoover in 1928.[5]

Nineteen twenty marked the Jews' highest proportion in Cleveland's population. The Jewish figure stood around 80,000 or nearly 10 percent of the city's population, owing, of course, to the intensive immigration of the previous twenty years. Extensive Jewish immigration continued during the immediate postwar years, when immigration to the United States was still free, but immigrants were not likely to come to Cleveland unless they had family there. By 1922 the Hebrew Shelter Home "was no longer called upon to serve its primary purpose of sheltering immigrant families coming through from ports of entry. . . ."[6] Later, as immigration was drastically restricted by law, the number who claimed foreign mother tongues also declined. There were 30,383 who gave Yiddish as their mother tongue in 1920, but only 19,319 in 1930.[7]

Nation-wide agitation against foreigners, Jews, and Catholics contributed to the passage of the Johnson Act of 1924, curtailing immigration sharply. Yet Cleveland, now composed mostly of such groups, generally shunned this movement. Thus, Henry Ford's anti-Semitic propaganda stirred anger and resentment when it began in 1920. A mass meeting at Woodland Avenue Presbyterian Church denounced the campaign, and a warm pro-Jewish statement came from the Reverend Joseph F. Smith, a future Auxiliary Bishop of the Catholic Archdiocese. The city even attempted to prevent the sale of Ford's *Dearborn Independent* on the streets, but was legally enjoined from this step.[8] Ford ultimately retracted, but the laws which ended free immigration were passed. A campaign of meetings and petitions and a City Council resolution against the 1921 bill, which would have barred all immigration for one year, saw the proposal fail.[9] The discriminatory racial provisions of the Johnson bill of 1924 were denounced by a 23-2 vote of the City Council, but it was enacted nevertheless. The two council dissenters had both received Ku Klux Klan endorsement.[10]

POPULATION, NEIGHBORHOODS, AND OCCUPATIONAL CHANGE

Cleveland Jewry was first counted systematically during the early 1920s. The Bureau of Jewish Social Research, commissioned by the Federation of Jewish Charities, included a population study in its monumental Jewish Community Survey of 1924. Unaided by the U.S. Census, statisticians had to devise other methods for arriving at the Jewish figures. One approach was based on computing the Jewish death rate. On this basis, Greater Cleveland had 86,540 Jews, 78,000 of whom lived within the city. Of the total, 36,797 (42.5 percent) were less than twenty years of age, and a mere 4,479 (5.2 percent) were aged sixty and over. A second method, based on the assumption that no Jewish child would attend school on Yom Kippur, pointed to a Jewish population of 89,400. The lower figure of 86,540 was the one generally adopted. An admittedly incomplete tabulation counted 11,949 Cleveland Jewish residences at the same date.[11]

This was the maximum population reached by Cleveland Jewry. Almost forty-five years before, there had been somewhat less than 3,000 Jews among 159,000 Clevelanders. The 1924 Cleveland population stood around 846,000.[12] Twenty-six years later, there were 1,465,511 in metropolitan Cleveland, while the number of Jews remained stationary; the general population would continue to rise, while the Jewish population declined slightly.[13]

Jewish population during the 1920s changed little, but neighborhoods shifted with unusual rapidity. East 55th Street was the main thoroughfare of the declining Jewish neighborhood in the mid-1920s, while the number of Jews around East 105th Street and Mount Pleasant-Kinsman was increasing. The older area, which extended from East 46th to East 66th Streets, and from Cedar to Grand Avenues (also bounded in other versions by East 40th and East 71st, and by Cedar and Kinsman), began to lose its Jewish population around 1918. It had over 17,000 Jews in 1924, but only 8,000 to 10,000 just three years later.[14] By 1928 we hear of "approximately 1,000 families [in] this deleterious environment."[15] Most Jews had quit the East 55th Street area, but it was expected that "a small nucleus of interested active persons" would continue to reside there, "whose economic status is such that they are tied to the neighborhood. . . ."[16] A canvass in 1929 turned up no more than 304 families, or somewhat over 1,400 individuals.[17] The area which had been fashionable at the beginning of the century thus became a poor backwater at the end of the 1920s.

Two areas were the principal successors of East 55th Street, East 105th Street and Mount Pleasant. The former was a relatively cosmopolitan area, adjacent to the University Circle complex of academic and cultural institutions, and was bounded by East 131st Street, Wade Park Avenue, Bratenahl, and Ansel Road. Here lived almost 32,000 Jews.[18] This during the late 1920s was

> the heart of the Jewish community life of Cleveland. It consists of many groups and classes. . . . there is a strata of artisans, small shopkeepers, and communally unattached and unorganized individuals. . . . No miraculous transformation has occurred in their lives by the simple act of moving from 55th Street to the 105th Street district. Some of them may be slightly better off economically. . . ."[19]

Nearby were the largest Jewish houses of worship, Mount Sinai Hospital, and other major Jewish institutions.[20]

Even newer than the 105th Street settlement was the Mount Pleasant area. As of 1925, it was

> a growing Jewish community of about twelve to fifteen thousand persons of working class status who are beginning to own their own homes and enjoy the beginnings of a better competence in life. They came originally from the Fifty-fifth Street area. The section is newly built, several synagogues have already been erected, and organized life along labor, fraternal, religious, and philanthropic lines has begun to spring up.[21]

In 1927 Mount Pleasant, as estimated by the methods of the 1924 study, contained the homes of over 22,000 Jewish residents along its agreeable, uncrowded streets.[22] The neighborhood had ethnic groups besides the Jews, including Italians and Czechs who were concentrated in its southern section, and there was inter-group friction, mainly among young people.[23]

Altogether some 71,000 of Cleveland's 78,000 Jews who lived within city lines in 1926 were included in three relatively limited neighborhoods. There were also several small concentrations such as that along Lake Shore Boulevard, particularly between East 148th and East 150th Streets. This entire area held about 1,200 Jews mostly "in moderate circumstances and occupationally . . . small shop keepers and artisans."[24] Of the 8,000 Jews reportedly living in Cleveland suburbs in 1926, 5,000 were found in Cleveland Heights and the remainder were scattered. Their economic position ranged from prosperous to opulent.

Thus, not only the immigrant Jew, obviously different from other Clevelanders, but also the fully acculturated Jew lived by choice in largely Jewish neighborhoods. Immigrant areas maintained the tradition of Jews dwelling together regardless of their wealth. By the 1920s Jews dwelt in neighborhoods as dictated by their means. A variety of housing suited different incomes.

Neighborhood changes were one sign of economic changes within the Jewish group during the 1920s. Thousands of Jews sought to leave their immigrant trades of peddling, tailoring, and carpentry. If they did not, their sons made the shift. The reported parental occupations of 267 poor children at the Federation's Camp Wise in 1926 gave 55 percent as peddlers, 13 percent in the building trades, and the balance scattered among other ill-paid employments. Only 23 percent of the fathers were born in the United States.[25] By the end of the 1920s, however, Camp Wise was finding it "almost impossible to fill camp with the class we have had. . . . Economic conditions and lack of immigration brought about the change."[26] The newer, more favorable economic picture was more nearly typified by the 1929 occupations of the parents of Jewish school children in the Collinwood section:

> The occupational classification of 166 parents [of the 214 on the school list] indicate that 54 are engaged in business (26 merchants, 8 grocers, 2 butchers, 6 druggists, 4 contractors, and 2 insurance); 33 are listed as salesmen; 5 are professional men; and 84 are workmen—the largest single groups are tailors (18) and carpenters (10).[27]

Definite changes were taking place in Cleveland Jewish occupations somewhat paralleling those visible in the neighborhoods. A sample drawn from Jewish occupations listed in the Cleveland City Directory of 1923 provides further confirmation.[28]

Category	% in 1923
Professional, technical, and kindred	8%
Managers, officials, proprietors	21%
Clerical	23%
Sales	13%
Craftsmen, foremen, and kindred	15%
Private household	0%
Service workers	1%
Laborers	4%
Total sample	(1,050)

However, the City Directory itself did not always clearly separate owners of businesses from those who worked in them.[29] Probably within every census category there were extensive shifts from trade to trade, and many of the "managers, officials, proprietors" experienced drastic changes for better or worse in their businesses. The considerable decline in "craftsmen, foremen, and kindred" and "laborers" is illustrated by the drop in the sample of needle trades employees between the 1923 and the 1930 directories from 83 to 65, among peddlers-hucksters from 46 to 27, and among laborers from 44 to 33. On the other hand, lawyers increased from 15 to 20, and salesmen from 39 to 60.[30] An estimated 165 of the 1,200 physicians of Cleveland in 1925 were Jewish. While 65 of the Jewish physicians were on the Mount Sinai Hospital staff, a mere 5 secured appointment to other hospitals, public and private.[31]

While we have an inkling of Jewish occupations and the shifts among them, Jewish incomes are unknown. However, the unionized Jewish tailors of Cleveland enjoyed a great improvement in their income and regularity of employment thanks to an extraordinary series of agreements between their unions and the Cleveland garment manufacturers, most of them Jews.

In 1925 the average men's and women's clothing tailors in the United States earned $1,173, and $1,384, respectively, which was 136 percent for the former and 146 percent for the latter of their real wages in 1914.[32] Perhaps Cleveland needle workers earned somewhat above the national average. Yet it is doubtful whether any but a few very skilled tailors reached the $1500 annual income which Professor (later Senator)

Douglas set in 1925 as the floor for "minimum health and decency;" most were at the "minimum subsistence" plateau beneath.[33]

When Cleveland's Garment Manufacturers Association at last accepted unionization, they did so on the basis of a unique series of agreements with the International Ladies Garment Workers Union. Piecework rather than timework continued, but complex production standards were devised to protect the workers' interests. All this could be done more readily in the large, well-regulated factories of the Cleveland industry than in the small sub-contractors' shops of New York. A 1921 agreement brought unemployment insurance and regularity of employment to the highly seasonal industry, as the cloak manufacturers guaranteed their workers forty weeks work yearly. They were to contribute 10 percent of their payrolls to establish a fund which would provide half the worker's minimum wage for each week of enforced idleness within those weeks. Both the ILGWU and the manufacturers intended to squeeze, although not to put out of business, the small outside shops, few of which could meet these union standards.[34] As the number of Jewish workers affected steadily declined, the Cleveland women's garment trade set new, imaginative standards for labor relations during the 1920s.[35]

In the men's clothing industry of Cleveland, 75 percent of the tailors were reported in 1918 to be Bohemian; probably some of them were Jewish.[36] The industry was unionized in 1918 by the Amalgamated Clothing Workers of America, and in 1920 the union signed a preferential shop agreement with the employers' association. The kaleidoscopic ethnicity of the labor force proved no obstacle. The union's general managers for Cleveland were Jews, as were five or six of the eighteen members of its executive.

> It is wonderful to watch the activity of the workers in this strike [in 1921]. We have a regular league of nations in that shop. You can find there Americans, Irish, Syrians, Italians, Jews, Bohemians, Russians, Poles, and Lithuanians.

The ACWA was proud of the loyalty of all these elements.[37] Major

Jewish-owned firms like Joseph and Feiss, Lion Knitting, and Richman Brothers nevertheless held out against unionization throughout the 1920s with extensive systems of efficiency rewards, bonuses, and welfare plans.[38] Richman Brothers had two large factories manufacturing clothing for its chain, which in 1929 numbered forty stores in thirty-eight cities. This firm sold its stock at reduced rates to employees, who profited nicely from the arrangement during the 1920s. The number of Jews among the tailors was meanwhile declining.

THE CONSOLIDATION OF COMMUNAL LIFE

Tendencies in Jewish communal life which were in evidence before the war period increased in strength after it. The East European Jewish stock constituted the large majority, and there was no question of treating them as clients of old-stock philanthropy. On the other hand, the power relations within the Jewish community between old stock and newcomers could not be quickly altered. The old guard of the Federation was changing as the significance of names like Eisenman, Joseph, Feiss, Mahler, and Hays declined due to death, the infirmities of age, or withdrawal from Jewish communal affairs. Some of the new leaders had the far-sighted ambition to make the Federation encompass all Jewish life, and their relative willingness to adapt and expand aided in the process of consolidation.

A personal factor also manifested itself in the presence in Cleveland of four communal leaders of remarkable vigor and magnetism who occupied strategic positions in Jewish life. Rabbi Abba Hillel Silver (1893–1963) had been at The Temple since mid-1917. Silver was born in Lithuania in 1893 and came to America in 1902. Raised by Orthodox parents on the Lower East Side of New York, where his father was a rabbi and Hebraist, he was active in Zionist clubs from his childhood. His decision to attend the Reform Hebrew Union College surprised his friends and chagrined his parents. He had barely come to Cleveland when his commanding presence and transcendent abilities electrified the Jewish community. Few Jews had imagined an incumbent of the classical Reform congregation's pulpit expertly addressing large groups in Yiddish, or winning recognition as a Hebrew orator. Moreover, the rabbi of The Temple demonstrated substantial scholarly capacities in his *History of Messianic Speculation in Israel: From the First Through the Seventeenth Centuries*, which he published in 1927. The subject concerned the thinking and the calculations which sought to penetrate the divinely fixed riddle of the time of the Messiah's advent to redeem Israel. Solidly based on an abundance of sources, the *History of Messianic Speculation* won Silver standing as a scholar; it remains the leading work of Jewish learning written by a Clevelander.[39]

In or out of his pulpit, Silver was an orator of overpowering force and brilliance and persuasiveness, ranking among the greatest ever heard in America, or in the Zionist movement. Meticulously preparing his addresses with facts and quotations, he appealed powerfully to the rationality and idealism of his hearers while assailing his opponents with withering sarcasm and irony. His command was as sure off the platform as on it. A tall man of leonine appearance, he was a scorching polemicist and an implacable opponent.

Besides serving The Temple which he dominated, and the Jewish community whose foremost figure he became within a decade of his arrival, and in addition to his Zionist work which won him an honored place in modern Jewish history, Abba Hillel Silver was a citizen of Cleveland who played a distinguished role in the city's affairs. Characteristically, he showed little interest in the merely proper and well-established institutions, preferring to devote himself to causes which he believed in. These included world peace, inter-religious understanding, birth control, and the problem of industrial labor.

It was in the latter field that Silver's contributions were the most significant. They began with his address in Public Square in 1919 denouncing the postwar open shop drive, and continued with his advocacy of trade unionism as the indispensable means to industrial peace and justice for working men. His sermon on "The Coming Industrial Struggle—The Open vs. the Closed Shop' in December, 1920, denied that the issue was one of inalienable rights of employer or employee. It was a question of "social utility and beneficence, from the point of view of the highest good of the commonwealth, of the people, of the community as a whole," and of labor's right to bargain collectively. While dubious of the closed shop and reprimanding trade unions for numerous failures to honor agreements, Silver endorsed "the shop where union labor is recognized as an agency for collective bargaining, or where, as in some instances, it is given a preferential position."[40] The garment unions, with their sharing in employers' concern for productivity and profits, and their welfare and unemployment provisions, well expressed Silver's conception of trade unionism. Richman Brothers' enlightened labor policies led him to disapprove of attempts to unionize their factories. General humane concerns, together with the experiences of Jewish workers in the seasonal garment trade, may have encouraged Silver's special interest in the problem of unemployment. Serving as chairman of the Ohio Commission on Unemployment Insurance, he became one of the American pioneers for this insurance concept. These multiple interests reinforced one another. Combined with his intellect and character, they secured a position for Abba Hillel Silver such as no other Jew ever attained in Cleveland.[41]

Rabbi Solomon Goldman (1893–1953) arrived in Cleveland in 1918 as rabbi of B'nai Jeshurun. With a personal background similar to Silver's, Goldman had become a Conservative rabbi, a graduate of the Jewish Theological Seminary. Like Silver, Goldman possessed notable oratorical ability and scholarly capacity; unlike Silver, he had stormy years with the two congregations he served during he decade in Cleveland. He sought to mold B'nai Jeshurun, the sometime Hungarian congregation, into a Jewish community center. Although admired and respected for his success in enlarging the congregation and in drawing younger people, he declined to remain in this often frustrating position and transferred to Anshe Emeth, now the Cleveland Jewish Center. There his leadership in transforming the half-century-old Orthodox congregation into a Conservative one encountered tenacious opposition which culminated in a lawsuit.

Rabbi Goldman, a man of fervor and vitality, was the leading supporter of modern Hebrew education in the city and was an effective advocate at the Federation of Jewish Charities of such new causes as the Orthodox Jewish Children's Home and the Bureau of Jewish Education. Socially, his role was that of spokesman and religious guide for Cleveland Jewry's new middle class, which rose out of immigrant ranks and did not enroll in Reform Temples. Goldman's potential as a Jewish communal leader was restricted by difficulties within his congregations and by the ascendancy of Silver. Perhaps these reasons led him to cut short his outstanding career in Cleveland and to leave for Chicago in 1929.[42]

Rabbi Louis Wolsey, once mildly rebellious against established Reform, had turned anti-Zionist and embraced classical Reform during the very years when the Reform constituency was shifting towards his earlier views. When Wolsey left for a Philadelphia pulpit in 1925 in an atmosphere of discord—although he strongly denied he and the Euclid Avenue Temple Board had clashed—his successor was of the new Silver-Goldman variety.[43] Barnet R. Brickner (1892–1958) was contemporary in age and personal background with his brilliant young colleagues: immigrant child, the Lower East Side of New York, traditional Judaism, Zionism. He had entered the rabbinate with experience in Jewish education and social work. Broadly conceiving religion as the inner moral control over man and civilization, the new rabbi of the Euclid Avenue Temple declared in his inaugural sermon in 1925 that "the most tragic spiritual occurrence of our times is the decided tendency of life and religion to drift apart. . . ." The "mighty protest" which once was Reform Judaism had sought

> to release the freeborn spirit of Jewish prophecy from the narrow Ghetto moulds into which historic necessity had forced it. . . . Its message was that Judaism is in consonance with reason and science, that it was free of dogmas and its creed was a life, lived in conformity with the principles of social justice, righteousness and brotherly love.

Reform, which aspired to have the Jews "again become a spiritual force in the world's life has deteriorated into a minority sect, and a cult within Israel." Rabbi Brickner brought to his new congregation's attention the rift between life and Judaism and Reform Judaism's loss of appeal to "the masses of the Jewish people." To meet these challenges he proposed to restore Reform's "original function of changing the spirit of Ghetto Judaism; and to make it the religion of all Jews to bring it into consonance with modern life." It was essential "to eliminate the intolerable dualism of double standard between profession and practice. . . ." The rabbi had in mind many young people, especially sensitive to social and intellectual currents, who were "lost in the fog of doubts" and placed their faith "in the hope of an indiscriminate cosmopolitan world brotherhood." He would assure them that "in and through Judaism they may find the best road to world fellowship."[44] To this large program Barnet R. Brickner devoted thirty-three years' service at the Euclid Avenue Temple, where his fervor and success as an educator were among his notable qualities. A strong and effective preacher who spoke extensively before many audiences, he possessed a personal warmth and geniality that attracted many to his congregation.[45]

The fourth leader was Abraham H. Friedland (1891–1939), yet another Lower East Side immigrant youth of traditional education, whose magnetic ability as a teacher in the Hebraic Zionist philosophy brought him to Cleveland to head the Cleveland Talmud Torah and the Bureau of Jewish Education. Poet, essayist, lecturer, and teacher par excellence, Friedland was the focal personality not only of Cleveland's Jewish education but of all Hebraic and Zionist cultural life in the city. More than his three rabbinic contemporaries, he raised disciples and followers, notwithstanding acute financial stress in his work. Friedland was a national leader of American Hebrew culture until his early death.

At the congregational level, the notable developments of the 1920s were the founding of Conservative Judaism in Cleveland and the very gradual trend back towards Jewish tradition on the part of Reform. Contrary to the situation in most cities, the Conservative congregations were not founded as such, nor were they declining Orthodox bodies seeking rejuvenation. Both were large and prospering when they officially altered their religious orientation, as most of their members had already done in their personal lives.

The two Conservative congregations were B'nai Jeshurun

and Anshe Emeth, Rabbi Margolies' former synagogue. The latter, as the Cleveland Jewish Center, erected a splendid building on East 105th Street with full educational provisions as well as an elaborate social and sports center. Rabbi Samuel Benjamin, trained in law and ordained by the Jewish Theological Seminary, wrathfully left the Center after two years, claiming that he was not receiving support in his religious and Zionist efforts; he then became rabbi of the large Orthodox congregation Oheb Zedek.[46] Under Rabbi Goldman, Benjamin's successor, the congregation's Orthodoxy was definitely breached. A bitter-end struggle took place over the symbolic issue of mixed seating, but the court's refusal to interfere in the majority's decision to seat men and women together left the Cleveland Jewish Center a Conservative congregation.[47]

Orthodox tradition at B'nai Jeshurun, on the other hand, had been less consistent. Rabbi Abraham Nowak, of Orthodox training but a Conservative rabbi, succeeded Goldman in 1923. The congregation built its Moorish-Byzantine brick edifice in Cleveland Heights at a cost of $1,000,000, dedicating it in 1926 —sixty years after Herman Sampliner's *minyan* first assembled in California Alley.[48] It assumed as its unofficial name, The Temple on the Heights.

One year earlier, Rabbi Silver had presided over the opening services of The Temple, newly built at East 105th Street and Ansel Road. It was in modified Byzantine style, with septagonal walls and interior arches supporting a great gold-tiled dome.[49] Contrary to the trend in other congregations at this time, The Temple relinquished all its activities which were not directly related to religious education and worship.[50] As the largest and socially the foremost congregation in Cleveland, with a membership which rose to 1,471 families in 1925, The Temple's policy stimulated its people to play active roles in communal life rather than focus on the synagogue as a place where their interests of whatever sort could be pursued.

Meanwhile, Euclid Avenue Temple also added members, as well as a wing for its existing structure. Never as "classical" in its Reform as The Temple, under Rabbi Brickner it began to restore "some of the more beautiful and significant customs which were inadvertently [!] omitted" by early Reform. These included Kol Nidre on the Day of Atonement and the Yizkor

memorial on some holidays for deceased relatives; a supposedly traditional "consecration service" for children beginning religious school was also introduced.[51]

Orthodox Judaism's adaptation to its American environment
proceeded slowly. A great many of its children quit the old-fashioned congregations, which lacked outward graces and were
wedded to Yiddish and East European ways, for Conservative
and   Reform places of worship, leaving old-timers and newcomers largely in control—a situation that tended to perpetuate
the original congregations' Orthodoxy. Oheb Zedek and Ohavei
Emunah, both reaching back to the early days of Russian immigration in the 1880s, relocated in the Glenville-East 105th Street
district,[52] as did Oer Chodosh Anshe Sfard, founded in 1897.[53]
Other Orthodox congregations included Tifereth Israel, Shomrei
Hadath, N'vai Zedek, and the Kinsman Jewish Center in that
area, and Sherith Jacob, Beth Hamidrosh Hagodol, Kenesseth
Israel, Anshe Marmoresh, Tetiever Ahavas Achim, Anshe
Grodno, Ahavath Zion, and Shomrei Shaboth in the Superior-
Thru area.[54] On the West Side, far from the Jewish neighborhoods, a little *minyan* (prayer assembly) existed from 1910
known as B'nai Israel. Its members succeeded in erecting a small
synagogue in 1926 on West 57th Street and Franklin Avenue for
the 214 Jewish families, approximately 1,000 individuals, who
lived in the area.[55]

A rabbinic arrival of 1925, Rabbi Israel Porath (1886–1974)
gradually became the central figure of the Orthodox rabbinate.
Born in the "old *yishuv*" of Lithuanian Jewry in Jerusalem and
given a traditional Talmudic education, Rabbi Porath had become a religious Zionist as a disciple of Rabbi Abraham Isaac
Kook. After playing a role in Jerusalem public life, particularly
in mitigating the hardships of World War I and its aftermath, the
rabbi arrived "temporarily" with his large family in 1923. In 1925
he assumed the rabbinate of Oheb Zedek, where he continued to
work on his multi-volumed *Mavo Ha-Talmud* (Introduction to
the Talmud), a topical exposition of the tractates of the Talmud
in clear, contemporary Hebrew.[56]

Jewish cultural life during the 1920's reached a level previously unknown. Zionism in Cleveland, thanks to its very firm roots

among local Hebraists, had a cultural emphasis perhaps stronger than anywhere else in the land. Hebrew-speaking groups met often.[57] The Cleveland Jewish Singing Society was an active amateur group founded about 1914. Frank Nowodworski and Morris Traeger were their guiding lights for many years.[58] Now and then Hebrew plays were presented, of which the most memorable were six performances by the Moscow Hebrew Art Players who visited Cleveland en route to settling permanently in Palestine as Habimah, the national theatre.[59] The most prominent activity of the secular, intellectual Yiddish Culture Gesellschaft was its Yiddish Dramatic Studio, which presented plays of a high standard. The Gesellschaft also conducted a children's literary and dramatic group; in addition, it heard regular lectures on political and cultural themes.[60] Other Yiddish plays were also performed in Cleveland, some of which were distinguished. Branches of the Cleveland Public Library housed in Council Educational Alliance buildings boasted collections of Judaica, mainly in Yiddish.[61] Cleveland Cultural Gardens, sponsored by the city's ethnic groups, contained a sylvan Hebrew Cultural Garden (Gan Ivri).[62] Its dedication in 1926 was adorned by the presence of Chaim Nachman Bialik, the great Hebrew poet, as the guest of honor.[63] The great composer Ernest Bloch (1880–1959) came to Cleveland in 1920 to establish and head the Cleveland Institute of Music. During his five years at this position Bloch continued to deepen his Jewish musical interests.[64]

It was characteristic of Jewish life in Cleveland of the 1920s that the Jewish community was not only an abstraction for the sum of its separate institutions. Already an organic entity was beginning to emerge.

In 1920 the Federation of Jewish Charities was still a comparatively simple organization which raised and disbursed funds for the principal Jewish charities of the city and for a few national institutions. Overseas aid was a temporary supplement. Of the $259,475 distributed by the F.J.C. in 1920, $189,500 went to Mount Sinai Hospital, the Hebrew Relief Association, the Educational Alliance, and Camp Wise, while $45,000 was appropriated to institutions for children and the aged.[65] The 1920s were a decade of far-reaching changes in the Federation itself and in its beneficiaries. Some of these changes came about subtly, and others by mature decision; a few were the result of insistent pressure.

The Federation joined the civic philanthropic establishment by affiliating in 1919 with the recently founded Cleveland Community Fund. The Jewish group, however, declined the Fund's suggestion that it consider a merger.[66] The theory was that combined fund-raising would save administrative expense and balance civic charities better—the original reasons for the Federation's existence. The Jewish partners must have welcomed their full share in this major civic enterprise, whose leaders were ranking names in Cleveland life.

It was to be a long-lived partnership, but one not without problems. When the Community Fund took over the Federation's list of contributors, it expected that they would contribute as least as well to the Fund as to the Federation: this was the financial foundation of the partnership. But this expectation was not fulfilled. President Charles Eisenman chidingly noted in 1922 that

> the Jewish community of this city had during the period of participation with the Community Fund, been relieved of a large financial responsibility and saved considerable money through having given a less amount to the Fund than was withdrawn for Jewish purposes . . . many had contributed to the Fund, while many more had escaped doing so, subscribing sums woefully inadequate to the needs and entirely out of accord with their respective resources.[67]

The first four years' affiliation resulted in more withdrawn for Jewish purposes than had been put in by Jewish donations.[68] This huge discrepancy was due mainly to large withdrawals for Jewish overseas aid which the Community Fund, essentially a local body, could not long finance. Probably many Jews were not yet accustomed to giving large enough amounts to a rather remote, non-Jewish institution, even when it provided for many of their needs. The Jewish record was embarrassing to the Federation, and also served to limit plans for unifying Jewish communal life by taking over the charities of the East European immigrants. Federation leaders felt, however, that the Community Fund was failing to develop its fund-raising methods, and that contributions were not adequate or not made at all because of inadequate techniques.[69] Yet the Community Fund, desiring to maintain the connection with the Jewish community, provided for the new Jewish agencies. Notwithstanding grave budgetary problems, it also permitted the Jewish Social Service Association to grant higher budgets for needy Jewish families than those given by the Associated Charities.[70] The Federation of Jewish Charities also saw the value of the affiliation. E.M. Baker, who succeeded to the Federation presidency upon Charles Eisenman's death in 1923, may have expressed it best when he

> appealed for a broad and generous support of the Community Fund as one of the best weapons conceivable with which to combat the potential dangers that arise out of group and class conflicts and petty jealousies. Mr. Baker pointed out further that no claim upon the Jews as a member of the community, was more vital or valid than that of the Community Fund.[71]

Yet the Federation was cramped in several respects by its alliance with the Community Fund. It could not take in the Bureau of Jewish Education, since religious education did not receive Community Fund support, and institutions which the Federation wished to support through the Fund were not matched by increased Jewish giving. Above all, the Community Fund was unable to do anything towards the overseas calls upon American Jewish generosity. Early in 1926 the Board of the Federation decided on a campaign combining overseas relief with improving Camp Wise for underprivileged Jewish children. Rabbi Silver carried the day for a still larger effort: "the time seemed ripe for an effort to unify all interests in the Jewish Community of Cleveland . . . " by taking in still other "Orthodox" institutions.[72] Seeing "the opportunity which such a combined drive would afford the Federation to establish the kind of a contact with the entire Jewish Community obtained prior to the organization of the Community Fund," the Federation trustees agreed.[73] The civic solidarity expressed in the Community Fund connection had its disadvantages:

Because of the long lapse which had ensued in Cleveland, especially, and in many other communities where foreign relief funds
had come from Community Chests and where the direct responsibility for the raising and subscription of these funds had been
lifted from the shoulders of the Jewish Communities, there had
been a relapse in the sense of obligation of Jews for their own
and this situation in turn had compelled communities everywhere
to unite a number of causes of local character with the foreign
relief appeal, the plea for all being made on the basis of a re-
vitalizing of Jewish consciousness and sense of responsibility.[74]

The result of the appeal far exceeded the hopes, as $700,000
was pledged by some 6,300 persons.[75] However, the Community
Fund was disturbed at the prospect of separate, successful Jewish appeals, and planned to make a great effort in 1929 to meet
local Jewish needs fully.[76]

The Federation's main internal interest lay in Jewish communal consolidation. It realized the "urgent necessity for some
action which will tend in the near future to harmonize . . .
social welfare work" within the Jewish community, and in
1923 decided on "a survey of the local philanthropic situation
by some unbiased outside authority provided that such a survey
were made under the auspices of all of the interests affected.
. . ."[77] The survey, directed by Samuel A. Goldsmith for the
Bureau of Jewish Social Research, was a landmark in the history of Cleveland Jewry. Besides making a population study
(quoted in Chapter 8) it examined thoroughly each Federation
institution and many unaffiliated ones. Above all, the survey
pointed out the lacunae and unfilled needs of Cleveland Jewish
life. A critical eye was also cast upon the Federation itself.
Underlying the manifold recommendations was the conviction
that the Jews required unity, that philanthropy could best unite
them, and that the Federation had the experience and prestige
to accomplish this. It had to rise above merely fiscal functions
to find and meet the needs of Cleveland Jewry in the fields of
welfare, health, recreation, and Jewish education.

The survey emphasized that the "Orthodox" (actually East
European immigrant, not necessarily Orthodox in religious observance) sub-community had to be regarded as the Jewish community of the future. "With the growing power and self-con-

sciousness of the Orthodox Jewish group, every large Jewish community has had to face the difficult problem of unifying and coordinating the efforts of sometimes divergent views or interests within the Jewish community."[78] Mount Sinai Hospital, for one, disregarded this need. "The personal customs of attitudes of the members of the board of trustees ought not to control its policy," and kosher food ought to be provided for its patients.[79] Meanwhile, the institution was greatly enlarged by the building of a nurses' home, a laboratory building, and an out-patient structure.[80] The survey further recommended that the Federation and its institutions should be closed on the Sabbath and Jewish holidays. Responsibility had to be undertaken in the field of Jewish education:

> From the standpoint of a full Americanization program, as well as from the standpoint of satisfying the wants of a considerable number of people in the Jewish community—a want that is to this considerable number of people a paramount need—Jewish education has come more and more to be of intense interest to all leaders of Jewish community welfare.[81]

To stir interest in Jewish education, and to improve Jewish schooling, a Board of Jewish Education was needed. Worthwhile recreation and social activities for all ages also required Federation initiative.

The Federation adopted virtually this entire program, which charted most of its direction until World War II. The Orthodox Home for the Aged, the Orthodox Jewish Orphan Asylum, and the Jewish Day Nursery became affiliated and seated representatives upon the Federation's Board; steps were taken to encourage the "kosherization" of the hospital and other affiliates; an active Functional Relations Committee and a Jewish Recreation Council scrutinized the work of most of its agencies. As Research Director, a young man of promise, Dr. John Slawson, provided executive and intellectual leadership for a productive four years.[82] To mark these far-reaching changes in its role, the Federation of Jewish Charities altered its name in 1926 to the Jewish Welfare Federation, while the Hebrew Relief Association likewise renamed itself the Jewish Social Service Association. The Federation's volume of business, to judge from the quantity of its records, must have trebled from its pre-World War I dimensions. With direct fund-raising now assigned to the Community Fund, it was understandable that the Federation should expand its activity into other areas. By 1929 the effects of Federation thought and planning could be felt throughout Cleveland Jewry.

Planning was often accompanied by controversy. Child care was a source of strife all through the 1920s. The Jewish Orphan Home was a B'nai B'rith regional institution over half a century old, boasted a wealthy Board of Directors including several leading Cleveland Jews, and was a notable example of an orphan home at its best. Its 280 children aged six to sixteen were brought up in an atmosphere of German-Jewish Reform. Under the direction of Michael Sharlitt, himself brought up in a Jewish orphanage, it relaxed its regimen to allow for unlimited visiting by relatives, individual clothing instead of uniforms, and longer education. Very different was the Orthodox Jewish Orphan Asylum, the creation of immigrant Jews who desired an unbringing for its thirty children in accord with their own ways. Unlike the Jewish Orphan Home, it was pinched for money and its methods and environment were sub-standard, which led to difficulties with the State Board of Charities' inspectors.

The Federation, however, was committed to foster homes, in accordance with the expert view of the time. Throughout the 1920s it urged, bickered, and even publicly disputed with the giant as well as the puny orphanage. Unable to secure the closing of the Orthodox home, it tried with slight success to control child placement and raise standards. The powerful Jewish Orphan Home was with difficulty prevailed upon to reduce the planned size of its new buildings from 350 to 250 beds—any thought of becoming a foster placing institution or of specializing in disturbed children was dismissed. In addition to its own resources it received $200,000 as a bequest from Col. Oliver H. Payne, a non-Jewish oil millionaire who admired the institution. After a decade of such embroilments over child care, the Jewish Welfare Federation succeeded neither in making the institutions change their policies nor in persuading them to cooperate with plans for centralizing local child care. While it was bickering with the Federation, the home was also contesting in the courts a zoning ordinance of University Heights which prevented its new buildings from being constructed. Convinced that the intention of the ordinance was discriminatory, the J.O.H. won the case against its constitutionality in the U.S. Circuit Court of Appeals. When the Supreme Court refused to hear the case in 1927, victory was final. Construction then began on what was to be known as the Bellefaire campus.[83]

EDUCATION AND COMMUNITY

One of the most far-reaching of the Survey recommendations was for founding "a Board of Jewish Education with full-time paid executive to deal with problems of Jewish education for the entire community."[84] There were of course numerous Jewish schools in the city, predominantly Sunday schools. In 1923 Euclid Avenue Temple enrolled 1,025 pupils and The Temple 1,023, and both were growing. These were among the best Sunday schools in the country, with paid teachers closely supervised by their rabbis, planned curriculum, and a full five-year course of study. The same number of pupils, 1,025, were enrolled in three free Sabbath schools of the Council of Jewish Women. Socially they were at the other end of the scale, meeting in the poorer Jewish neighborhoods on Saturday afternoons. The Council Sabbath schools imitated the Temples' Sunday schools but lacked direction and supervision. Their yearly turnover exceeded 50 percent of enrollment.

Arising from East European orthodoxy was the Yeshivah Adath B'nai Israel. It had some 300 boys in two schools and appears to have remained as little affected as possible by the new winds of education. It seems to have been more or less a large *heder* and provided Bar Mitzvah preparation for its youthful clientele. Far different was the Workmen's Circle Folk Schule in Mount Pleasant. Committed to secular, Yiddish-speaking ethnicity, it taught

a couple of hundred pupils. . . . Their program is entirely Yiddish, yet they do accomplish something in the direction of acquainting the Jewish child with traditional Jewish culture. There is a movement going on now amongst the radical Jewish groups for the introduction of the Hebrew language and, thereby, also the religious phase, into the curricula of their schools.[85]

The Jewish National Workers' Alliance for a time operated a Yiddish school in a Zionist spirit.[86]

The Cleveland Hebrew School (Talmud Torah) burst forward during the early 1920s to attain its maximum growth. In 1920 it paid $58,000 for the spacious Gesangverein on East 55th Street,[87] and it also had five branches. Next year Abraham H. Friedland arrived from New York as the school's Educational Director, thus placing upon the Cleveland scene a brilliant and magnetic individual. His pedagogic gifts were also manifest in several dozen little books of children's Hebrew stories which Friedland wrote for schools.

The enrollment for daily sessions at the Hebrew School multiplied from 867 in 1919[88] to 2,300 four years later.[89] The curriculum was a model for its time, with the children progressing from simple beginnings to studying the Biblical prophets and modern Hebrew literature. A Hebrew high school was built upon the Talmud Torah. Throughout, the emphasis lay upon Hebraic humanism, and neither traditional orthodoxy nor even modernized tradition loomed large in the program. It was fitting that when the Palestine Mandate was ratified in 1922 the children of the Hebrew Schools marked the event by a parade through the Jewish neighborhood. Thousands heard bands and singing, and observed three floats which depicted the gloom of exile, the signing of the Mandate, and the flourishing farms and vineyards of reborn Palestine.[90]

Friedland was quite candid in his views with his own committee:

> after many years of contemplation, he is of the conviction that the only product worth preserving in what is spoken of as Jewishness, is Jewish culture; that Hebrew is the most significant group integrator; that Hebrew is probably the only language making for individual Jewish creativeness; that language and literature are progressively becoming the only distinguishing features of an ethnic culture.[91]

Under its dynamic principal, the Cleveland Hebrew School established a salary scale by which teachers could earn up to a nearly unheard of $200 a month, and head teachers and principals $300.[92] Thus, the institution had a corps of able teachers for its well-designed curriculum.

The accomplishments of the Hebrew School became known all over the country, but it was hag-ridden by a deficit which increased yearly. By 1926 the debt reached $60,000.[93] For all his talents, Friedland was not financially skillful. He preferred to employ funds available from appeals to expand the school rather than to retrench and pay debts. At the same time his institution was slowly undermined by declining enrollment, which fell from 2,300 in 1923 to 1,500 by 1929.

The Bureau of Jewish Education first organized in 1924, and Rabbi Abba Hillel Silver was its first Chairman.[94] It was generally agreed, in the spirit of the Community Survey, that the Bureau (a designation more self-limiting than Board) should not take "its primary duty" to be the financing of existing schools, but should promote "more efficient utilization of present facilities and a program to encourage the demand for Jewish education so that more of the 12,000 Jewish children of school age not now receiving such education, might be brought in touch with the schools."[95] Since the Community Fund did not support religious education, the Federation only promised benevolent interest.[96] The Bureau thus had to raise its own funds, but the four largest congregations pledged their support.[97] Before 1930 the Bureau conducted two moderately successful public campaigns, raising $65,000 and $51,000. In effect, the Bureau was controlled by the Hebrew Schools; A. H. Friedland became Executive Director of the Bureau and most funds were allegedly channeled to that institution. Many in the native Reform group were distressed with the "intensive Hebrew education curriculum," which, however, "with longer stay in this country . . . might be subject to a great deal of modification." The Talmud Torah's leaders replied that it was the community-sponsored Sunday schools which were "foreign and unnatural," and that this form of education "is a new one with the Jewish masses. . . ."[98] As the Hebrew Schools' financial position worsened, ideological conflicts became sharp and open, in turn followed by semi-public personal quarrels.[99] By 1929 the way lay open for the tragic dissensions and decline of the 1930s.

X

Depression Crisis and Communal Expansion, 1929–1945

THE economic disaster which struck America and the world in 1929 was foreshadowed in Cleveland. Business and industry in the city declined in 1927, while unemployment rose there and in other heavily industrial cities.[1] By 1928 the number of families requiring assistance from the Jewish Social Service Bureau (the former Hebrew Relief Society) seems to have gone up nearly 50 percent from the preceding year or two.[2] The new clients were probably distressed for some time before turning to the Bureau; over 75 percent of the Bureau's cases were skilled craftsmen and businessmen, who presumably had some resources in time of need.[3] The Cleveland Hebrew School was in deep fiscal trouble in 1929 "on account of the present depressed financial conditions which is [sic] more noticeable among the parents of the Hebrew Schools' pupils," who came from the poorer classes.[4]

This was the overture to the disaster beginning in the winter of 1929–1930. Jewish distress was part of the general distress of the city and state. Early in 1930 3,000 unemployed men, incited by Communist speakers, attempted to storm City Hall.[5] Factories were discharging workers en masse. Conditions in the ladies' garment industry persuaded employers in 1931 to discontinue the elaborate system of production standards and return to piecework, and the union could do nothing to prevent this decision.[6]

As the economic collapse continued, "a tremendous increase in the number of material relief families due to the industrial situation . . ." was reported by the Jewish Social Service Bureau.[7] There was "every indication that the demand for help during this Winter and the ensuing year [of 1931] will be greater. . . ."[8] The city's unemployment rate for males of gainful employment age stood at 14.8 percent in 1930 and leaped the next year to a terrifying 35.1 percent—the highest in any major American city. This figure, moreover, omitted those who could secure only part-time work.

The unemployment was frightening not only because of its extent, but also due to the social groups which it struck. Early in the bleak year of 1931, "insistent and increasing demand" for aid was coming from families whose sources of income have been affected not alone by unemployment but also by the inroads of present day business operations upon their means of livelihood as merchants and tradesmen."[9] One man who had been president of a large synagogue and gave a $10,000 contribution to Palestine in 1924 was destitute in 1934. These ruined businessmen were often older men, and it seemed that their misfortune might "present . . . needs of a more permanent character."[10]

> Our Jewish people have asked help later because they are tradesmen. They will buy and sell as long as there are those to trade with. Coming to us now in increasing numbers are the small merchant, the builder and real estate dealer. In fact, a new clientele is being created—the so-called "white collar" class. There has been an intensification and increase of the various problems of distress and maladjustment among our Jewish families. Economic dislocation, widely distributed, has resulted in increasing the area of dependency. Increased unemployment and the reduction or discontinuance of income for many families have slowly exhausted the self-maintaining resources of ever-widening groups of our Jewish population. . . . a period such as we are passing through takes its toll in various forms of physical illnesses, particularly that of undernourished children, to say nothing of mental conflict and mental illness, depression and despondency and the increasing number of problems of delinquency.[11]

It soon became clear that aid from private charity, whatever might be said of it during normal times, was impossible during the crisis. There was noted "a return of unorganized and individualistic forms of friendly assistance . . . [by] those who are touched by the distress and suffering of their neighbors. . . ."[12]

No one knew just how many were unemployed. Rabbi Abba Hillel Silver, extremely well-informed, estimated that 60,000 families, or 300,000 to 350,000 persons had their breadwinner

unemployed in April, 1932. Such a catastrophe had never before been known. The city of Cleveland had to look to the conservative Republican administration of the State of Ohio for
public aid to the unemployed. However, the amounts granted
were so inadequate and the terms so onerous that the unemployed were stirred to a resentment which many feared (and
some hoped, in those days) boded social revolution. Public
funds were granted to private agencies for distribution; the
State Relief Commission gave to the Cuyahoga County Joint
Committee on Relief Measures, which subsidized the welfare
organizations. Early in 1933, before the New Deal revolution-
ized public policy towards unemployment relief, the Jewish
Social Service Bureau was strongly pressed by the Ohio State
Relief Commission to cut back its standards. Otherwise, the
Commission threatened, it would be "unwilling to recommend
further funds to be administered by that agency on the present
basis."[13] The Commission objected especially to the Jewish
agency's raising the monthly family cost from $39.21 in the sum-
mer of 1932 to $45.10 by December of the same year.[14] It re-
iterated the question why Jewish clients feasted on a weekly
food budget of $6.50 for a family of five compared to the $4.25
given by the Associated Charities, and why Jews were provided
with minuscule rent, fuel, and electricity subsidies contrary to
accepted practice.[15]

Appealing to public opinion, Rabbi Silver assailed the policy
which required destitution before any public aid would be given.
He denounced the pitiful relief being granted—$3.48 weekly for
a family of four—and predicted future problems of illness, mal-
nutrition, and moral damage. Cleveland contrasted poorly with
other American cities, and America did worse than did England
with her unemployed. In April, 1932, Silver demanded higher
relief based on higher income taxes, an extensive program of
work for the unemployed, and higher wages and shorter hours
rather than excess speculative profits.[16]

Such liberal ideas began to be put into effect a year later in
the New Deal. The State of Ohio, however, declined to support
the Jewish community's desperate effort to prevent its carefully
wrought structure of social service from sinking to paltry hand-
outs. The Relief Commission decided to withhold relief money

from Cuyahoga County until the Jewish Social Service Bureau ceased its extravagance and kept its family budgets within 10 percent of the Associated Charities average; allowances were to be lowered from $37 per month to a maximum of $21.[17] Word of the decree was published in newspapers. Cleveland banks were shut and a new president was about to enter the White House when, on March 3, 1933, Cleveland Jewish unemployed rioted at the office of the Jewish Social Service. Bureau.[18]

The six months which followed the courageous resistance of the Jewish Social Service Bureau, led by its president, Marc Grossman, produced a remarkable vindication. By the end of March, 1933, the Jewish Social Service Bureau was granted the full food budget it requested, and shortly afterwards it was enabled to receive some State funds for its clients' rent, fuel, and electricity.[19] As the New Deal's relief measures took over from the exhausted private organizations, the food standards of the Jewish agency were not only continued but were explicitly applied to all Cleveland cases.[20] Its central role in raising public relief standards was thankfully recognized.[21]

The crisis of the 1930s not only shook the economic order but also impelled many to rethink the social assumptions by which they had lived. Wealthy leaders of Jewish social welfare, generous at heart while pronouncedly conservative in their social views, changed their mind over the vital question of the government's role in society, particularly in times of distress. Already in 1928 Mrs. Siegmund Herzog, President of the Jewish Welfare Federation, had declared that "the policy of 'laissez faire' in social work is as bad as it is in the fields of economics and business."[22] In 1931, however, as the depression was deepening, Mrs. Herzog's successor, Sol Reinthal, looked back over a year "of great concern and loss to us all. No one could have escaped the back-swing of the pendulum from the peak which was reached in over speculation in business and over indulgence in private life." Linking economic suffering to moral excess in conservative moralistic fashion, Reinthal stressed the obligations of private charity.[23] Cleveland's leading rabbis addressed themselves to the ills of the day. Rabbi Nowak and Rabbi Brickner joined Rabbi Silver. Brickner, for example, spoke in 1934 of "socialized capitalism" and a "new social order," while

Silver assailed with names and facts the Van Sweringen brothers and other financial malefactors who had swindled Cleveland's common people of their meager savings.[24]

Concern rose over the plight of jobless, demoralized youth. Walter L. Solomon, headworker of the Council Educational Alliance in Mount Pleasant, reporting early in 1934, saw deeply into the state of mind of the Jewish youth:

> As I observe the young people in this fourth year of the depression I am appalled by their cynical acceptance of things as they are. They are not avid for tools of understanding; they reject opportunities for vocational preparation, seeing, as they do, that fitness is no guarantee of work. . . . Our day classes lose in popularity as the depression drags on. The ever increasing group of idle high school graduates who have never worked is little interested in serious preparation for industrial or political life. They see no hope of participation in the first and are quite disillusioned about the latter. Their long hours of dull loafing are punctuated only by the search for pleasure and more pleasure—anything to add spice to the unending monotony of the days.[25]

VOCATIONAL AND RESIDENTIAL SHIFTS

Notwithstanding the prevasive gloom and sense of futility about preparing for a blank future, the occupational distribution of Cleveland Jewry continued to shift. The categories employed by the U.S. Census, when applied to a sample of the city's Jews, show little outward change during the depression years:

Category	% in 1936	% change from 1923
Professional, technical, and kindred	9%	+1%
Managers, officials, proprietors	29%	+8%
Clerical and kindred	17%	−6%
Sales	19%	−6%
Craftsmen, foremen, and kindred	12%	−3%
Private household	0%	0%
Service workers	7%	+6%
Laborers	3%	−1%
Total sample	(981)	(1,050)

The "managers, officials, and proprietors" include 100 listed as "presidents" and "proprietors" of firms which were a new Directory category. Together with independent grocers and other food dealers, the number of independent Jewish businessmen, whatever their prosperity, increased considerably. Most of the new recruits to "service" appear to have been drivers, while the uncertainty of categories suggests that many who were in "sales" may have been shopkeepers. The older Jewish immigrant trades continued their decline, on the other hand. Peddlers and hucksters, numbering 46 in the 1923 sample and 27 in that of 1930, dropped still further to 20 in 1936. The number of tailors fell precipitously; 83 in 1923 and 65 in 1930, it was merely 31 in 1936. Carpenters and bricklayers, 33 in 1923 and again in 1930, fell to 15 in 1936. Economic conditions perhaps drove some unemployed tailors and carpenters into other fields, but it is more probable that these were aging craftsmen whose places were not being taken by fresh Jewish recruits.[26] Clerical and managerial work and small business were the prevailing sources of livelihood.

The number of Jews in professions rose steadily. A careful estimate for 1938 showed a remarkable increase in Jewish physicians to 402, from 165 in 1925. With the Jews approximately 7.7 percent of Cleveland's total population, their representation in professions was heavy:[27]

	Number of Jews	Proportion of Cleveland Total
Physicians	402	20.8%
Dentists	208	17.8%
Lawyers	658	23.1%
Teachers	253	4.7%
Pharmacists	370	26.1%
Engineers	31	2.2%
Architects	12	5.0%

To the 1,944 Cleveland Jews who practiced these seven professions could be added one to two hundred rabbis, social workers, and Jewish educators.

Taking the entrepreneurial picture as a whole, Cleveland Jews were prominent in department stores, service trades, film distribution and exhibition, scrap metal, and building and real estate. The city's industrial scene showed extensive Jewish representation in printing and publishing, paints, plumbing fixtures, garments, meat packing, and textiles. Such men as I. F. Freiberger and Edgar A. Hahn, a lawyer, were important in banking.[28]

During the decade of economic crisis the city's population grew at the slowest rate in its history. From 902,700 in mid-1930, the number of Clevelanders reached 994,700 in mid-1940.[29] In 1937, when the population was estimated at 967,100, there were 25,304 Jewish families, or 91,073 Jewish individuals, in Cuyahoga County. Within the decade which began in 1924, Jewish child population of elementary and high school age shrunk by a reported 22 percent to stand at 14,531 in 1934. The conclusion was drawn that birth control had become prevalent, especially after the economic downturn, which occurred from 1926 in Cleveland. So sharp a decline in the number of prospective Jewish adults for the 1940s and later was likely to mean still fewer children and an aging Jewish population.[30]

The suburban movement, which would sweep Cleveland Jewry beyond the city's limits between 1945 and 1960, was under way in limited form.[31] By 1940 Cleveland Heights ranked second as a Jewish neighborhood, and during the World War II years the movement into the area continued. It was recognized that "Cleveland Heights is the future principal center of Jewish residence in Cleveland, if it has not already become so."[32] In 1945 the Glenville-East 105th Street area was reported to be two-fifths Jewish, two-fifths non-Jewish white, and one-fifth black, and communal institutions in the area began to close and move as the trend continued.[33] Kinsman-Mount Pleasant's Jews also decreased by one-third between 1937 and 1944.[34] Of Jewish families, 17,193 lived within the city, while 4,252 could be found in Cleveland Heights, 1,191 in East Cleveland, and 873 in Shaker Heights.[35] The heaviest Jewish concentration continued to be Glenville-East 105th, followed by Kinsman-Mount Pleasant; the old immigrant neighborhoods had disappeared. More prosperous Jews were moving further east; thus, The Temple on East 105th Street and the Euclid Avenue Temple on Euclid Avenue and East 82nd Street had very few of their members nearby. The Jewish Center, on the other hand, was surrounded by the homes of its people, and the same could be said of the other Orthodox and Conservative congregations.[36] "Suburban neighborhoods were considered far more predominantly native born than that of Cleveland itself. . . . The suburbs have attracted the younger, native" Jews, who occupied "higher economic brackets and [are] more mobile than their aging foreign parents."[37] Illustrative of Jewish neighborhood concentration were Columbia and Chesterfield elementary schools and Glenville Senior High School, where more than 75 percent of the pupils were Jewish; nine other schools were at least one-third Jewish. On the other hand, 107 of Cleveland's 155 public schools had 1 percent or less Jewish pupils.[38]

The period between 1930 and 1945 may be called a demographic slowdown. In comparison with what occurred before and after these fifteen years, change was limited. Few persons during most of the 1930s were able to move to better neighborhoods; many were compelled to move to smaller, less costly dwellings. The indefatigable local demographer, Howard Whipple Green, also took note of the type of dwelling preferred by Cleveland Jews:

One third of all Jewish families . . . lived in two-family dwellings, up and down, as contrasted with 36% of all families living in such accommodations. The 26 per cent living in large apartment houses may be contrasted with the 13 per cent [among non-Jews] . . . and the 20 per cent living in one-family dwellings with the 36 per cent of all families in one-family dwellings.[39]

Mass immigration was a memory. The only Jewish immigrants from abroad who were reaching Cleveland came from Nazi Germany and numbered at least 1,000 in 1939. Some arrived after enduring concentration camps, especially after the infamous Kristallnacht (Night of Broken Glass) of November, 1938.[40] As a middle-class group of German culture fleeing from murderous oppression, they differed greatly from most Cleveland Jews. Moreover, during an era of mass unemployment it was extremely difficult for them to find even menial jobs, and to avoid creating the impression that they were displacing native Americans. False rumors flew that local department stores were discharging workers en masse in order to employ German-Jewish refugees, and "some Jews have complained about individual families whom they thought arrogant or unwilling to

accept positions which they thought they should take."[41] For the
déclassé German Jews, the 1930s were the worst of times to
settle in the United States. Hostility and scurrilous rumors
were inevitable during those bleak years even among some
Jews, notwithstanding the loathing felt by all Jews and the vast
majority of Americans for Nazism and its works. The Jewish
Social Service Bureau worked together with a special board to
find employment for the refugees, while the Council of Jewish
Women provided relief where needed. The newcomers aided one
another and, led by Rabbi Enoch H. Kronheim, one of their
number, established their own Gates of Hope Congregation
(later Mayfield-Hillcrest Temple).

Participation in Urban Society

Jews continued throughout the period to pursue an active
role in Cleveland life, but a dimension of concern over their
security appeared among them which had not been known before. To a large extent the Jewish concern was nourished by
foreign events. Persecution of Jews in backward Eastern Europe
seemed "normal" in their perception, but no one was morally
prepared for the triumphal march which brought Nazism to
power and Germany to barbarism. Already in 1931 the Jewish
Welfare Federation trustees met specially and "discussed at
length the spread of anti-Semitism in Germany," the ancestral
land of many present.[42]

Yet there was much reason to feel security and satisfaction,
and quite little objectively to stir real fear. Jews held positions
of prominence and distinction in the city's public life, although
the old established civic bodies for art, music, and higher education found little if any place for Jews. The one-time impoverished immigrant boy, Manuel Levine (1881–1938), a police
court judge from 1908, rose within the judiciary to become a
judge of the Ohio Court of Appeals in 1923. His judicial colleagues throughout the state elected him in 1931 Chief Justice
of the Courts of Appeals. The energetic, liberal Levine contributed notably by establishing the State's first probation department, pioneered in court-sponsored conciliation, founded
domestic relations courts, and led the way in citizenship prepara-

tion for immigrants.[43] Joseph H. Silbert (b. 1894) and Samuel H. Silbert (distantly related; 1882–1974) were both long-time members of the bench. "Judge Sam," who began in public life in 1909 as a City Council candidate, served as Common Pleas judge from 1924 to 1969, the last fifteen of these forty-five years as chief justice. Joseph Silbert began his long service on the Common Pleas bench in 1935, after serving a term in the State Legislature. Maurice Bernon was another judge of Common Pleas.[44] Ezra Shapiro (1903–1977) as a young lawyer functioned as City Law Director from 1933 to 1935, once serving by virtue of his office as acting mayor. He was also one of Cleveland's leading Zionists. Alfred A. Benesch, a veteran of public life, gave long, distinguished service on the elective Board of Education (1925–1962) and as State Director of Commerce (1935–1939). His interest in education led Benesch to champion teachers' rights to oppose compulsory military drill.[45]

Within organized business, Jews occupied a favorable position. Such key bodies as the Chamber of Commerce, the Rotary Club, the Better Business Bureau, the Kiwanis, and the Cleveland Stock Exchange had numerous Jewish members and officers, and a few presidents. The same could be said of some nonpartisan political groups such as the Foreign Affairs Council and the City Club, and of veterans' mass organizations like the American Legion and the Veterans of Foreign Wars. Such old-line bodies as the Daughters of the American Revolution and the Sons and Daughters of the Civil War were quite friendly. All in all, Jews also stood well in the professional societies of physicians, dentists, lawyers, engineers, and architects. In many they were active members and committeemen, and even presidents, reflecting their respected professional position and aiding their careers. Nevertheless, there were leading law firms, hospitals, and universities where there was no chance for a Jew to be employed except, occasionally, as a "token." Cleveland's newly organized Committee for Industrial Organization (CIO) was considered "completely friendly" while the Cleveland Federation of Labor was "friendly, but some of its leaders are anti-Semitic." On the other hand, the Associated Industries was a bastion of "strong anti-labor and anti-Communist Red-baiting" industrialists. "Individual leaders [were] suspected of anti-Semitic feeling." One of them, James F. Lincoln, a large electrical manufacturer, early in 1933 assailed three prominent advocates of unemployment insurance—Rabbi Silver, William M. Leiserson, and Isaac M. Rubinow—as Russian-born and therefore lacking the proper American spirit of individual responsibility and initiative. Denounced by Rabbis Brickner and Davidowitz (Silver was abroad), Lincoln again indicted the Russian birth of his opponents. This nativist identification of Jews with Russians, and of Russians with Communism, and that in turn with social legislation, was not unknown among political reactionaries.[46]

The pattern of exclusion at the social level was firmly rooted in Cleveland. The upper-class Union Club and University Club admitted no Jews, while the Athletic Club took in a few. Most of the forty Masonic lodges with 30,000 members admitted few or no Jews, and the Elks accepted none at all. The Moose, Eagles, and Odd Fellows were more cordial, while the Knights of Pythias, with 20,000 Cleveland members, had three all-Jewish lodges and was friendly to Jews who were scattered among its other lodges. The Jewish Excelsior Club expired in 1930, and its successor as the Jewish upper-class social center was the Oakwood Club.

During the 1920s and 1930s a comity developed between segments of Cleveland Judaism and Protestantism, mainly between Reform and upper-class liberal churches. These relations, which reached back to Rabbi Moses J. Gries' efforts during the 1890s, were institutionalized in such forms as the Reform Temples' annual institutes for Jewish study which Protestant ministers attended, and reciprocal visiting among young people to the Temples and churches. Regular discussions and meetings were held, and Rabbis Silver and Brickner were periodic speakers before church groups. The Protestant ministers were outspoken against Nazism and anti-Semitism. In general Cleveland was considered "fortunate in that its leading Protestant ministers are unusually cordial in their relations with Jews."

Relations were less cordial between Jews and Catholics, who now constituted the majority of the city's population and were, like most of the Jews, very much an immigrant group. The opposition of Jews to released time from the public schools for religious training and Jewish sympathy with the Spanish Loyalists, both contrary to Catholic views, contributed to tension and resentment.[47] In local lodges of the Knights of Columbus, the Catholic fraternal body, these Jewish views stirred "some sharp feeling and comment." The clerical leadership of the Archdiocese of Cleveland reflected some of this Catholic feeling by allowing its organ, "The Catholic Universe Bulletin," to give friendly prominence for some time to Father Coughlin's anti-Semitic utterances and to slur Leon Blum. At the same time Archbishop Joseph Schrembs in public strongly condemned anti-Semitism, and Auxiliary Bishop McFadden, while supervising the offensive archdiocesan newspapers, also frequently appeared at meetings with messages of good will. The impression to be gained is that the Catholic Archdiocese firmly disapproved of anti-Semitism but was unhappy over Jewish support for secularist movements hostile to Catholic interests, and did not wish to alienate itself from its faithful by striking out too sharply at the prejudices some of them held.[48]

The Jewish response to Nazism from the first was fear and loathing, and it was of some comfort to realize that Nazism was generally despised in Cleveland. The daily press, the Bar Association, and the Fellowship of Faiths were among those who denounced the Hitler regime from its accession to power. The press and organizations of Cleveland's many ethnic groups of Central and East European origin were also generally anti-Nazi, especially as Nazi conquest pressed ever deeper into their homelands. This had the effect of diminishing any anti-Semitic feeling which existed. Individual groups ranged, however, from those like the anti-Nazi Czechs and Serbs, who were free of anti-Semitism, to the Slovaks and Russians, who tended strongly to the contrary. Already in 1933 a mass parade and protest meeting with notable Jewish and non-Jewish speakers nearly filled cavernous Public Hall.[49] The giant pogrom of November, 1938, was condemned on all sides.[50] After initial hesitation, Cleveland became a bastion of the anti-Nazi boycott, organized locally by the League for Human Rights against Nazism, which also exposed sympathizers with Nazism to obloquy. While nonsectarian, the League received strong Jewish support.[51] Jewish managers of Cleveland's major department stores were called upon to join the boycott notwithstanding manifest commercial difficulties in doing so.[52]

Nazi anti-Semitism stirred horror, and its manifestations far away were disturbing, but what inevitably hurt most was anti-Semitism restricting the possibility of finding a job. Blatant employment discrimination existed. Jay Iglauer of Halle Brothers department store learned from a teacher in John Hay High School what the Jewish graduate faced in seeking a job:

> She tells me that in almost seventy-five per cent of the cases where request is made for graduates, the stipulation is made that they will not take Jewish students, and that at least half of the Jewish firms themselves make this stipulation.
>   It has been her practice when a request comes from a Jewish firm to insist that they consider Jewish applicants. . . .[53]

Jewish youngsters, harassed by slurs and hostile acts, occasionally had to fight it out with their peers. Some of this behavior fell into the general pattern of inter-ethnic rivalry and hostility.[54]

Accusations of anti-Semitism spilled into politics, not always reputably. Thus, Mayor Harry L. Davis supposedly referred to an opponent as an anti-Semite, which he denied when the charge was bitterly refuted.[55] A few years later Mayor Harold H. Burton was charged with hostility to Jews in making appointments. In the course of his indiscriminate attendance at all manner of local meetings he once visited the German-American Bund and gave routine praise to their activities. The thoughtless Burton had difficult amends to make after the furor which erupted.[56]

Despite friction and occasional incidents, Jewish status in Cleveland remained essentially unshaken. The strength of national and local democratic traditions, and militant defense of democracy and the rights of all citizens, no doubt helped. No anti-Semitic leader emerged, and anti-Semitism was branded as utterly disreputable, even though a substantial stratum of prejudice remained.

A good deal of hesitancy could be found among Jews, however, concerning the general community's reaction to them. Thus a proposal in 1938 to try introducing Hebrew as a foreign language in Cleveland high schools provoked a revealing, wide-ranging debate. Advocates of Hebrew emphasized not only its educational benefits but, even more, its value "in creating a respect for the language . . . [as] a living tongue which has a culture. It is likely to have a good will effect upon our general population." The dissemination of Hebrew in the school system would dispel any impression that Jews were "secretive. . . . Will it not have an emancipating, clarifying, wholesome effect?" Opponents of promoting Hebrew in the high schools, however, feared that "we are going to fan the certain unreasoning elements, the rising tide and flame of anti-Semitism. . . ." At present, argued another, "the Jewish community should not make itself too conspicuous, too demanding and too assertive. . . . We should try to be good citizens and make no private and individual demands." Alfred A. Benesch dismissed the latter assertions, regarding them "of the same type with the complaint about the unduly large immigration into this country, and the complaints of too many Jews in public life. I have no sympathy with the public relations argument at all. If the project merits approval, it should have that approval regardless of any other consideration." To think in other terms "is an admission of an inferiority complex." Benesch, the leading Cleveland Jew in public office, ploughed ahead. "Nor am I worried about the argument that too many Jews are seeking public office. If they are the right kind of Jews, they deserve support. That argument emanates more from our group than from the non-Jewish group."[57] The Jewish community, or some of its members, apparently lacked assurance how they stood in their city.

RESTRUCTURING JEWISH COMMUNAL LIFE

The depression for years dissipated interest in the affairs of the local Jewish community. When two large banks where most Cleveland Jews' savings and commercial accounts were concentrated could not reopen after the bank holiday of March, 1933, the personal affairs of thousands of Jews were paralyzed. Understandably, they could not then worry over the Jewish institutions whose funds were frozen in the same banks.[58] The Jewish Welfare Fund trustees discussed this point in 1934 after indifferent results in the campaign they had just concluded. They inquired of other local Jewish communities and were advised of similar conditions.[59] The sheer struggle for economic survival preoccupied thousands of Jews who would have contributed, or once had contributed, money and energy to Jewish purposes. Others were drawn into the throbbing excitement of public affairs in New Deal days and regarded Jewish matters as of little consequence. Finally, the growing peril to Jews abroad and the development of Palestine tended to divert interest from more humdrum affairs at home, such as hospitals and child care and social service. But the middle 1930s brought new ideas into the Jewish community and broadly expanded the communal structure.

Some of the new energy could be found in Zionist youth organizations, or among the young people meeting in cultural clubs at such places as the Council Educational Alliance, more than in the synagogues or the well-established philanthropies. The dynamic A. H. Friedland and such pedagogic idealists as Harry Schuster and Mordecai Medini raised a small but impressive group of young people who identified themselves with Hebraic idealism, and pursued their Hebrew studies at an advanced level. These teachers and youth were the organizers of the League of Jewish Youth to which about 4,000 youngsters in dozens of organizations became connected.[60] Another devoted group were the Orthodox young men of the little Jewish Orthodox Rabbinical Seminary, brought to Cleveland from New Haven in 1929 by Rabbi Judah Levenberg.[61] Several rabbis and educators completed their Talmudic studies before the school ended its career with Rabbi Levenberg's death in 1938. Perhaps it was a decline in adult prestige which brought about the Jewish Young Adult Bureau, founded in 1939 by the Jewish Community Council. It sought "to provide cultural, athletic, social and recreational activities for the Jewish young adults of Cleveland" on the model of a Young Men's Hebrew Association. However, it lacked a building of its own.[62] Hakoah (strength), also founded in 1939, consisted of young German refugees. It aimed "to act as a bridge for newcomers between the old and American way of life," and to assist social adjustment "between ourselves and their fellow American youth."[63] World War II, however, adjourned these promising starts.

Separate Jewish campaigns continued for purposes not covered by the Jewish Welfare Federation's affilation with the Community Fund. One in January, 1931, was the local appeal by the

Joint Distribution Committee for Eastern Europe and the Jewish Agency for Palestine.

> Inasmuch as it appeared rather certain . . . that the need repre-
> sented by the Allied Jewish Campaign would continue for sev-
> eral years and that Annual Campaigns would be recurring
> events, it was recommended that the Executive Committee [of
> the Jewish Welfare Federation] consider the feasibility of join-
> ing with this annual appeal, the further demands which the Jew-
> ish Community of Cleveland were called upon to subscribe to
> annually, other than those provided through the Community
> Fund. This would in fact result in the establishment in Cleveland
> of a Jewish Welfare Fund such as those already in operation in
> . . . other cities. . . .[64]

The sole local cause, with the "orthodox" institutions now members of the Jewish Welfare Federation at last, was the financial orphan, the Bureau of Jewish Education. Its inclusion in the Jewish Welfare Fund, founded in 1930, annoyed those dissatisfied with the local Bureau or disinterested in Jewish education, as well as others who felt that its priority was not urgent enough for the new Fund.[65] The retention of the Bureau of Jewish Education, and the preference it sometimes received during the first years of the Jewish Welfare Fund, were largely due to the persuasion and influence of Rabbis Brickner and Silver.

The Jewish Welfare Fund was founded by the Jewish Wel-fare Federation to advance the aims of the parent body as a fund-raising arm. Its campaign organization was established during the dark days of late 1930. Judge Maurice Bernon was campaign chairman, Irwin N. Loeser was associate chairman, and Louis Bing, Jr., became treasurer.[66] A statement of pur-pose was promulgated:

> The Object of the Jewish Welfare Fund of Cleveland is to further
> project the idea and principles of the Jewish Welfare Federation
> under whose auspices the Fund has been created; to promote a
> plan of centralized budgeting and control in the relations of the
> Federation and the Jewish Community of Cleveland, with Jew-
> ish Philanthropic and Educational Causes, Emergency Needs
> of National and International Scope, and such other Causes as

do not come within the purview of the Cleveland Community Fund;
and thereby encouraging the Community's support through
such means, of all purposes having a just claim on the Cleveland
Jewish Community. . . .[67]

During the Fund's first year a meager $128,618 was garnered
from 2,611 contributors, and next year produced a depression-
starved $52,982.[68] Only $37,635 could be allotted in 1933.[69] A
bare $86,550 was collected in 1934.[70] Notwithstanding extensive
efforts, the pall of depression and its Federation-centered management deprived the Jewish Welfare Fund of some of its attractiveness. Its allotments were apportioned among beneficiaries more on the basis of compromise than unanimity and
enthusiasm. The catastrophic events in world Jewry during the
later 1930s and the 1940s finally stirred the devotion and near-
unanimity of purpose that brought the Jewish Welfare Fund to
dominant importance in Cleveland Jewry.

Far-reaching changes in Jewish communal structure were
in the offing during the depression. Serious questioning of well-
established social and economic authority, which could not
foresee or cope with a great economic disaster, was endemic.
Many one-time authorities lost wealth or credibility, or both.
The New Deal reforms were based in part upon this widespread
disillusion. It was not remarkable, therefore, that those who had
long governed Jewish affairs in Cleveland by virtue of their
wealth, inheritance, and social and political connections abdi-
cated some of their power by extensively restructuring the
Jewish communal edifice.

In November, 1933, the Trustees of the Federation heard informally from Rabbi Harry S. Davidowitz about the "Pittsburgh
Plan" recently adopted in that city. It provided for a broad reconstruction of the Federation by bringing in representatives
from the gamut of organized Jewish life in the city.

The Plan as further proposed anticipated various forms of taxa-
tion for communal purposes somewhat upon the basis of those
which had obtained in the European Jewish communities. One of
the major items . . . Rabbi Davidowitz said, "would be the
problem of study and redirection wherever possible of the voca-
taional pursuits of young Jewish men and women with the pur-

pose in mind of deterring large numbers from the ambitions and training for the professions." Involved with this would of course be the question of the attitude in general and especially among Jewish businesses and industries towards the employment of Jews.[71]

This proposal, which the Trustees of the Federation would no doubt have dismissed out of hand five years before, became the basis of Federation planning for the following six years. Such a fusion of self-abnegation, forethought, and conciliation was indeed statesmanship.

The needs of the time also aroused a feeling of Jewish solidarity which required institutional expression:

> Frequently the Jewish Community finds itself embarrassed and disadvantaged by the expressions of self-appointed spokesmen and leaders who are quoted in the public press . . . ; or in broadcasting matters of specifically Jewish concern such as the questions of Kashruth, shechita, and the jurisdictional disputes of the different elements of Jewry. These matters should be dealt with by proper authorities and should not be exposed to outside curiosity and ridicule.[72]

However, "Federations must undergo radical alterations in their basic structure" if they were to become "the authoritative leader of a community program. . . ."[73] The social basis of Federation leadership was too narrow:

> By and large the present Federation represents only the wealthier elements. Labor, the middle classes, the professions, and various functional groups are not represented at all; or at best, in a very minor degree. It would seem axiomatic, that if the Federation wishes to exercise the kind of leadership and authority present conditions increasingly demand, it must represent, in fact as well as in theory, all elements in the Community.[74]

President Louis S. Bing enumerated new directions for transforming a philanthropic institution into a communal voice. The Federation Board had to be enlarged to represent all Jewish groups, thus giving these organizations the required "community attitude." For "problems have arisen and will arise, where Jews will require an organized voice," and this did not yet exist. "Greater economic security in Jewish life" was needed; "there are special Jewish problems of unemployment and re-employment, and special Jewish economic sores that should be treated and cured."[75] Quite interesting was the last of Bing's points for the new communal agenda:

> To foster Jewish life and culture. 1933 has made many Jews Jewish-conscious for the first time. A great world of Jewish culture and accomplishment lies not only in the past, but is in the making today. Surely, some significant adjusted type of Jewish life and education will arise from the interplay of the many forces active in America.[76]

With a prescience perhaps stimulated by previous service as president of the Bureau of Jewish Education where he had encountered ideas and personalities unwonted to a pillar of the Reform Temple, Bing addressed the Federation's Committee on Policy and Reorganization:

> The Federation was gradually losing out in those things that were the keystone of original Federation activity, such as material relief which is now furnished by the County. He felt generally that the things that called Federations into being have been undertaken by other agencies. The Cleveland Federation as an institution is well organized . . . but in spite of these advantages it has lost a certain contact with the rank and file of the Jewish community. The community regards the Federation as removed from the newer things in Jewish life.[77]

Among these communal leaders a consensus emerged which favored "a Community Council consisting of representatives of important Jewish organizations throughout the City sponsored by the Federation."[78] The decision to proceed was taken in December, 1934. "It was emphasized that the process would have to be a slow one, with a maximum of participation by the entire Community in the organization of the Council, from the beginning."[79] Over the next year, the Jewish Community Council was assisted towards its birth by six conferences,

> including the Rabbis and Presidents of the Temple and Synagogue Congregations and Activity Groups, Lodges and Social

Clubs, Philanthropic and Benefic [*sic*] Societies, local chapters of National and International Organizations, and the Editors of the Jewish Newspapers. In all, a total of 130 persons had been contacted in this way, representing 67 organizations, or 86 if Auxiliaries and Temple Activity Groups were counted independently.[80]

"Perhaps about 10,000" Jews were reached through these conferences.[81] During the deliberations

> Rabbi Silver asked whether a Council based upon individual membership obtained through contributions to the Jewish Welfare Fund might not be more advisable than one consisting of delegates from the various Jewish organizations. . . . in this way the delegates might avoid the intense partisanship that the delegates from organizations would carry to the meetings, and a deliberative body chosen by the membership would be qualified to speak for the entire Jewish Community on the broad basis of Community interest. . . .

Rabbi Silver forebore to press his point, which came into its own fifteen years later.[82]

The Jewish Community Council vigorously took over its role as spokesman without and policeman within the Jewish community. Its Jewish Conciliation and Arbitration Court was established to adjudicate cases having a bearing on the Jewish community or its good reputation. A Committee on Fictitious Jewish Political Issues saw that attempts to inject spurious Jewish issues into political life for ulterior motives were repressed. Defense against anti-Semitism was gradually concentrated in a Community Relations Committee. And *kashrut*, the subject of ugly fraud and racketeering highlighed in the courts and the press in 1933,[83] began to be brought under communal regulation.

While the Jewish Community Council was expanding its role, the Jewish Welfare Fund was reorganized. Rabbi Silver had pointedly questioned its organization, implying that this was responsible for the poor results obtained, and Rabbi Brickner had offered the radical suggestion "that the fund should be divorced entirely from the Federation and administered by an independent Board or Committee," preferably by the Jewish

Community Council then about to be created.[84] Although there was no enthusiasm for this step, the Fund was reorganized with Rabbis Silver and Brickner becoming Campaign Chairman and Associate Campaign Chairman, respectively.[85] With effective organization, aided by the fervor and eloquence of the two renowned rabbis, the resulting campaign at last exceeded its goal. A total of $137,500 was raised from 6,980 individual contributions—"the greatest number ever to give to a single Jewish Cause in Cleveland."[86]

Within the year, the Federation overcame its apprehensions that the Jewish Community Council might come under the domination of "extremists" and decided to affiliate with the body it had created.[87] The Jewish Welfare Fund and the Jewish Community Council formed a potent new combination which represented the popular, East European, pro-Zionist, politically left-of-center masses in the Jewish community. By the end of the 1930s it had great influence in the affairs of the Jewish community.

AN ACTIVE COMMUNITY

While the structure of the Jewish community changed, its individual units were glad if they could hold their own during the hard years. The old Reform Temples weathered hard times without much strain, as did well-established social agencies, once public funds under New Deal programs took over the burden of the unemployed. Yet the Council of Jewish Women, whose members were from a prosperous social stratum, lost half of them within three years, after its dues rose in 1930 from $3.00 to $4.00.[88] Little Orthodox congregations were long accustomed to meager finances. It was the newer institutions which had expanded rapidly and erected large structures during the 1920s that went to the wall during the 1930s, conspicuously the Bureau of Jewish Education and the Cleveland Hebrew Schools.

The great majority of Jews had some Jewish affiliation, although 4,727 families had none. There were 9,047 Jewish families represented in one Jewish organization, 4,171 in two, 2,446 in three, and 1,531 in four. Cleveland Jewry also had its "joiners": 2,489 Jewish families were found in five to nine Jewish organizations, and there were as many as 252 families whose members were enrolled in ten or more! Affiliation or its absence could be found almost uniformly in dense as well as scattered Jewish neighborhoods.[89] Many of these connections were only casual or habitual, or dutifully continued a family tradition. For a great many others, however, activity in Jewish life was their central interest.

Cleveland's synagogues and their rabbinic leadership did not change much. The two Reform Temples' membership declined slightly, but their rabbis' careers flourished. The Jewish Center and the Temple on the Heights, with 845 and 806 member families respectively, both definitely in the Conservative fold, changed rabbis during this period. Rabbi Harry Davidowitz, who succeeded Rabbi Goldman in 1929, resigned in 1934 in order to settle in Palestine. Young Rabbi Armond E. Cohen succeeded Rabbi Davidowitz and gave a long career of service to the Jewish Center and, as it later became, Park Synagogue. Rabbi Rudolph A. Rosenthal came to the Temple on the Heights in 1933, likewise to devote many years to his congregation. Rabbi Abraham Nowak, whom the Temple on the Heights discharged in 1933, led a group of 25 men to found the Community Temple in that year. While traditional in worship, the new congregation asserted a liberality in social outlook by eliminating set membership dues. Adding Beth Am (People's House) to its name, the congregation reached 305 members by 1938. It chose to define itself as a Conservative congregation; Rabbi Harold Goldfarb succeeded Rabbi Nowak, who left in 1936 for New Rochelle, New York.[90]

In addition there were several communally significant Orthodox congregations, mentioned previously, while numerous conventicles served their limited membership. On Woodland Avenue in the long abandoned immigrant neighborhood, Sherith Israel Chevra Thilim, founded by poor Jews in 1927, somehow kept alive with five members in 1940. Ahavath Zion was a synagogue which grew out of a Zionist society. Typical of many moderate-size Orthodox synagogues, Oer Chodosh Anshe Sfard carried on without a rabbi after old Rabbi Gittelsohn's death in 1932. However, it engaged a cantor to attract worshippers, especially for the High Holidays.[91] In the Kinsman area a group deriving from the Anshe Marmoresh B'nai Jacob founded in 1928 B'nai Jacob-Kol Israel (Sons of Jacob-All Israel), emphasizing by the latter half of their name that they did not wish to be a specially Hungarian congregation. Under energetic lay leadership, they assumed the name of Kinsman Jewish Center and succeeded in erecting a synagogue during the years of depression. Rabbi David L. Genuth began a long career as an Orthodox rabbi at the Kinsman Jewish Center in 1933. He was reported "able to cope successfully with the somewhat radical labor elements which he found in the locality."[92] Young Israel, a national Orthodox movement seeking especially to attract the young, conducted some small activity in Cleveland from 1917, consisting mainly of Jewish study groups. Its major phase began in 1937, when it acquired a small building and a full-fledged congregation began to flourish. With its appeal to youth, abandonment of Yiddish, and fervid congregational singing, Young Israel was a harbinger in Cleveland of thoroughly acculturated Orthodoxy.[93] In addition to the yeshiva he headed, Rabbi Levenberg, a scholar and orator, functioned as chief rabbi for a group of Orthodox congregations. The gifted man, however, was embroiled in controversies concerning the control of *kashrut* and the scope of his authority until his premature death.[94]

The congregations by no means exhausted the content of Jewish life. A quite contrary trend, the socialist laborite non- (or anti-) Zionist Workmen's Circle had 361 members. It was centered in the Mount Pleasant area, where it had a building for its activities and its Yiddish school.[95] The socialist Zionists had 113, the Orthodox religious Zionists of Mizrachi and Hapoel Hamizrachi counted 351 men, and Hadassah had 1,110 women. While Cleveland was a strongly Zionist Jewish community, its Cleveland Zionist District was almost paralyzed by protracted strife. Talented men and loyal Zionists bickered bitterly for years, and their quarrels spilled into the Bureau of Jewish Education where many of them were active. At the center was the brilliant, stormy Abba Hillel Silver. Through the rival Cleveland Zionist Society he established in 1936, he rapidly came to dominate the Zionist scene. His Society had 745 members in 1937 to the 521 of the Zionist District. With Rabbis Silver and Brickner dominating Reform Judaism and prominent in Federation and Welfare Fund affairs, local sources of anti-Zionism were neutralized or weakened.

Nearly every charity had its organized supporters, and quite a few benevolent societies could be found. Their interests were largely confined to supporting their particular charity or aiding each other, and few played a communal role. B'nai B'rith, however, had long discontinued its mutual benevolent features and became an organization to serve the general and Jewish community by combatting anti-Semitism and promoting democratic practices, sponsoring Hillel Foundations at universities, and fostering good will. Its 1,663 male members in four lodges were joined by 929 woman in four auxiliaries.

The 1930s were harsh years in Jewish education.[96] The leading institution, the Cleveland Hebrew School, saw its enrollment decline and its indebtedness, much of it in pay due to teachers, mount steadily. Still, under Friedland's charismatic direction, the Bureau of Jewish Education conducted a high school, a teacher-training program, youth clubs, children's shows in theatres before the Jewish holidays—all in addition to supervising its schools. Demographic changes were unfavorable, however.[97]

The first of numerous studies of Jewish education in Cleveland, done in 1936, established that the 6,646 children attending some Jewish school, out of 10,600 in public elementary grades, was roughly twice the proportion in Chicago and New York. This high proportion was mainly due to Cleveland's large Sunday schools, which nearly 70 percent of the children were attending. The Council of Jewish Women's Sunday school continued to function at several branches. Yiddish radical schools grew, somewhat "due to the fact that socialist groups which formerly followed an assimilationist or indifferent policy with reference to Jewish matters have . . . tended to develop a deeper sense of Jewish self-consciousness." Intensive Jewish education, however, focused in the Cleveland Hebrew Schools, was declining. There had been 1,505 pupils in 1929, and the number dropped continuously to 716 in 1936, due to neighborhood changes and social conditions:

a. The [Hebrew week-day] schools are situated in immigrant

sections from which young parents are steadily moving away. No branches have been opened in the new neighborhoods. . . .

b. Forty per cent of the children enrolled in the Hebrew Schools are from relief families, the schools thus becoming "schools for the poor" and their social prestige has further been lowered.

c. As a result of the depression also, private schools have been opened in which unemployed persons—frequently ill prepared—give instruction in ivri [Hebrew reading], broches [blessings] and bar mitzvah at a pittance, and these schools compete with the Hebrew schools. Some who were able to pay formerly, but now cannot, prefer to give their children such "private instruction" rather than to accept what might be termed charity.[98]

The report belittled the alleged distinction between "religion" and "nationalism" in Jewish education, setting aside the frequent charge that Friedland was teaching secular Jewish nationalism. It found "that the intensive weekday instruction is much more effective than the one-day-a-week instruction in developing positive Jewish attitudes and interests."[99] Yet it tied intensive Hebrew education to a declining era of American Jewish life. It considered the congregational school was "an important, perhaps the chief, Jewish educational instrument," and advocated that such schools be given a larger role in the Bureau of Jewish Education.

The Berkson-Rosen report thus justified the social arguments of those opposing the Friedland philosophy, even while it endorsed the educational accomplishment of pupils who underwent the full intensive Hebrew curriculum. However, similar to Talmud Torahs in other cities, only one-tenth completed the six-year course of study, while two-thirds stayed less than three years. The embattled Friedland, almost single-handedly running the Hebrew Schools and the Bureau of Jewish Education under a mountainous debt, reaffirmed his credo:

We are becoming more and more reassured that intensive Hebrew education is striking root in this American soil. All statements made in the past that the daily Hebrew School is an East

European importation and will pass with the passing of the immigrant generation lose their validity. We are already dealing with the children of the second generation. . . . Only a Jewish education based upon our rich cultural values can distract the attention of our young people from the spectres of antisemitism, discrimination, and persecution that constantly assail their mental and spiritual stability. The serenest Jewish youth today is to be found among the graduates of the daily Hebrew schools. . . . The soundest and sanest leadership in Jewish life . . . comes from their midst. . . . These rising and intelligent young Jews in our midst offer an inalienable source of optimism and faith and unchallengeable confidence in our ultimate triumph.[100]

The Bureau of Jewish Education remained torn by personal and ideological strife for years to come. Rabbi Brickner, its head from 1932 to 1940, labored with little success to bring harmony to flaring disagreements. Friedland somehow had the inner resources during his last years to publish a long series of Hebrew educational literature for children, some of it in collaboration with Rabbi Solomon Goldman, and a book of Hebrew poems, sonnets, and stories.[101]

WORLD WAR II AND AFTER

Morally the Jews had been at war for years when America entered the conflict in December, 1941. Participation in the war meant, above all, military service. At the war's end in August, 1945, the local branch of the Jewish Welfare Board, which rendered services to men in uniform, counted up and found that 9,823 Cleveland Jews had served in the armed forces. Of them, 178 had lost their lives and 65 were missing in action; there were 50 prisoners and 265 had suffered wounds. Decorations were awarded to 322. Like all statistics of war, these figures concealed heroism and suffering. Thus, Julian M. Goodman as a young physician was captured by the Japanese in the Philippines and endured a prison camp. In November, 1944, he was transported on a horrible prison ship to Japan, where he remained until the liberation.[102] Arthur Heinz Gottschalk, who was killed in action in France, had come to Cleveland as a refugee youth with his family from Coblenz.[103]

Most Jewish organizations, not to mention families, took part in the U.S. war effort by sending packages to soldiers, making blood donations, donating to war service appeals, purchasing U.S. war bonds, and demonstrating heartfelt interest in the triumph of American arms in the theatres of war. The impact of war, however, intensified the "disruptions of family living that come with separation of parents, with mothers working, with children unsupervised. . . ." Case workers also noted "increased adolescent unrest and uneasiness . . . although actual delinquency has not occurred. . . ."[104] Jewish education and social work especially suffered from manpower shortages, but planned new programs for the coming of peace.[105]

Cleveland Jews shared in the economic changes and the prosperity which World War II helped to bring. Even during the war, as we have seen, Jewish neighborhoods shifted, with the new areas providing better and more expensive homes for their inhabitants than the old. Cleveland Heights and Shaker Heights ranked among the best residential districts of Greater Cleveland. An increase of Jewish women in Federal jobs was reported, and also of men in war-related light industry.[106] Jewish vocations and entrepreneurship as a whole during the war period are suggested by the Jewish Welfare Fund's list of prospects for 1943:

Amusement	400
Attorneys	711
Bankers and brokers	194
Brass metal products	180
Builders (and construction trades)	1,062
Dentists	288
Downtown retail stores	550
Drugs	659
Dry goods	621
Food	1,078
Furniture	474
Insurance	500
Iron and steel	368
Knit goods	270
Men's apparel	325
Oils, paints, autos	513
Physicians	322

Printers	339
Real estate	269
Social service	277
Temples and schools	742
Women's apparel	288

These were independent businessmen and salaried or self-employed professionals, since an additional 5,036 persons were classified as "employees of stores and factories." It seems likely that the large majority of Jewish businessmen was included.[107] The Jewish trade unions by this time were mostly a memory. Butchers and bakers had their Jewish Bakers-Local 56 and the Jewish Butchers' Welfare Society. The Jewish Carpenters Union and the Painters and Decorators Masters represented the carpenters and painters. Among major industrial unions, only the Amalgamated Clothing Workers of America still had a noticeable number of Jewish members in Cleveland. Beryl Peppercorn (1892–1969), the longtime manager of its Cleveland Joint Board, was an important figure in the local labor movement. Employment in trades and crafts for Jews was dwindling away indeed.

During the World War II years of manpower shortage, anti-Semitic job discrimination fell off sharply. The problem persisted in upgrading, however, and the quota system was still being followed by many companies. Moreover, "instances of anti-Jewish prejudice" were said to be numerous, with "conclusive evidence that these instances represent intensive anti-Semitic reaction in the community. . . . Anti-Semitic doggerel and anonymous defamatory literature have been circulated in the war plants, public buildings and non-Jewish neighborhoods." Under the blanket of patriotic unity in wartime, and with anti-Semitism identified as an enemy ideology, in Cleveland this hatred reached a disturbing level.[108]

Cleveland Jewry, like American Jewry generally, was deeply involved in the American war effort and apprehensive of the anti-Semitic undercurrent. The truth about the Nazi mass murder of European Jewry was widely known during the war, but one does not discern any major effort towards rescue or towards influencing America's immigration policy, which was then much more restrictive in practice than even the Johnson

Act required. The principal reaction before 1945 to the horrible events in Europe was increased giving to the Jewish Welfare Fund. Another was the great growth in Zionist membership, for only the Zionist program seemed to offer hope for real rescue and rehabilitation once the war ended. By 1944 over 7,000 Cleveland Jews belonged to Zionist organizations. Rabbi Abba Hillel Silver in 1943 became co-chairman of the American Zionist Emergency Council, beginning his epochal service at the head of American (and, in effect, world) Jewry's struggle which culminated in the establishment of the State of Israel in 1948 and its victorious War of Independence in 1948–1949.

Other divisions healed in the community. Overseas exigencies and increasing income brought more harmony to the allocation of Welfare Fund receipts. The Bureau of Jewish Education at last began to experience the blessings of cohesion. With A. H. Friedland's death and Silver's absorption in Zionist work, it became possible to reconstitute a broadly representative Bureau. Azriel L. Eisenberg, an able educator, brought a broad community viewpoint as Executive Director, and improved finances aided him to implement his plans.[109]

Two new Orthodox educational institutions began their careers in Cleveland. Students and teachers of the Telshe Yeshiva, destroyed in its native Lithuania, reached America via Shanghai in 1941. A small nucleus led by Rabbi Chaim M. Katz and Rabbi Elijah M. Bloch reestablished their famed academy at an unpromising location on East 105th Street. In 1941 Cleveland hardly appeared a likely site for a rigorously Orthodox yeshiva. Possessing little but militant determination and the sometimes skeptical goodwill of local Orthodox leaders, the refugee teachers and the students who gradually joined them pursued full-time advanced Talmud study. The Rabbinical College of Telshe, as it was later named, was a forerunner of the post-World War II Orthodox revival, and it was to gain a national reputation. The Hebrew Academy of Cleveland was an Orthodox day school, a type of intensive Jewish education which was beginning to flourish in many cities. It was under the educational direction of the Telshe Yeshiva, and had approximately 100 children in 1945. The older Yeshivath Adath B'nai Israel, the strongly Orthodox afternoon school, began introducing modern Hebrew for its 262 pupils, who by then included girls in a separate department.[110]

At the close of World War II most of Cleveland Jewry's economic troubles had been eased. The portents of post-World War II period were somewhat visible: concentration in business and the professions, movement to the suburbs, Orthodox revival, education becoming more a congregational than a communal function. The tension between old-stock and new-stock Cleveland Jews had mostly disappeared, and a rationalization of communal functions could now replace most of the ideologically based divisions of the past. The Council Educational Alliance, adjusting to the new realities, merged with the Y.M.H.A. movement which had had a spasmodic existence for half a century. From this combination the Jewish Community Center of Cleveland was to emerge. The age of harmony that seemed to be dawning made some people—frequently they were the youth—look wistfully upon the two generations of issues and conflict in Jewish life which had ended. Relations among Cleveland's many ethnic and religious groups also improved greatly, and anti-Semitism apparently decreased sharply.

From 1945 to 1950 all eyes were upon the remnant of European Jewry and the land of Israel. Cleveland Jews played a creditable role in that epochal story, which must be told elsewhere. The Cleveland Jewish horizon, with that of American Jewry, became world-wide, and the widest meanings of American citizenship and Jewish peoplehood presented themselves for thought and endeavor.

Afterword

A Cohesive Jewish Community

THE Jewish community of Cleveland was created out of the imagination and labors of generations of individuals joined in collective Jewish life. What emerges from this volume is much more than the birth and development of a Jewish community in the American Mid-West. As we study this record of Cleveland Jewry's history from its beginnings until the watershed period following the Second World War, we can better understand the cohesiveness which is the hallmark of the present-day community. The substance of this cohesiveness, which evolved out of the past detailed in these pages, is visible corporate identity: involvement in civic life, engagement in American Jewish concerns, commitment to the needs and aspirations of Jews throughout the world. In this respect the Jewish Community of Cleveland, guided by a succession of determined and innovative leaders, professional and volunteer, is emulated by many sister communities in the United States and in other parts of the Diaspora.

Mid-twentieth century American Jewish life was marked by the most pronounced surge of Jewish group affiliation in its three hundred year history which, in turn, led to a transformation of Jewish communal purpose and organization. The potential for these developments was inherent in American pluralistic society and American Jewry's inner growth, but their compelling force could be found in the response to the unprecedented events of twentieth century *world* Jewish history. East-West migration and the destruction of European Jewry made the Jewish community of America the most vital center of the Diaspora. The rise of the State of Israel confronted it with historic opportunity and spiritual challenge.

As we review the reformulations of priorities for action of the organized Jewish community during this period, one of its most inspiring chapters—I would contend its most animating

321

precept—was responsibility for Jews everywhere, interrelationship with "our Jewish brothers wherever they may be," in the traditional phrase, *Aheinu B'nai Yisrael b'Khol Makom sh'Hem.* Yet, while American Jewry became profoundly involved in world Jewish destiny, its inner creative capacities flowered as well. Unable to replace the annihilated centers of European Jewry, Jewish "city-communities" in the United States rose to accept ever-widening responsibilities with the avowed determination to forge their unique link in the chain of Jewish generations. The content of Jewish life in America was intensified through synagogue and school even as commitment was expanded to hasten the reconstruction of Jewish life in Europe and to intensify personal and collective bonds with the Jewish community in *Eretz Yisrael.* Such intensity of commitment to a weighty task brought forward a prescient leadership for a maturing American Jewish generation.

Local community histories constitute the basis for national and world Jewish history. By isolating those elements which invest the Jewish community of America with its special significance —the constants, mutations, continuities, and discontinuities—one can grasp more profoundly the meaning of the larger Jewish experience in America. Whatever else may help determine the character of a Jewish community, primary account must be taken of place and historic configuration. "The Bible itself"— observed the late Professor Allan Nevins, first Policy Director of the American Jewish History Center—"for all its grand personages and their transcendant significance, is local history writ large."

But what constitutes a "Jewish Community"? As Professor Gartner has stated elsewhere: "The Jews of America are a community by virtue of their internal social communication which leads them to share and develop Jewish ideas, values, and practices." This means that while not all people *make* history, all people are *of* history. In the present volume, Professor Gartner brings to the fore the people themselves—many of them hitherto known only to the historian and archivist. It is the interplay between individual and group that creates community.

This has been the thrust of the Jewish Theological Seminary's Regional History Series, of which *The History of the Jews of*

Cleveland is the fourth volume, following communal histories of Milwaukee, Los Angeles, and the agricultural settlements of New Jersey: to study Jewish communities in America in their indigenous context; their reaction to the environing culture and their adjustment to it; their changing responses to the emergent needs of the Jewish People on the national and international scene. All these factors make for important dissimilarities not only among established Jewish communities in different parts of the world, but even within the same country; indeed, they help to define the unique qualities of diverse communities.

The path of Jewish life has ever been past-minded and future-directed; and history binds past and future together. As we turn, and return, to these pages of collective memory. and as we add to it the record of the contemporary era, we learn how this distinctive Jewish community served, and continues to serve, as a guarantor of Jewish group consciousness in Greater Cleveland—and beyond.

Institute of Contemporary Jewry   Moshe Davis
The Hebrew University of Jerusalem

Appendix I

The following passenger list was located by the late Abe L. Nebel and deciphered by Rabbi Malclm H. Stern. The full transcription is in Box 2369, American Jewish Archives.

The ship *Howard* carried three cabin and 111 steerage passengers. Among the latter, five were Saxons, and the remainder were Bavarians. They came from small towns more or less the size of Unsleben and Heinsfort, Reckendorf, and Steinhart were the most prominently represented. To judge from the names listed, approximately two-thirds of the passengers were Jews.

DISTRICT OF NEW-YORK—PORT OF NEW-YORK

[Handwritten parts underlined, remainder printed]: I, *O.H.* [?] *The*[?] Flor do solemnly, sincerely, and truly *swear* that the following List or Manifest of Passengers, subscribed with my name, and now delivered by me to the Collector of the Customs for the District of New-York, contains, to the best of my knowledge and belief, a just and true account of all the Passengers received on board the *Ship Howard* whereof I am Master, from *Hamburg. Sworn* to the *12th July 1839.* Before me *J.B.*—[?], D[rector of] C[ustoms]. LIST OR MANIFEST of all the PASSENGERS taken on board the *Ship Howard* whereof *O.H.*[?] *Flor* is Master from *Hamburg* burthen   tons.

324

[All that follows is handwritten]

No.	NAMES	AGE	PLACE OF NATIVITY	Country from whence they have come	To what nation they belong and owe allegiance	THEIR OCCUPATION	DESCRIPTION OF THEIR PERSONS
				Cabin Passengers			
70.	L. Kopfmann	42	Unsleben	Bavaria	Bavaria	merchant	)2 trunks,
71.	S. Kopfmann	63	"	"	"		)5 chests,
72.	Jenni Kopfmann	24	"	"	"		)2 casks,
73.	Fanny Kopfmann	25	"	"	"	weaver	)1 cloke bag
74.	Sophie Kopfmann	18	"	"	"		)1 gun
75.	Meyer Thormann	30	"	"	"		)beds
76.	Simon Thormann	21	"	"	"	saddler	)
77.	R. Thormann	26	"	"	"	farmer	)
78.	Regina Klein	24	"	"	"		
81.	B. Fleischhauer	26	"	"	"		1 trunk, 1 cask
82.	Janette Dinckel	27	"	"	"	butcher	1 chest, beds
							1 trunk, 1 chest
							beds
83.	Moses Rosenbaum	32	"	"	"	shoemaker	)2 trunks,
84.	Hanne Rosenbaum	18	"	"	"		)beds
85.	M. Alsbacher	34	"	"	"	dier [!]	)2 chests,
86.	Jette Alsbacher	21	"	"	"		)1 trunk, 1 cask,
87.	Jette Alsbacher	1	"	"	"		)1 basket, beds,
88.	Babette Salb	23	"	"	"		)2 chests
89.	Carl Salb	3	"	"	"		)

Appendix II

ECONOMIC LIFE IN 1914
JR&O, XL, No. 42 (Oct. 9, 1914), p. 7

The Jewish population of Cleveland is prominently identified with the commercial development of the city, being identified with some of the largest wholesále and retail establishments.

They are pioneers in the clothing business and are among the best known manufacturers of men's and women's clothing, not only in Cleveland but throughout the country. Among them are The Joseph Feiss and Co.; Charles Eisenman Co., known also as The K. and E. Blouse Makers; Kohn Bros. and Co.; Freedman Bros.; Bloch Co.; Richman Bros. Co., and Schaffner Bros., manufacturers of men's clothing. In the manufacture of women's clothing Landesman-Hirscheimer Co., The H. Black Co., The M. T. Silver Co., John Anisfield and Co., Schwartz, Huebschman and Forney, J. P. Kohn and Co., S. Korach Co., Printz-Biederman and Co., L. N. Gross Co., Cohn-Goodman Co., Greenhut Cloak Co., Max G. Wertheim and The Sunshine Cloak and Suit Co., together with many others, have contributed much toward making Cleveland a great center of the garment manufacturing industry.

The leading department stores are The Halle Bros. Co., The May Co and The Bailey Co. and are owned by our co-religionists. Among the dry goods stores are The Strauss Bros. and Oppenheim and Collins and Seigels and The Lindner Co., and these are among the best known firms carrying ready-made garments for women. The Steran Co. is one of the best known stores of the kind, not only in the state, but in the country.

The Acme Foundry Co., The Empire Plow Co., The Cleveland Worsted Mills, The Cleveland and Sandusky Brewing Co., The Glauber Brass Co., The Atlas Brass Co., The Monarch Brass Co., The Rickersberg Brass Co., The Wolf Envelop Co. and The Superior Foundry are enterprises conducted by our co-religionists.

The Friedman-Blau-Farber Co., The Bamberger-Reinthal Co., N. J. Rich and Co., The Keller Knitting Co. and The Standard Knitting Co. have achieved a well known reputation in the knit good market and there are numerous other Jewish firms who are well known for the high grade of goods they carry in this line. Mandelbaum, Wolf and Lang are well known in the business circles of the city.

Among some of the prominent brokers are E. M. Baker, B. Mahler & Co., and W. S. Halle & Co.

Mr. A. F. Hartz, the manager of the Opera House, has been instrumental in securing the best dramatic productions for Cleveland.

Mr. Dan S. Wertheimer, the publisher and printer of the Opera House, Colonial, Hippodrome, Prospect, and Metropolitan theater programs, has been in that business for thirty-five years. He is also publisher and proprietor of *The Jewish Review and Observer*.

In the real estate business the names of A. Wiener & Son, Joseph Laronge, The J. Timendorfer Co., M. C. Stone & I. N. Stone, S. Scheuer, Scheuer & Dewey Co., H. S. Bloch, Adolph Bernstein, Albert Salberg, Joseph Goodhart, Goakes Dettelbach & Co., and I. J. Rothschild and J. Rothschild occupy a prominent position.

The Solomonson Optical Co., C. R. Fishel, and The Kluger Optical Co. have gained much prominence in this line of business.

In the ranks of the insurance business there are Lewis Hartz, Herman Koppel, The D. Jankau Co., Weil & Son; G. Kanner, manager of the Canadian Life Insurance Co., Herman Moss of the Equitable Insurance Co., Max Wurtenberg of the Northwestern, and E. N. Newburger are all eminently identified in the insurance interests of the city.

Mr. Max Levi is treasurer of the German-American, Mr. L. C. Haas, of Central National bank, and Mr. Louis Kaufman of, The Guardian Savings & Trust Co.; George Lomnitz is assistant treasurer of The Citizens.

Many of our co-religionists are members of the board of directors of different banks in the city.

Among the well known jewelers are Arnstine Bros., Charles Ettinger, J. H. Heiman, Jewelers Manufacturing Co., Goldsmith Bros., and Rosenthal Jewelry Co.

Mr. A. D. Rheinheimer is among the well known ladies tailors.

Mr. Louis Rorheimer, of the Rorheimer-Brooks Studio, and The Newman Photo Studio, are well known.

There is scarcely a phase of mercantile activity in the city that has not within its ranks some of our co-religionists. Mr. Morris A. Black is president of the Chamber of Commerce. Mr. M. A. Marks is president of the Federation of Charities and Philanthropies of the city of Cleveland, and Mr. Edward M. Baker is president of the Stock Exchange.

Notes

AJA	*American Jewish Archives*
AJHQ	*American Jewish Historical Quarterly*
AJYB	*American Jewish Year Book*
AmIsr	*American Israelite*, Cincinnati
CJN	*Cleveland Jewish News*
F.J.C.	Federated Jewish Charities
HO	*Hebrew Observer*
JInd	*Jewish Independent*
JMess	*Jewish Messenger* (New York)
JR	*Jewish Review*
JR&O	*Jewish Review and Observer*
J.W.F.	Jewish Welfare Federation (merged into Jewish Community Federation
OSAHQ	*Ohio State Archaeological and Historical Quarterly*, Columbus; intermittently, *OAHQ* : *Ohio Archaeological and Historical Quarterly*
PAJHS	Publication of the American Jewish Historical Society (later, *AJHQ*)
PD	*Cleveland Plain Dealer*
YV	*Yiddisher Velt*

Manuscript sources, unless otherwise specified, are deposited at the Jewish Community Federation, Cleveland; or The Cleveland Jewish Archives, Western Reserve Historical Society; and those of Tifereth Israel-The Temple deposited at that institution.

CHAPTER I

1. James H. Kennedy, *A History of the City of Cleveland* (Cleveland, 1896), p. 1; W. G. Rose, *Cleveland: The Making of a City* (Cleveland, 1950), p. 64; Stewart H. Holbrook, *The Yankee Exodus: An Account of Migration from New England* (New York, 1950), pp. 25–38.

2. Samuel P. Orth, *A History of Cleveland, Ohio*, 3 vols. (Chicago-Cleveland, 1910), I, p. 113.

3. D. F. Bradley, "Protestant Churches," in Orth, *op. cit.*, I, p. 349; see also Holbrook, *op. cit.*, p. 39, and Lois Mathews Rosenberry, *The Expansion of New England* (Boston-New York, 1909), p. 192.

4. Orth, *op. cit.*, pp. 114, 115.

5. Rose, *op. cit.*, pp. 76, 166–68.

6. J. P. B. McCabe, comp., *Directory: Cleveland and Ohio City, For the Years 1837-38*, pp. 50, 56, 60; Rose, *op. cit.*, p. 169; Harry N. Scheiber, "Urban Rivalry and Internal Improvements in the Old Northwest," in *idem*, ed., *The Old Northwest: Studies in Regional History, 1787–1910* (Lincoln, Nebraska, 1969), esp. p. 264.

7. *Herald and Guardian*, February 7, 27, 28, 1838, quoted in Works Progress Administration, *Annals of Cleveland, 1818–1935*, 1837, Vol. XXI, Part I (Cleveland, 1939); *Herald and Guardian*, March 13, 1829, quoted *op. cit.*, 1838, Vol. XXII, Part I (Cleveland, 1939); George Roberts Taylor, *The Transportation Revolution 1815–1860* (New York, 1950), pp. 161–62, 253.

8. Quoted by Charles F. Thwing, "Cleveland," in *Historic Towns of the Western States*, ed. Lyman P. Powell (New York, 1901), pp. 31, 32; Rose, *op. cit.*, pp. 196–202.

9. Rose, *op. cit.*, p. 187. See Baird Still, "Patterns of Mid-Nineteenth Century Urbanization in the Middle West," *Mississippi Valley Historical Review*, XXVIII, No. 2 (September, 1941), 187–206.

10. *Cleaveland Register*, March 16, 1819, quoted in Works Progress Administration, *Annals of Cleveland 1818–1935*, 1818, 1819, 1820, Vol. I (Cleveland, 1939), No. 930.

11. *Cleaveland Register*, March 30, 1819, quoted *loc. cit.*

12. *Cleaveland Herald*, October 7, 1825, quoted *loc. cit.*, Vols. VI, VII, VIII, Part I (Cleveland, 1938).

13. *Cleveland Whig*, December 31, 1834, quoted *op. cit.*, Vols. XV, XVI, XVII, Part I (Cleveland, 1938) No. 3, p. 285.

14. *Cleveland Herald*, August 18, 1846, quoted *op. cit.*, Vol. XXIX (Cleveland, 1938), No. 245.

15. *Cleveland Herald*, October 17, 1836, quoted *op. cit.*, 1835–1836, Vols. XVIII–XIX, Part I (Cleveland, 1938).

16. *Cleveland Herald*, October 18 and December 15, 1836, quoted *loc. cit.*; *Cleveland Herald*, January 3, 1837, quoted *ibid.*, Vol. XX, Part I (Cleveland, 1938).

17. *Cleveland Herald and Gazette*, November 3, 1837, quoted *ibid.*

18. *Jewish Encyclopedia*, s.v. "Joachimsen, Philip J." On emigration from Europe to the United States during this period, the great work is Marcus Lee Hansen, *The Atlantic Migration 1607–1860* (Cambridge, Mass., 1940; paper ed., 1961).

19. Many instances are cited in Rudolf Glanz, "Source Materials on the History of Jewish Emigration to the United States, 1800–1880," *YIVO Annual of Jewish Social Science*, VI (1951), Nos. 1–19, 25–30, 33–45; *idem*, "The German Jewish Mass Migration 1820–1880," *American Jewish Archives*, XXII, No. 1 (April, 1970), pp. 49–66; see also Jacob Toury, "Jewish Manual Labour and Emigration: Records from some Bavarian Districts (1830–1857)," in Leo Baeck Institute, *Year Book*, XVI (1971), pp. 45–62, esp. Tables VII, VIII.

20. Lazarus Kohn to Moses and Jetta Alsbacher, May 5, 1839 (German MS in possession of Jewish Community Federation, Cleveland). Invaluable information about Unsleben is in Baruch Zvi Ophir, *Pinkas Hakehillot: Encyclopedia of Jewish Communities . . . Germany-Bavaria* (Hebrew; Jerusalem, 1972), pp. 396–97.

21. *Allgemeine Zeitung des Judenthums*, May 25, 1839, p. 256. The village of Unsleben lies on the Streu River near the Thuringian border of Bavaria. Its bearings are 50.22 N by 10.15 E.

22. *Occident*, September, 1852, p. 305. When Simile Thorman, a member of the Unsleben party, died in 1890, the *American Israelite* noted that he was "one of a committee to bring the first Torah in Cleveland from Europe." April 10, 1890.

23. Joseph L. Blau and Salo W. Baron, *The Jews of the United States 1790–1840: A Documentary History* (New York and Philadelphia, 1963), III, pp. 864–65, 989–90; Jacob Neusner, "The Role of English Jews in the Development of American Jewish Life, 1775–1850," *YIVO Annual of Jewish Social Science*, XII (1958–1959), pp. 131–56; Peixotto reminisced in an address at the Jewish Orphan Asylum, *PD*, July 10, 1888.

24. The 1840 Jewish estimate derives from adding up the Unsleben group as well as seven or more Jews known to have been in Cleveland by that date; others were certainly present. For 1850, see *PD*, April 22, 1850.

25. Family document of Mr. Charles J. Colman (b. 1890), in Abe L. Nebel Collection, American Jewish Archives, Cincinnati, Ohio, questions 5, 6, 23.

26. Colman document, questions 6, 12; *JR&O*, July 22, 1904.

27. *JR&O*, April 30, 1897.

28. *HO*, March 26, 1897; June 17, 1897.

29. *AmIsr*, January 22, 1891; January 2, 1896.

30. *JR&O*, May 1, 1914.

31. *JR&O*, February 2, 1900.

32. Rudolf Glanz, "The 'Bayer' and 'Pollack' in America" and "German-Jewish Names in America," in *Studies in Judaica-Americana* (New York, 1970), pp. 187–202, 278–304 (esp. p. 282).

33. *JR*, March 7, 1902.

34. Some of his children retained this family name, notably the gynecologist Marcus Rosenwasser, while other successful sons (Edward Rosewater, journalist, and Joseph Rosenwater, engineer) illustrated its mutations. *JR&O*, September 9, 1910.

35. *AmIsr.*, March 31, 1898.

36. *PD*, September 3, 1880.

37. *JR*, September 17, 1897; *HO*, September 16, 1897.

38. *AmIsr*, January 17, 1889; *JR&O*, May 27, 1904.

39. *HO*, July 29, 1892.

40. Arnstein's Oath of Identity, Certificate of Service, and a note concerning his land claim are in the Abe L. Nebel Collection, American Jewish Archives.

41. J. G. Buttner, *Der Staat Ohio: Eine geographisch-statistisch-topographische Beschreibung für Einwanderer und Freunde der Länder-und Völkerkunde* (Bayreuth, 1849). The quotation is from pp. i–ii of the preface, dated August 6, 1848.

42. The local figure for 1852 was taken in a city census reported in the *PD*, August 3, 1886, and the Jewish one was reported by Joseph Levy in the *Occident*, September, 1852, pp. 308–10. Isaac M. Wise, who visited Cleveland many times, is the source for the 1858 and 1860 Jewish figures. *AmIsr*, August 20, 1858; July 20, 1860.

43. *JR&O*, December 8, 1905; *AmIsr*, May 7, 1896, October 12, 1899; *PD*, August 9, 1886; for the family emigration, see Rudolf Glanz, "The German Jewish Mass Emigration: 1820–1880," *loc. cit.*, and Adolf Kober, "Jewish Emigration from Württemburg to the United States of America (1848–1855)," *PAJHS*, XLI, No. 3 (March, 1952), 225–73.

44. *JR&O*, February 10, 1905.

45. Jacob Bloom, an immigrant of 1850, reportedly sailed 45 days. *JInd*, December 3, 1915.

46. See obituary in *HO*, December 16, 1892.

47. *Isr*, July 13, 1855; see below, pp.

48. *Isr*, August 19, 1859.

49. T. Čapek, *The Čechs (Bohemians) in America* (New York, 1920), pp. 42 f.

50. This and previous quotations are from the unpublished "Autobiography of Kaufman Hays," March 9, 1910, in American Jewish Archives, Cincinnati, Ohio. This document is approximately 3,500 words in length.

51. *PD*, February 23, 1885.

52. *JR&O*, January 1, 1904; December 7, 1906.

53. *JR&O*, September 11, 1908.

54. Louis J. Swichkow and Lloyd P. Gartner, *A History of the Jews of Milwaukee* (Philadelphia, 1963), pp. 46–49; Morris A. Gutstein, *A Priceless Heritage: The Epic Growth of Nineteenth Century Chicago Jewry* (New York, 1953), pp. 61–65, 283–85.

55. The only exceptions derive from the umlaut; Loeb for Löb, Hexter for Höchster.

56. Hays autobiography, *loc. cit.*

57. Colman document, question 9.

58. *JInd*, December 24, 1915; *JR&O*, July 24, 1908; March 31, 1916.

59. *AmIsr*, February 19, 1891; on Cleveland Germandom and the limited Jewish participation within it, see Carl Wittke, "Ohio's Germans, 1840–1875," *Ohio Historical Quarterly*, LXVI, No. 4 (October, 1957), pp. 339–54.

60. Allan Nevins, *John D. Rockefeller: The Heroic Age of American Enterprise*, 2 vols. (New York, 1940), I, pp. 96–97.

61. Herbert Croly, *Marcus Alonzo Hanna, His Life and Work* (New York, 1912), p. 57.

62. Cf. Allan Nevins, *The Ordeal of the Union*, Vol. II: *A House Dividing* (New York, 1947), p. 247.

63. Rose, *op. cit.*, p. 155.

64. Works Progress Administration, *Annals of Cleveland, Court Record Series*, Vol. III, 1858–1860 (Cleveland, 1939), pp. 261–62.

65. *Jewish Chronicle* (New York), March 30, 1860, p. 311.

66. Works Progress Administration, *loc. cit.*, pp. 28–29; for a similar, unpleasant case in 1858 between Moses Schwab and John B. Franklin (probably not a Jew) who were partners in Mansfield, see *ibid.*, pp. 89–90.

67. See *Cleveland Morning Leader*, April 23, 1857; October 29, 1857; December 2, 1857; November 1, 1863; *PD*, August 11, 1852; July 1, 1853; January 3, 1856; January 4, 1865; September 29, 1866; May 14, 1926 (W. G. Rose, "All in the Day's Work").

68. *PD*, July 1, 20, 1854; February 23, 1855; January 22, 1856; *Daily Leader*, September 11, 1857.

69. *PD*, September 27, 1852; July 1, 1853; January 3, 1854; January 4, 1859.

70. *PD*, September 22, 1847; May 28, 1850; August 30, 1852; September 21, 1852; January 3, 1853; March 7, 1855; June 9, 1855; September 21, 1855; July 27, 1859; May 28, 1861; September 11, 1861; March 19, 1862; August 26, 1862; July 7, 1864; June 27, 1865; March 5, 1866; April 14, 1866; July 5, 1867; *Daily Leader*, March 6, 1857; Tifereth Israel, Minutes, October 16, 1859; January 29, 1865.

71. *Cleveland Leader*, December 2, 1857; January 5, 1869; *PD*, August 21, 1855; March 1, 1859; March 24, 1860; May 31, 1861; July 1, 1861; August 27, 1862; February 15, 1862.

72. *PD*, February 21, 1885. See also *AmIsr*, January 17, 1889; August 10, 1893; *HO*, August 11, 1893, p. 4; Rose, *op. cit.*, p. 183.

73. Works Progress Administration, *Court Record Series* (Cleveland, September, 1938), p. 47.

74. *Ibid.*, Vol. IV, 1861-1866 (Cleveland, 1939).

75. See *AmIsr*, December 21, 1893; see also *JR&O*, July 7, 1900 (obituary of Mahrum Mittelberger).

76. Rosenberry, *op. cit.*, p. 155.

77. PD, May 22, 1904; *JR&O*, May 27, 1904. Twelve of the sixteen incorporators were Jews.

78. Nevins, *Rockefeller*, I, p. 212.

79. *JR&O*, June 23, 1899; Works Progress Administration, *Annals, 1818-1935* Vol. I, 1837-1850 (Cleveland, June, 1939) pp. 233-34; Aaron Lowentritt's widow survived her husband fifty-two years and died in 1918. *JInd*, March 1, 1918.

80. A detailed account of Peixotto's diplomatic and communal career is in Lloyd P. Gartner, "Roumania, America and World Jewry: Consul Peixotto in Bucharest," *AJHQ*, LVIII, No. 1 (September, 1968), pp. 25-117.

81. *AmIsr*, October 18, 1894; *B'nai B'rith Magazine*, February, 1938, pp. 176-77; *JInd*, September 7, 1906; April 23, 1909; *JR&O*, September 7, 1906; Guido Kisch, *In Search of Freedom* (London, 1949), pp. 125-26; M. S. Rosewater, "Autobiography," in American Jewish Archives, Cincinnati, Ohio, pp. 10, 11, 40.

82. See memoirs of Simon Wolf, *Presidents I Have Known* (Washington, D.C., 1918); *JInd*, June 8, 1923; *JR&O*, October 26, 1906.

83. Willoughby University of Lake Erie, Trustees' Minutes, July 11, 1835, MS. 2352, Western Reserve Historical Society; *Herald and Guardian*, July 29, 1837, in Works Progress Administration, *Annals, 1818-1935*, 1837, Vol. XX, Part I (Cleveland, 1938).

84. *Herald and Guardian*, February 7, 27, 28, 1838, *loc. cit.*, Vol. XXI, Part I (Cleveland, 1938); Trustee's Minutes, April 10, 1838.

85. *Herald and Guardian*, March 13, 1839, *loc. cit.*, Vol. XXII, Part I (Cleveland, 1938).

86. I. J. Benjamin, *Three Years in America 1859-1862*, 2 vols. (Philadelphia, 1956), I, pp. 51-53; Isaac S. and Suzanne A. Emmanuel, *History of the Jews in the Netherland Antilles*, 2 vols. (Cincinnati, 1970), I, pp. 424-26; II, pp. 1076-77.

87. Korn, *American Jewry and the Civil War* (Philadelphia, 1951), p. 4; Benjamin Rabinowitz, "The Young Men's Hebrew Associations (1854-1913)," *PAJHS*, XXXVII (1947), pp. 223, 224.

88. *Isr*, November 30, 1860; April 19, 1861; April 1, 1864; April 15, 1864; *AmIsr*, March 31, 1883; *JMess*, December 14, 1860; *JR&O*, September 11, 1908; *Occident*, April, 1861, pp. 41, 42.

89. Rabinowitz, *loc. cit.*

90. *Isr*, January 31, 1868; January 1, 1869; January 8, 1869.

91. *Isr*, March 7, 1862; June 24, 1864; April 29, 1870; *JMess*, June 17, 1870, p. 5; *Jewish Times* (New York), April 29, 1870; *Cleveland Leader*, March 5, 1862; June 30, 1864; *Isr*, March 7, 1862.

92. *Isr*, April 29, 1870; *JMess*, June 17, 1870; *Jewish Times* (New York), April 29, 1870.

93. *Isr*, January 1, 1869 cf. Rudolf Glanz, "The Rise of the Jewish Club," *loc. cit.*, pp. 169-86.

94. Bloom V. Richards, 2 Ohio State, p. 387 (quotation on pp. 390, 391).

95. Cincinnati V. Rice, 15 Ohio Reports, p. 225.

96. *Jewish Times* (New York), August 12, 1870.

97. *Isr*, May 3, 1867 see also M. U. Schappes, *A Documentary History of the Jews in the United States, 1654–1875* (New York, 1950), pp. 510, 511. The Cleveland Committee to cooperate with the committees of other Jewish communities consisted of: A. Wiener, A. Jankau, S. Newmark, M. Liebenthal, K. Hays, M. Halle, A. Schwab, M. L. Peixotto, M. Moses, and S. Mann. E. Budwig was secretary.

98. James G. Heller, *Isaac M. Wise: His Life, Work and Thought* (New York, 1965), p. 276.

99. *Cleveland Leader*, October 22, 1857; see Schappes, *op. cit.*, pp. 315–24.

100. *Cleveland Leader*, February 12, 15, 1859.

101. Bertram W. Korn, *op. cit., passim*; Kenneth E. Davison, *Cleveland During the Civil War* ([Columbus], 1962); Andreas Dorpalen, in "The German Element and the Issues of the Civil War," *Mississippi Valley Historical Review*, XXIX, No. 1 (June, 1942), 55–76, notes that Germans (including Jews) generally supported Lincoln's candidacy in 1860 but that German businessmen, like other businessmen, distrusted Republican fervor and preferred Douglas.

102. Sefton D. Temkin, "Isaac Mayer Wise and the Civil War," *AJA*, XV, no. 2 (November, 1963), 120–42.

103. Nevins, *The Ordeal of the Union*, Vol. II, pp. 128, 131; Roy F. Nichols, *The Disruption of American Democracy* (1948); paper ed., New York, 1962), pp. 99, 214, 499, 500.

104. Thomas Kessner, "Gershom Mendes Seixas: His Religious 'Calling', Outlook and Competence," *AJHQ*, LVIII, No. 4 (June, 1969), pp. 445–71; Archer H. Shaw, *The Plain Dealer: One Hundred Years in Cleveland* (New York, 1942), pp. 124–25; Davison, *op. cit.*, pp. 14–15.

105. Korn, *op. cit.*, p. 34; *PD*, May 15, 1861; see also *JInd*, July 22, 1921, *JR&O*, May 27, 1904; cf. Emerson D. Fite, *Social and Industrial Conditions in the North during the Civil War* (New York, 1910), pp. 278–80.

106. Tifereth Israel, Minutes, December 29, 1861; July 27, 1869.

107. Fite, *op. cit.*, pp. 47, 57, 88, 217n., 220, 227–29.

108. Elroy McKendree Avery, *A History of Cleveland and its Environs*, 3 vols (Chicago-New York, 1918), II, 190; Rose, *op. cit.*, p. 598; *PD*, July 9, 1880; *AmIsr*, February 8, 1894; October 5, 1899; *HO*, February 27, 1891; *JInd*, October 2, 1953; *JR&O*, February 16, 1900; May 27, 1904; May 5, 1905; February 9, 1923; December 7, 1923. On Slesinger's service against the Indians, see Henry Cohen, "A Brave Frontiersman," *PAJHS*, VIII (1900), p. 59; General A. G. Forsyth, "A Frontier Fight," *Harper's Monthly Magazine*, June, 1895, p. 43; Charles Reznikoff, "The Search for the Indian Scout," *Menorah Journal* (Spring 1948), pp. 218. It was the custom of Cleveland Lodge No. 16, B'nai B'rith to decorate the graves of Jewish soldiers. Those memorialized in 1912 were: Jacob Arnstein (Mexican War, see *supra* note 40) Michael Bodenheimer, Jacob Brown, David Dauby, Samson Goldberg, Herman Goldsmith, Leopold Goldreich, Solomon Green, Isaac Gross, Joseph Koch, Moses Koch, Marx Leopold, A. J. Marx, Moses Marx, F. Muhlhauser, J. J. Newman, Joseph Perley, Isaac Richman, H. Rosenbaum, Jacob Rosenberg, Sol Sloss, Joachim Steiner, Samuel Steiner, Abram Straus, H. L. Straus, Morris Ullman (Confederacy), Louis Weinberg, *JR&O*, May 24, 1912. These sources contain inconsistencies, many of which arise from different spellings of family names and changes of surnames. Other Civil War veterans were Felix Rosenberg, who fought for the Confederacy and settled in Cleveland around 1880 (*JR&O*, March 31, 1916), and Herman Stern, who likewise moved to Cleveland, after service in the Union Army (*JR&O*, February 9, 1923).

109. These resolutions were reprinted from an untraceable source in *JInd*, February 11, 1916; Daniel J. Ryan, "Lincoln and Ohio," *OAHQ*, XXXII, No. 1 (January, 1923), pp. 7 ff.

CHAPTER II

1. Ahram Vossen Goodman, "A Jewish Peddler's Diary, 1842-1843," *AJA*, III, No. 3 (June, 1951), p. 85.

2. A photostat of the document of sale is in the Abe L. Nebel Collection, American Jewish Archives, Cincinnati, Ohio.

3. Related by I. M. Wise, in *AmIsr*, August 20, 1858, of a visit in Cleveland; his source was doubtless local informants, and the event was a comparatively recent "first" which therefore was accurately recalled. An 1888 report, however, mentions one Morris Marks as the first person interred in 1840. *AmIsr*. July 6, 1888. In 1856 there were 20 interments, and 32 in 1857. *Cleaveland Leader*, January 3, 1857; January 4, 1858. With a population reasonably estimated no higher than 200 families (*AmIsr*, August 20, 1858), most of the deceased could only have been children. A brief, useful study is Allan Peskin, *This Tempting Freedom: The Early Years of Cleveland Judaism and Anshe Chesed Congregation* (Cleveland, ca. 1973).

4. *Occident*, September, 1852, p. 6.

5. *Occident*, June, 1844, p. 144; September, 1852, p. 306. "In the house on the first street, Mr. Kelley reported a bill to incorporate the Anshi Chesed congregation of the city of Cleveland." *Cleveland Herald*, February 7, 1842, in Works Progress Administration, *Annals of Cleveland*, Vol. XXV, Part I (Cleveland, 1938), No. 377.

6. *Cleveland Herald*, February 7, 1842, p. 2; *JR&O*, March 22, 1912, Part I, p. 2.

7. *JR&O*, March 22, 1912, Part I, p. 2; this account appears to be based upon available congregational records. Aid came from two New York congregations; Hyman B. Grinstein, *The Rise of the Jewish Community of New York 1654-1860* (Philadelphia, 1945), p. 522.

8. The document is in the Cuyahoga County Recorder's Office, Deeds, Vol. 34, p. 412.

9. *Cleveland Herald*, October 7, 1845.

10. Edmund H. Chapman, *Cleveland: Village to Metropolis. A Case Study of Problems of Urban Development in Nineteenth Century America*, (Cleveland, 1964), pp. 73-82.

11. *Cleveland Herald*, October 7, 1845, p. 2; *Occident*, March, 1845, p. 599; October, 1846, p. 358; *Jewish Chronicle* (London), May 2, 1845, p. 158; *Voice of Jacob* (London), May 9, 1845, p. 158; *Allgemeine Zeitung des Judentums*, (Leipzig) January 5, 1840, p. 21; Rachel Wischnitzer, *Synagogue Architecture in the United States*, (Philadelphia, 1955), p. 42.

Those present at an incorporation meeting on May 18, 1846, were Joel Engelhart, Aaron Lowentritt, Gerson Strauss, A. Lewin, Asher Lehman, Jacob L. Richard, Michael Wiener, I. Stern, Kalman Roskopf, David Heller, D. Frank, W. Riglander, R. Strauss, Moses Moses, Michael Baer, L. Ehrlich, Moses Schott, Simon Newmark, A. Tuch, S. Erlanger, Frederick Goldsmith, Jacob Silverman, Joseph Grumpan, I. Ansel, Jacob Frank, Simson Thorman, Isaac Hoffman, Simon Hoffman (Hopfermann), S. L. Colman, Moses Alsbacher, N. Tuch, M. Lowenthal, I. Michael, and Seligman L. Stern. *JInd*, March 15, 1912. The same list is given in *JR*, February 21, 1896, except that "Riglander" is "Richlander"; R. "Strauss" is "Strouse"; M. Thorman and N. Strauss are added; and for Joel Engelhart, "I. Engelhart" appears three times.

12. *PD*, August 7, 1846.

13. An account of Kalisch's career may be found in Louis J. Swichkow and Lloyd P. Gartner, *History of the Jews of Milwaukee* (Philadelphia, 1963), pp. 39–40, 42–44, and notes *ad loc.*

14. The first charter was secured that year. (The congregation was later incorporated in 1853 under an act passed the previous year.) Another meeting was held October 6, 1850, at which the following were elected officers: A. Schwab, president; K. Koch, vice-president; G. A. Davis, treasurer; E. Pincus, secretary; S. Stein, *shamus* (sexton); and the following were elected trustees: G. A. Davis (for three years); K. Koch (for two years); D. Hexter (for three years); S. Loeb (for two years); I. Engelhart and W. Richlander (for one year each). Tifereth Israel, Minutes, October 6, 1850. See the report of a meeting at the house of Joseph Greenebaum on "Senecka Street," at which the following were elected: S. Hexter, president; A. Lehman, vice-president; L. Wolf and M. Nusbaum, trustees; and the "meeting requested that the said President and Trustees shall apply for a Charter for the Congregation to be called Tifereth Israel Society." Tifereth Israel, Minutes, July 15, 1850; *JR&O*, November 9, 1906. The latter quotes a record of Cuyahoga County, dated July 17, 1850, in which the members of the Tifereth Israel Society are stated to have met at the house of Joseph Greenebaum on Seneca Street, elected S. Hexter, president; A. Lehman, vice-president, I. Wolf and M. Nusbaum, trustees, and applied for a charter through E. Pincus, their secretary.

15. Tifereth Israel, Minutes, November 17, 1850; *Occident*, December, 1850, p. 479. Leeser was dubious of these arrangements and implied that this was approach to Reform. He thought highly of Rabbi Kalisch, an opinion he was shortly to revise. *Ibid.*, p. 480. Actually, this arrangement, a sort of adaptation of a *bet din* tribunal, was probably the work of Orthodox members who suspected Kalisch's Reform proclivities. No record shows that the "assistant rabbis" actually functioned as such.

16. Tifereth Israel, Minutes, June 9, 1850; September 22, 1850.

17. *AmIsr*, April 30, 1880; *JMess*, April 30, 1880; *Occident*, September, 1852, p. 307; March, 1855, p. 618; *JR&O*, March 22, 1912, Part I, p. 2.

18. Tifereth Israel, Minutes, May 26, 1850; June 9, 1850.

19. *Ibid.*, January 3, 1852. It is not clear whether *rishon* would be an Aaronide and *sheni* a Levite, as tradition demanded.

20. *Cleveland Daily Leader*, September 29, 1861.

21. Swichkow and Gartner, *loc. cit.*; *AmIsr*, April 30, 1880.

22. *Occident*, September, 1857.

23. *JMess*, July 7, 1882.

24. *Occident*, September, 1852, pp. 307–8.

25. *PD*, September 20, 1849; such statements are made about the High Holidays but, significantly, not about other Jewish holidays.

26. Allan Nevins, *John D. Rockefeller: The Heroic Age of American Enterprise*, 2 vols. (New York, 1940), p. 88.

27. *Occident*, April, 1852, p. 45; *JInd*, May 5, 1911; *JR&O*, November 15, 1907; November 29, 1912.

28. *JR&O*, May 27, 1904.

29. Nevins, *op. cit.*, I, p. 118.

30. *Forest City Democrat*, February 7, 1854; *Occident*, April, 1854, pp. 55, 56; *JR&O*, November 15, 1907; Bertram W. Korn, *The Early Jews of New Orleans* (Waltham, Mass., 1969), p. 256. The will is given in Morris U. Schappes, *A Documentary History of the Jews in the United States 1654–1875*, rev. ed. (New York, 1952), pp. 333–41, clause 50.

31. Tifereth Israel, Minutes, May 11, 1854; *Cleveland Leader*, May 26, 1855; No-

vember 1, 1855; January 5, 1856, *Isr*, January 4, 1856; Wischnitzer, *op. cit.*, p. 45.

32. Levy wrote in Hebrew under the Hebrew date Heshvan 14, 5612 (October, 1851), and it was published in the *Occident* of June and July, 1852; the translations are taken from the *Asmonean*, July 9, 1852. On Levy's rabbinic ordination, see *Occident*, April, 1852, p. 45; since he refers to finding a fine synagogue, Levy must have arrived after 1846.

33. Letter by Kalisch to *Asmonean*, September 10, 1852, supplemented by *PD*, October 4, 1851.

34. *PD*, October 4, 1851.

35. *PD*, October 23, 1851.

36. *Occident*, April, 1852, p. 45; Emanuel Goldsmith, letter to ed., *Asmonean*, September 24, 1852. The issuance of a Jewish bill of divorce, which is a legally complicated and morally responsible operation, is a function confined to men learned in the Law. In autonomous or centrally organized Jewish communities, only their recognized authorities may perform the act; privately arranged divorces, even by a rabbi, would be invalid and the participants punished. For an authoritative exposition, see Louis M. Epstein, *Marriage Laws in the Bible and Talmud* (New York, 1942).

37. On this occasion he signed himself Ab Bet Din, perhaps with reference to his two "assistant rabbis," or to emphasize his claim to be the sole rabbinic authority. *Asmonean*, September 10, 1852. Jewish law actually requires a tribunal: one rabbi and two others familiar with matters of divorce law (*tiv gittin*).

38. Tifereth Israel records contain no reference to this episode.

39. *AmIsr*, October 26, 1855. On the gathering, see Moshe Davis, *The Emergence of Conservative Judaism: The Historical School in Nineteenth Century America* (Philadelphia, 1963), pp. 130–33; to Davis' list of participants (*ibid.*, p. 422, n. 36) should be added Rabbi Leo Merzbacher of New York; *Cleveland Herald*, October 18, 1855; *AmIsr, loc. cit.*; *Occident*, December, 1855, pp. 421–22; *ibid.*, May, 1856, pp. 75–76.

40. *AmIsr, loc. cit.*

41. *Cleveland Herald*, October 19, 1855.

42. October 23, 1855.

43. *Cleveland Herald*, October 22, 1855; dispatch of October 25 in *Isr*, November 2, 1855.

44. *JR&O*, March 22, 1912, Part I, p. 2.

45. Tifereth Israel, Minutes April 12, 1857; April 4, 1858; June 23, 1861; *Isr*, April 5, 1861; *JMess*, October 24, 1862; *Occident*, September, 1857.

46. *Isr*, December 21, 1860, p. 198.

47. *Isr*, April 30, 1863; Grinstein, *op. cit.*, pp. 256–57; Cohen was probably the first American composer of Jewish music. His collected compositions include:

a. *The Orphtus, or Musical Recreations, for the Family C'rcled Public Worship with Piano and Organ Accompaniment. An Entire New Collection of Songs, Duets, Choruses, Hymns & Psalms.* Undated, it is dedicated to Benjamin F. Peixotto, Grand Sar of B'nai B'rith, an office he held in 1863–1864.

b. *Sacred Harp of Judah: A Choice Collection of Music for the Use of Synagogues, Schools, and Home. Part I—Sabbath Liturgy/The Result of 25 Years' Experience and Worship* (Cleveland, n.d. [probably late 1860s]).

c. *Musical Relaxations for the Family Circle, for the School and Public Service* (MS, n.d.). Songs for holidays, both original hymns and settings of liturgical texts.

d. *The Sacred Harp of Judah or Musical Recreations, for the Family Circle and Public Worship with Piano and Organ Accompaniment. An Entire Collection of Songs, Duets, Choruses, Hymns & Psalms* (Cleveland, 1878). The Preface states that some of the music is drawn from other sources, especially Congregation Beth Elohim of Charleston, S.C., and "Dr. Wise's Hymn Book." The simplicity of the music is emphasized by the author.

The works of this unobtrusive composer, like the rest of nineteenth century American Jewish music, appear to merit musicological-historical attention.

48. Tifereth Israel, Minutes, November 30, 1859; April 9, 1860; September 13, 1860; *JMess*, August 3, 1860. The incense formula (*pittum ha-ketoret*) and an Aramaic invocation (*Berikh shemey*) were omitted. The Aaronides' recitation of the priestly blessing ("*dukhan*") was retained, however.

49. A Cincinnatian from 1844 until 1851 or later, he had been an official of Bene Israel congregation in that city. Schappes, *op. cit.*, p. 650.

50. The bitter words are Isaac Leeser's in the *Occident*, May, 1861, pp. 87–88. His anger was unusual—Leeser had become sorrowfully accustomed to synagogues turning towards Reform—and is probably explained by his previous satisfaction over the state of traditional Judaism in Cleveland. Another sentence by Leeser is significant:

The philanthropist Judah Touro, when he bequeathed $3,000 to this congregation, never dreamed that his money would be eventually appropriated to effect so shameful and outrageous an innovation on [*sic*] our worship as the converting of a Synagogue into the style of a Christian church, and the inauguration of radical changes in the creed, faith and ritual of the Jewish religion. We question the legality of the act according to the laws of Ohio or the United States. (*Ibid.*)

Leeser had played an important role from a distance in framing the will of the New Orleans merchant, who acquired Jewish interests only a few years before his death in 1854. Quite possibly, he endorsed the struggling Cleveland congregation's appeal to Touro by means of a word to Gershom Kursheedt, the confidant and executor. Leeser's fury suggests that he felt personally betrayed by what he regarded as a misappropriation of the bequest. Korn, *op. cit.*, pp. 245–58. On the other hand, reports from Cleveland to the *Isr* first exaggerated and then underestimated the force of the drive for Reform. *Isr*, April 5, 12, 1861.

51. Tifereth Israel, Minutes, April 9, 1861.

52. *Ibid.*, July 14, 1861.

53. *Ibid.*, August 11, 1861.

54. *Ibid.*, April 20, 1862.

55. Grinstein, *op. cit.*, pp. 362–63; Musaph was the "additional" service on the mornings of Sabbaths and Festivals. Tifereth Israel, Minutes, April 12, 1863.

56. *Ibid.*, September 27, 1863. Clearly, few if any individuals bought the biblically mandated "four species."

57. *Ibid.*, April 16, 1865.

58. *Ibid.*, October 8, 1865. Such covenants of Sabbath observance are known from Cincinnati, San Francisco, and elsewhere; Schappes, *op. cit.*, pp. 392–94, 677 n.2; I. J. Benjamin, *Three Years in America, 1859–1862*, 2 vols. (Philadelphia, 1951), I, p. 82. The petition implies that Jewish merchants did not fear Christian competition when closing on Saturday.

59. Tifereth Israel, Minutes, October 15, 1865.

60. *Ibid.*, November 4, 1865.

61. *Isr*, October 16, 1863. See also *JR&O*, March 22, 1912, Part I, p. 2.

62. *JR&O*, March 12, 1897.

63. Tifereth Israel, Minutes, June 21, 1866.

64. *Ibid.*, December 15, 24, 1865; *JR*, March 12, 1897. Early in 1865 consideration was given to electing Ferdinand Sarner rabbi. *Isr*, February 17, 1865; July 13, 1866.

65. *JR&O*, March 22, 1912, Part I, p. 2; *Jewish Times* (New York), August 12, 1870. The three-year cycle was an ancient practice, long abandoned in Ashkenazic Jewry. Its revival was intended to shorten the weekly Torah reading and in the context of its adoption represented a step towards Reform.

66. Tifereth Israel, Minutes, July 22, 29, 1866; August 23, 26, 1866; October 7,

1866. Wise's was the most traditional of the Reform prayer books, and the meeting of July 29, 1866, which adopted it, altered some of its contents: "everything appertaining to the bodily resurrection, the bodily Messiah, rebuilding of the temple and the sacrifices [several words removed] which was unanimously adopted." The missing words can only be "deleted" or a synonym. Moshe Davis, *Yahadut Amerika Be-Hitpathutah* [The Shaping of American Judaism] (New York, 1951), pp. 307–17, compares and analyzes these prayer books.

67. *AmIsr*, October 19, 1866. *Aufrufen* are callings to the Torah reading (*aliyot*) on occasions required by custom: a bridegroom on the Sabbath before marriage, a father upon the birth of a child, a family member thirty days after the death of an immediate relative or on the anniversary of such a death, a boy at his thirteenth birthday, and several others.

68. *AmIsr*, July 26, 1867.

69. Tifereth Israel Minutes, February 10, 28, 1867.

70. *Ibid.*, February 3, 1867. In his recollections thirty years later, Cohen states that he returned from Milwaukee directly to Anshe Chesed, thus glossing over the humiliating episode at Tifereth Israel. *JR*, March 12, 1897. The ultimate exposure of his dazzling replacement could have given him some satisfaction.

71. *AmIsr*, February 22, 1867.

72. See, for example, the *Cleveland Leader*, September 20, 1869, p. 2; September 30, 1869, p. 2. Anshe Chesed, thanking the learned Rabbi Marcus Jastrow (1829–1903) of Philadelphia for "masterly" sermons as a guest preacher "which were more of an intellectual treat than we ever enjoyed," pointedly added that "his words . . . are such as not to break down the holy faith of our ancestors, but to build up the holy ark of Judaism . . . ." *AmIsr*, November 27, 1868. This observation would be gratuitous if it did not refer to Rabbi Mayer, who had come to Cleveland the previous year.

73. Tifereth Israel, Minutes, September 13, 1868; October 13, 1870; *Isr*, October 21, 1870; *Jewish Times* (New York), August 12, 1870.

74. See, for example, an extract from one of Mayer's sermons in the *Cleveland Leader*, February 28, 1870.

75. *Cleveland Leader*, November 9, 1869.

76. *Occident*, September, 1857; see also *JMess*, August 3, 1860.

77. *PD*, September 5, 1887; *JInd*, April 26, 1912, Sect. III, p. 24 (but the date of foundation in 1867 is mistaken); *JR&O*, September 23, 1910, Part III, p. 4. See also M. J. Gries, "The Jewish Community of Cleveland," in S. P. Orth, *A History of Cleveland, Ohio*, 3 vols. (Chicago-Cleveland, 1910), I, p. 380; this may be the "Polish Kahal" seen by the traveller I. J. Benjamin in 1862, and the seed of the later Anshe Emeth. *JR&O*, June 3, 1904; Benjamin, *op. cit.*, II, p. 281.

78. *PD*, February 9, 1864.

79. August 12, 1870.

80. *PD*, September 5, 1887, *JInd*, April 26, 1912, Sect. III, p. 24; *JR&O*, September 23, 1910. See also Gries, *loc. cit.*

81. *Cf.* Swichkow and Gartner, *op. cit.*, pp. 30, 49, showing a far lower proportion in Milwaukee; a comparison of Jewish population estimates and the single synagogue and one *minyan* in Rochester, N.Y., suggests an even lower percentage. Stuart E. Rosenberg, *The Jewish Community in Rochester 1843–1925* (New York, 1954), pp. 41, 52, 148.

82. Mordecai Eliav, *Ha-Hinnukh ha-Yehudi be-Germaniah bi-Ymey ha-Haskalah veha-Emanzipaziah* [Jewish Education in Germany in the Period of Enlightenment and Emancipation] (Jerusalem, 1960), pp. 179–208 passim.

83. W. G. Rose, *Cleveland: The Making of a City* (Cleveland, 1950), pp. 206, 244.

84. Swichkow and Gartner, *op. cit.*, p. 52.

85. *Occident*, September, 1849, p. 331.

86. *Occident*, September, 1852, pp. 305–7. His teacher was Rabbi Hirsch Kunreuther, rabbi of Gelnhausen near Frankfort from about 1820 until 1848, who conducted a yeshiva. M. Strauss, *Festschrift zum 200 jahrigen Jubiláum der beiden Gemiluth-Chasodim v. Kabronim in Gelnhausen* (Gelnhausen, 1911), p. 21.

87. The catechism is probably Judah Lob Ben Sew, *Religionslehrbuch für die jüdische Jugend beiderlei Geschlechts* . . . (Darmstadt, 1834), containing only the German text of the author's *Jesode Hadath* [*sic*]: *Kolel 'Ikarey ha-'Emunah* . . . , 3rd ed. (Vienna, 1823). The latter, which is the original version, contains two introductions; the text is facing Hebrew, and German in Hebrew script. Although the doctrines inculcated are formally Orthodox, the catechism places emphasis on Judaism as a natural, enlightened religion and on the civic duties of the Jews. It hardly mentions or cites the Talmud or other rabbinic literature, and does not refer to a Jewish condition of exile or to messianic-redemptive hopes. Teaching by catechism was a sharply disputed innovation. See Isaac Barzilay, "National and Anti-National Trends in the Berlin Haskalah," *Jewish Social Studies*, XXI, No. 3 (July, 1959), 177, and Jakob J. Petuchowski, "Manuals and Catechisms of the Jewish Religion in the Early Period of Emancipation," in *Studies in Nineteenth Century Jewish Intellectual History*, ed. Alexander Altmann (Cambridge, Mass., 1964), pp. 45–64.

88. *Allgemeine Zeitung des Judentums*, October 25, 1852, p. 527; *Cleveland Leader*, November 2, 1855; *Occident*, September, 1849, p. 331; September, 1852, pp. 307, 308; R. Glanz, "Jews in Relation to the Cultural Milieu of the Germans in America up to the 1880s," in *Studies in Judaica Americana* (New York, 1970), pp. 245–46.

89. *Occident*, September, 1857.

90. *Daily True Democrat*, December 18, 1849.

91. *Plain Dealer*, April 22, 1850; *ibid.*, May 6, 1850, praises Adam in flowery terms.

92. *Cleveland Leader*, November 2, 1855.

93. *Daily True Democrat*, May 7, 1851.

94. Tifereth Israel, Minutes, June 1, 1856.

95. Mark A. DeWolfe Howe, *James Ford Rhodes, American Historian* (New York and London, 1929) pp. 30–31. Rose, *op. cit.*, pp. 276, 278.

96. *Isr*, August 20, 1858. See also *Occident*, September and December, 1857.

97. *Occident*, June, 1858; Tifereth Israel, Minutes, November 7, 1858; April 24, 1859; *Isr*, December 21, 1860; *JMess*, August 3, 1860; *Occident*, November, 1858, pp. 407, 408; December, 1858, pp. 455, 456; April, 1861, p. 41; March, 1862, p. 568.

98. *PD*, July 10, 1888.

99. *Isr*, August 9, 1861.

100. *Isr*, October 25, 1861.

101. *JMess*, October 24, 1862; *Isr*, November 6, 1863; *PD*, July 18, 1864.

102. *Isr*, November 14, 1862.

103. Tifereth Israel, Minutes, October 15, 1865; April 1, 1866; May 16, 1867; March 31, 1869; December 30, 1869; April 17, 1870.

104. On these day schools, see Davis, *Emergence*, pp. 37–41; Grinstein, *op. cit.*, pp. 228–46; *idem*, "Studies in the History of Jewish Education in New York City (1728–1860)," *The Jewish Review*, II, Nos. 1 and 2–3 (April, July-October, 1944), pp. 41–58, 187–201; Morris A. Gutstein, *A Priceless Heritage; The Epic Growth of Nineteenth Century Chicago Jewry* (New York, 1953), pp. 211–26; Lloyd P. Gartner, *Jewish Education in the United States: A Documentary History* (New York, 1969), pp. 7–10, 61–65, 80–84; *idem*, "Temples of Liberty Unpolluted: American Jews and Public Schools, 1840–1875," in *A Bicentennial Festschrift for Jacob Rader Marcus*, ed. Bertram Wallace Korn (Waltham, Mass., and New York, 1976), pp. 157–91.

105. *Occident*, September, 1853, pp. 308–10.

106. *JR&O*, November 15, 1907; November 29, 1912.

107. Davis, *Emergence*, pp. 78–79; S. W. and J. M. Baron, "Palestinian Messengers in America, 1849–1879," *Jewish Social Studies*, V, No. 2 (April, 1943), 141; *Cleveland Leader*, June 26, 27, 1854; *Occident*, August, 1854, pp. 264–65; September, 1854, pp. 324–25.

108. "Autobiography of Joseph Hays," American Jewish Archives, Cincinnati, Ohio; *Occident*, July, 1855, p. 200.

109. *Isr*, January 6, 1860; November 29, 1861; October 12, 1866; November 8, 1867; *Occident*, April, 1861, p. 42; *JR*, March 12, 1897.

110. *Isr*, February 9, 1866.

111. *Isr*, July 13, 1860; July 26, 1861; March 13, 1863.

112. *JR&O*, October 31, 1913. Word soon reached the old country; *Ben Chananja*, 1865, No. 14, p. 232, cited from Gotthard Deutsch catalogue, American Jewish Archives, Cincinnati, Ohio.

113. Its charter name was the Ungarischer Frauen Unterstützungs Verein. *AmIsr*, May 18, 1893.

114. See Isaac M. Wise's colorful account in *Isr*, July 17, 1868.

115. Report of trustees of the District Grand Lodge No. 2, *Isr*, February 21, 1868.

116. *AmIsr*, July 24, 1868.

117. *Ibid.*

118. William Kriegshaber in *AmIsr*, October 8, 1868.

119. *AmIsr*, January 13, 1869.

120. *AmIsr*, June 18, 1869.

121. *Ibid.*

122. See David J. Rothman, *The Discovery of the Asylum: Social Order and Disorder in the New Republic* (Boston, 1971), for the theory of the custodial institution. The memoirs of Edward Dahlberg, *Because I Was Flesh* (New York, 1963), pp. 65–91, contain a hostile description of the author's years at the asylum from 1912 to 1917.

CHAPTER III

1. Rollin Lynde Hartt, "The Ohioans," *The Atlantic Monthly*, No. 505 (November, 1899), p. 681; on economic development, see Philip D. Jordan, *Ohio Comes of Age 1873–1900*, in *History of the State of Ohio*, Vol. V (Columbus, 1943), pp. 222–23, 233–37.

2. *JR&O*, September 23, 1910, Part I; cf. *JR&O*, October 9, 1914.

3. *PD*, January 14, 1882.

4. *PD*, May 6, 1904.

5. *PD*, April 15, 1881.

6. *PD*, November 9, 1882.

7. *PD*, March 21, 1884; April 8, 1884.

8. *PD*, March 30, 1883.

9. E.g., *PD*, May 8, 1883.

10. *PD*, December 5, 1883.

11. *PD*, April 11, 1883.

12. For example, *PD*, December 15, 17, 1884, advts.

13. *PD*, October 24, 1884.

14. *PD*, December 1, 1884.

15. *PD*, January 26, 1885.

16. *PD*, December 5, 1884.

17. *PD*, May 22, 1902.

18. *PD*, January 14, 1886; April 4, 1886; April 25, 1886; June 3, 1886; July 1, 1886; October 24, 1886; January 11, 1887; February 27, 1887; May 29, 1887; March 3, 1892.

19. *AmIsr*, February 4, 1887.

20. *PD*, December 31, 1899.

21. *PD*, October 17, 1888.

22. *PD*, May 15, 1890; October 8, 1890; of other failures, *PD*, February 20, 1892; January 8, 1895.

23. For example, see report on the difficulties of Rosenheim and Manche, *PD*, October 8, 1890.

24. *PD*, October 1, 1892.

25. *PD*, December 21, 1886.

26. *PD*, June 11, 1887.

27. *AmIsr*, August 15, 1885; January 15, 1887.

28. Excelsior saw fit to publish this and other missives in its advertisement, *PD*, December 15, 1884.

29. *PD*, December 17, 1884.

30. *PD*, October 29, 1884.

31. *PD*, June 2, 1888.

32. *PD*, April 13, 1882; July 18, 1882; April 26, 1884; January 5, 1886.

33. *AmIsr*, December 24, 1896; June 3, 1897; *HO*, January 22, 1897.

34. *JR&O*, May 13, 1910.

35. *PD*, June 4, 1880; his unexplained suicide was reported here.

36. *PD*, March 3, 1879; March 5, 1880; July 18, 1882; July 19, 1882; January 17, 1883; January 5, 1886; March 24, 1888; October 16, 1890.

37. *PD*, February 18, 1904, showing all five incorporators of the Retail Merchants' Protective Association as Jewish.

38. *PD*, January 11, 1896.

39. Records of Jacob Perkins estate in Works Progress Administration, *Annals of Cleveland, Court Record Series*, Vol. III, 1858–1860 (Cleveland, 1939), p. 172.

40. *PD*, July 14, 1892.

41. *Ibid*,; *JR&O*, September 11, 1908.

42. W. G. Rose, *Cleveland: The Making of a City* (Cleveland, 1950), p. 597.

43. *PD*, May 22, 1905, Section IV; Anshe Chesed, Special Board Meeting, Minutes, August 27, 1912.

44. *PD*, December 7, 1902; December 4, 1905; *JR&O*, February 25, 1910.

45. Jews appear to have been among the small oil producers in Pennsylvania who were devoured by Standard Oil during the 1870s. Myer Lowentritt and Moses Koch were among them, while Manuel Halle testified to chaotic conditions in the industry before it was controlled by Rockefeller and his fellow-monopolists. Allan Nevins, *John D. Rockefeller: The Heroic Age of American Enterprise*, 2 vols. (New York, 1940), I, p. 212.

46. *PD*, July 11, 1896; *JR&O*, September 11, 1908; September 23, 1910.

47. *JR&O*, April 28, 1905; March 6, 1908; February 2, 1917.

48. *PD*, July 14, 1892; the following data are also taken from this valuable account.

49. *PD*, September 3, 1880.

50. *PD*, November 11, 1893.

51. *JR*, November 17, 1897.

52. *JR&O*, May 30, 1902; September 15, 1905; *PD*, November 26, 1896.

53. *JR&O*, June 15, 1917.

54. *PD*, May 22, 1902.

55. Rose, *op. cit.*, p. 699.

56. *Ibid.*, p. 797.

57. *Ibid.*, p. 617.

58. *Ibid.*, p. 477; Hays autobiography, American Jewish Archives, Cincinnati, Ohio.

59. *PD*, December 12, 1886.

60. Central National, Guardian Trust, Guarantee Title and Trust, Colonial National, Federal Trust.

61. They were Louis Black, Martin A. Marks, A. Stearn, Sol M. Hexter, and M. J. Mandelbaum director of two. *PD*, May 22, 1902, Part 3, pp. 8–9. Kaufman Hays was the only Jewish director in the banks with which he was connected.

62. *PD*, January 16, 1902.

63. *PD*, January 6, 1898; *JR&O*, December 26, 1913.

64. *PD*, May 22, 1904; *JR&O*, February 1, 1924.

65. *JInd*, November 3, 1916.

66. *JInd*, September 8, 1916.

67. *PD*, September 25, 1909. The Exchange closed on Yom Kippur in deference to its Jewish members.

68. *JInd*, November 13, 1908; September 7, 1923.

69. *JR&O*, May 17, 1901.

70. *Ibid.*; *PD*, October 25, 1904.

71. *JR&O*, September 12, 1913; *PD*, January 13, 14, 15, 1879; October 23, 1883; January 12, 1884; May 1, 1884; November 27, 1893; George A. Myers to James Ford Rhodes, April 30, 1920, in John A. Garraty, ed., "The Correspondence of George A. Mayers and James Ford Rhodes, 1910–1923—III," *Ohio Historical Quarterly*, LXIV, No. 3 (July, 1955), 285.

72. *PD*, February 23, 1896; December 29, 1895; February 11, 1900; *JR&O*, November 24, 1911.

73. Frederic C. Howe, *Confessions of a Reformer* (New York, 1925), pp. 213–15.

74. Address at Federation of Jewish Charities meeting, *JInd*, January 21, 1910.

75. Annual Report to Federation of Jewish Charities, *Ibid.*

76. *JR&O*, January 27, 1911; the newspaper editorially deplored this "disgrace to the civilization" and assailed the landlords, "many of whom are pillars of the church and leaders of society" who allegedly drew "immense rents. . . ." It advocated private investment in good working-class housing. *JR&O*, February 24, 1911.

77. *JR&O*, January 21, 1916.

78. *Ibid.* On businessmen's social outlooks and their claim to national leadership, see Robert H. Wiebe, *Businessmen and Reform: A Study of the Progressive Movement* (Cambridge, Mass., 1962), pp. 19, 164, 180–93, 206–24.

79. *PD*, June 22, 1886; June 21, 1887; July 16, 1892; June 20, 1882.

80. *PD*, April 26, 1886.

81. *JR&O*, August 14, 1914.

82. *PD*, July 14, 1892.

83. *Ibid.*

84. *PD*, September 10, 1885.

85. *PD*, September 27, 1896; Rose, *op. cit.*, p. 411. The family name was subsequently changed to Rorimer.

86. *PD*, September 29, 1895; Samuel Isham, *The History of American Painting* (New York, 1905), pp. 480, 483. Other promising artists included J. Levy and Max Joseph Spero. *PD*, January 21, 1889; June 5, 1904.

87. *PD*, January 10, 1904.

88. *PD*, July 26, 1889; June 16, 30, 1901; October 24, 1904.

89. *PD*, November 3, 1895; March 29, 1896; February 3, 1901; Rose, pp. 379, 402, 557, 767.

90. *PD*, November 27, 1898.

91. *JR&O*, September 4, 1908.

92. His views may be found in "Status of the Modern Hebrew: I. The Secret of his Immortality," *The Arena*, XXIV (1900), 421-31 ("prejudice and violence" is first used there); "The Twentieth Century Jew: An Observation," *Lippincott's Monthly Magazine*, LXXXI (1908), 268-70; *Ghosts of Yesterday: A Reappraisal of Moral Values and of Accepted Standards in this Changing World* (New York, 1935). A later, unsuccessful novel about lawyers is *The Jugglers* (New York, 1920); oral statement of Ezra Z. Shapiro, Brudno's first cousin, Jerusalem, April, 1977.

93. *JR*, June 10, 1898.

94. Rose, *op. cit.*, pp. 654, 655, 754; *JR*, April 9, 30, 1897; *PD*, September 1, 1879; *JR&O*, July 27, 1917; *CJN*, May 12, 1967.

95. Dr. John H. Lowman, "Dr. Marcus Rosenwasser," *Cleveland Medical Journal*, n.d., reprinted in *JR&O*, October 7, 1910; *JR&O*, September 9, 1910; *PD*, December 5, 1896; October 25, 1889; July 28, 1892. Family tradition has it that Dr. Rosenwasser was compelled to leave the deanship on account of anti-Semitism.

96. *PD*, June 12, 1888; October 25, 1889; *HO*, August 15, 1894.

97. *PD*, April 22, 1905; *JR&O*, April 29, 1905.

98. *PD*, October 25, 1889; July 21, 1892; August 23, 1892; *AmIsr*, April 29, 1887.

99. Rose, *op. cit.*, p. 766; *HO*, August 10, 1894; *PD*, February 24, 1904.

100. *Cleveland Leader*, June 20, 1877.

101. *PD*, June 9, 1881; July 15, 1881.

102. *PD*, December 13, 1889.

103. Quoted in Leonard A. Greenberg and Harold J. Jonas, "An American Anti-Semite in the Nineteenth Century," *Essays in Jewish Life and Thought in Honor of Salo Wittmayer Baron*, ed. Joseph L. Blau *et al.*, (New York, 1959), p. 281.

104. *Cleveland Federation for Charity and Philanthropy as Proposed by The Committee on Benevolent Associations of The Cleveland Chamber of Commerce January Seventh 1913* consists mainly of Marks' speech; see also Roy Lubove, *The Professional Altruist: The Emergence of Social Work as a Career 1880-1930* (Cambridge, Mass., 1965), pp. 186-88.

105. Tifereth Israel, Minutes, October 19, 1896.

106. *Ibid.*, October 1, 1893.

107. *Ibid.*, October 21, 1894.

108. *Ibid.*

109. *HO*, December 11, 1891.

110. Oral interview, January 25, 1972.

111. Jordan, *op. cit.*, pp. 472-73; Cleveland Council of Sociology, *Program and Revised Membership List*, 1906-1907 and 1911, MS 3090, Western Reserve Historical Society.

112. Records of Franklin Club, MS 445, Western Reserve Historical Society.

113. Family names, often including several family units, were Austrian, Feiss, Hahn, Halle, Hays, Joseph, Koch, H. Kohn, I. Levy, Machol, Mandelbaum, A. A. Michelson (the scientist), Moses, Richman.

114. *Cleveland Social Directory*, 1885-1886; *Cleveland Blue Book*, 1895; James B. Whipple, "Cleveland in Conflict: A Study in Urban Adolescence" (Ph.D. diss., Western Reserve University, 1951), pp. 321-22.

115. *PD*, October 17, 1883.

116. In 1889 Rabbi Machol referred to this as occurring "a few years ago." *PD*, May 24, 1889.

117. *PD*, June 15, 1882; *Wächter und Anzeiger*, August 9, 1902.

118. *JR&O*, May 15, 1903.

119. *PD*, January 20, 1893; July 12, 1893.

120. *PD*, July 12, 1893.

121. Rudolf Glanz, "Jews in Relation to the Cultural Milieu of the Germans in America before 1880," in *Studies in Judaica Americana* (New York, 1970), pp. 226–43; Louis J. Swichkow and Lloyd P. Gartner, *History of the Jews of Milwaukee* (Philadelphia, 1963), pp. 133–36. German was still taught in 1902 at the Jewish Orphan Home which Wolfenstein directed. *Wächter und Anzeiger*, August 9, 1902, p. 67.

122. *PD*, April 24, 1904.

123. *The Pythian Knight*, quoted in *PD*, July 14, 1889.

124. *PD*, May 23, 1889.

125. *PD*, May 24, 1889.

126. *PD*, May 23, 1889; naming the lodge after the Hungarian liberal leader suggests that these Jews were Hungarian.

127. *PD*, May 24, 1889; for further qualified denials, see *PD*, May 25, 1889.

128. Quoted in *PD*, July 14, 1889.

129. *PD*, June 27, 1889. Wheeler's diatribe may be the first manifestation of this charge against the Jews, later to become familiar.

130. *AmIsr*, January 23, 1886.

131. *AmIsr*, June 19, 1885.

132. *PD*, January 1, 1909.

133. Its membership roll of 1887 shows not more than four members from countries other than Germany and Bohemia. *PD*, January 1, 1888.

134. The Standard Club was a less plush Jewish club, founded in 1908. *JR&O*, September 23, 1910.

135. *JInd*, October 26, 1906.

136. *Ibid.*—a fighting article. In 1931 the club sold its building to the university, which called it Thwing Hall.

137. John Higham, *Send These to Me: Jews and Other Immigrants in Urban America* (New York, 1975), pp. 144–57; *PAJHS*, XLVII, No. 1 (September, 1957), 11–17; Glanz, "The Rise of the Jewish Club in America," *op. cit.*, pp. 169–87; Morton Rosenstock, *Louis Marshall: Defender of Jewish Rights* (Detroit, 1965), pp. 234–39; oral interview with Alfred A. Benesch, tape recording at Jewish Community Federation, Cleveland.

138. *JInd*, January 31, 1908.

139. *JR&O*, October 10, 1913. The principal attempted to make light of the assault as an "annual event," but the offenders were brought to trial. *YV*, October 6, 7, 1913.

140. *JInd*, May 1, 1908.

141. *HO*, May 3, 1895.

142. *JInd*, January 17, 1908.

143. *AmIsr*, July 6, 1888.

144. Cf. Swichkow and Gartner, *op. cit.*, pp. 146–47; Max Vorspan and Lloyd P. Gartner, *History of the Jews of Los Angeles* (San Marino, Calif., 1970), pp. 50, 78–79, 137–38; Morris A. Gutstein, *A Priceless Heritage: The Epic Growth of Nineteenth Century Chicago Jewry* (New York, 1952), p. 424; Wm. J. Akers, *Cleveland Schools in the Nineteenth Century* (Cleveland, 1901), pp. 418–24.

145. Matthew Holden, "Ethnic Accommodation in a Historical Case," *Comparative Studies in Society and History*, VIII (January, 1966), 168–80; this suggestive study, however, draws too far-reaching conclusions solely from Cleveland's 36 mayors between 1836 and 1900; Jordan, *op. cit.*, p. 206; for interesting notes on Ohio politics, see also Irwin Unger, *The Greenback Era: A Social and Political History of American Finance 1865–1879* (Princeton, 1964), p. 87 and *passim*.

146. *AmIsr*, October 22, 1891.

147. *HO*, April 1, 1892.

148. *PD*, September 23, 1893.

149. Wellington G. Fordyce, "Nationality Groups in Cleveland Politics," *OSAHQ*, XLVI (1937), 110–12; James B. Whipple, "Municipal Government in an Average City: Cleveland, 1876–1900," *OSAHQ*, LXVIII, No. 1 (January, 1953), 1–25. Note the rebuke to "our co-religionists who have been here for many years" who "encourage the newly arrived immigrants to be followers of the political demagogues," and "to form political organizations dominated [*sic*] as Jewish political clubs." *JR&O*, May 16, 1913.

150. Howe, *op. cit.*, pp. 80–84.

151. Oral interview, January 14, 1972 *loc. cit.*

152. Lincoln Steffens, *Autobiography* (New York, 1931), pp. 470–81; Howe, *op. cit.*, pp. 73–166; a series by Eugene C. Murdock in *OSAHQ*, LXII, No. 4 (October, 1953), 323–33; LXIII, No. 4 (October, 1954), 319–35; LXV, No. 1 (January, 1956), 28–43; LXVI, No. 4 (October, 1957), 375–90; LXVII, No. 1 (January, 1958), 35–49.

153. John D. Buenker, "Cleveland's New Stock Lawmakers and Progressive Reform," *Ohio History*, LXXVIII, No. 2 (Spring, 1969), 116–37, 154–56; idem, *Urban Liberalism and Progressive Reform* (New York, 1973), pp. 34–35, 56–69, 94–95, 99–100, 105–7, 182–83, 192–93.

154. Important statements on Progressives and immigrants are Richard Hofstadter, *The Age of Reform: From Bryan to F.D.R.* (New York, 1955), pp. 175–214; John Higham, *Strangers in the Land: Patterns of American Nativism 1860–1925*, 2nd ed. (paper, New York, 1970), pp. 116–22, 174–76, 178–80; Lawrence A. Cremin, *The Transformation of the School: Progressivism in American Education 1876–1957* (New York, 1961), pp. 58–59. Interesting material is in Rudolf Glanz, "The Muckrakers and Jewish Social Conditions," *op. cit.*, pp. 384–407.

CHAPTER IV

1. *PD*, December 29, 1879.

2. The monthly accounts of the Emigrant Detective, who met arriving trains and supervised immigrants passing through, appeared in the *PD* on the second or third of the following month, e.g., September 2, 1879, for August, 1879. Furthermore, the first week of each year saw publication of an annual report, e.g., *PD*, January 5, 1896, for 1895.

3. On Jewish migrations during this period, see Salo W. Baron, *The Russian Jew under Tsars and Soviets* (New York, 1964), pp. 76–89 and *passim*; E. Tcherikover (Tcherikower), *History of the Jewish Labor Movement in the United States* (Yiddish), 2 vols. (New York, 1943–1945), Volume I; transl., rev., and abr. version in English is Elias Tcherikower and Aaron Antonovsky, *The Early Jewish Labor Movement in the United States* (New York, 1961), Parts I and II; Raphael Mahler, "The Economic Background of Jewish Emigration from Galicia to the United States," *YIVO Annual of Jewish Social Science*, XII (1952), 255–67; Samuel Joseph, *Jewish Immigration to the United States, 1881–1910* (New York, 1914); Moses Rischin, *The Promised City: New York's Jews 1870–1914* (Cambridge, Mass., 1962), pp. 19–47; Mark Wischnitzer, *To*

Dwell in Safety: The Story of Jewish Migrations Since 1800 (Philadelphia, 1949), pp. 37–141; Lloyd P. Gartner, The Jewish Immigrant in England 1870–1914 (London and Detroit, 1960; 2nd ed., London, 1973), pp. 15–56; Joseph Kissman, "The Immigration of Rumanian Jews Up to 1914," YIVO Annual of Jewish Social Science, II–III (1947–1948), pp. 160–79; Salo Wittmayer Baron, Steeled by Adversity: Essays and Addresses on American Jewish Life, ed. Jeannette Meisel Baron (Philadelphia, 1971), pp. 274–313, 341–48, 373–89, with rich bibliography; the following studies by Zosa Szajkowski: "How the Mass Migration to America Began," Jewish Social Studies, IV, No. 4 (October, 1942), 291–310; "Jewish Emigration Policy in the Period of the Rumanian Exodus, 1899–1903," loc. cit., XIII, No. 1 (January, 1951), 47–70; "The Attitude of American Jews to East European Jewish Immigration (1881–1893)," PAJHS, XL, No. 3 (March, 1951), 221–80; "The European Attitude to East European Jewish Immigration," PAJHS, XLI, No. 2 (December, 1951), 127–62; Lloyd P. Gartner, "Immigration and the Formation of American Jewry," in Jewish Society Through the Ages, ed. H. H. Ben-Sasson and S. Ettinger (New York, 1971), pp. 297–312; Simon Kuznets, "Immigration of Russian Jews to the United States: Background and Structure", Perspectives in American History, IX (1975), pp. 35–124.

4. PD, August 6, 1881; see also PD, November 23, 1880, and January 18, 1881; cf. Louis J. Swichkow and Lloyd P. Gartner, The History of the Jews of Milwaukee (Philadelphia, 1963), pp. 133–38.

5. PD, May 13, 19, 20, 1881; June 1, 17, 1881; September 21, 1881; October 3, 1881. In addition to the literature cited supra, n. 3, the pogroms of 1881–1884 are described in S. M. Dubnow, History of the Jews in Russia and Poland, II, (Philadelphia, 1916), pp. 243–323; Eliahu Tcherikover, Yehudim be-Itot Mahpekhah [Hebrew; Jews in Revolutionary Times] (Tel-Aviv, 1955), pp. 341–66.

6. PD, February 25, 1882.

7. PD, January 5, 1882.

8. PD, September 9, 1882.

9. PD, June 17, 1882; further views, and those of other newspapers, appear in PD, June 9, 10, 23, 1882; July 30, 1882. On newspapers and politics, see Philip D. Jordan, Ohio Comes of Age: 1873–1900 (Columbus, 1943), p. 206; James B. Whipple, "Cleveland in Conflict: A Study in Urban Adolescence" (diss., Western Reserve University, 1951) pp. 131–38.

10. JMess, January 20, 1882; AmIsr, January 20, 1882.

11. PD, February 11, 1882.

12. PD, July 8, 1882. If the latter is correct, the absence of a middle class and of any suggestion of material comfort among Russian Jewish immigrants for at least the following ten years requires explanation.

13. PD, October 27, 1882. Cf. the alarm and anger of Milwaukee Jews at the unexpected arrival of 218 Russian Jewish refugees on June 29, 1882; Swichkow and Gartner, op. cit., pp. 76–84.

14. AmIsr, January 26, 1883.

15. AmIsr, November 23, 1883, reporting a meeting which took place "a few weeks ago."

16. AmIsr, June 13, 1884.

17. PD, January 5, 1886; April 26, 1884.

18. JMess, March 14, 1884; W. Gunther Plaut, The Jews in Minnesota: The First Seventy-five Years (New York, 1959), pp. 96–109.

19. AmIsr, November 23, 1883; Berg Street, which no longer exists, was near the present Terminal Tower.

20. PD, September 3, 1883.

21. Before the 1890s, virtually all names mentioned in Hungarian societies were those of Jews, as during the Hungarian festival of 1887; e.g., *PD*, July 18, 25, 29, 1887; September 12, 13, 1887. Cf. Yeshayahu Jelinek, "Self-identification of First Generation Hungarian Jewish Immigrants," *AJHQ*, LXI, No. 3 (March, 1972), pp. 218-20. The first Hungarian churches in Cleveland were founded in 1891, twenty-five years after the Hungarian synagogue; Wellington G. Fordyce, "Immigrant Institutions in Cleveland," *OSAHQ*, XLVI (1937), 93.

22. Gilbert Osofsky, "The Hebrew Emigrant Aid Society of the United States (1881-1883)," *PAJHS*, XLIX, No. 2 (March, 1960), 173-87.

23. *PD*, July 28, 1885; August 27, 1885.

24. *PD*, April 15, 1887.

25. *PD*, August 23, 1886. Trains bearing immigrants arrived at unpredictable hours, and the protection of the immigrants from scamps and cheats remained a continuous problem. See [City of Cleveland], Department of Public Safety, [First] *Annual Report of the Bureau of Immigration . . . ,* 1913, pp. 3-4.

26. *PD*, December 3, 1886.

27. *HO*, August 15, 1890. On this decree, see Dubnow, *op. cit.*, pp. 399-413; Wischnitzer, *op. cit.*, pp. 67-70.

28. *HO*, June 26, 1891.

29. *AmIsr*, July 2, 1891; *HO*, July 3, 1891; January 22, 1892; *PD*, October 12, 1891; on the ambitious but short-lived Jewish Alliance, which was based in Philadelphia, see Moshe Davis, *The Emergence of Conservative Judaism: The Historical School in 19th Century America* (Philadelphia, 1963), pp. 265-68, 388-92; Wischnitzer, *op. cit.*, pp. 72-74.

30. *HO*, July 17, 1891.

31. *AmIsr*, October 8, 15, 1891; December 24, 1891; *HO*, June 26, 1891; October 16, 1891; January 22, 1892.

32. *HO*, May 21, 1897; *PD*, September 4, 1905.

33. *JInd*, January 21, 1910. The Home gradually became a way-station for Jewish vagabonds. Federation of Jewish Charities, Executive Committee, Minutes, October 19, 1922.

34. *AmIsr*, October 6, 1892.

35. *HO*, December 11, 1891.

36. These figures are found in Tifereth Israel's return to the Board of Delegates of American Israelites, Box 2384-B, American Jewish Archives, Cincinnati, Ohio. The original return shows "cannot be estimated" for Jews under 21, and "about 2,000" written alongside by a contemporary hand. Perhaps this was done after repeated inquiry.

37. *AmIsr*, July 6, 1888.

38. *AmIsr*, February 20, 1885.

39. *PD*, January 24, 1895.

40. *AmIsr*, September 19, 1895.

41. *HO*, August 26, 1897.

42. *The Jewish Encyclopedia*, 12 vols. (New York, 1903-1907); IV, s.v. "Cleveland"; XII, s.v. "United States of America."

43. *PD*, January 24, 1895; *AmIsr*, January 10, 1895. Miss Davis' remarks may be compared with some of those quoted in Swichkow and Gartner, *op. cit.*, pp. 83-92, 151; Rischin, *op. cit.*, pp. 95-103; Robert A. Rockaway, "Ethnic Conflict in an Urban Environment: The German and Russian Jew in Detroit, 1881-1914," *AJHQ*, LX, No. 2 (December, 1970), pp. 133-50; Zosa Szajkowski, "The Attitude of American Jews" *loc. cit., passim.*

44. *HO*, August 13, 1897.

45. *PD*, September 20, 1895.
46. *PD*, September 23, 1896; April 7, 1896.
47. *HO*, March 31, 1899; *AmIsr*, April 6, 1899.
48. *PD*, January 2, 1904; July 15, 17, 1904; October 10, 17, 1904; *JInd*, August 13, 1920.
49. *PD*, July 3, 1887.
50. *PD*, May 15, 1895.
51. *PD*, July 28, 1902.
52. *JR&O*, May 29, 1903; see Philip Ernest Schoenberg, "The American Reaction to the Kishinev Pogrom of 1903," *AJHQ*, LXII, No. 3 (March, 1974), 262–83.
53. *PD*, January 26, 1904.
54. *PD*, January 11, 1904.
55. *JInd*, October 19, 1906; March 1, 29, 1907; April 5, 1907.
56. *PD*, February 12, 1904.
57. A recent study is Gary Dean Best, "Financing a Foreign War: Jacob H. Schiff and Japan, 1904–05," *AJHQ*, LXI, No. 4 (June, 1972), 313–24.
58. *PD*, February 4, 12, 1904.
59. *PD*, February 14, 1904.
60. *PD*, December 1, 1904; it later supported the national campaign to revoke the Russo-American Treaty of 1832 on account of discrimination against American Jews holding U.S. passports. *PD*, February 12, 1911; *JR&O*, February 24, 1911.
61. The protest meetings are reported in detail in *JR&O*, November 24, 1905.
62. Federated Jewish Charities, Minutes, November 15, 1905; January 29, 1906; *JR&O*, November 17, 1905; *PD*, February 23, 1906; *JInd*, August 31, 1906; September 28, 1906.
63. *JInd*, July 27, 1906; on Maksim (Shimon Klevansky, 1878–post 1924?), see Henry J. Tobias, *The Jewish Bund in Russia: From Its Origins to 1905* (Stanford, 1972), pp. 336, 350.
64. Wischnitzer, *op. cit.*, pp. 98–140, 289ff.
65. A stimulating contribution on this subject is Josef J. Barton, *Peasants and Strangers: Italians, Rumanians, and Slovaks in an American City* (Cambridge, Mass., 1975).
65A. *HO*, August 13, 1897.
66. Taped oral memoirs of Ezra Z. Shapiro, in Archives of Jewish Community Federation, Cleveland, supplemented by interviews in Jerusalem, April, 1977.
67. Max Sandin, "I was Sentenced to Be Shot" (Memoirs), in Max Sandin Papers, No. 3542, Western Reserve Historical Society, Cleveland, pp. 20–26 with omissions. Sandin's English has been slightly repunctuated, and some grammatical errors removed. The title of the memoirs refers to a court-martial sentence passed upon him during World War I for insubordination, which was commuted to a short sentence following a public outcry. A brief memoir of a 1903 immigrant from Kovno is Frank Stein, "Remembrance of Things Past," *CJN*, October 4, 1968.
68. *PD*, March 3, 1905. Reflecting the hardships of life, immigrant lore punned ironically on city names. Thus, Dallas was "Daless"—poverty—while Cleveland became "Kelevland"—"dogland."
69. *PD*, March 3, 1905; i.e., two suicides of immigrants on one day.
70. On the operations of the I.R.O., see generally Samuel Joseph, *History of the Baron de Hirsch Fund* (New York, 1935), pp. 184–205.
71. For examples of the I.R.O. in other cities, see Swichkow and Gartner, *op. cit.*, pp. 157–60; Max Vorspan and Lloyd P. Gartner, *History of the Jews of Los Angeles* (San Marino, Calif., 1970), pp. 111–12, 320–-21; Robert A. Rockaway, "Worthy Sir: A

Collection of Immigrant Letters from the Industrial Removal Office," in *Michael*, III (Tel-Aviv, 1975), pp. 152–71; Council Educational Alliance, Annual Meeting, Minutes, January 15, 1905. As extensive correspondence shows, this collaboration had its tensions, especially around 1912–1913.

72. *PD*, January 15, 1904.

73. The figures available follow:

Year	Ohio	Cleveland
1901	152	not given
1902	350	not given
1903	726	141 [cumulative?][a]
1904	622	188
1905	765	257 (134 "cases" and 33 families)
1906	1,020	330
1907	1,065	386 (230 "cases" and 52 families)
1908	352	156
1909	419	[173][b]
1910	680	260
1911	613	270
1912	802	322
1913	1,207	329
1914	585	[158][c]

a. This figure appears in the 1903 Annual Report in a context which suggests it may be cumulative for 1901, 1902, 1903.

b. The Annual Report supplies no figure for Cleveland. However, since 44.3% of those sent to Ohio in 1908 went to Cleveland, and 38.2% in 1910, it was decided to average the two percentages and apply it to the missing 1909. This average, 41.2%, applied to 419 proceeding to Ohio, yields 173 for Cleveland. This seems a reasonable conjecture.

c. The Annual Report supplies no figure for Cleveland, while those for 1915 and 1916 could not be located. Since 27% of those sent to Ohio in 1913 went to Cleveland, it was decided to apply this percentage to the 585 who went to Ohio in 1914.

There are many problems about these figures as a whole. The Annual Reports give 330 for 1906 and 386 for 1907, while local reports (*infra*) mention approximately 150 for 1906 and 249 for 1907. Perhaps New York headquarters kept better records than the off-and-on Cleveland office, but this is by no means definite.

74. The following letter is from General Manager, New York, to Ulrich Richter, Agent, Cleveland, January 2, 1905. This and all letters cited below are from the Cleveland file, Baron de Hirsch Fund Archives, American Jewish Historical Society, Waltham, Massachusetts. I would like to thank Nathan M. Kaganoff, Librarian, and Bernard Wax, Director of the Society, for their aid and courtesy in making this material usable.

75. Industrial Removal Office, *Annual Report, 1905*, p. 6.

76. *JR&O*, January 10, 1908.

77. D. M. Bressler, General Manager, to A. S. Newman, New York, December 3, 1909.

78. *Ibid.*

79. H. Hollander, to D. M. Bressler, Cleveland, January 10, 1907.

80. D. M. Bressler to A. S. Newman, New York, March 10, 1908.

81. A. S. Newman to D. M. Bressler, Cleveland, March 25, 1908.

82. H. Hollander to D. M. Bressler, Cleveland, January 9, 1907.

83. A. S. Newman to D. M. Bressler, Cleveland, July 10, 1908.

84. D. M. Bressler to A. J. Halle, New York, March 16, 1914.

85. *Ibid.*

86. *HO*, August 13, 1897.

87. United States Immigration Commission, *Reports*, 41 vols. (Washington, D.C.: Government Printing Office, 1908–1913), XXV (*Immigrants in Cities*, I), p. 519 (cited hereafter as *Immigrants in Cities*, I or II, the latter volume being XXVI of the *Reports*).

88. *Immigrants in Cities*, II (*Reports*, XXVI), p. 173, Table 165.

89. *Ibid.*, p. 161, Table 156; p. 167, Table 162; p. 173, Table 165; p. 176, Table 167; p. 176, Table 168; pp. 184–85, Tables 180–81; p. 187, Table 184.

90. [Mildred Chadsey], *An Investigation of Housing Conditions of Cleveland's Workingmen*, Department of Public Welfare of the City of Cleveland, Monograph Series, No. 1, April, 1914, p. 5 ("The Best/The Average/The Worst"). Cf. *Housing Conditions in Cleveland: Report of Progress Submitted by The Housing Committee of the Cleveland Chamber of Commerce January 1st 1904*, not dealing with Jewish neighborhoods, which identifies the problem as the overcrowding of one and two-family houses.

91. *Immigrants in Cities*, II (*Reports*, XXVI), pp. 190–92, Table 188; p. 197, Table 192.

92. Eleanor E. Ledbetter, *The Czechs of Cleveland* (Cleveland, 1919), p. 35; Charles W. Coulter, *The Poles of Cleveland* (Cleveland, 1919), p. 10; *idem, The Lithuanians of Cleveland* (Cleveland, 1920), *passim*; Thomas Čapek, *The Čechs (Bohemians) in America* (New York, 1920; reprinted 1970), pp. 71–72.

93. Joseph Morgenstern, "Cleveland Fifty Years Ago: Reminiscences of Immigrant Life," *Jewish Currents*, XII, No. 1 (January, 1958), 19–20.

94. *Ibid.*, p. 20.

95. *JR&O*, May 20, 1910.

96. *PD*, January 8, 1911, Magazine.

97. Thomas F. Campbell, *Daniel E. Morgan, 1877–1949: The Good Citizen in Politics* (Cleveland, 1966), pp. 18–19.

98. Mr. Judah Rubinstein was kind enough to extract this information from the *City Directory*, 1912.

99. Rose Pastor Stokes, "The Little Breadwinner" (Memoirs), *Jewish Currents*, XII, No. 6 (June, 1958), 10. Her full memoirs are preserved in MS in the Archives Room, Sterling Memorial Library, Yale University.

100. *PD*, September 2, 1880; October 26, 29, 1880; November 6, 1880; April 21, 1883; June 15, 1887; August 13, 1890; November 22, 1892.

101. Morgenstern, *loc. cit.*, pp. 20–21.

102. *Ibid.* For a description of Jaffa Maier's dirty cigarmaking shop, where "spiritual life" was less noticeable, see *PD*, November 8, 9, 1895.

103. Brisker-Grodner Society, Minutes, 1911–1919, *passim*.

104. Rischin, *op. cit.*, p. 66; Edna Bryner, *The Garment Trades*, Cleveland Education Survey (Cleveland, 1916), pp. 47–48.

105. *PD*, January 8, 1911, Magazine.

106. Bryner, *op. cit.*, p. 20.

107. Abraham Stearns to "Dear Sam & Bertha," November 13, 1900, in Stearns letter copy book, at Jewish Community Federation, Cleveland.

108. It is likely that Anisfield was employing a variant not of the derogatory slang "kike" but of "keek," which Webster's Unabridged, Second Edition, defines as a clothing trade term for one whom a manufacturer employs to spy out the latest fashions of rivals. "Kuk," or, in its double diminutive form, "kukele"—with the "u" of Lithuanian Yiddish transformed to "i" in Galician-Hungarian Yiddish—is "peek" (n.). Uriel Weinreich, *Modern English-Yiddish Yiddish-English Dictionary* (New York, 1968), p. 425, col. 2. Anisfield was born "near Vienna" in 1860, and Viennese Jews generally

had a Galician past. Samuel P. Orth, *A History of Cleveland*, Vol. II, *Biographical* (Chicago & Cleveland, 1910), pp. 806–7.

109. Report ca. 1908 in Hiram House Papers, Western Reserve Historical Society.

110. Bryner, *op. cit.*, pp. 22–23.

111. *PD*, May 20, 21, 1896. On the relative absence of hostility to trade unionism in Cleveland see Herbert G. Gutman, "The Workers' Search for Power: Labor in the Gilded Age," in *The Old Northwest: Studies in Regional History*, ed. Harry N. Scheiber (Lincoln, Neb., 1969), pp. 362–95.

112. Bryner, *op. cit.*, p. 53.

113. *PD*, May 18, 1894; cf. *PD*, June 11, 1890.

114. *PD*, April 29, 1896; the names of the local United Garment Workers leaders were Max Appel, John Tomachek, Lewis Bierman, Charles Benjamin, Charles Kurlander, F. Neubauer, John Meyer, Alex Ramm, and Abe Abrahamson.

115. *PD*, March 16, 1896; April 29, 1896.

116. *PD*, June 12, 23, 26, 27, 30, 1896.

117. *PD*, August 15, 1904; August 21, 22, 23, 26, 1904; *cf. PD*, February 15, 1904.

118. *JInd*, July 26, 1907.

119. Louis Levine, *The Women's Garment Workers: A History of the International Ladies' Garment Workers' Union* (New York, 1924), pp. 208–17, 360–64; Bryner, *op. cit.*, p. 55; *PD*, June 10, 1911, carried an advertisement by the manufacturers; *Cleveland Citizen*, October 28, 1911. Useful sidelights may be found in Workmen's Circle, Branch 79, *Thirty-fifth Anniversary Jubilee. Sunday, October 15, 1939* (souvenir journal, mostly in Yiddish).

120. *Cleveland Press*, July 3, 24, 1918; Levine, *op. cit.*, pp. 364–68.

121. *PD*, April 8, 1904.

122. *Cleveland Citizen*, July 27, 1912.

123. *JR&O*, January 7, 1910.

124. *Cleveland Citizen*, December 17, 1910.

125. *YV*, August 7, 1913.

126. *Cleveland Citizen*, June 8, 15, 1912.

127. *JInd*, June 21, 1907.

128. *Cleveland Citizen*, December 17, 1910.

129. *Cleveland Citizen*, January 21, 1911.

130. *JInd*, March 17, 1911; July 30, 1909.

131. *YV*, August 15, 1913; September 5, 1913; *AJYB, 1911–1912*, lists the "Hebrew Bricklayers' and Stonemasons' Union," organized in February, 1905.

132. *City Directory*, 1912; by courtesy of Mr. Judah Rubinstein. In 1905, No. 184 was known as Ore Handlers; *Cleveland Citizen*, May 20, 1905.

CHAPTER V

1. W. G. Rose, *Cleveland: The Making of a City* (Cleveland, 1950), p. 436.

2. Rose, *op. cit.*, p. 508; *AmIsr*, September 26, 1895.

3. Rose, *op. cit.*, p. 786; *JInd*, June 22, 1923.

4. The statistics are given in forms returned to the Board of Delegates of American Israelites "for the year ending September 18, 1876 [5636]," deposted in Box 2384-B, American Jewish Archives, Cincinnati, Ohio.

5. *JR*, January 7, 1898.

6. *JMess*, July 7, 1882.

7. *PD*, September 29, 1884; October 13, 1891. In 1885 "both of the leading synagogues were densely crowded. . . . notwithstanding many of our prominent merchants

had their places of business open and striving hard for those few dollars taken in.
. . ." *AmIsr*, September 18, 1885.

8. *AmIsr*, September 30, 1887.
9. *AmIsr*, October 8, 1891.
10. *AmIsr*, March 30, 1888.
11. *JR*, November 8, 1895.
12. *AmIsr*, October 14, 1887.
13. *AmIsr*, March 23, 1888.
14. *AmIsr*, March 30, 1888.
15. *AmIsr*, October 29, 1886; this formed part of his address in German at the corner-stone laying of Anshe Chesed on Scovill Avenue.
16. *PD*, March 15, 1889.
17. *PD*, March 14, 1889.
18. *Ibid.* We hear of the funeral of Mrs. A. Pollock being conducted jointly by Rabbi Aaron Hahn and Lyman C. Howe, the Boston spiritualist. *PD*, March 5, 1890.
19. *PD*, March 18, 1888; *AmIsr*, January 2, 1880.
20. *PD*, February 4, 1889. Machol taught his candidates the principles of Judaism; the act of conversion required a confession of faith, but apparently not immersion.
21. *PD*, October 22, 1886. In 1890 Zucker contributed to a symposium in the Rochester (N.Y.) *Jewish Tidings* on the Sunday Sabbath, reprinted in *PD*, May 3, 1890. It was an idea which he "radically opposed . . . for the members of our religious nationality. . . . If the idea was to take a step towards the direction of a universal religion then perhaps I would be in favor of the idea, but as long as our faith is worth upholding, the distinctive part of it, the observance of the seventh day with all its attendant religious ceremonies, should be faithfully clung to." When the issue became heated in 1897, Zucker no longer resided in Cleveland.
22. *JR&O*, October 16, 1908.
23. *PD*, March 21, 1896; Frederick C. Howe, *The Confessions of a Reformer* (New York, 1925), p. 84.
24. *JR&O*, March 26, 1915.
25. Moritz Tintner served for three months in 1874 as rabbi but was discharged, apparently for more than trivial defects of character. *AmIsr*, March 6, 1874; July 31, 1874; October 9, 1874; *Reformer and Jewish Times*, August 8, 1879.
26. *JR&O*, November 10, 1916; *AmIsr*, October 5, 1888.
27. Aaron I. Abbell, *The Urban Impact on American Protestantism* (Cambridge, Mass., 1943); Robert D. Cross, ed., *The Church and the City 1865–1910* (Indianapolis and New York, 1967), Introduction. A somewhat different emphasis is found in Winthrop S. Hudson, "The Church Embraces the World: Protestantism Succumbs to Complacency," in *The Great Tradition of the American Churches* (New York, 1953), pp. 195–225, and Henry Steele Commager, *The American Mind: An Interpretation of American Thought and Character since the 1880's* (New Haven, 1950), pp. 162–95; who observes that "it is scarcely an exaggeration to say that during the nineteenth century and well into the twentieth, religion prospered while theology went slowly bankrupt" (p. 165).
28. Isaac M. Fein, *The Making of an American Jewish Community: The History of Baltimore Jewry from 1773 to 1920* (Philadelphia, 1971), pp. 111–12.
29. *Jewish Times* (New York), August 6, 1875.
30. *Die Gottesbegriffe des Talmud und Sohar sowie der vorzuglichsten theosophischen Systeme* (Leipzig, 1869), p. 46.
31. *Sefer Okrey Harim. The Rabbinical Dialectics. A History of Dialecticians and Dialectics of the Mishnah and Talmud* (Cincinnati, 1879).
32. Tifereth Israel, Minutes, April 25, 1886; October 18, 1889; *AmIsr*, June 13, 1884; June 11, 1886; November 12, 1886; February 4, 1887; March 23, 1888; *PD*, December 26, 1887; December, 21, 1888; January 2, 1889.

33. This matter reached the press and became a shortlived sensation: *PD*, August 26, 28, 1887; September 1, 5, 1887; *AmIsr*, September 9, 1887.

34. *AmIsr*, October 14, 1887; September 28, 1888; cf. *PD*, September 14, 15, 1880.

35. Tifereth Israel, Minutes, October 14, 1895.

36. When Rabbi Spitz of St. Louis spoke during Hahn's absence, the reporter referred ironically to "no lack of a 'little change' in our pulpit," and found that the guest was "in voice, has a good delivery, and speaks to the point." It seems quite pointed. *AmIsr*, September 10, 1887.

37. Central Conference of American Rabbis, *Yearbook*, I (1890), quoted in *Retrospect and Prospect: Essays in Commemoration of the Seventy-Fifth Anniversary of the Founding of the Central Conference of American Rabbis 1889-1964*, ed. Bertram W. Korn (New York, 1965), pp. 110-11.

38. Tifereth Israel, Minutes, October 18, 1891.

39. Tifereth Israel, Minutes, October 25, 1891; February 14, 1892; February 16, 1892; May 1, 1892.

40. *A Course of Lectures delivered by Dr. Aaron Hahn . . .* , Vol. I, Nos. 1 and 2, (Cleveland, 1892); at Hebrew Union College Library.

41. *HO*, April 21, 1893.

42. *AmIsr*, September 28, 1893; March 15, 1894; *HO*, April 21, 1893; oral statement by Mr. Henry Rocker. Hahn appeared at the dedication of The Temple in 1925.

43. *PD*, December 5, 1885; May 3, 1886; *AmIsr*, April 30, 1886; *JR&O*, March 22, 1912, Part I, p. 2; August 30, 1912.

44. Anshe Chesed, Minutes, January 6, 1907; *PD*, May 2, 1878; September 15, 1880; *AmIsr*, July 19, 1878; February 2, 1883; November 23, 1883; October 7, 1887; September 28, 1888; June 13, 1889; October 17, 1889; November 7, 1889; October 15, 1891; *HO*, October 16, 1891; October 23, 1891; *JMess*, July 7, 1882. However, a proposal to eliminate the deep-rooted Ashkenazic custom—not religious law—of the Yizkor memorial service on the Day of Atonement "was overwhelmingly defeated." *AmIsr*, October 13, 1892.

45. *JR*, November 8, 1895.

46. *JR&O*, March 22, 1912.

47. His parting words at his successor's installation also imply this. *JInd*, September 6, 1907.

48. The Gries papers in the American Jewish Archives contain little but sermons, and also some interesting family letters of the 1850s and 1860s.

49. Edward M. Baker, "Judaism and the American Spirit," *The Arena*, XXVII (1904), 166 ff., reprinted in *PD*, August 14, 1904.

50. *HO*, December 2, 1892.

51. *AmIsr*, December 15, 1892.

52. *AmIsr*, December 30, 1897.

53. Tifereth Israel, Minutes, August 12, 1894; May 6, 1895.

54. *American Hebrew* (New York), July 21, 1893; *AmIsr*, October 24, 1895; March 23, 1893; September 27, 1894; October 4, 1894.

55. *AmIsr*, October 4, 1894.

56. Tifereth Israel, Minutes, February 25, 1894; *HO*, March 16, 1894.

57. Tifereth Israel, Congregation Minutes, October 1, 1893.

58. Tifereth Israel, Congregation Minutes, October 19, 1896; Board Minutes, November 2, 1896; Cross, *op. cit.*, p. xvi.

59. *HO*, January 27, 1899; *AmIsr*, December 29, 1898 (a bitter comment on the social and religious life of middle-class Cleveland Jews).

60. *HO*, December 30, 1897; on the Sabbath question, cf. Moshe Davis, "Jewish Religious Life and Institutions in America," in *The Jews*, ed. Louis Finkelstein, 2 vols. (3rd ed. New York, 1960), pp. 518-19; *idem, The Emergence of Conservative Judaism* (New York, 1963), pp. 275-78; and the varied viewpoints quoted in Stuart E. Rosen-

berg, "*The Jewish Tidings* and the Sunday Services Question," *PAJHS*, XLII, No. 4 (June, 1953), 371–85.

61. *JR&O*, October 7, 1904; *Anshe Chesed: In Commemoration* (Cleveland, 1896), p. 15.

62. This trend did not pass without sharp local criticism. When Anshe Chesed described its belief "in a reform which is of a purely progressive nature, and eschewing all which savors of Nihilism and destructiveness," it was pointing at its fellow Reform congregation.

63. Tifereth Israel, Minutes, 1871, 1894, 1898; *JR&O*, September 23, 1910; there were about 800 member families when Rabbi Gries retired in 1917.

64. *JR&O*, April 17, 1914; November 10, 1916; Cross, *op. cit.*, pp. xxv, xxxv–vi.

65. *HO*, July 24, 1896. An extreme in the identification of Judaism with regional traditions of religious liberalism is in *Growth and Achievement: Temple Israel 1854–1954*, ed. Arthur Mann (Boston, 1954), pp. 45–84.

66. *JInd*, November 22, 1907.

67. Annual Message, Tifereth Israel, Minutes, October 19, 1896.

68. *AmIsr*, June 16, 1898.

69. *HO*, December 23, 1897.

70. *JR&O*, March 25, 1904.

71. *PD*, November 7, 1904.

72. *PD*, February 1, 1904.

73. *JR&O*, October 5, 1906.

74. *JR&O*, June 14, 1912.

75. He addressed a Zionist women's group: *JInd*, May 21, 1909; see also *JR&O*, June 18, 1909.

76. *JInd*, November 13, 1908. It is not known what, if any, specific criticism prompted these sharp words. However, Rabbi Stephen S. Wise's conflict with the Trustees of Temple Emanu-El in New York was well publicized. See *Louis Marshall: Champion of Liberty*, ed. Charles Reznikoff, 2 vols. (Philadelphia, 1956), II, pp. 831–37; *Stephen S. Wise: Servant of the People, Selected Letters*, ed. Carl Hermann Voss (Philadelphia, 1969), pp. 25–34.

77. *JR&O*, December 24, 1909.

78. *JInd*, June 10, 1910; Norman Bentwich, *For Zion's Sake: A Biography of Judah L. Magnes* (Philadelphia, 1954), pp. 20–118.

79. *Cleveland Leader*, December 4, 1909, published Wolsey's sermon; Gries' retort is in *JR&O*, December 17, 1909. The issue arose from Wolsey's opposition to the Central Conference of American Rabbis' seeming sanction of intermarriage as a means to proselytism.

80. *JR&O*, December 24, 1909.

81. *JR&O*, January 7, 1910; other exchanges are in *JR&O*, January 14, 1910.

82. *PD*, April 11, 1904; see also *PD*, April 4, 1904.

CHAPTER VI

1. *PD*, September 29, 1887; quotations that follow are also from this article, which excels for its clear observation and, unusual for the general press, its transcription of Hebrew names and terms.

2. Chap. II, n. 77.

3. Chap. II, n. 76.

4. *AmIsr*, June 8, 1883. The same newspaper's list of synagogues, their location and ministers, included the regional background of each one: e.g., "The Tiffereth [*sic*] Israel Congregation (German). . . ." *AmIsr*, September 14, 1888.

5. Tactfully, he did not say "in this city," but he would have been correct if he had.

6. *JR&O*, June 3, 1904.

7. *JR&O*, June 14, 1912.

8. The Jewish immigrant population was too small to follow the New York custom of establishing congregations based upon the town of origin. An intimate view of one immigrant synagogue during this period is Abraham J. Karp, "An East European Congregation on American Soil: Beth Israel, Rochester, New York, 1874–1886," in *A Bicentennial Festschrift for Jacob Rader Marcus*, ed. Bertram Wallace Korn (New York, 1976), pp. 263–302.

9. *HO*, October 6, 1898.

10. It appears to have been a converted church. *AmIsr*, June 13, 1884; see also *PD*, May 31, 1884; *AmIsr*, November 23, 1883.

11. *AmIsr*, June 13, 1884.

12. *AmIsr*, October 21, 1887. This seems to be the concrete meaning of the comment that Chevra Kadisha "suffered the consequences of the 'New Era,' in which so much was devoted to show, and where it became a matter of fashion to belong to an up-to-date congregation. . . . [it] lost some of its members who might have been of some value, particularly in a pecuniary way." *HO*, October 6, 1898.

13. *JInd*, October 13, 1916.

14. *AmIsr*, October 13, 1916; August 18, 1916.

15. *AmIsr*, January 16, 1880. This newspaper note refers to a building supposedly purchased by the congregation, which is apparently a misleading reference to the rented hall on Michigan Street.

16. *PD*, September 5, 1887.

17. *Ibid.*

18. *PD*, July 14, 1884.

19. *PD*, September 5, 1887.

20. *Ibid.*, Wise's challenge to traditional law could have been met, although not in the terms of solely Biblical Judaism on which he insisted.

21. *PD*, September 13, 1887.

22. *PD*, October 25, 1904, copied in *JR&O*, October 28, 1904; *JInd*, May 4, 1906.

23. *JR&O*, July 14, 1905; April 17, 1908.

24. *JInd*, December 10, 1909; a brief biography is in *JR&O*, October 1, 1915.

25. *JR&O*, September 23, 1910, Part III, p. 4.

26. *Ibid.*

27. *JR&O*, April 24, 1908.

28. Samuel Schwartz, "Tell Thy Children," MS autobiography, American Jewish Archives, Cincinnati, Ohio, 1951, pp. 43–47.

29. *JInd*, May 21, 1909.

30. *JR&O*, April 5, 1912; he received a long, honeyed reply assuring him that differences of opinion "always rested on the foundation Rock of Ages [*sic*]." Congregation Bene Jeshurun to Rabbi Samuel Schwartz, April 18, 1912, in *JR&O*, May 3, 1912. In his memoirs, cited above, Schwartz says that the congregation's president was his chief critic, "and that is fatal to a rabbi." *Op. cit.*, p. 46.

31. *JR&O*, August 30, 1912.

32. *JInd*, March 2, 1919; May 31, 1918. Rabbi Klein next became an insurance agent. *JInd*, September 6, 1918.

33. *PD*, May 1, 1880.

34. *PD*, May 10, 1880.

35. *Ibid.*, during the tempest stirred by Hahn's announced intention to address B'ne Jeshurun bare-headed, he referred to dedication sermons he had delivered in "one Bohemian, one Hungarian, and two Polish synagogues, which means four dedicatory sermons in exclusively orthodox congregations, and all were delivered with uncovered head." *PD*, August 28, 1887. Why did Orthodox congregations permit this? Probably it was due to their insecurity before established, acculturated Judaism, notwithstanding their own stubborn adherence to the old ways. His previous bare-headed sermons do partially explain why Hahn reacted so indignantly to B'ne Jeshurun's refusal to permit this already customary practice.

36. *PD*, March 12, 15, 1881; December 6, 1887; *AmIsr*, September 28, 1888; November 28, 1889.

37. *PD*, August 14, 1885; David Levy served as cantor during the 1870s. *JR&O*, April 13, 1906. On Paltrovich, see Selig Adler and Thomas E. Connolly, *From Ararat to Suburbia: The History of the Jewish Community of Buffalo* (Philadelphia, 1960), pp. 190, 434; Nathan M. Kaganoff, "American Rabbinic Books Printed in Palestine," in Korn, *op. cit.*, pp. 253–54.

38. *PD*, August 14, 15, 1885; *AmIsr*, August 2, 1885.

39. *PD*, August 6, 1886.

40. *PD*, February 22, 1888.

41. *JR&O*, April 13, 1906.

42. *PD*, September 26, 1888.

43. *PD*, *ibid.*; October 24, 1887; February 10, 22, 1888; September 26, 1888; March 18, 1889; *AmIsr*, August 31, September 28, 1888. Both the "reform" president and secretary of Anshe Emeth moved to New York just at this time. While this was unrelated to congregational storms, it must have weakened the reforming party. *PD*, October 7, 1888; March 12, 1889.

44. There were 900 seats for men and 300 for women; *JR&O*, September 11, 1903. See also *JInd*, August 3, 1906; *JR&O*, June 3, 1904; *PD*, May 30, 1904.

45. For example, *JR&O*, September 30, 1904.

46. *JR&O*, August 25, 1904. See also his views on the Sabbath, *ibid.*, November 11, 18, 1904. Rabbi Hirsch Werner, who became rabbi of Anshe Emeth in 1897, was actually a competent English speaker. *HO*, May 21, 1897.

47. *JR&O*, February 3, 1905.

48. *JInd*, October 27, 1916.

49. *JInd*, October 27, 1917; July 13, 1917.

50. *JInd*, October 27, 1916.

51. *PD*, September 11, 1893.

52. *PD*, July 23, 1897; *HO*, September 5, 1890.

53. *JR&O*, August 20, 1909.

54. *JR&O*, September 2, 1910.

55. *JR&O*, September 30, 1910.

56. *JInd*, July 17, 1914.

57. *JInd*, February 1, 1907; cf. *AmIsr*, January 31, 1889.

58. *AmIsr*, March 6, 1890; April 3, 1890; April 17, 1890; the account is contemptuous and sarcastic.

59. They are *Ha-Poteah ve-ha-Hotem* (New York, 1898), a collection of Talmudic discourses on *Halakha* and *aggadah* for the conclusion of Torah scrolls as well as Mishnah and Gemara, which mention biographical details in Part I, pp. 18 and 24; *Seder Haggada shel Pesah 'im Be'ur Nagid ve-Nafik* (Jerusalem, 1904), a detailed commentary on the Passover *haggadah*. The latter book, very well printed by I. N. Lewy,

includes a printer's colophon urging Hebrew authors to assist Eretz Israel by having their books printed there; see also Kagauoff, *loc. cit.*, pp. 242–43, 247. In general both books are abstracted from contemporary affairs. However, the haggadah commentary inserts a warning against the friendliness of modern nations which would lead Jews to final assimilation (p. 25a). Scholarly articles in the contemporary Hebrew press are cited, as are the learned notes by S. P. Rabinowitz to Graetz's history of the Jews (p. 53ab). Some of the discourses in *Ha-Poteah ve-ha-Hotem* were delivered before Cleveland congregations (Part II, pp. 13b, 17b, 44a, 47b, 48a). While the author refers (*ibid.*, Part II, p. 19a) to his MS commentary on the prayer book, there is no record of its publication. Dr. Dov Levin kindly supplied information on Trashkun (Troshkunay).

60. *AmIsr*, November 3, 1892.

61. *JInd*, March 29, 1907.

62. *JR&O*, November 12, 1915.

63. *JR&O*, September 2, 1904.

64. *PD*, December 31, 1904.

65. *AJYB*, 1909–1910, p. 359; *JInd*, August 21, 1914; also *PD*, August 29, 1904.

66. Besides the old Willet Street burial ground, the two Reform temples collaborated in the United Jewish Cemeteries. There were also the cemeteries of Anshe Chesed; B'nai Abraham; one at Lansing Avenue used by five congregations; Chevra Kadisha (Bohemian); two of Ohab Zedek; Ohavei Emuna; and Shaarei Torah. For the earlier situation, see *AmIsr*, July 6, 1888. Private individuals held a controlling interest in at least one of these cemeteries, as seen by a lawsuit against three owners for wrongful burial of a parent in a disreputable location. *PD*, September 4, 1895.

67. *PD*, March 5, 1904. The reference to a braid is to the rule of burying men in their tallit over the shroud. The tallit is first rendered unfit for other use by tearing off one of its fringes.

68. *Cleveland Citizen*, June 15, 1907. On such traditional forms of protest retained in urban, industrial society, see Herbert G. Gutman, "Work, Culture, and Society in Industrializing America, 1815–1919," *American Historical Review*, LXXVIII, No. 3 (June, 1973), 531–88, esp. 576.

69. *PD*, December 9, 1893.

70. *PD*, December 26, 1892.

71. One example is in *PD*, March 12, 1890; April 4, 1890.

72. *JInd*, April 26, 1907.

73. *JInd*, April 19, 26, 1907.

74. *AJYB*, 1909–1910, pp. 354–356.

75. *JInd*, June 21, 1907.

76. *JInd*, August 24, 1906.

77. *WPA* Church Records Inventory, Western Reserve Historical Society.

78. *JInd*, August 24, 1906.

79. WPA Church Records Inventory, Western Reserve Historical Society; Lubavich was nearly the only Hasidic group to organize congregationally with any success. Nusach Ari is a characteristic Hasidic name, while Zemach Zedek bears the title of a learned work by the fourth of the Lubavich rabbis. The difference in reported dates of founding may simply be the gap between birth and public notice. Louis J. Swichkow and Lloyd P. Gartner, *The History of the Jews of Milwaukee* (Philadelphia, 1963), pp. 206, 207.

80. *CJN*, May 3, 1974.

81. Data from WPA Church Records Inventory, Western Reserve Historical Society.

82. *JR&O*, October 17, 1913; December 26, 1913; July 9, 1915; *JInd*, May 15, 1914.

The contemporary Taylor Road Synagogue originated as Oheb Zedek and was founded in 1904 (see above). It absorbed several immigrant congregations: Chibas Jerusalem (1952), Agudath B'nai Israel Anshe Sfarad (1953), Shaaray Torah (1955), Agudath Achim (1953), Kenesseth Israel (1955). *Jewish News*, January 4, 1970, p. 19.

83. *JInd*, June 14, 1918; March 7, 1919.

84. *JR&O*, June 3, 1904.

85. *JR&O*, May 28, 1915. On the religion of other Cleveland immigrants, see Josef J. Barton, *Peasants and Strangers: Italians; Rumanians, and Slovaks in an American City* (Cambridge, Mass., 1975); on immigrant religion, Rudolph J. Vecoli, "Prelates and Peasants: Italian Immigrants and the Catholic Church," *Journal of Social History*, II, No. 2 (Spring, 1969), 217–68; Oscar Handlin, *Boston's Immigrants*, rev. ed. (New York, 1974), pp. 124–50, 161–66; Richard M. Linkh, *American Catholicism and European Immigrants (1900–1924)*, (Staten Island, New York, 1975).

CHAPTER VII

1. *PD*, September 25, 27, 1901.

2. *JInd*, April 2, 1915; Eugene Lipman, "The Conference Considers Relations between Religion and the State," in *Retrospect and Prospect:: Essays in Commemoration of the Seventy-Fifth Anniversary of the Founding of The Central Conference of American Rabbis 1889-1964*, ed. Bertram W. Korn (New York, 1965), pp. 114–128; on the other hand, Louis Marshall, the foremost American Jewish leader of the time and a noted constitutional lawyer, favord Bible readings provided they were very tactfully arranged. *Champion of Liberty: Louis Marshall*, ed. Charles Reznikoff, 2 vols. (Philadelphia, 1956), II, pp. 967–70. The more widespread view, that advocated by Rabbis Gries and Wolsey, is expressed many times in the pertinent sections of the *American Jewish Year Book*.

3. *JR&O.*, November 18, 1910.

4. Tifereth Israel, Board Minutes, October 2, 1870.

5. *AmIsr*, September 7, 1888; September 7, 1893; *HO*, August 25, 1893; the delay was one day, in conformity with Reform Jewish practice.

6. *JR&O*, March 22, 1907.

7. *PD*, February 1, 1889.

8. Herbert Adolphus Miller, *The School and the Immigrant* (Cleveland, 1916), pp. 32–33.

9. *Ibid.*, pp. 40–52.

10. Timothy L. Smith, "Immigrant Social Aspirations and American Education, 1880–1930," *American Quarterly*, XXI, No. 3 (Fall, 1969), 523–43, emphasizing Slavic and Italian immigrants.

11. Two Jewish children are on record as attending parochial schools. United States Immigration Commission, *Reports*, 41 vols. (Washington, D.C., 1908–1913) Vol. XXX (*The Children of Immigrants in Schools*) II, p. 759. One wonders which was the parochial school, or more likely, whether it was error on the part of careless enumerators or two confused children.

12. *JR&O*, June 16, 1905.

13. *The Children of Immigrants in Schools*, II, p. 882. The categories are Hebrew, German; Hebrew, Polish; Hebrew, Rumanian; Hebrew, Russian; and Hebrew, Other. Since 40 of the 80 are "Hebrew, Other" it is clear that a major territorial origin is meant. In the Cleveland Jewish context this would mean Hungary and, to a lesser extent, Bohemia. Elsewhere in Immigration Commission statistics, only two

categories, "Hebrew, Russian" and "Hebrew, Other", are employed; "Other", therefore covers more ground.

14. E.g., *PD*, June 21, 1887; June 22, 1895; September 11, 1892.

15. *The Children of Immigrants in Schools*, II, p. 759. The division here is "Hebrew, German," 939, probably including most foreign-stock Hungarians and Bohemians; "Hebrew, Polish," 548 '[surprisingly small, perhaps only Austrian Poland-Galicia]; "Hebrew, Russian," 3,332.

16. Miller, *op.cit.*, pp. 79–80.

17. Walter L. Solomon, Headworker of Council Educational Alliance, in F.J.C., Minutes, May 15, 1919.

18. Franklin Bobbitt, *What the Schools Teach and Might Teach* (Cleveland, 1915), pp. 94–95.

19. Charles H. Judd, *Measuring the Work of the Public Schools* (Cleveland, 1916), pp. 47-52; Leonard P. Ayres, *School Organization and Administration* (Cleveland, 1916), *passim*.

20. The five volumes of *The Children of Immigrants in Schools*, devote many pages to statistical grappling with the "retardation" of immigrant school children and attempt to correlate it positively or negatively with length of time in the U.S. They ignore cultural and historical factors bearing on the children's achievement in school. The many tables say very little that is useful concerning immigrant children and a great deal concerning the Commission's bias against recent immigration. See Maldwyn Allen Jones, *American Immigration* (Chicago, 1960), pp. 177–183; Oscar Handlin, "Old Immigrants and New" in his *Race and Nationality in American Life* (Boston, 1957). The Council of Jewish Women pioneered in schooling for retarded children, opening special classes for them in 1914. Council of Jewish Women, Minutes, February 3, 1914.

21. Judd, *op.cit.*, pp. 85–87; Miller, *op.cit.*, pp. 79–80.

22. One of these schools, Outhwaite, also excelled in a selective mathematics test. Judd, *op.cit.*, p. 118. Of the 96 elementary schools, Kennard was lowest, Central eighth lowest, and Case-Woodland ninth; quite inexplicably, Longwood, tied for second place in spelling, with 47.4% presumably slow learners, was the worst in the city. Leonard P. Ayres, *Child Accounting in the Public Schools* (Cleveland, 1915), p. 47.

23. Judd, *op.cit.*, pp. 146–47.

24. Miller, *op.cit.*, pp. 62–66.

25. Lawrence A. Cremin, *The Transformation of the School: Progressivism in American Education, 1876-1957* (New York, 1961), pp. 66–75; with impressionistic eloquence, Oscar Handlin, *The Uprooted* (Boston, 1952), pp. 240–49.

26. *The Children of Immigrants in Schools,* II, pp. 833, 844.

27. Hiram House Papers, Container 30, Folder 4, MS 3319, Western Reserve Historical Society.

28. *PD*, January 31, 1909, Magazine section.

29. Hiram House Papers, Container 33, Folder 5, *loc. cit.*

30. Hiram House Papers, Container 31, unnumbered folder, *loc. cit.*

31. *JInd*, December 13, 1912.

32. *JR&O*, May 13, 1910.

33. Oral interview, January 14, 1972; tape at Jewish Community Federation.

34. *The Children of Immigrants in Schools*, V, pp. 740, 773, 776, 789.

35. *JR&O*, November 23, 1906.

36. *JR&O*, October 18, 1912.

37. *PD*, November 18, 1904.

38. *JR&O*, April 29, 1910.

39. *JR&O*, May 20, 1910; January 22, 1909.

40. The five-fold division was: Hebrew, Russian, 1,497; Hebrew, Polish, 218; Hebrew, other foreign, 185; Hebrew, German, 50; Hebrew, Rumanian, 26. Miller, *op. cit.*, p. 88. A fond, popular novel about night school is Leonard Q. Ross (Leo C. Rosten), *The Education of H*y*m*a*n K*a*p*l*a*n* (New York, 1937).

41. *JInd*, February 12, 1932; January 31, 1919; Zorach's memoirs, *Art is My Life* (Cleveland, 1967), include poignant passages on his early years.

42. *JR&O*, April 14, 1905.

43. *JR&O*, October 1, 1909.

44. Cited in Tifereth Israel's report in MS to the Board of Delegates of American Israelites, Box 2384-B, American Jewish Archives, Cincinnati, Ohio.

45. *AmIsr*, August 6, 1886.

46. *AmIsr*, July 30, 1875.

47. An example from Anshe Chesed is in *AmIsr*, June 5, 1885.

48. *AmIsr*, June 26, 1885.

49. Tifereth Israel, Congregation Meeting, Minutes, October 5, 1890.

50. *JR&O*, September 23, 1910; April 16, 1915.

51. Tifereth Israel, Congregation Meeting, Minutes, September 25, 1888; October 18, 1889.

52. It is unclear whether enrollment figures refer to the opening or end of the school year, or to average attendance. *AmIsr*, May 15, 1885; August 6, 1886; Tifereth Israel, Congregation Meeting, Minutes, October 1, 1893; Rabbi Wolsey to Anshe Chesed members, n.d. (but clearly 1908).

53. *HO*, October 10, 1890.

54. *Ibid.*

55. *HO*, January 1, 1892; February 12, 19, 1892.

56. *AmIsr*, July 6, 1893.

57. Tifereth Israel, Board Minutes, April 1, 1895; October 7, 1895; *AmIsr*, October 18, 1895.

58. Tifereth Israel, Congregation Meeting, Minutes, October 1, 1893.

59. *JR&O*, November 3, 1905.

60. Tifereth Israel, Board Minutes, October 7, 1901. A loophole existed for those who claimed inability to pay.

61. Tifereth Israel, Board Minutes, June 30, 1902.

62. *Ibid.*

63. *JInd*, December 13, 1912.

64. *JR&O*, November 10, 1916.

65. Tifereth Israel, Board Minutes, September, n.d., 1920.

66. *PD*, August 30, 1885.

67. *AmIsr*, August 10, 1883.

68. On immigrants and education, see Marcus Lee Hansen, *The Immigrant in American History* (Cambridge, Mass., 1940), pp. 93–94, 133–34, 203–7; Timothy L. Smith, *op. cit.*

69. *AmIsr*, June 13, 1884; November 26, 1886; *PD*, December 12, 1887; *JInd*, October 19, 1906.

70. *JR&O*, September 23, 1910.

71. Samuel Schwartz, "Tell Thy Children" (memoirs), MS, American Jewish Archives, Cincinnati, Ohio, pp. 45, 46.

72. *JInd*, December 13, 1912.

73. *PD*, November 30, 1885; Rabbi Hahn, interestingly, is listed among the speakers.

74. *PD*, May 16, 1886.

75. *HO*, June 5, 1896.
76. *HO*, May 7, 1897; *JInd*, January 24, 1908; Henrietta Joseph, "History of the Council Religious Schools 1894–1947," MS in Bureau of Jewish Education records.
77. *HO*, May 7, 1897.
78. *JR&O*, January 22, 1909.
79. *JInd*, November 29, 1906, which includes a photograph of part of the front page; *JInd*, October 4, 1907.
80. Cleveland Hebrew Schools, Minute Book, December 1, 1902; December 3, 1904; *JInd*, February 1, 1907. The subject of matzot appears frequently in financial discussions and reports as late as 1938.
81. *JInd*, April 12, 1907.
82. *JInd*, October 4, 1907.
83. *JInd*, November 8, 1907.
84. Oral interview with Ezra Z. Shapiro, February 26, 1972; tape at Jewish Community Federation.
85. *Ibid.*
86. *JInd*, September 8, 1916.
87. Miller, *op. cit.*, p. 44.
88. Cleveland Hebrew School, Board of Education, Minutes, October 30, 1919.
89. *Ibid.*
90. *Ibid.*, January 20, 1917; March 31, 1917; April 1, 1918.
91. *Ibid.*, August 12, 1919.
92. *JInd*, November 5, 1909; February 6, 1914; an attempt by Rabbi Schoenbrun to found an advanced yeshiva at Kenesseth Israel did not succeed. *PD*, November 14, 1904.
93. *JR&O*, September 3, 1915; *JInd*, August 25, 1916.
94. Cleveland Hebrew School, Minutes, April 23, 1918; *JR&O*, September 14, 1917.
95. *JInd*, January 24, 1908.
96. Miller, *op. cit.*, p. 43.
97. *JInd*, December 10, 1909.
98. *JR&O*, May 2, 1915.
99. *PD*, September 6, 1887; on German Jewish fondness for theatre, see Rudolf Glanz, *Studies in Judaica Americana* (New York, 1970), pp. 239–43.
100. H. Avner, "Die geshikhte fun idishen teater in Klivland un zayn tsukunft," *YV*, December 30, 1913. This is the account of an experienced observer.
101. M. Weidenthal, "The Drama," in S. P. Orth, *A History of Cleveland, Ohio* (Cleveland, 1918), p. 449. *JR&O*, June 1, 1906; Adler and his company returned four years later in three productions. *JR&O*, May 6, 1910.
102. *JInd*, January 11, 1907.
103. *JR&O*, March 11, 1910.
104. *JInd*, May 10, 1918.
105. *PD*, February 4, 1904.
106. Avner, *loc. cit.*

CHAPTER VIII

1. I have adopted the term from Howard Mumford Jones, *The Age of Energy: Varieties of American Experience 1865–1915* (New York, 1970), as defined on p. xii: "the discovery, use, exploitation, and expression of energy, whether that be of personality or of prime movers or of words," as the "central . . . stand-point from which to survey the tumult of the age."
2. *JR&O*, March 7, 1924.

3. *JR&O*, May 13, 1910.

4. Joseph Morgenstern, "My First Years in Cleveland (Memoirs)" (Yiddish), *Yiddishe Kultur*, XIX, No. 7 (August-September, 1957), 53.

5. *HO*, November 10, 1893.

6. *JR&O*, June 14, 1912.

7. *HO*, November 10, 1893; January 19, 1894.

8. Ezra Shapiro, oral recollections, February 26, 1972; tape at Jewish Community Federation.

9. This account is provided by *JInd*, March 23, 1906.

10. *JInd*, January 16, 1914; *CJN*, July 30, 1971.

11. *YV*, July 18, 1913.

12. *YV*, October 26, 1913.

13. *YV*, August 8, 1913.

14. *YV*, October 7, 1913.

15. *YV*, November 22, 1913.

16. *YV*, December 7, 1913.

17. *JR&O*, August 20, 1915.

18. *Ibid.*

19. *JR&O*, February 16, 1917.

20. *JR&O*, June 4, 1915.

21. *JR*, March 12, 1897.

22. *JR*, March 26, 1897.

23. *JR&O*, March 24, 1905.

24. Sigmund Shlesinger in *JInd*, January 7, 1910; *Anshe Chesed—In Commemoration of the Semi-Centennial of the Scovill Avenue Temple, 1846–1896*, p. 31.

25. *JInd*, January 7, 1910, quoting the Society's minutes of that date, now no longer traceable.

26. *HO*, September 2, 30, 1892; October 7, 1892; *PD*, October 3, 1892; *AmIsr*, October 6, 1892.

27. *JR&O*, January 13, 1905.

28. *Ibid.*

29. *HO*, September 29, 1893.

30. *JInd*, January 8, 1909.

31. *JInd*, January 7, 1910.

32. *HO*, August 26, 1897.

33. *HO*, February 27, 1891.

34. *HO*, October 8, 1897.

35. *JInd*, October 16, 1914; *JR&O*, December 7, 1923; May 15, 1930.

36. *JInd*, January 7, 1910.

37. *PD*, January 9, 1905.

38. *JR&O*, January 12, 1906; probably to plead their cases. Perhaps professionalism was not gladly accepted by the poor, nor even by long-time volunteers.

39. A. S. Newman in *JInd*, January 9, 1914.

40. *JR&O*, January 17, 1913.

41. *JInd*, January 9, 1914.

42. *JInd*, January 10, 1919.

43. *JR&O*, January 17, 1913.

44. J. H. Greenberg to S. Hartman, July 24, 1912, in J.C.F. Historical Correspondence file.

45. Jewish Community Survey, 1923, I, p. 104; F.J.C., Minutes, September 11, 1924.

46. *HO*, April 2, 1897; July 15, 1897.

47. *PD*, August 5, 1901; *JR&O*, August 9, 1901; *JInd*, January 4, 1907.

48. *JR&O*, March 22, 1907; February 19, 1909; September 23, 1910; January 13, 1911; *JInd*, January 7, 1910.

49. *JR&O*, January 14, 1916; letter, Max Rosenblum, President.

50. *PD*, January 28, 1905; July 10, 1905; January 10, 1906; *JR&O*, September 23, 1910; January 15, 1915; Salo W. Baron, *The Jewish Community: Its History and Structure to the American Revolution*, 3 vols. (Philadelphia, 1942) II, pp. 326–27; III, p. 210.

51. *PD*, April 30, 1905; June 17, 1905.

52. *JInd*, September 28, 1906; *JR&O*, September 21, 1906.

53. *JInd*, April 3, 1914.

54. *JInd*, September 23, 1910; October 22, 1915.

55. *JR&O*, April 23, 1915.

56. A historical resume is in *JInd*, May 9, 1924; *HO*, November 23, 1894; Minute Books.

57. They were Rabbi Moses J. Gries, Dr. Marcus Rosenwasser, Sol Reinthal, Charles Eisenman, Julius Feiss, Sigmund Shlesinger, Samuel Friedman, Leopold Einstein, Meyer Weil, Jacob Mandelbaum, Nathan Loeser, Belle (Mrs. Abraham) Wiener, Flora (Mrs. M. B.) Schwab, Bertha (Mrs. Abraham) Stearn, Mary (Mrs. Leopold) Einstein.

58. Judith A. Trolander, "Twenty Years at Hiram House," *Ohio History*, LXXVIII, No. 1 (Winter, 1969), 25–37, 69–71.

59. By way of illustration, the Warden's (George Bellamy) report to the Board of Trustees, January 11, 1906, pp. 6–7: "It is interesting to observe the effect of the Settlement Christmas upon the Jewish people. The old idea of giving presents—of even [!] recognizing the Christmas Day—was scarcely known among them. . . . many of them are now exchanging gifts and celebrating at heart the birth of Christ. True, there is not a great mental recognition of the spirit, but they are unconsciously absorbing the Christian conception of loving service, and of expressing it in their lives and, in time, will express it in their thoughts." Hiram House Papers, Container 37, Folder 5, MS 3319, Western Reserve Historical Society.

60. *PD*, August 14, 1904.

61. C.E.A., Board Minutes, February 14, 1909.

62. C.E.A., Board Minutes, August 12, 1903.

63. C.E.A., Board Minutes, November 9, 1903; the issue appeared several times, e.g., *ibid.*, December 10, 1905; April 8, 1907; February 13, 1911; November 13, 1911.

64. *Charity Fair Journal*, ed. Nathan Loeser, November-December 1897, quoted in draft MS of 40th anniversary pageant, 1939. On this and other conceptions of the problem of poverty see Robert H. Bremner, *From the Depths: The Discovery of Poverty in the United States* (New York, 1956), pp. 50–66.

65. 40th anniversary pageant MS, *loc. cit.*

66. Annual Report, 1914; *JR&O*, April 17, 1914.

67. Address at the Annual Meeting, C.E.A., Minutes, January 15, 1905.

68. *Ibid.*

69. Annual Report, 1914, *loc. cit.*

70. Cf. Allen F. Davis, *Spearheads for Reform: The Social Settlements and the Progressive Movement* (New York, 1967); Emanuel Sternheim headed the C.E.A. for one year, and spoke in relatively radical political terms.

71. C.E.A. Annual Meeting, Minutes, February 2, 1911.

72. S. Rocker to Eisenman, January, 1912; *YV*, January 7, 1912, translated by S. Rocker and enclosed in letter.

73. *JInd*, March 1, 1912.

74. *HO*, January 1, 1897.

75. Robert H. Wiebe, *Businessmen and Reform: A Study of the Progressive Movement* (Cambridge, Mass., 1962), pp. 16–23, 41, 65–67, 97–100, 206–24; Richard Hofstadter, *The Age of Reform: From Bryan to F.D.R.* (New York, 1955), pp. 173–84, 202–12; George E. Mowry, *The California Progressives* (Berkeley and Los Angeles, 1951), pp. 86–104.

76. F.J.C., Minutes, May 30, 1903.

77. F.J.C., Minutes, December 21, 1903; January 12, 1904.

78. F.J.C., Minutes, February 2, 1905.

79. F.J.C., Minutes, November 30, 1903.

80. F.J.C., Minutes, February 4, 1914.

81. Mahler's resignation appears in C.E.A., Board Minutes, December 7, 1903. Six days later the minutes record action taken at a special C.E.A. meeting to alter the by-laws. On January 11, 1904, Mahler's refusal to reconsider his resignation was reported. C.E.A., Board Minutes, January 11, 1904.

82. F.J.C., Minutes, October 17, 1906.

83. F.J.C., Minutes, June 26, 1905.

84. F.J.C., Minutes, February 21, 1905.

85. F.J.C., Minutes, January 10, 1908.

86. F.J.C., Minutes, February 26, 1915.

87. F.J.C., Minutes, January 25, 1904.

88. F.J.C., Minutes, January 14, 1920.

89. F.J.C., Minutes, January 7, 1917. Goldhammer's memoirs, *Why Doncha Write a Book: A Half-Century of Experience in Jewish Communal Life* (offset; Cleveland, 1963), provide interesting sidelights, mainly about fund-raising.

90. F.J.C., Minutes, March 7, 1904.

91. F.J.C., Minutes, October 28, 1912; January 9, 1913; *JR&O*, January 24, 1913.

92. F.J.C., Minutes, December 5, 1906.

93. *JInd*, January 31, 1908.

94. The minutes do not mention this decision, but an Emergency Fund account was emptied in 1914; F.J.C., Minutes, November 30, 1914.

95. F.J.C., Minutes, March 7, 1904; February 11, 22, 1906.

96. F.J.C., Minutes, October 30, 1913.

97. F.J.C., Minutes, February 13, 1908.

98. F.J.C., Minutes, March 6, 11, 1914.

99. F.J.C., Minutes, April 26, 1907.

100. F.J.C., Minutes, April 30, 1918; May 3, 7, 1918.

101. *PD*, October 1, 1892.

102. *JR&O*, March 7, 1924.

103. F.J.C., Minutes, April 2, 1907; on medical affairs, see the chronicle by Clyde L. Cummer, "Medical Societies in Cleveland from 1890 to 1945," *OSAHQ*, LVII, No. 4 (October, 1948), 344–78, in which Jews, for whatever reasons, do not figure.

104. F.J.C., Minutes, April 9, 1907; November 4, 1908.

105. F.J.C., Minutes, January 24, 1910.

106. F.J.C., Minutes, March 22, 1910.

107. F.J.C., Minutes, January 26, 1911; February 1, 6, 7, 1911.

108. F.J.C., Minutes, June 23, 1913.

109. Eisenman to Margolies, June 20, 1913, in Jewish Community Federation Correspondence.

110. F.J.C., Minutes, July 13, 1922. The Kosher hospital project raised merely

$2,500, and charges were heard of financial irregularities. *YV*, October 7, 1913; November 22, 28, 1913.

111. F.J.C., Minutes, May 25, 1914.

112. F.J.C., Minutes, January 14, 1915.

113. F.J.C., Minutes, February 2, 1915; May 5, 1916; September 8, 1916.

114. *JInd*, June 11, 1915.

115. F.J.C., Minutes, May 15, 1919.

116. F.J.C., Minutes, November 15, 1905; E. M. Baker to Jacob H. Schiff, November 13, 1905.

117. F.J.C., Minutes, January 19, 1913.

118. F.J.C., Minutes, January 9, 1913.

119. On this effort and subsequent attempts to restrict immigration, see John Higham, *Strangers in the Land: Patterns of American Nativism 1860–1925*, 2nd ed. (New Brunswick, N.J., 1955), pp. 110–16; Naomi W. Cohen, *A Dual Heritage: The Public Career of Oscar S. Straus* (Philadelphia, 1969), pp. 152–64.

120. F.J.C., Minutes, May 18, 1906.

121. Baker to Cannon, Telegram, June 22, 1906, in Historical Correspondence file, Jewish Welfare Federation, Cleveland. The "exemption clause" in the British Aliens Act of 1905 guaranteed admission to immigrants arriving "solely to avoid prosecution or punishment on religious or political grounds, or for an offense of political character, or persecution involving danger to life and limb. . . ." See Bernard Gainer, *The Alien Invasion: The Origins of the Aliens Act of 1905* (London, 1972), pp. 144–65.

122. T. E. Burton to Moses J. Gries, June 25, 1906, *loc. cit.*

123. F.J.C., Minutes, June 19, 1906; February 26, 1907; Higham, *op. cit.*, pp. 128–29.

124. F.J.C., Minutes, October 17, 1906; February 6, 1908.

125. Accounts of charities and federations in other local Jewish communities may be found in Louis J. Swichkow and Lloyd P. Gartner, *The History of the Jews of Milwaukee* (Philadelphia, 1963), pp. 215–34; Isaac M. Fein, *The Making of an American Jewish Community: The History of Baltimore Jewry from 1773 to 1920* (Philadelphia, 1971), pp. 213–20; Selig Adler and Thomas E. Connolly, *From Ararat to Suburbia: The History of the Jewish Community of Buffalo* (Philadelphia, 1960), pp. 222–23, 227–36; W. Gunther Plaut, *The Jews in Minnesota: The First Seventy-five Years* (New York, 1959), pp. 221–30; Max Vorspan and Lloyd P. Gartner, *History of the Jews in Los Angeles* (San Marino and Philadelphia, 1970), pp. 171–83. A bureaucratically oriented study is Harry L. Lurie, *A Heritage Affirmed: The Federation Movement in America* (Philadelphia, 1961), treating mainly the more recent period.

126. *JInd*, July 1, 13, 20, 27, 1906.

127. *JInd*, December 28, 1906.

128. *JInd*, December 28, 1906; March 15, 1907; January 31, 1908.

129. *JInd*, March 29, 1907; April 5, 1907.

130. *JInd*, June 1, 1906; July 13, 1906.

131. *JInd*, January 31, 1908.

132. *JInd*, February 21, 1908.

133. *JInd*, April 16, 1909.

134. Aaron Garber to J. L. Magnes, n.d.; Magnes to Garber, November 19, 1913, in Magnes Archives, Historical Society of Israel, F 22–L 142. Dr. Arthur Goren was kind enough to bring these to my attention. His *New York Jews and the Quest for Community: The Kehillah Experiment 1908–1922* (New York, 1970) provides a description of the Clevelanders' model.

135. *JInd*, February 27, 1914.

136. *YV*, November 19, 1913.

137. *JInd*, January 24, 1919.

138. F.J.C., Minutes, July 13, 1922.

139. *PD*, January 20, 1880.

140. *HO*, February 13, 1891.

141. The discussion which follows began in the *Leader*, November 18, 1895, and was reprinted and amplified in *HO*, November 22, 1895.

142. See Naomi W. Cohen, "The Reaction of Reform Judaism in America to Political Zionism (1897–1922)," *PAJHS*, XL (1950–1951), 361–94.

143. The notice sent by Jacob de Haas, Herzl's English secretary, appeared in *HO*, April 9, 1897. The Hebrew writer and bibliographer Ephraim Deinard was agitating for Zionism in Cleveland in 1895: Jacob Kabakoff, "Documents from the Deinard Collection," in *Michael: On the History of the Jews in the Diaspora*, Vol. III, ed. Lloyd P. Gartner (Hebrew; Tel-Aviv, 1975), p. 31.

144. *JR*, June 25, 1897.

145. *HO*, July 30, 1897.

146. *HO*, September 9, 1897.

147. *YV*, July 18, 1913.

148. *HO*, November 5, 1897.

149. *HO*, December 16, 1897; the last-named may have been the young son of Rabbi B. Gittelsohn, who had a long career as a physician.

150. *HO*, December 1, 1898.

151. *Ibid.*

152. *HO*, September 8, 1899.

153. *HO*, August 25, 1899.

154. *JR&O*, December 29, 1899.

155. *JR&O*, February 9, 1900.

156. *JR&O*, February 28, 1902.

157. Yonathan Shapiro, "The Zionist Faith," *AJA*, XVIII, No. 2 (November, 1966), 107–27, and his *Leadership of the American Zionist Organization, 1897–1930* (Urbana, Ill., 1971), pp. 24–77; other studies of American Zionist history during this period are Marnin Feinstein, *American Zionism 1884–1904* (New York, 1965); Avyatar Friesel, *The Zionist Movement in the United States 1897–1914* (Hebrew; Tel-Aviv, 1970); Isidore S. Meyer, ed., *Early History of Zionism in America* (New York, 1958); Naomi W. Cohen, "The Maccabean's Message: A Study in American Zionism until World War I," *Jewish Social Studies*, XVIII, No. 3 (July, 1956), 163–78. All the community histories cited above (n. 125) include Zionist activity in their respective cities.

158. *JR&O*, January 10, 1902; February 28, 1902.

159. *JR&O*, July 22, 1904; *PD*, July 24, 1904.

160. *PD*, August 21, 1905.

161. *JR&O*, May 27, 1910; June 17, 1910; besides Tiphereth Zion, founded 1903, other known groups were Buds of Zion, Blossoms of Zion, Sisters of Zion, Herzl Society (founded 1902), B'nai Zion, Ezras Chovevei Zion (pre-1897), Young Lovers of Zion, Alt-Nailand Club, Zionist Literary Circle. No doubt their names and memberships shifted a great deal, and some may have only existed on paper.

162. *JR&O*, December 18, 1903; November 17, 1905.

163. *JR&O*, September 23, 1904.

164. *JR&O*, January 10, 1902; December 18, 1903.

165. *JR&O*, August 10, 1906; March 13, 1908; *JInd*, March 13, 1908.

166. Timothy L. Smith, "Immigrant Social Aspirations and American Education, 1880–1930," *American Quarterly*, XXI, No. 3 (Fall, 1969), 532.

167. The example of the Slovaks is well presented in Josef J. Barton, *Peasants and Strangers: Italians, Rumanians, and Slovaks in an American City* (Cambridge, Mass., 1975).

168. *PD*, June 4, 1904.

169. Pre-convention stories are in *PD*, February 21, 29, 1904; March 31, 1904; April 11, 1904; May 2, 1904 [lecture by Jacob de Haas]; June 1, 1904; on the convention, *PD*, June 4, 5, 6, 7, 8, 1904.

170. *PD*, June 6, 1904.

171. *PD*, July 6, 1904.

172. *JR&O*, July 22, 1904.

173. *Cleveland Citizen*, September 17, 1904; November 17, 1904.

174. *Ibid.*, June 24, 1905.

175. *Ibid.*, March 23, 1907; August 31, 1907.

176. *Ibid.*, November 21, 1907.

177. *Ibid.*, January 28, 1911. See the debate over the effectiveness of these activities in *YV*, August 15, 22, 1913.

178. *Cleveland Citizen*, March 2, 1912.

179. *Ibid.*, February 15, 1913.

180. *Ibid.*, November 7, 1914.

181. *Ibid.*, January 25, 1908; February 15, 1913.

182. For the New York example, see Goren, *op. cit.*, pp. 186–213; Hyman Berman, "The Cloakmakers' Strike of 1910," in *Essays in Jewish Life and Thought Presented in Honor of Salo Wittmayer Baron*, ed. Joseph L. Blau *et al.* (New York, 1959), pp. 60–90; Moses Rischin, "The Jewish Labor Movement in America: A Social Interpretation," *Labor History*, IV (Fall, 1963), 227–47.

183. A. S. Sachs, *Di Geshikhte fun Arbayter Ring*, 2 vols. (New York, 1925), II, end pages viii, xxx.

184. Workmen's Circle, Karl Marx Branch 559, *20th Jubilee*. Sunday, December 15, 1940 (souvenir journal), n.p.

185. *JInd*, August 24, 1906; cf. *JR&O*, November 23, 1906, reporting the Herzl Society's discussion of the subject.

186. *JR&O*, December 9, 1910.

187. *YV*, July 18, 1913; *JInd*, April 30, 1915.

188. *YV*, July 18, 1913.

189. *JInd*, March 8, 1907; Joseph Morgenstern, *loc. cit.*, p. 53.

190. *JInd*, May 8, 15, 1908.

191. *JR&O*, October 4, 1907; for a reply by Rabbi Margolies, see *JInd*, October 25, 1907.

192. *JR&O*, February 28, 1908.

193. *JInd*, June 18, 1915.

194. *JInd*, February 24, 1911.

195. Letters from Achuzah, No. 1, Cleveland, June 5, 1913, February 2, 15, 1914, Hebra le-Hakhsharat ha-Yishuv, L18/256, Central Zionist Archives, Jerusalem.

196. *JInd*, December 21, 1906.

197. *JInd*, March 6, 1908.

198. *JR&O*, February 16, 1912; March 8, 1912; April 12, 1912.

199. *YV*, October 19, 20, 22, 1913. On the trial, see Maurice Samuel, *Blood Accusation: The Strange History of the Beiliss Case* (Philadelphia, 1966).

200. *JInd*, October 7, 1914; *PD* and *Leader* for October 8, 1914, cited in Alpheus Thomas Mason, *Brandeis: A Free Man's Life* (New York, 1946), p. 672, n. 24.

201. Brandeis to De Haas, October 9, 1914; to Israel J. Biskind, November 6, 28, 1914; in *Letters of Louis D. Brandeis*, Vol. III (1913–1915), *Progressive and Zionist,*

ed. Melvin I. Urofsky and David W. Levy (Albany, 1973), pp. 319–20, 349–50, 375. To Abraham Kolinsky, Brandeis addressed an interesting responsum on the propriety of lawyers contributing to a judge's election campaign. December 1, 1914, *ibid.*, pp. 378–79.

202. *JInd*, August 7, 1914.

203. *JInd*, November 6, 1914.

204. *JInd*, September 18, 25, 1914; October 9, 1914.

205. Besides Federation leaders, representatives appeared from B'nai B'rith, The Temple, Euclid Avenue Temple, B'ne Jeshrun, Hungarian Aid Society, and the Kehillah. F.J.C., Minutes, November 9, 1914.

206. *Ibid.*

207. *JInd*, December 4, 11, 1914.

208. *JInd*, January 22, 1915; on efforts at the time, *JInd*, February 12, 19, 1915.

209. *The People's Relief of America: Facts and Documents 1915–1924* (Yiddish; New York? 1924?), pp. 583–98, provides a full chronicle; figures are on p. xxx.

210. *JInd*, February 11, 1916.

211. *JR&O*, February 25, 1916.

212. *JInd*, January 7, 1916.

213. *JInd*, January 12, 1917.

214. *JR&O*, August 13, 1915.

215. Carl F. Wittke, *German-Americans and the World War (with Special Emphasis on Ohio's German-Language Press)* (Columbus, Ohio, 1936), pp. 29–30, 51, 59, and *passim.*

216. *JR&O*, July 23, 1915.

217. *JR&O*, October 29, 1915.

218. *Ibid.*

219. *JInd*, November 19, 1915; December 3, 1915; he had argued this at the Central Conference of American Rabbis; *JInd*, July 2, 1915.

220. *JR&O*, April 14, 1916.

221. On this movement, see Swichkow and Gartner, *op. cit.*, pp. 268–85; Vorspan and Gartner, *op. cit.*, pp. 184–92; Oscar I. Janowsky, *The Jews and Minority Rights (1898–1919)* (New York, 1933), pp. 161–90; Jonathan Frankel, "The Jewish Socialists and the American Jewish Congress Movement," in *YIVO Annual of Jewish Social Science*, XVI (*Essays on the American Jewish Labor Movement*, ed. Ezra Mendelsohn) (New York, 1976), pp. 202–341.

222. *JInd*, September 17, 1915.

223. George A. Myers to James Ford Rhodes, March 16, 1917, in John A. Garraty, ed., "The Correspondence of George A. Myers and James Ford Rhodes," *Ohio Historical Quarterly*, LXIV, No. 3 (July, 1955), p. 240.

224. *JInd*, March 30, 1917.

225. *JInd*, March 23, 1917.

226. *JInd*, April 7, 1917.

227. *JInd*, April 13, 1917.

228. *JInd*, August 17, 1917.

229. Elbert J. Benton, "The Cleveland World War Machine," *OSAHQ*, XXXVIII, No. 3 (July, 1929), p. 451.

230. *JInd*, March 15, 1918.

231. Jewish Welfare Board to Abba Hillel Silver, October 28, 1919, in Federation of Jewish Charities file, Silver Archives, The Temple.

232. *JInd*, April 19, 1918; June 21, 1918.

233. F.J.C., Minutes, February 28, 1918.

234. F.J.C., Minutes, September 17, 1919; January 11, 1920; February 1, 1921.

235. Richard A. Folk, "Socialist Party of Ohio—War and Free Speech," *Ohio History*, LXXVIII, No. 1 (Winter, 1969), 104–15, 152–54.

236. *Ibid.*, p. 112.

237. John D. Buenker, *Urban Liberalism and Progressive Reform* (New York, 1973), pp. 183–84.

238. Wittke, *op. cit.*, pp. 130, 135, 136, 153–54, 168, 171, 175, 178–79, 185, 186.

239. *JInd*, September 28, 1917; Elias A. Gilner, *War and Hope: A History of the Jewish Legion* (New York, 1969), p. 172.

240. The pamphlet paid tribute to Judge Manuel Levine and others of the Immigration League of 1911, who did the first Americanization work in the city and "probably the most important early movement in America." *Americanization in Cleveland*, n.p.

241. *JInd*, May 4, 1917.

242. *JInd*, May 18, 1917.

243. *JInd*, May 25, 1917.

244. *JInd*, June 15, 1917.

245. On the elections in other local Jewish communities, see Vorspan and Gartner, *op. cit.*, pp. 190–91; Swichkow and Gartner, *op. cit.*, pp. 279–80; Plaut, *op. cit.*, pp. 250–53.

246. *JInd*, November 23, 1917.

247. *JInd*, February 1, 8, 22, 1918; March 1, 1918.

248. *JInd*, May 3, 1918.

249. Irving Levitas, "Reform Jews and Zionism—1919–1921," *AJA*, XIV, No. 1 (April, 1962), 15; Wolsey to Rabbi Henry Berkowitz, January 14, 1919, American Jewish Archives, Box 1893, Folder W. I am indebted to Dr. Irving Levitas for his kind assistance. On the other hand, Rabbi Gries, of impeccable classical Reform principles, did not apparently take part in this group; *JInd*, September 13, 1918; October 11, 1918.

250. *JInd*, December 28, 1917.

251. E.g., *JInd*, December 13, 1918.

252. *JInd*, May 30, 1919.

253. *JInd*, November 29, 1919.

254. Thomas F. Campbell, *Daniel E. Morgan: The Good Citizen in Politics* (Cleveland, 1966), pp. 72–73.

255. *JInd*, January 24, 1919.

256. *JInd*, May 27, 1921.

257. Shapiro, *Leadership of the American Zionist Organization*, pp. 135–79. Melvin I. Urofsky, *American Zionism from Herzl to the Holocaust* (Garden City, N.Y., 1975), pp. 246–98; George L. Berlin, "The Brandeis-Weizmann Dispute," *AJHQ*, LX, No. 1 (September, 1970), pp. 37–68; *JInd*, June 10, 1921, adds a few details.

258. Hebrew was included with Yiddish, but it could have been the native tongue of a negligible proportion. The totals divide foreign-born speakers (16,408 Yiddish and Hebrew) from native born with one or two foreign-born parents (13,975 Yiddish and Hebrew). U.S. Bureau of the Census, *Fourteenth Census of the United States . . . 1920 . . .*, Vol. II, *Population 1920* (Washington, D.C., 1922).

CHAPTER IX

1. Only 76,762 of the metropolitan area's 637,425 in 1910 lived beyond the city line. By 1920 the corresponding figures were 146,654 of 943,495.

2. Yearly population figures are in Howard Whipple Green, *Population by Census Tracts in Cleveland and Vicinity* (Cleveland, 1931), p. 4.

3. Cleveland Chamber of Commerce, Industrial Development Department, *A Decade in the History of Metropolitan Cleveland* (Cleveland, n.d. [ca. 1930]).

4. Blake McKelvey, *The Emergence of Metropolitan America 1915–1966* (New Brunswick, N.J., 1968), pp. 53–54.

5. Edgar Eugene Robinson, *The Presidential Vote 1896–1932* (Stanford, Calif., and London, 1934), p. 293.

6. F.J.C., Executive Committee Minutes, October 19, 1922.

7. The declines were even greater for other ethnic groups: the 43,000 who spoke Czech in 1920, 65,000 Polish, and 120,000 German were reduced by 1930 to 14,000, 25,000, and 37,000 respectively.

8. On Henry Ford's anti-Semitism, see Morton Rosenstock, *Louis Marshall, Defender of Jewish Rights* (Detroit, 1965), pp. 128–200; John Higham, *Strangers in the Land: Patterns of American Nativism 1860–1925*, 2nd ed. (New Brunswick, 1963), pp. 282–85.

9. *JInd*, February 4, 1921.

10. See in general Rosenstock, *op. cit.*, pp. 201–33; Higham, *op. cit.*, pp. 264–330.

11. Jewish Community Survey, I, pp. 28, 31, 36.

12. Green, *loc. cit.*

13. The Jewish population of the Great Lakes cities from Buffalo to Minneapolis has also remained stationary for some fifty years, with the exception of Detroit, where it has not actually declined.

14. Council of Jewish Women, Minutes, November 2, 1920; Annual Report of Executive Director in C.E.A., Board Minutes, April 25, 1926; J.W.F., Functional Relations Committee, Jewish Recreation Conference, Minutes, October 26, 1927, Exhibit A. On the other hand, the Research Secretary's Annual Report, in J.W.F., Minutes, January 9, 1927, speaks of 16,000 Jews still in the area, although the contradictory suggestion is made of a 50© decrease during the preceding five years. There was no question of a sharp decline.

15. Report of Executive Director, in C.E.A., Board Minutes, March 21, 1928.

16. Letter, Leonard S. Levy, Secretary, C.E.A., in J.W.F., Minutes, February 28, 1929.

17. Annual Report of Executive Director for 1929 in C.E.A., Board Minutes, March 20, 1930.

18. Jewish Recreation Conference, "Statement of Studies and Surveys Committee on E. 105th Street Situation," in J.W.F., Minutes, October 18, 1926. St. Clair Avenue seems a likelier northern boundary than Bratenahl.

19. Annual Report of Executive Director in C.E.A., Board Minutes, April 25, 1927.

20. Nostalgic neighborhood recollections are "Greatest of Neighborhoods—E. 105," *CJN*, April 6, 1973.

21. Annual Report of Executive Director, 1925, in C.E.A., Board Minutes, no date (ca. March, 1926).

22. J.W.F., Functional Relations Committee, Jewish Recreation Conference, Minutes, October 26, 1927, Exhibit A; cf. Annual Report, Research Secretary, J.W.F., Minutes, January 9, 1927. Two nostalgic memoirs are "How Life Was Among the 'Kinsman Cowboys,'" and "More Memories of 'Kinsman Cowboys,'" *CJN*, January 7, 21, 1972.

23. C.E.A., Board Minutes, February 19, 1930; *idem*, Annual Report, 1932.

24. Jewish Recreation Conference, in J.W.F. Minutes, December 18, 1928; January 18, 1929. Residents of the area claimed as many as 4,000 Jews, but their eye was on persuading the Federation to help them to establish a Jewish community center. See also J.W.F., Research Department, Report of Lake Shore Jewish Center and Recreation Subcommittee [Studies and Surveys Committee] on Jewish Center Project, Ex-

hibits B and C, in J.W.F., Minutes, March 21, 1929. Exhibit B contains useful occupational data.

25. Camp Wise, Minutes, n.d. (ca. 1927).

26. Camp Wise, Minutes, October 5, 1929.

27. Research Department, Report on Lake Shore Jewish Center, Exhibit B, in J.W.F., Minutes, March 21, 1929.

28. The Distinctive Jewish Names method was employed, by which the possessors of 34 exclusively Jewish names are employed as the representative sample. There were 3,480 bearers of DJNs in the 1923 Directory, and 3,437 in 1930. Every third person was counted. Mr. Edward L. Greenstein assisted in these calculations. For an example of its application elsewhere see Max Vorspan and Lloyd P. Gartner, *History of the Jews of Los Angeles* (San Marino and Philadelphia, 1970), pp. 126–28 and notes thereto.

29. In general workers in a trade were designated by an "er" suffix, while owners were usually described by the article or service they offered, e.g., "overall co.," "gloves," "cleaning."

30. The number of physicians declined from ten to seven. This appears inexplicable, since other sources make clear, as will be seen presently, that the number was rising sharply. It may be that the increase of specialization led physicians to be listed as internists, orthopedists, etc., and the method used here is not of fine enough mesh to "catch" two internists or one orthopedist in a thousand Jewish names.

31. Jewish Community Survey, I, pp. 209–10, where it is also observed that a higher proportion of Jewish than non-Jewish physicians held hospital appointments. Director, Mount Sinai Hospital, to Functional Relations Committee, in J.W.F., Minutes, November 27, 1925; January 14, 1926.

32. Paul H. Douglas, *Real Wages in the United States 1890–1926* (Boston and New York, 1930), pp. 126–27, 129, 263–67.

33. Quoted in Irving Bernstein, *The Lean Years: A History of the American Worker 1920–1933* (Boston, 1960), pp. 64–65.

34. John R. Commons *et al.*, *History of Labor in the United States*, Vol. III, by Elizabeth Brandeis (New York, 1935; reprinted New York, 1966), pp. 262–66; Jesse Thomas Carpenter, *Competition and Collective Bargaining in the Needle Trades, 1910–1967* (Ithaca, N.Y., 1972), pp. 84, 116–17, 125.

35. Sumner H. Slichter, *Union Policies and Industrial Management* (Washington, D.C., 1941), pp. 393–430. Louis Levine, *The Women's Garment Workers* (New York, 1924), pp. 360–81.

36. Amalgamated Clothing Workers of America, *Proceedings of Third Biennial Convention . . . Baltimore . . . May 13 to 18, 1919* [*sic*; should be 1918].

37. *Ibid.*, 1922, pp. 166–69.

38. *Ibid.*, 1926, pp. 122–23; 1928, p. 55; *JR&O*, September 20, 1929.

39. The work was reissued in 1959 with a new introduction by the author, and in a paperback edition.

40. This sermon is in the Silver Archives, The Temple.

41. The Temple contains the excellently arranged archives of Silver. His sermons, in the course of publication, now include *Therefore Choose Life* (New York, 1971). *In The Time of Harvest* (New York, 1963) is a festschrift on his seventieth birthday which became the year of his death. Pending the full biography which he abundantly requires, there is a fine memoir by Leon I. Feuer, *AJA*, XIX, No. 2 (November, 1967), 107–26, supplemented by *AJA*, XX, No. 2 (November, 1968), 127–28.

42. *JInd*, June 9, 23, 30, 1922; *JR&O*, March 29, 1929.

43. *JInd*, February 6, 1925; *JR&O*, February 20, 1925.

44. *JInd*, October 16, 1925; October 2, 1925.

45. *JInd*, February 27, 1925; October 2, 16, 1925.

46. *JInd*, February 10, 1922; June 30, 1922.

47. Harsh memories abide: Letter, Hannah Katz Engelberg, in *CJN*, June 27, 1969.

48. *JInd*, March 2, 1923; *JR&O*, September 3, 1926.

49. In 1974 The Temple was placed on the National Register of Historic Places, thus making it proof against razing. *CJN*, September 20, 1974.

50. The Temple, *Annual Report*, 1930; *JR&O*, May 31, 1929.

51. *JR&O*, April 11, 1930.

52. *JInd*, March 18, 1921; August 4, 1921.

53. *CJN*, March 16, 1973.

54. The first-named small congregation indirectly shows that the Temple's original name, also Tifereth Israel, was virtually forgotten. The present Warrensville Center Synagogue incorporates several of these congregations: Tetiever Ahavas Achim, Bnai Jacob-Kol Israel (Kinsman Jewish Center), N'vai Zedek, Sherith Jacob Israel (Eddy Road Jewish Center-Memorial Synagogue); *CJN*, June 25, 1971; May 3, 1974.

55. *JR&O*, November 5, 1926.

56. *JInd*, September 4, 1925; *CJN*, December 24, 1971.

57. On Hebrew activities, see *Hadoar* (New York), May 2, 1930; June 13, 1930.

58. *CJN*, May 10, 1974; *JR&O*, August 26, 1921.

59. *JR&O*, May 13, 20, 1927.

60. C.E.A., Minutes, October 16, 1929; March 20, 1930; idem, Executive Director's Report, 1931; *Survey of Group Work Resources* (1945), I, p. 165.

61. *JInd*, August 28, 1931. On the Yiddish books, see *CJN*, April 5, 1974. A curious Yiddish publication is Rabbi A. Y. Zhitnik, *Di Iden in Sovet-Rusland*, published in 1925 as the first and only one of five projected volumes by the Orthodox rabbi who founded and led the "All-Russian Union of the Toiling Jewish Masses" in the Ukraine, 1918–1921. The small book was intended to justify his activities, and was published by the "Publication Committee for Rabbi Zhitnik's Works." The rabbi, however, lived in New York City. See Zvi Y. Gitelman, *Jewish Nationality and Soviet Politics: The Jewish Sections of the CPSU* (Princeton, 1972), pp. 239–41.

62. *JInd*, April 15, 1927.

63. *JR&O*, April 30, 1926.

64. Grove's *Dictionary of Music and Musicians*, s.v. "Bloch, Ernest." Some local Jewish sources claim that Bloch's resignation from his position was due to anti-Semitism.

65. F.J.C., Minutes, January 14, 1920.

66. James R. Garfield to Charles Eisenman, August 25, 1919, in F.J.C., Minutes, August 25, 1919; *ibid.*, August 28, 1919; Charles Eisenman to James R. Garfield, August 28, 1919, in *ibid.*, August 28, 1919; *ibid.*, September 19, 1919; October 14, 1919.

67. F.J.C., Minutes, October 19, 1922.

68. F.J.C., Minutes, September 26, 1923.

69. F.J.C., Minutes, May 23, 1924; October 9, 1924; April 1, 1925.

70. J.W.F., Minutes, September 27, 1928, Exhibit A.

71. F.J.C. Annual Meeting, Minutes, March 16, 1924.

72. J.W.F., Executive Committee Minutes, February 8, 1926.

73. J.W.F., Board Minutes, February 23, 1926.

74. *Ibid.* The Community Fund was not unwilling to take in the Orthodox Jewish Orphans Home, the Jewish Day Nursery, and the Orthodox Home for the Aged. The Federation, however, would not guarantee the extra $50,000 required, especially because the institutions' supporters were unlikely to give as much as they had brought to the offices of the institutions directly. The Jewish campaign was to provide 1 1/2 years' support for the three institutions, following which, the Community Fund having

seen that they could draw the needed monies through a combined appeal, they would become full beneficiaries from January 1, 1928. J.W.F., Letter to Community Fund, in Minutes, March 9, 1926.

75. J.W.F., Financial Report at Annual Meeting, Minutes, January 9, 1927.

76. J.W.F., Minutes: Budget and Finance Committee, April 12, 1928; Finance Committee, June 11, 1928; Budget and Finance Committee, August 29, 1928; Report to Community Fund Council on Jewish Welfare Federation's 1929 Budget Request, copy in J.W.F., Minutes, October 1, 1928.

77. F.J.C., Executive Committee, Minutes, April 12, 1923.

78. Jewish Community Survey, I, p. 208.

79. *Ibid.*

80. *JR&O*, May 26, 1926.

81. Jewish Community Survey, I, pp. 17–18.

82. He later served as Executive Vice President of the American Jewish Committee from 1943 to 1967.

83. *JR&O*, December 2, 1927.

84. Jewish Community Survey, II, p. 538.

85. Report on the Activities of the Bureau of Jewish Education, n.d. (early 1925), by Alfred H. Sachs, Executive Director.

86. Bureau of Jewish Education, Executive Committee Minutes, November 1, 1927.

87. *JInd*, June 18, 1920; July 2, 1920.

88. Cleveland Hebrew School, Annual Meeting, April 17, 1919; 367 pupils were free and the remainder paid between 25c and $3.00 monthly.

89. Remarks of Friedland to Federation Trustees, in F.J.C., Minutes, September 3, 1923.

90. *JR&O*, September 15, 1922.

91. Joint Jewish Education Committee, Minutes, June 22, 1928.

92. Cleveland Hebrew Schools, Board of Education, Minutes, December 25, 1922.

93. Cleveland Hebrew Schools, Board of Directors, Minutes, February 18, 1926.

94. Organizing Meeting, Minutes, April 16, 1924; Board Meeting, Minutes, October 9, 1924.

95. Organizing Meeting, *loc. cit.*

96. The anomaly and communal danger of this situation were noticed in an article by Slawson in *Jewish Social Service Quarterly*, 1927, quoted in J.W.F, Minutes, November, 1927.

97. *JR&O*, November 20, 1925.

98. Joint Jewish Education Committee, Minutes, June 22, 1928.

99. Joint Jewish Education Committee, Minutes, June 29, 1928, Exhibit B; October 19, 1928; Memorandum, A. Simon to Rabbi A. H. Silver, November 21, 1928; all in J.C.F. transfer file.

CHAPTER X

1. Irving Bernstein, *The Lean Years: A History of the American Worker 1920–1933* (Boston, 1960), pp. 59, 70–72.

2. J.W.F., Executive Committee Minutes, March 8, 1928.

3. J.W.F., Minutes, September 27, 1928, Exhibit A. The figure of 75% was from 1925.

4. Cleveland Hebrew School, Board of Directors, Minutes, October 20, 1927; September 12, 1929. The great impact on American Jewry of the depression of the

1930s remains unstudied except for contemporary reports mainly by social workers; see Max Vorspan and Lloyd P. Gartner, *History of the Jews of Los Angeles* (San Marino and Philadelphia, 1970), pp. 193–208; *Trends and Issues in Jewish Social Welfare in the United States, 1899–1958*, ed. Robert Morris and Michael Freund (Philadelphia, 1966), pp. 279–462.

5. Bernstein, *op. cit.*, p. 426.

6. Sumner H. Slichter, *Union Policies and Industrial Management* (Washington, D.C., 1941), pp. 431–32.

7. Jewish Social Service Bureau to J.W.F., January 24, 1930, in J.W.F., Minutes, *ad loc.*

8. Budget Committee of J.W.F. to Community Fund Investigating Committee, September 29, 1930, in J.W.F., Minutes, September 19, 1930.

9. J.W.F. Budget and Finance Committee, to Kenneth Sturges, General Manager of Community Fund, n.d., in J.W.F., Minutes, March 31, 1931.

10. *Ibid.*

11. Jewish Social Service Bureau to J.W.F., n.d., in J.W.F., Minutes, March 28, 1931.

12. Report of Executive Director at Annual Meeting, J.W.F., Minutes, January 25, 1933.

13. E. O. Braught, Executive Sec. Ohio State Relief Commission, to A. V. Cannon, Chairman Joint Committee on Relief Measures, n.d., copy in J.W.F., Minutes, January 5, 1933.

14. *Ibid.*

15. J.W.F., Minutes, January 24, 1933.

16. Sermon, "Why Cleveland Is Not Taking Care of Its Own," April 3, 1932, Silver Archives, The Temple. There is an extensive file documenting his vigorous efforts at the Associated Charities to keep up the size of family allowances.

17. J.W.F., Minutes, February 16, 1933.

18. They had heard that matzot for Passover would be denied them.

19. J.W.F., Minutes, March 17, 24, 1933; April 17, 1933.

20. J.W.F., Minutes, August 18, 1933; September 11, 1933.

21. *PD*, July 15, 1936.

22. Address at Annual Meeting, J.W.F., Minutes, February 19, 1928. This address was also issued as a brochure.

23. President's address at Annual meeting, J.W.F., Minutes, February 16, 1931.

24. Sermon, November 12, 1933, Silver Archives, The Temple. These sermons brought many simple, moving letters of gratitude from non-Jews, most of them victims of the depression.

25. Report of Walter Leo Solomon, Headworker, 1934; MS at Jewish Welfare Board, New York City, later published after Solomon's death in 1934 as "Retrospect: Jewish Center Ideals" in *The Jewish Center*, March, 1938; for the situation slightly later, see Charles E. Hendry and Margaret T. Svendsen, *Between Spires and Stacks* (Welfare Federation of Cleveland, 1936), a study of youth in Tremont, a poor, mostly Slavic and Italian working-class area near Cleveland's center.

26. The source and method of this calculation may be found in Chap. 9, n. 28. The "Honor Roll" of the Joseph and Feiss Co. clothing firm listed 144 employees serving in the armed forces in 1945. No more than 20 names appear Jewish, and the rest Slavic and Italian.

27. Lee J. Levinger, "Jews in the Liberal Professions in Ohio," *Jewish Social Studies*, II, No. 4 (October, 1940), 401–34.

28. "Questionnaire for Local Surveys," p. 1, in O/Cleveland (General), American Jewish Committee Archives, New York.

29. Howard Whipple Green, *Population by Census Tracts Cleveland and Vicinity with Street Index* (Cleveland, 1941), p. 4.

30. (A. H. Friedland), Report on the . . . Jewish School Population of Cleveland," in Bureau of Jewish Education, Minutes, January 24, 1935.

31. Warren S. Thompson, *Migration within Ohio, 1935–1940: A Study in the Re-Distribution of Population*, Scripps Foundation Studies in Population Distribution, No. 3 (Miami University, 1951), pp. 15–29.

32. Report of Executive Director, C.E.A., March 15, 1944.

33. C.E.A., Staff meeting, Minutes, October 5, 1945.

34. *Survey of Group Work Resources Available to the Jewish Community of Greater Cleveland*, 2 vols. (1945), I, p. 67. This survey was commissioned by the Social Agency Committee of the Jewish Welfare Federation and taken by the National Jewish Welfare Board. It is abbreviated here as *Survey*, 1945.

35. Green, *op. cit.*, pp. 4, 64, 121.

36. *Ibid.*, maps, p. 29ff.

37. *Survey*, 1945.

38. *Ibid.*, pp. 81–82, Table 9.

39. Green, *op. cit.*, p. 1.

40. A few personal accounts are in *CJN*, November 3, 1972.

41. "Questionnaire for Local Surveys," pp. 24–25, *loc. cit.*

42. J.W.F., Trustees' Minutes, May 13, 1931.

43. Material concerning Levine may be found in the index to the Hiram House Papers, Western Reserve Historical Society; *Cleveland News*, September 16, 1930; October 10, 1935; *New York Times*, May 7, 1938.

44. *CJN*, March 6, 1970; December 10, 1971.

45. *PD*, August 26, 1937; October 20, 1937; November 3, 5, 1937.

46. *PD*, January 11, 12, 30, 1933.

47. Cleveland Study Committee, Community Study, 1944, p. 29 (mimeographed).

48. The information in the paragraphs above is drawn mainly from the "Questionnaire for Local Surveys," *loc. cit.* The words "from E. M. Baker" are faintly pencilled in the upper corner of Page One. As a veteran member of the American Jewish Committee his authorship of this document appears probable. Moreover, Baker was the long-time president of the Cleveland Stock Exchange and well informed on the city's life, especially at its upper level. A valuable study of anti-Semitism in American society during the 1930s and of American Jewish Committee endeavors in connection with it is Naomi W. Cohen, *Not Free to Desist: The American Jewish Committee 1906–1966* (Philadelphia, 1972), pp. 193–226; see also Charles Herbert Stember *et al.*, *Jews in the Mind of America* (New York, 1966), and Seymour Martin Lipset and Earl Rabb, *The Politics of Unreason: Right-Wing Extremism in America, 1790–1970* (New York, 1970), pp. 150–208. Relevant Catholic thinking is ably presented in Aaron I. Abell, *American Catholicism and Social Action: A Search for Social Justice, 1865–1950* (Notre Dame, Ind., 1963).

49. *PD*, May 14, 1933.

50. *PD*, November 9, 11, 12, 1938; *Cleveland Press*, November 12, 1938; *JInd*, November 18, 1938.

51. "Questionnaire for Local Surveys," *loc. cit.*, p. 13; letter, League for Human Rights against Nazism to Jewish Welfare Federation, n.d., in J.W.F., Minutes, Vol. XI; Moshe Gottlieb, "The Anti-Nazi Boycott Movement in the United States: An Ideological and Sociological Appreciation," *Jewish Social Studies*, XXXV, No. 3–4 (July–October, 1973), 198–227, esp. 208–10.

52. J.W.F., Informal Trustees' meeting, Minutes, March 15, 1934.

53. J.W.F., Trustees' Minutes, April 10, 1930. The Jewish firms' alibi was that "too

many" Jews in their employ "would cripple them on the three or four Jewish holidays." *Ibid.*

54. For example, *CJN*, April 5, 1968 [p. 20].

55. *PD*, November 6, 7, 1933.

56. Jewish Community Council Committee on Fictitious Jewish Political Issues, Minutes [in J.W.F., Minutes], June 25, 1937.

57. Bureau of Jewish Education, Board of Trustees, Minutes, November 7, 1938. The effort was not pursued and was abandoned in 1949, owing to the general decline in foreign language study and the dwindling number of Jews in the city's schools. *Ibid.*, January 30, 1949.

58. A. H. Friedland to Ben Rosen, March 22, 1933, Bureau of Jewish Education records.

59. J.W.F., Trustees' Minutes, July 30, 1934.

60. *PD*, February 25, 1935; October 28, 1935.

61. *JR&O*, October 25, 1929; Isaac Ever, *Ha-Rav Y. H. Levenberg* (Yiddish; Cleveland, 1939), informative although panegyrical.

62. Jewish Young Adult Bureau, "Rules and Regulations," Preamble; Harold Arian, "A Community-Wide Experiment in Decentralized Group Work—The Jewish Young," Adult Bureau of Cleveland (M.A. thesis, School of Applied Social Sciences, Western Reserve University, 1941).

63. Martin Rosskamm and Eric Hirschfield, Hakoah, to Herbert A. Rosenthal, Jewish Young Adult Bureau, December 2, 1940, J.Y.A.B. file at Jewish Community Federation.

64. J.W.F., Trustees' Minutes, April 10, 1930. For a summary of contributions made by Cleveland Jews to the Community Fund ($429,960), the Bureau of Jewish Education ($43,696), and national Jewish and foreign Jewish organizations, see J.W.F., Minutes, September 29, 1929, Exhibit C. The total of $246,136 is quite incomplete.

65. J.W.F., Minutes, December 5, 1930; June 8, 1932; June 20, 1932; January 19, 1933.

66. J.W.F., Minutes, December 17, 1930.

67. J.W.F., Budget & Finance Committee Minutes, December 15, 16, 1930.

68. J.W.F., Jewish Welfare Fund Committee Minutes, January 19, 1932; Budget & Finance Committee Minutes, June 2, 1932; tables of funds received and allotted, *passim.*

69. J.W.F., Minutes, September 28, 1933.

70. J.W.F., Budget and Finance Committee Minutes, July 30, 1934; April 8, 1935.

71. J.W.F., Informal Trustees' meeting, Minutes, November 16, 1933.

72. From an analysis of S. Goldhammer of proceedings at National Council of Jewish Federations and Welfare Funds, in J.W.F., Minutes, January 22, 1934.

73. *Ibid.*

74. *Ibid.*

75. The reference is probably to alleged Jewish overcrowding in trade and excessive ambitions to enter the professions.

76. President's Address at Annual Meeting, J.W.F., Minutes, February 25, 1934.

77. J.W.F., Committee on Policy and Reorganization Minutes, March 15, 1934.

78. *Ibid.*, September 20, 1934.

79. *Ibid.*, November 13, 1934; Trustees' Minutes, December 7, 1934.

80. J.W.F., Committee on Policy and Reorganization Minutes, March 4, 1935.

81. *Ibid.*

82. *Ibid.*, March 4, 1935.

83. *PD*, January 20, 23, 1933; October 2, 9, 1933.

84. J.W.F., Jewish Welfare Fund Committee Minutes, February 14, 1935.

85. J.W.F., Trustees' Minutes, February 19, 1935; Welfare Fund Committee Minutes, March 28, 1935.

86. J.W.F., Annual Meeting, Minutes, February 5, 1936.

87. J.W.F., Report of Special Committee . . . to Consider Affiliation with the Jewish Community Council, September 27, 1935; Trustees' Minutes, September 26, 1935.

88. Council of Jewish Women, Minutes, February 3, 1933; March 8, 1933.

89. Green, *op. cit.*, pp. 11ff. In 1944 an estimated 50,000 members belonged to 100 Jewish organizations; *Survey*, 1945, I, pp. 171ff.

90. *PD*, June 19, 21, 1936; Works Progress Administration, Ohio Historical Records Survey, Church Records (incomplete survey; at Western Reserve Historical Society).

91. *CJN*, March 16, 1973.

92. Elmer Louis, A Study of the Organized Recreational Education, Leisure Time Activities, Sponsored by the Jewish Community in the Mount Pleasant Area, Cleveland, Ohio, 1937 (M.A. thesis, School of Applied Social Sciences, Western Reserve University, 1940), pp. 23–24.

93. Much of the preceding is from Church Records, *loc. cit.*

94. Ever, *op. cit.*

95. Workmen's Circle, Branch 79, *Thirty-Fifth Anniversary Jubilee. Sunday, October 15th, 1939*; Louis, *op. cit.*, pp. 28–31.

96. Oscar I. Janowsky, "The Cleveland Bureau of Jewish Education: A Case Study (1924–1953)," *AJHQ*, LIV, No. 3 (March, 1965), 323–57.

97. *JInd*, December 11, 1931, provides a broad description.

98. Ben Rosen and Isaac B. Berkson, "Digest of Summary and Recommendations, 1936 Education Survey of Cleveland," Part I; other sections of this illuminating socioeducational discussion are reprinted in Lloyd P. Gartner, *Jewish Education in the United States: A Documentary History* (New York, 1969), pp. 174–77. The 1935 report presented by Friedland (*supra*, n. 30) points to similar conditions.

99. "Digest of Summary Recommendations . . . ," Part II.

100. *9th Annual Cleveland Hebrew School Banquet Program*, December 1937. Friedland's faith in the Zionist, Hebraist foundation of his educational work also did not waver:

> Somehow one cannot help feeling that the opportunities in Palestine have come to us with a timeliness that baffles the sobrieties of reason. The beginning of the twentieth century left us woefully depleted of our spiritual reservoirs. . . . Religion as a super-natural force, as a uniquely Jewish possession, lost its hold upon us. Our national culture lost the promise of survival in the face of overwhelming local cultures. Then the World War came and with it the Balfour Declaration reaffirming our historic rights to Palestine.
>
> The faith of spiritual Zionism seeks to kindle to new religious incandescence, the aspirations towards the good, the true and the beautiful on the part of a people that is today the most downtrodden and tormented. . . . Out of the depths of despair, we call unto the Lord. From the nadir of oppression we climb to the very heights of spiritual triumph.

Testimonial Dinner Tendered to A. H. Friedland, June 2, 1936, *Program*; A. H. Friedland to Solomon Goldman, December 24, 1936, in Bureau of Jewish Education files.

101. *Sippurim* (Tel-Aviv, 1939); *Sonetot* (Tel-Aviv, 1939); *Shirim* (Tel-Aviv, 1940). *Sefer Zikkaron le-H. A. Friedland*, ed. Menahem Ribalow (New York, 1941).

102. *PD*, undated clipping, late 1945. A 1949 estimate of 14,000 World War II veterans in a Jewish community of 85,000 appears exaggerated.

103. *PD*, February 27, 1945.

104. Cleveland Study Committee, *Community Study Prepared for the Joint Annual Meeting . . . Cleveland, Ohio, May 17–21, 1944.*

105. The 1944 study, cited here, is one example, as is the 1945 *Survey of Group Work Resources.* See also Jewish Young Adult Bureau, Report of the Executive Director, January 26, 1943, and C.E.A. Director's Report, March 17, 1942.

106. Cleveland Study, 1944, p. 9.

107. 2,238 were classified as opaque "miscellaneous," for a grand total of 15,342. *Survey*, 1945, I, p. 71.

108. Cleveland Study, 1944, p. 31; Stember *et al., op. cit.*, pp. 110–35.

109. Azriel L. Eisenberg, "The Coordination Program of the Bureau of Jewish Education of Cleveland, 1941–1945," December 6, 1945 (MS); Janowsky, *op. cit.*, pp. 336–42.

110. Bureau of Jewish Education, Minutes, December 18, 1944.

Index

379

INDEX